Transnational corporations
and endogenous development

Transnational corporations and endogenous development
Effects on culture, communication, education, and science and technology

JEAN-LOUIS REIFFERS,
Director of
the Centre d'Économie et de Finances Internationales (CEFI),
Faculty of Economic Sciences of the University of Aix-Marseilles-II

André Cartapanis,
William Experton and
Jean-Luc Fuguet, researchers

unesco

Published in 1982 by the United Nations
Educational, Scientific and Cultural Organization
7 place de Fontenoy, 75700 Paris

Composed by Gerbaud, Paris
Printed by Offset-Aubin, Poitiers

ISBN 92-3-101853-1
French edition: 92-3-201853-5
Spanish edition: 92-3-301853-9

© Unesco 1982
Printed in France

PREFACE

Conscious of the need to highlight the endogenous nature of development and the variety of ways in which it can be brought about, the General Conference of Unesco has called for a study of the effects of the activities of the transnational corporations on the development process, especially in the Organization's spheres of competence. If development is to be endogenous, the different societies concerned must retain their own identity, drawing their strength from their own specific forms of thinking, and acting and setting themselves goals that are consonant with those values and with the needs they feel and the resources they possess. This is the spirit in which this study has been undertaken. The study is based on an extensive bibliography, which calls on the findings of a large number of studies on the activities of the transnational corporations, including those carried out by Unesco and the United Nations Centre on Transnational Corporations. It takes stock of our knowledge of the socio-cultural impact of the transnational corporations' activities and is a starting-point in the bid to identify the effects they have more clearly.

The interdisciplinary research team of the Centre d'Économie et de Finances Internationales of the Faculty of Economic Sciences of the University of Aix-Marseilles-II, under the direction of Professor Jean-Louis Reiffers, has brought together the work produced by a large number of specialists from various regions of the world. While remaining mindful of the integrated and global character of development, the research team has focused its analysis more particularly on the effects which the activities of the transnational corporations have on culture, communications, education, and science and technology, and has drawn from it conclusions in respect of methodology and quantitative and qualitative assessments which should furnish guidance to researchers, specialists and officials responsible, both nationally and internationally, for development policies. This study may also contribute to the drafting and implementation of a relevant code of conduct by the competent authorities.

In addition to their personal contribution, the researchers associated with the study have made a point of maintaining close links with the competent regional and international institutions that have amassed considerable experience and well-tested knowledge in their fields of competence. National case-studies have enabled essential references to be made to specific situations.

The authors are responsible for the choice and the presentation of the facts contained in this book and for the opinions expressed therein, which are not necessarily those of Unesco and do not commit the Organization.

CONTENTS

Foreword 11
General introduction 13

PART ONE
Overview of the impact of transnational corporations on socio-cultural development 17

Chapter 1. An economic force versus an idea: the contrapuntal relationship between TNCs and endogenous development 19

Section 1. The general characteristics of transnational corporations 19
   Number 21
   Speed 24
   Flexibility 26
   Magnetism 27

Section 2. What is endogenous development? 30
   The emergence of a multidimensional representation of dependence 30
   The general features of the concept of endogenous development 33

Section 3. Assessing the effects of TNCs on endogenous development: the search for national ways of transforming external impulses 40
   Four working hypotheses 40

Chapter 2. The strategic conflict between TNCs and nation-states 49

Section 1. Endogenous development in practice 49
   Establishing a viable memory-storage, information and communication system consonant with the historical heritage 51
   Promoting a co-ordinated vision of society, in terms of its identity and differences 54
   Adaptability, creativity and the state's search for coherence 55

Section 2. TNC growth in practice, and the conflicts to which it gives rise ... 58
    TNCs and the effort to accede to a higher level of capability:
        the organizational shock ... 59
    The main lines of socio-cultural conflict from the standpoint
        of the TNCs' strategies ... 79

Chapter 3. The changing system of interactions: the role of cultural values and of communication, education, science and technology ... 93

Section 1. The scenario based on extrapolation: spontaneous national responses to the worldwide dissemination of socio-cultural characteristics transmitted by TNCs ... 94
    Pointers to the socio-cultural characteristics of the future
        world system ... 95
    Unconscious national responses ... 105

Section 2. The controlled scenario: consciously planned national responses through the maintenance of cultural values and the control of communications, education, science and technology ... 110
    The need for a completely different methodological approach ... 110
    Consciously planned action: the protection of cultural values,
        and action in regard to communications, education,
        science and technology ... 115

PART TWO
    The impact of TNCs on cultural values and communication,
        education, science and technology ... 121

Chapter 4. The influence of TNCs on cultural values and communication in the developing countries ... 123

Section 1. National cultural values and TNCs: the terms of a contradiction ... 124
    The social and mental basis of cultural values ... 124
    Communication: different forms but the same issue ... 125
    The culture shock ... 127

Section 2. Communication media and cultural dependence ... 129
    The TNCs' dominant position *vis-à-vis* the developing
        countries in regard to control over the media ... 130
    The underlying rift between transnational communication
        corporations and the cultural identity of developing countries ... 147

Section 3. Extroversion of tastes: TNCs and consumer patterns— an overview ... 154
    Consumer patterns and cultural identity ... 155
    The structuring of patterns of consumption and acculturation ... 156

Section 4. How to preserve cultural values from the influence of TNCs: guidelines for action ... 163
    Some general principles ... 164
    Some key areas for application ... 167

Chapter 5. The impact of TNCs on education   183

Section 1. The transmission of an educational model by TNCs   189
    Firms specializing in the sale of educational goods
      and services   189
    Direct TNC educational action   192
    The indirect impact of TNCs on education through the interplay
      between training and employment   208

Section 2. TNCs and educational development   212
    TNCs and the splintering of education systems   212
    TNCs and the extroversion of education systems   225

Section 3. Promoting endogenous educational development   231
    Conservation measures   232
    Measures to promote endogenous educational development   232

Chapter 6. The role of TNCs in the production of knowledge and the division of labour in the developing countries: science and technology   243

Section 1. The nature of scientific and technological development   245
    The sphere of innovation   245
    Endogenous innovation   247
    Assimilation and utilization   248

Section 2. The influence of TNCs on science and technology   249
    Ways and means of transferring technologies   249
    The effects of the firm's strategy   252
    The forging of links: relations between the subsidiary
      and the scientific, technological and industrial potential
      of the host country   259

Section 3. The influence of TNCs on labour   261
    The link between the technology employed and the technical
      division of labour   262
    The spread of wage-earning   265
    The problem of urban unemployment   266
    The twofold division of the labour market   267

Section 4. Ways of achieving an endogenous technology   268
    Intermediate technology   269
    Proposals   270

General conclusion   281

General bibliography   283

FOREWORD

This work is one of a series of studies carried out by Unesco since 1975, pursuant to resolutions adopted by its General Conference, concerning the effects of the activities of transnational corporations in its fields of competence. Two meetings of experts have been held on the subject. The first, held at Unesco Headquarters in 1976, had as its theme 'The Impact of Transnational Corporations on Development and International Relations within the Fields of Competence of Unesco'. The purpose of the second meeting, held at Helsinki (Finland) in 1978, was to evaluate and orient Unesco studies concerning the influence of the activities of transnational corporations in the Organization's fields of competence.

As a preliminary to this work, the Centre d'Économie et de Finances Internationales (CEFI) was asked to prepare a critical annotated bibliography and a methodological analysis on the theme: 'Transnational Corporations and Educational Systems in Developing Countries'. This work was carried out by A. Cartapanis, W. Experton and J.-L. Fuguet, and resulted in two publications by Unesco's Division for the Study of Development.

The present work is the product of a team effort: A. Cartapanis has been mainly concerned with questions relating to cultural values and communication, W. Experton with educational questions and J. L. Fuguet with questions of science and technology. The authors wish to thank Mrs Nathalie Roux for her general contribution to the first part of the work and for her substantial contribution to Chapter 2 in particular. Mention should also be made of two studies—one carried out in Singapore by Dr Wong Kum Poh of the University of Singapore and the other in Tunis by Dr Fayçal Lakhoua of the University of Tunis—which have provided the authors with additional guidance in their approach to the subject and which are published separately by Unesco's Division for the Study of Development.

Jean-Louis REIFFERS

GENERAL
INTRODUCTION

Our language is permeated by such metaphors from life as order, disorder and noise. As this century draws to a close, human beings act as though they feel a growing need to be reassured about the forms taken by the relationship which they have progressively built up with their fellow beings. If natural organisms pursue their development along paths that appear to follow a preset pattern, and if they succeed in setting up defence mechanisms against external aggression, why then cannot the collective organization of relations between people be endowed with the same properties? Why should it not also be able to reverse the flow of time and define the present by reference to the future? But then, if the present is governed to a greater extent by the future than by the past, what pole or configuration of the future is such as to exert an attractive force on human societies?

Arising out of this sense of disquiet is the desire to visualize the configuration, identify the pole and bring the collective organization of relations into harmony with it. The desire becomes a conscious project or design, which is where paradox comes on the scene. Since those who visualize the projected point of attraction are situated within the system and since, therefore, their awareness of the future is drawn from the past, where is their freedom of action? Moreover, the accomplishment of the project is clearly situated in a causal universe, hence in a chain sequence in which the previous state generates the subsequent state. Should the idea of a conscious project therefore be abandoned in favour of a determinism governed by the past? That would be a sad prospect, but fortunately it is becoming increasingly remote as a result of the work done by scientists on living matter. This suggests that it might no longer be necessary to visualize the point in the future, to spell out the goals towards which it was directed and to develop the 'programme' needed to reach it, since the living system would be endowed with the specific property of determining, and itself modifying, both the goals towards which it was directed and its organization. Provided it was sufficiently complex, it would derive possibilities for further development alike from external assaults and internal disorders. Each form it took would be higher than that preceding it: it would be impossible to move backwards, and hence the movement would be irreversible. Optimism would only be tempered by death. That death would come about because of the inability to adapt, or else because the system was closed down. Here again, only a constantly evolving internal organization can ensure a longer lease of life. The design and the goals would consequently be such as were most likely to ensure the constantly evolving quality of the organization. However, it is arguable whether what holds true for living organisms applies, in the same terms, to collective organizations composed of human beings. There is an essential difference: when scientists analyse nature and the contradictions, conflicts and perturbations which mark its evolution, they observe them, whereas when human beings give thought to their collective organization, they know that they are producing something that they will live through. Hence, they cannot remain indifferent to the path taken by developments and they seek to steer the conflict and contradiction in the direction of their own aims. They know that there are several possible paths, each of which is characterized by a specific resolution of the conflicts involved. The design or project can no longer involve abstract organizational principles alone, but is bound up with a quest for power.

When the international community entertained and recognized the demand for a new international order, these, in fact, were the difficulties with which it was confronted. After the first optimistic flush of independence, the developing countries came to realize that the way the worldwide system was evolving merely perpetuated their unfavourable relative position in it, and they embarked on a struggle to secure a better share in the progress being made. That fact itself, combined with objective reasons having to do with the world crisis, culminated in the project for a new international order, an ambitious project which, among other things, looks forward to some 25 per cent of world industrial output being in the hands of the developing countries by the year 2000. It seems *a priori* as if some of the questions suggested by that goal have been neglected. Defining an order or an end-purpose for a worldwide system means pondering on the dynamics of the events that will lead up to it. There are grounds for thinking that the new order will derive a good many of its features from the past. It is arguable that the goal will be credible only if it is coupled with some conception of the way in which the structures concerned are to develop. It would also be possible to imagine the organizational principles underlying the worldwide system which would enable that goal to be attained. Although, to our knowledge, none of the approaches suggested above has been systematically investigated, the international community has behaved like a living organism. Rather than define ways and means, predict the way in which structures will evolve or reformulate comprehensive organizational principles, it takes note of the demand and allows the contradiction free rein; in short it progressively reorganizes itself by enacting rules that set the seal on a given state in the process.

This study represents a particular juncture in these developments. It is a juncture at which, paradoxically, the path to reorganizing the world system lies in organizing and defending national autonomy. It is a paradox only in appearance for those who are familiar with living things, and who know full well that the diversity and autonomy of the component parts are the guarantors of the unity and complexity of the whole, and hence of its evolution. It is urgent, in fact, to organize the autonomous differentiation of nations in a world system built around transnational corporations (TNCs). It is likewise urgent to raise the issue of endogenous development at the socio-cultural level when the phenomenon holding the world system together is essentially economic in character. This indeed is the only way of visualizing national autonomy from the standpoint of the world system. However, information comes before self-organization or reorganization, and it is primarily a contribution to information that this study seeks to make.

PART ONE

Overview of the impact of transnational corporations on socio-cultural development

Regardless of whether they are a freak symptom of civilization, the product of a world that has been narrowed down by transport and communications, or else an objective prerequisite for the survival of the economic systems of the developed countries, the transnational corporations whip up a storm.[1] Subjected as they are to the worldwide dissemination of information, which has also enabled them to assume international proportions, they are the subject of arguments that are equally impassioned, whether they are for or against. When analysis is undertaken on a scientific plane, the catch-phrases of journalists give way to the heavy batteries of theory. All this makes our knowlege of the effects of transnational corporations one of the most motley collections of information imaginable. Facts, messages and viewpoints are delivered up in a selective stream and are taken in through the specific codes characterizing a large number of social groups. This host of differing appraisals goes hand in hand with a multitude of conflicting conceptions and, ultimately, a deep sense of uncertainty, which is bound to encourage the retreat into abstraction. The difficulty becomes even more acute when an essentially economic phenomenon is related to the socio-cultural sphere.

No analysis of the effects of the TNCs on the socio-cultural sphere can be content merely with listing the immediate effects engendered by the role which they play in education, science and technology, communications and culture. Although this study is designed to approach the question from the standpoint of Unesco's fields of competence, it cannot but pay attention to the indirect effects consequent on the new organizational forms adopted in regard to production systems, work methods and consumption patterns. Assuming it is possible to visualize those effects and hence to shed light on the interlinking system of relationships existing between the economic and socio-cultural spheres, it is still necessary to inquire into the nature of the influences undergone by one or other of those spheres in order to trace the laws governing the development of the system that brings them together.

Moreover, the concept of endogenous development, seen as a principle for guiding the action of the nation-states and international organizations responsible for keeping the TNCs in check, is unimaginable without taking the development of the world economy into account. Each national entity is linked up with the other entities in the world system. The goals of autonomy and independence accordingly have to be spelt out, without overlooking the totalizing dimension which in part determines them and provides their justification. The permanent contradiction between the unity of the system as a whole and the diversity of its parts, in other words the nations, has to be kept in mind.² In any event, this is the only analytical framework that will make it possible to move ahead in the search for realistic answers consonant with the demands of cultural identity, and this is in fact the framework that Unesco has adopted in its Medium-Term Plan.³ Lastly, false opposites have to be eliminated from the discussion. The path to endogenous development cannot be traced in a Manichean setting where inherited culture is set against imported modernity. There is no contradiction between basing one's arguments on the strategic behaviour of the protagonists and seeking the laws governing the development of the system of interrelationships characterized by more abstract fields or categories. Even attempts to draw too systematic a distinction between the socio-cultural and economic spheres are scarcely meaningful in the traditional communities so dear to anthropologists. All these difficulties militate in favour of adopting an approach with a marked empirical content. Once certain preconceived ideas have been banished, this approach should make it possible to obtain a clearer picture of the consequences of the growth of multinationalization and to catch a glimpse of the answers that can be made to some of the questions most fundamentally important for the future. Will the power of the TNCs and their considerable homogenizing capacity be matched by a strength and coherence on the part of nation-states sufficient to hold in check, channel and eventually assimilate the external impulse the TNCs transmit? And will the TNCs themselves, when they come to realize this resistance, re-examine their organization and practices in order better to accommodate national demands for the preservation or strengthening of socio-cultural identity?

NOTES

1. R. Vernon, *Storm over the Multinationals. The Real Issues*, Cambridge, Mass., Harvard University Press, 1977.
2. E. Morin, *La méthode I. La nature de la nature*, pp. 105 et seq., Paris, Seuil, 1977; A. Atlan, 'On a Formal Definition of Organization', *Journal of Theoretical Biology*, Vol. 45, p. 19.
3. *Thinking Ahead*, Paris, Unesco, 1977.

Chapter 1

An economic force versus an idea: the contrapuntal relationship between TNCs and endogenous development

The problem to be considered can be formulated in terms of a straightforward observation: faced with an essentially economic phenomenon which represents a considerable mass and is growing at considerable speed, nation-states are endeavouring to lay down procedures to enable them to pursue uninterrupted development that will respect their cultural identity. This 'endogenous development' involves complex long-term processes which are liable to be seriously perturbed by the force that currently shapes the world economy. Two preconceived ideas must accordingly be avoided.

The first consists in believing that the structural configuration of the world system built up by the TNCs is already so complete that national reality no longer has an existence of its own, the day of the nation-state is past and nations are no more than impersonalized entities for reproducing and accumulating capital.

By contrast, the second boils down to asserting that there are no limits on what politically sovereign nations can achieve and that no breakdowns in socio-cultural structure are irreversible.

A considerable proportion of the literature on the subject is divided on the issues of idealism versus materialism and universalism versus culturalism. Rather than take one or other of these viewpoints as our reference, we have preferred to inquire into the relationship existing between the economic force represented by the TNCs and the idea of endogenous development, in sufficiently comprehensive fashion to provide a framework for analysing the effects of the TNCs on the socio-cultural identity of the developing countries.

Section 1

The general characteristics of transnational corporations

The first broad definition of firms operating internationally stemmed from the report of the Group of Eminent Persons convened by the Secretary-General of the United Nations,[1] namely: 'Multinational corporations are enterprises which own or control production or service facilities outside the country in which they are based. Such enterprises are not always incorporated or private; they can also be co-operatives or state-owned enterprises.' This definition embraces all enterprises established in two or more countries. At the fifty-seventh session of the United Nations Economic and Social Council, in 1974, the term multinational was replaced by transnational, in order to mark the fact that they were enterprises transcending national boundaries from a given national territory. Although the task of making this definition more precise still forms part of the programme of work of the Commission on Transnational Corporations established as a result of that session of the Economic and Social Council, we have adopted it for this study, on the understanding that it covers both private and state-owned companies and that those affiliates or subsidiaries of transnational corporations will be regarded as affiliates that are established with foreign-equity participation.[2] In a sense, this definition has the merit of being wide-ranging. Inasmuch as it does not imply that the corporations defined as such have a large number of affiliates abroad (whereas at least six affiliates are necessary for a corporation to be considered as multinational according to the definition of the Harvard Group) and that all their functions, including research and development and top management, are multinationalized, it enables the whole phenomenon of the internationalization of capital to be encompassed.

Without going so far as to assert, like the United States Tariff Commission, that the spread of international business is, together with the development of the steam engine, electricity and the automobile, one of the major events of modern economic history, it has to be acknowledged that the TNC phenomenon has, since the 1950s, marked world economic history to a greater extent than any other. This significant growth is in the first place due to endogenous factors and, in that regard, it is the outcome of what can be termed a 'push effect'. From the macro-economic standpoint, it can scarcely be denied that the TNCs have enabled the industrialized countries to maintain substantial growth rates as a result of the natural and manpower resources which they were able to mobilize, the broadening of the market for their products, and the size of the financial earnings which they have repatriated. From the micro-economic standpoint, the TNCs are currently the 'ideal' management model: as efficient, flexible and diversified ventures, they represent the outcome of a sequential process bound up with long-term corporate planning which, as a rule, prompts a large-scale national corporation to develop its domestic operations on a 'multi-plant' basis, sell licences and their associated technical applications, develop a portfolio of investments abroad, and finally engage in productive activities on an international scale. However, the euphoria which dominated host-country reactions to the TNCs then gave way to a period of apprehension and, not long afterwards, to one of hostility. The reason for this lies in the fact that the effects on employment and industrialization, which were originally regarded as being positive, were frequently offset by the nation-states' loss of their independent decision-making power, their awareness of the increasing instability of the resulting growth patterns and appreciation of the socio-cultural distortions introduced. Taking the world system as a whole, there can be little denying that its interdependence, and indeed its economic integration, have been significantly reinforced by the spread of the TNCs. Some circles even go so far as to claim that if that trend were to continue, the world would become an integrated unit, a 'global supermarket' controlled by a handful of very large corporations.[3]

These comments suggest that the TNCs primarily pose a problem of force. This force and the power accompanying it are the first point to be borne in mind in attempting to visualize the general background to the problem of the socio-cultural effects which they can bring in their wake. In order briefly to signify what this means, we shall consider that the TNC phenomenon derives its power from four main features: its mass, its speed (in other words its rate of growth), its flexibility and hence its ability to adapt, and its magnetism, which is taken as meaning its ability to integrate and co-ordinate the world system.

Number

On the basis of the foregoing definition it was reckoned in 1973 that there were some 9,500 TNCs throughout the world. Of these, 4,532, or some 48 per cent of the total, were situated in the European Economic Community (EEC) and 2,567, or about 27 per cent, in the United States.[4] Few of the TNCs were widely established throughout the world (60.6 per cent have affiliates in one or two countries). Only 324 companies can be said to be really worldwide enterprises in that they are represented in more than twenty countries. If we consider the ranking of the first 50 firms, the importance of the United States emerges much more clearly, in that 22 of them are American companies, and 11 of these are among the first 15.

It is always extremely difficult to gain a precise idea of the importance of the TNCs in terms of the major economic aggregates. We cite below some of the most recent evaluations. That of the Commission of the European Communities (Table 1) confirms the dominant place occupied by the United States and emphasizes the significant share which Japan has now taken as a home country.

TABLE 1. Distribution, by home country, of TNCs' turnover, assets and number of personnel employed

	Turnover[1] %	Assets[1] %	Personnel employed[2]	
			Number	%
United States	46.7	28.7	19 592 094	42.6
EEC	33.4	42.4	20 962 875	45.6
France	5.1	6.2	3 357 133	7.3
Fed. Rep. of Germany	9.4	12.4	5 409 369	11.7
United Kingdom	11.5	14.9	7 937 152	17.3
Japan	13.9	15.9	1 717 851	3.7
All countries	100	100	58 976 474	100

1. Sample of 4,531 firms.
2. Sample of 5,105 firms.
Source: Commission of the European Communities, *Étude sur les entreprises multinationales*, pp. 33 and 34, July 1976.

According to the above estimates, the TNCs can be said to employ some 58 million people in all. The United Nations, on the other hand, gives a figure of 10 million for the number of people directly employed by TNCs in foreign affiliates in 1976, including 3 to 4 million in the developing countries (the corresponding estimates by the International Labour Office are 13 to 14 million and 2 million, respectively (See Table 2).[5] Over the past few years, TNCs have emerged which have their headquarters in certain developing countries, such as Brazil, Hong Kong, India, Mexico and the Philippines, and these in their turn have become exporters of direct investments.[6] The socialist countries themselves cannot be excluded from this pattern, though in their case, the forms taken by internationalization chiefly involve participation for the purpose of setting up communication networks and providing financial, transport and technical services.[7] Some idea can be gained of the scale of the whole phenomenon when it is borne in mind that the fifteen leading TNCs produce goods to a value ranging between 10 and 15 per cent of the industrial output of the market economies in 1975,[8] that the direct investment stock, which is an indicator significantly underestimating the phenomenon, represents some 7 per cent of the combined gross national product of the market-economy in industrialized countries,[9] that 50 per cent of all corporate earnings of British firms are derived from overseas activities,[10] and that the turnover of the TNCs chiefly engaged in manufacturing activity, and having their headquarters in the Netherlands, the United Kingdom, Japan and the United States, represents an amount corresponding to 68.8, 52.3, 45.8 and 41 per cent respectively of those countries' gross domestic product.[11]

The first finding emerging from the worldwide distribution of the activities of the TNCs (Table 2) is that they are mainly centred on the developed countries, only about a quarter being located in the developing countries. However, since those countries account for only 7 per cent of world manufacturing output, the relative importance of the place which the TNCs represent in them is often far greater than that which they represent in the developed countries.

TABLE 2. Stock of direct investment abroad of developed market economies, by host country, 1967–75

Host country and country group	Distribution of stock (%)		
	1967	1971	1975
Developed market economies	69	72	74
Canada	18	17	15
United States	9	9	11
United Kingdom	8	9	9
Federal Republic of Germany	3	5	6
Other	30	32	33
Developing countries	31	28	26
TOTAL	100	100	100
Total value of stock ($ billions)	105	158	259

Source: United Nations, *Transnational Corporations in World Development. A Re-examination*, 1978, p. 237 (doc. E/C. 10/38).

The pattern of distribution of the direct investment stock within the group of developing countries shows that the greater part of that stock is received by the 'new industrialized countries', in the meaning of that term as used by OECD (Table 3).

From the standpoint of the sectors involved, it can clearly be seen that the manufacturing sector still occupies an overwhelming position, in spite of a substantial increase in TNC operations in services. The relative importance of the TNCs in the developing countries is borne out by certain national data. For example, the share held by foreign enterprises is as follows:[12]

Nigeria: 70 per cent of assets in 1968 (data on the 625 largest manufacturing firms).

Malaysia: 62 per cent of assets in 1961.

TABLE 3. Direct investment stock in developing countries by host country, 1967–75, and distribution by sector for certain countries (percentage)

	1967	1975	Distribution of stock by sectors				
			Extractive sector	Manufacturing sector	Service sector	Other	Total
OPEC countries[1]	27.7	22.9					
Venezuela	10.6	5.9					
Indonesia	0.6	5.1	37.5	57.0	10.3	—	100[3]
Nigeria	3.3	4.3	63.3	25.2	10.3	1.2	100[4]
Iran	2.1	1.8					
Tax havens[2]	7.0	13.0					
Other developing countries	65.3	64.1					
Brazil	11.3	13.3	2.5	76.5	18.6	2.0	100[3]
Mexico	5.5	7.0	4.1	77.5	18.1	0.2	100[5]
India	4.0	3.5	4.2	92.0	3.7	—	100[6]
Malaysia	2.1	3.4					
Argentina	5.5	2.9	5.6	65.0	24.5	4.5	100[4]
Singapore	0.6	2.5					
Peru	2.4	2.5					
Hong Kong	0.9	1.9	—	100.0	—	—	100[3]
Philippines	2.1	1.8	12.6	48.7	34.0	4.7	100[3]
Trinidad and Tobago	2.1	1.8					
Total above ten countries	36.5	40.6					
GRAND TOTAL	100	100					

1. Algeria, Ecuador, Gabon, Indonesia, Iran, Iraq, Kuwait, Libyan Arab Jamahiriya, Nigeria, Qatar, Saudi Arabia, United Arab Emirates and Venezuela.
2. Bahamas, Barbados, Bermuda, Cayman Islands, Dutch West Indies and Panama.
3. 1976. 4. 1973. 5. 1975. 6. 1974.
Source: United Nations, *Transnational Corporations in World Development. A Re-examination*, 1978, pp. 254, 259 (doc. E/C. 10/38).

Ghana: 50 per cent of sales in 1974.

Brazil: 49 per cent of the sales of the 1,000 largest firms and 29 per cent of the assets of the 5,113 largest non-financial firms in 1974.

Central American common market: 31 per cent of sales in 1971.

Peru: 46 per cent of sales in 1969.

Singapore: 24.5 per cent of the GNP and 90 per cent of the value added of industry in 1978.[13]

Argentina: 31 per cent of sales in 1972.

Mexico: 27 per cent of sales in 1972.

The importance of foreign participation by sectors is also very significant:[14]

Argentina: 75 per cent in rubber; 82 per cent in non-electrical machinery and 84 per cent in motor vehicles in 1969.

Mexico: 87 per cent in rubber and 67 per cent in chemicals in 1973.

Peru: 67 per cent in chemicals and 88 per cent in rubber in 1969.

Singapore: 46 per cent in chemicals and 76 per cent in rubber.

In order to complete this brief overall picture, it should be added that the TNCs primarily enter industries in which the main features are heavy concentration, a high level of research and considerable labour skills. In these industries, they usually engage in more research, employ larger numbers of skilled labour, have a higher proportion of management-level staff and produce above-average operating results. Moreover, while most TNCs are diversified horizontally, many firms are diversified vertically, especially those with a strong research component. Lastly, the geographical origin of the TNCs is reflected in some of their characteristics, such as differences in size (United States), the number of links with the host country (United Kingdom, Federal Republic of Germany and Switzerland) and the intense pace of research (United States and Japan).

Speed

While it is true that the TNCs have existed for a considerable length of time, they only really began to develop with the Second World War. Hence, it has been rightly stressed that there has been no economic organization in post-industrial society that has grown as quickly.[15] The only phenomenon that might conceivably be described as similar was the emergence of cartels and trusts at the turn of the twentieth century. However, the latter were mainly national in character and their international operations were conditional on agreement being reached between major groups rather than on planning integrated and visualized on a worldwide scale by a single top management.[16] Figure 1 illustrates this phenomenon and shows in particular that the slight slackening-off in the transnationalization of American capital which can be observed at the end of the period was picked up again by European and Japanese firms and, in the past few years, by firms from the developing countries.

This movement has even grown stronger in recent years, since the world stock of direct investment has risen from $105 billion in 1967 to $287 billion in 1976, making an average annual growth rate comparable to that of the GNP for all the developed market-economy countries combined, which also increased over the latter part of the period (Table 4).

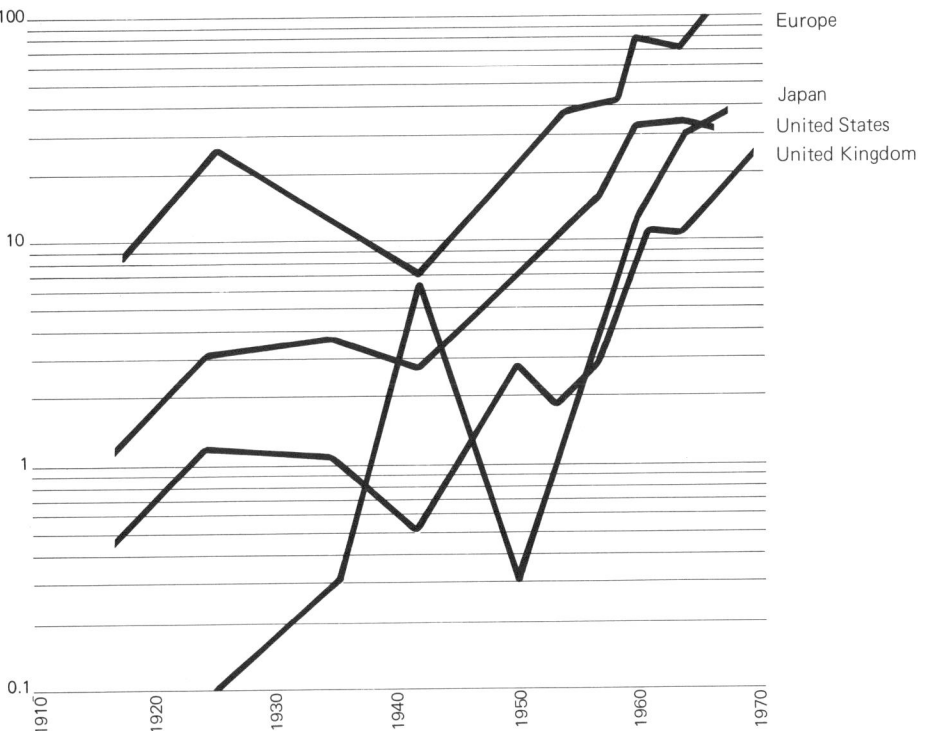

FIG 1. Average number of new affiliates created, by home regions and by year (after P. J. Buckley and M. Casson *The Future of the Multinational Enterprises*, London, Macmillan, 1976).

TABLE 4. Average percentage annual growth rate of developed countries

	1967–71	1971–76
GNP of developed countries	9.1	13.5
Direct investment stock	10.7	12.7

Source: United Nations, *Transnational Corporations in World Development. A Re-examination,* 1978, p. 36 (doc. E/C. 10/38).

These observations call for a basic preliminary comment in regard to the nature of the relationship between the TNCs and socio-cultural conditions in the developing countries. Without unduly anticipating the points that will be examined further on in this study, it is plain that the evolution of a national culture is a long-drawn-out process difficult to co-ordinate, in that it stems from a host of frequently small-sized determining factors, unless there is a break in continuity or a sudden shock, such as a colonial-type invasion. What this brief survey clearly shows is that, over the past thirty years, that process has undergone massive, co-ordinated and very rapidly expanding influence from outside. In this connection, it would be almost tempting to make reference to an elementary physical law and to point out that the resultant of the two forces involved is bound to follow, at least partially, the movement imposed by the stronger, more coherent and swifter force.

Flexibility

Flexibility could be defined as being the speed of adaptation of a phenomenon. From this point of view, the TNCs are a remarkable example, in that they have displayed a considerable ability to adapt. This assertion is borne out by three features that are symptomatic of current developments: namely, diversification, mobility and changing forms of establishment.

All the recent studies underscore the fact that there is a widespread tendency towards greater diversification. The introduction of new product lines is a pattern that can be seen in virtually all TNCs, whether they be American, European or Japanese. This diversification often even extends beyond the confines of the industry concerned. Companies in food industries have gone into chemicals, oil companies have engaged in tourism, hotel management and even home-building, and companies based on mining have invested downstream in the manufacturing sector in a bid to secure outlets. Conversely, specifically industrial companies have come to control upstream sources of supply. There has been considerable diversification into services and it is becoming more and more frequent for banks to invest in non-banking activities. It is possible to obtain some idea of the widespread character of this movement when it is noted that:

Until 1970, the 180 largest United-States-based TNCs controlled 1,822 manufacturing affiliates in the developing countries. These produced 2,184 product lines, making 1.2 products per affiliate. In 1975, the same corporations controlled 1,463 affiliates engaged in 2,451 product lines, so that the product/affiliate ratio rose to 1.68.

In 1970, the 135 leading European corporations controlled 1,009 manufacturing affiliates in the developing countries engaged in 1,001 product lines (a ratio of 1) while, in 1975, they controlled 936 affiliates involving 1,079 products (a ratio of 1.15).[17]

This trend, combined with the geographical spread in activities, clearly reflects considerable adaptability, as is emphasized in the above-cited United Nations report: 'More products, combined with a substantial increase in the proportion of many firms' activities that are foreign, have produced a situation in which the flexibility of the parent company in response to changing world conditions is greatly enhanced.'

Mobility is taken as meaning the scope which firms have for switching the location of their foreign affiliates and changing their number. In 1977 J. P. Curhan, W. Davidson and R. Suri evaluated this phenomenon for the 180 largest United States TNCs (Table 5).

Over the entire period 1967–75, while these 180 TNCs added 4,700 affiliates to their networks, in other words twice as many as the number of affiliates operating in 1966, 2,400 affiliates were 'liquidated', sold or nationalized.

TABLE 5. Affiliates added to or eliminated from the networks of 180 American TNCs (annual average)

	1951-66	1967-69	1970-71	1973-75
Affiliates added to network	456	254	801	563
Affiliates eliminated from network	50	258	267	281

Although American TNCs are the most mobile, this feature must be regarded as being shared by European and Japanese firms, and as being a source of concern to the developing countries, which look upon it as an impediment to the stability of the operations set up in those countries.[18] As a result, in many instances, states negotiating the setting up of activities with TNCs have included provisions to protect them against disinvestment practices.

However, the flexibility of the TNCs is probably best mirrored in the change occurring in the forms of establishment. As J. Dunning has pointed out,[19] the traditional pattern of internationalization, based on large, capital-intensive American and European firms exercising 100 per cent control over their affiliates, is gradually giving way to a form of internationalization in which Japan and the new industrial nations are taking an increasing part. This is based on smaller subsidiaries covering a broader spectrum of sectors, and less tightly controlled. This last-mentioned point is worth stressing, as we are now witnessing a significant increase in the number of joint ventures, based on an often substantial participation of host-country firms or governments, and even many forms of agreement which do not entail the setting up of a company in the host country. These agreements range from licensing contracts and franchise or management agreements to more complex combinations, including the setting up of industrial projects, manufacturing contracts, joint research-and-development operations, joint production, joint distribution and after-sales service, and so on. The importance of this trend is borne out by Table 6, from which it will be noted that there has been an increase in the proportion of minority-holding affiliates and a decline in the proportion of 100 per cent controlled affiliates. This trend is less clear cut, however, in the case of the American TNCs.

In the light of these observations, therefore, it can scarcely be denied that the TNCs have adapted themselves well to the changing environment and particularly to the new forms of control imposed by the developing countries. However, the theoretical significance of the flexibility concept will have to be investigated further in the course of this study: it may reflect either a firm's willingness to subordinate its operating practices to the political will of the host countries (this view, which is held by many authors, finds expression in particular in the report of the United Nations Centre on Transnational Corporations), or its power.

Magnetism

The last essential feature of the TNCs is their ability to set up a field of

TABLE 6. Ownership patterns of 1,276 manufacturing affiliates of 391 TNCs established in developing countries

Home country and type of ownership	Number of cases as a percentage of total			
	Before 1951	1951–60	1966–70	1971–75
Affiliates of 180 United-States-based TNCs				
Total number	100.0	100.0	100.0	100.0
Wholly-owned	58.4	44.5	46.2	43.7
Majority-owned	12.2	21.4	17.8	17.3
Co-owned	5.6	7.9	11.2	10.4
Minority-owned	11.2	18.8	21.5	28.1
Unknown	12.6	7.4	3.3	0.5
Affiliates of 135 TNCs based in Europe and the United Kingdom				
Total number	100.0	100.0	100.0	—
Wholly-owned	39.1	31.6	18.9	—
Majority-owned	15.4	20.1	16.4	—
Co-owned	5.3	6.6	6.6	—
Minority-owned	9.8	27.9	42.1	—
Unknown	30.4	13.8	16.0	—
Affiliates of TNCs in 76 other countries				
Total number	100.0	100.0	100.0	—
Wholly-owned	27.4	16.7	6.1	—
Majority-owned	8.2	26.1	8.2	—
Co-owned	12.3	7.1	7.5	—
Minority-owned	16.4	42.9	74.2	—
Unknown	35.6	7.1	3.9	—

Source: United Nations, Transnational Corporations in World Development. A Re-examination, 1978, p. 299 (doc. E/C. 10/38).

attraction, and this is undoubtedly the most important element contributing to the structure of the world system.

The physical reality of this field of attraction can be readily shown by observing the relative importance of the internal relations of the TNCs compared with the whole range of international economic relations. For instance, the share of intracompany exchanges in exports and imports in the United States has been evaluated at 50 and 46 per cent respectively. Similarly, information is available which indicates that 29 per cent of Swedish exports in 1975, 30 per cent of United Kingdom exports in 1973, and 59 per cent of Canadian exports in 1971 corresponded to intracompany exchanges.[20] Although there are no comprehensive data on the developing countries, many studies have shown that, in some sectors, sales within a single firm may account for a substantial amount of a country's exports.

Table 7 gives a more precise picture of this structural pattern on the basis of the amounts traded between affiliates of American TNCs, compared with the latters' total sales. It is noteworthy that the sales of affiliates outside the United States to their parent companies occupy a more important place in cases where those affiliates are situated in the developing countries, whereas the share of interaffiliate sales is relatively greater in instances where those affiliates are situated in the developed countries. This doubtless points to the affiliate being more dependent on the parent company in the former case.

The volume of these interaffiliate sales has significant repercussions at the management level, and entails, among other things, the introduction of monitoring procedures at a higher-ranking level than that of the affiliates. Such monitoring procedures are also more widely disseminated.

However, the magnetism of the TNCs can also be seen in the fact that they are responsible for a mimetic effect on the part both of other firms of the same type and of local firms. Instances have frequently been observed where, whenever a TNC gained a foothold in a particular market, other TNCs looked with favour at the idea of setting up affiliates engaging in the same activities in the same market. This behaviour pattern is by no means irrational, but suggests a determination to minimize the risk involved. This is a fairly widespread practice on markets dealing in standardized products where, owing to the magnitude of the fixed production costs, one of the main fears of firms is to see their competitors succeed in cutting their costs.[21] It is for reasons of this type—though the arguments are often based on a less sophisticated analysis—that local firms are prompted to imitate the general features of foreign affiliates or subsidiaries. The presence of such affiliates tends to cause their forms of organization and behaviour patterns to become widespread among local firms, even where the nature of the activities involved would have made it possible to manage without them. This phenomenon is still perceptible long after these affiliates have been nationalized. It is indicative of the lasting nature of the mark left by the

TABLE 7. Share of intracompany sales of majority-owned foreign affiliates of United-States-based TNCs, 1971–75 (percentages)

	Share of affiliate exports to parent in total affiliate exports to the United States		Share of affiliate exports to other affiliates in total affiliate exports to other countries	
	1971	1975	1971	1975
World	74	74	53	42
Developed market economies	76	65	60	60
Developing countries	69	82	42	30
Latin America	69	85	56	73
Africa	79	95	73	74
Middle East	59	43	23	14
Asia	93	100	74	65

Source: United Nations, Transnational Corporations in World Development. A Re-examination, 1978, p. 221 (doc. E/C. 10/38).

TNCs and suggests that, whatever may happen hereafter, their impact has been powerful enough to influence the future socio-cultural development of the nations concerned.

Section 2

What is endogenous development?

Confronted as they were with the economic force which we have just described, the nation-states gradually elaborated the concept of endogenous development, a concept taken over and progressively legitimated by the international organizations and in particular by Unesco. As always happens in such cases, this concept had its origins in critical reflection on the theoretical paradigm which was used to justify the phenomenon, following which the more constructive task was undertaken of exploring ways of finding a possible alternative. In its present state, the concept of endogenous development is still imbued with a marked idealistic content. As counterweight to the economic force described above, states therefore have primarily an idea based on the critical analyses conducted on theories of dependence, the concept representing a synthesis of those theories in the advanced state they have reached and, at the same time, of some of their ambiguities. If it is really to act as a guide for state action or make it possible to analyse in concrete terms the dialectical process involving on the one hand the TNCs and their activities and on the other the socio-cultural development of nation-states, the concept of endogenous development will have to discard something of its abstract and immaterial character. For this purpose more penetrating consideration will have to be given to three themes: that of total development, i.e. development that is both economic and socio-cultural; that of unity amid the diversity of the internal and external fields; and that of the relationship between modernity and historical heritage. These are the themes that will feature in the ensuing discussion on the origins of the concept, its content and its operational status.

The emergence of a multidimensional representation of dependence

It was unquestionably the theoretical debate on dependence that took place after the Second World War which served to identify the main criteria that were subsequently to fill out the concept of endogenous development. The debate originated in Latin America in the discovery that the ill-effects of underdevelopment persisted long after political independence had been won, and it developed in the first place as a reaction against the neo-classical paradigm and hence against the idea whereby the free circulation of goods on the basis of comparative advantage would be conducive to worldwide maximum collective advantage of the type postulated by Pareto. The task force of the United Nations Economic Commission for Latin America argued that on the contrary the terms of trade of the developing countries were progressively deteriorating owing to the structural conditions underlying international trade and in particular the monopolistic structure of the industrialized countries. The outcome of this line of thinking was to make the national entity the focus of analysis, to visualize the world economy as being a field of conflictual and asymmetrical relations between a centre and a periphery (an idea elevated to the status of a theory by F. Perroux in 1948), and to advocate industrialization through import substitution.

However, while this initial work seems to have had the merit of relaxing the straitjacket of orthodox thought, it still had three major shortcomings. In the first place, it was based exclusively on an economic view of development, and this caused it to rule out socio-cultural differences and especially the role of class structures from the discussion. Secondly, it made internal underdevelopment dependent on external causes alone and displayed little interest in the relationship existing between the internal impediments to development and those that were international in origin. Thirdly, since its arguments were based exclusively on trade flows, it could not take into account the structural changes in the world economy and, in particular, the consequences of the internationalization of capital.

The remarkable development of the dependence theory and its spread to Africa and Asia were due to the failure of the industrialization policy based on import substitution, secondly to the realization that that policy had been instrumental in enabling transnational corporations to become established in sectors that could seldom be regarded as pace-setters and, thirdly, the desire to give added impetus to the structuralist standpoint while broadening its scope to cover the analysis of social classes. However, this theoretical field was constructed in a rather haphazard manner in that, on the one hand, it borrowed the analysis in class terms from the Marxist approach and, on the other, attempted to broaden the structuralist outlook on the basis of general systems theory, thus bearing out the contention that this composite formulation is a conceptual scheme, an interlinking set of hypotheses and an overview rather than a theoretical model based on a corpus of formal propositions that are capable of being tested.[22]

In spite of the large number of schools involved and the debates that set them against each other, such as the Latin American school of F. H. Cardoso, O. Sunkel and T. Dos Santos, and the African school of Samir Amin, the theme of dependence will be considered in this study as being organized in its present-day form round the following:[23] (a) the concept of development is an all-embracing one; (b) internal development and external development are joined in one and the same system of interactions; (c) modernity must seek its roots in the diversity of existing cultures.

The first principle is now taken for granted, at least on paper. No one adhering to this trend of thought would any longer profess economism in the narrow sense. The approach is bound to be many-sided and cannot be compartmentalized into its economic, sociological and political aspects. This is why the terminology used in systems theory, such as open system, integration–disintegration, control and so on, is increasingly encountered. The first outcome of this was fairly widespread criticism of the traditional forms of development: 'In fact, what had been considered plusses in the traditional approaches, became minuses when looked at through dependence "glasses".'[24] The question of technological dependence, the mass media and adoption of the organizational norms, criteria and models specific to the industrial countries was raised in terms of social and cultural segmentation. Studies were made of the way in which the new middle classes had emerged at the expense of the rest of society, 'partly by preserving the pre-existing local institutions and culture, and partly by destroying them in order to generate an abundant supply of cheap labour'.[25] In instances where the writer drew his inspiration more directly from Marxism, the accent was especially placed on the social relations accompanying a given level of development of the productive forces, and hence on the manner of controlling the means of production, the form of worker participation, and even the scope for the personal and collective emancipation of all those concerned. These critical analyses provided the basis from which the outlines of a new theory of development were progressively drawn. This theory posed the question afresh from a historical standpoint, set about characterizing the societies investigated in terms of their specific socio-cultural features, and increasingly acknowledged the need to modulate the laws governing the growth of capitalism according to the goals being studied. Concern over growth in quantitative terms was superseded by the development-type concept based on the ability of the process to accommodate the deep-felt aspirations of the population. It was realized that, if development was to succeed, it entailed the effective participation of all those engaged in the life of society and hence mobilization of the different social groups.

The second principle requires the analysis to be focused on the manner in which the internal and external structures are linked. As a consequence of this requirement, the dependence of a given society was considered as capable of being characterized by a set of complex interrelationships in which the external dimensions were generally regarded as being decisive,[26] since the internal structures draw part of their significance from the functional place they occupy in this system of dependence. A standard example is that provided by the case of local élites:

Historically, it has been rare on the periphery for local interests to develop which are capable of charting a successful policy of self-sustained development. This is the case because dominant local interests, given the nature of class arrangements emerging from the characteristics of peripheral economies, tend to be those which favour the preservation or re-articulation of patterns of dependency which are clearly in their interests.[27]

Without underestimating the significant differences of opinion over the theoretical status of this external determining factor,[28] it will be noted, for the purpose of this study, that dependence theory now situates it within the framework of a system linking both the national and international domains. This rules out, therefore, both the nationalist viewpoints marked by culturalist attitudes and those viewpoints that are exclusively founded on the economic rationality of a world system linked together by a dominant mode of production.

The third principle is based on recognition of the fact that modernization, on the one hand, and heritage and identity, on the other, are compatible. Hence, it runs counter to those approaches that analyse the failures of modernization in terms of socio-cultural impediments. Such approaches usually draw a distinction between two types of society: first, modern societies that are characterized by neutral and universal models for action, a highly developed division of labour, a marked degree of social and occupational mobility, an extensive network of communications, and political structures that are considerably differentiated and have a rationally determined legal basis;[29] and, second, traditional societies, in which the individual members are held to behave irrationally, to be heavily influenced by nonspecific, emotionally inspired and particularist action models, and to be organized along the lines of an extended kinship structure having a variety of functions. In such societies, the division of labour is not very developed, social, occupational and spatial mobility is slight, and authority is based exclusively on a person's rank in the hierarchy.

In these approaches, this distinction is taken as a basis for regarding the obstacles to development as bound up with traditional structures and attitudes and with all the inherited forms of differentiation. In the long run, they come to assimilate the success of a modernization process to a society's ability to import a standardized behaviour model.

By contrast, the dependence perspective sees modernization as a gradual process of adaptation drawing its sustenance, at one and the same time, from inherited particularisms, all kinds of differentiation and selectively imported behaviour patterns and discoveries. Hence, there can no longer be said to be 'values and attitudes which contribute to the absence of entrepreneurial activities or to institutional arrangements reinforcing underdevelopment. . . . Individuals in widely different societies are capable of pursuing rational patterns of behaviour, able to assess information objectively in the pursuit of utilitarian goals.'[30] While this point of view is not unduly optimistic, it is an invitation to seek ways and means of rendering modernism and cultural heritage compatible with one another, and it recognizes, in particular, that it is necessary to

confront the monolithic block of science with the more loosely organized cultural system in which we find the partial determinisms specific to the major cultural spheres (language, literature, the arts, political and religious ideologies, etc.) criss-crossed by the richly varied links between those spheres or between them and science—expressing at once the unity and the diversity of the society's cultural models—and also by the ties of interaction between values and political, educational, economic and family institutions.[31]

The general features of the concept of endogenous development

It has now become common practice to contrast the homogenizing processes consequent to the growing interpenetration of the world system with the variety of development patterns. That variety can only be maintained if it is considered desirable to do so, through the 'endogenous development' of nation-states. Although some authors have thought that they detected in the concept of endogenous development traces of earlier ideas drawn from the economic sphere, such as the ideas of self-sufficiency and self-sustained or auto-centred development, its primary significance is cultural. At the first attempt to spell out its meaning, by the Panel of Counsellors on Major World Problems and Unesco's Contribution to Solving Them, it was stated:

The problems of peace, of the rights of man, and of the survival of mankind are not to be separated from the problems of development itself. For this reason we should look beyond economic development. What is necessary is to seek an optimal and global socio-economic solution which will benefit all mankind. We must therefore give up thinking of the centres of economic power as the sole repositories of truth, civilization and universality. . . . Once it is seen as global, development can no longer be the direct extension to the whole world of the knowledge, ways of thought, life-styles or experiences specific to a single region of the world; each local development must be related to its own values and culture.[32]

This was put in even more explicit terms by Amadou-Mahtar M'Bow, Director-General of Unesco, at the fourteenth session of the United Nations Economic Commission for Africa in March 1979:

This is why the criteria used to establish investment priorities did not generally reflect an attempt gradually to remove existing imbalances but were more often based on abstract imbalances seen in the light of a classical model borrowed from the industrialized societies. Modernization was thus injected into the economy but did not always take into account the internal logic of the processes set in motion or the relevance of the projects chosen to the country's material resources and needs.

Independence from external economic influence was not the real objective. For instead of seeking to establish an equilibrium at the national or regional level, by diversifying production, a greater effort was made to develop the production of raw materials for export, whether mineral or agricultural, in an attempt to diversify the range of customers in order to escape certain pressures.

This approach inevitably had three consequences—in my opinion, very serious ones. First of all, modernization seen as a purely economic phenomenon tended to stifle the specific genius of peoples whose productive activity had, in traditional societies, formed an integral part of the wider sphere of their creative activity as a whole. Secondly, industrial development, when it was undertaken, was launched without taking agricultural development into account. Agriculture was then unable to supply the urban and industrial centres with a large enough surplus of foodstuffs or, consequently, to become the main outlet for the products of the new industries.

Finally, industrial plant and the corresponding technical structures were often chosen without regard for the size of the labour force which they would be able to absorb. If the alternatives were a series of labour-intensive co-operative projects for crafts or manufactures and a single industrial project providing work for far less employees, the second alternative was generally favoured.

The population of the countryside thus continues to shift to the towns, where unemployment is always on the increase. The little that used to be provided by a subsistence economy is now no longer always guaranteed and today's needs, created by the production/consumption model of the industrial countries, are out of reach for the majority, who do not have the necessary purchasing power.

Towards a social definition of culture

Seeking to find what lies beyond economic development accordingly entails in the first place taking up a clear position on what we understand by culture.

Anthropologists have taught us that culture has a cognitive content. As a representation of learned behaviour models with inherited and legitimized components, culture influences all individual perceptions. This gives culture its first dimension, which is to convert the sense-data of the world into symbolic forms. The objects accompanying these symbolic forms, which are identifiable in any society, are what we call cultural works. They appear in the form of written language (literature and philosophy), graphic signs (painting and the plastic arts), and audio-images or signs (music, popular songs and traditional rhythms). These cultural works are symbolic objects, because they differ from other objects on account of the values (moral, political or aesthetic norms) that they convey and that are attributed to them alone.[33] Their content consequently expresses the sensibility of a nation or ethnic group as that sensibility has come to be built up through the history of the nation or group or the crises it has experienced. This can only be a starting-point however. A large proportion of cultural works appear in the wake of a process of legitimation initiated principally by élites, institutions and other learned circles, or through the commercial forms that they may take. If culture is viewed through such works, it gives the impression of being selective because it proceeds by exclusiveness, with the society of culture being divided into insiders and outsiders, into those who have the purchasing power and those who have not. Hence, the protection of these cultural works does not guarantee the preservation of all the values of a civilization.

An initial way of broadening the definition is to take a psycho-sociological standpoint. The idea is no longer solely to explore a cognitive process, but to grasp the linkage between perception, cognition (knowledge and representations) and behaviour. Although this linkage poses a large number of theoretical problems, it enables the social domain to be covered more thoroughly, since it is concerned with the whole range of behaviour. This approach is exemplified in practice in work done by the Inter-Futures Group of OECD).[34] The method it uses involves contrasting values with demands and behaviour patterns: 'Values express underlying preferences such as those possessed by an individual as a result of his personality, the particular society in which he lives . . . and an archetype held desirable by a particular group. Demands, on the other hand, are the responses of individuals and groups to the interaction of their values and the environment in all its forms.' The study of the relationship between values and demands then makes it possible, at one and the same time, to identify more closely certain forms of segmentation (the formal and informal sector in the language of the Inter-Futures Group), explore the cognitive processes and analyse behaviour patterns as a translation of the demands. The concept of culture then sees its scope significantly widened, in that it will explain and characterize a set of behaviour patterns in a given concrete situation.

It is the socio-cultural perspective, however, that adds the final dimension to the concept of culture. The aim of the sociology of culture is to ascertain the processes by which societies or social groups recognize themselves in symbolic works, choose values and have particular attitudes or behaviour patterns. The central point of the method it uses is to posit that these processes have a large number of causes. In the view of M. Kaplun for instance, they can be accounted for by four theoretical sub-systems, namely ideology, social structure, technical and economic structure, and personality.[35] Many other bundles of causes can be envisaged, and we shall be expressing an opinion on this point further in this study. For the moment, it is important to stress the fact that cultural processes have their roots in several spheres, especially in the economic sphere. The concept of culture is accordingly at the crossroads where the features of a civilization come together. This was the standpoint adopted by Unesco in its Medium-Term Plan when it asserted:

Narrow, élitist definitions of culture, viewed as the system of fine arts and literature, a luxury reserved for the privileged few, must be superseded. Culture, in the full sense of the term, is a fundamental component of the vitality of any society; it is the sum total of a people's creative activities, its methods of production and of appropriation of material assets, its form of organization, its beliefs and sufferings, its work and its leisure, its dreams and its successes.'[36]

Culture and endogenous development

On the basis of the above definition, it becomes possible to state the two general principles of endogenous development.

The first principle is that of cultural identity. It implies recognition of each nation's right to conserve its own culture. This does not mean that communities should withdraw into their shells but, on the contrary, signifies 'mutual appreciation of the values of all peoples, fuller integration in development and, in the case of communities that are today rejected or in a marginal position, the right to existence and dialogue on a footing of equality.'[37] Cultural identity refers back, therefore, to the twofold requirement of conserving a heritage and of displaying receptiveness. It is based on the acceptance of cultural pluralism. It played a part in the struggle for liberation from colonialism and is now the best safeguard for the new states' continued existence as nations. Although the status of cultural minorities within those states gives rise to problems in many cases, cultural identity and endogenous development are linked together at the level of the nation as a whole. Failing some measure of cultural coherence, the nation-state as such can have no existence. Respect for cultural minorities should not be a reason, therefore, for not endeavouring to bring about integration at that level. Failure in this respect would signify the break-up of society and hence increased segmentation and cultural marginalization and would, in any event, make it impossible to conceive of endogenous development.

The second principle concerns the implementation of endogenous development. This must be participatory in nature, instigated by the people themselves. The development and representation of cultures in their authentic form must come essentially from within. Cultural values have to be interpreted and updated by the groups that enter into them. It is in this way that endogenous development will be integrated and that it will become a genuinely human blueprint for civilization. Endogenous development accordingly implies acceptance of a process of self-creation, and that process is incompatible with non-selective adoption of imported forms of culture.

Yet a series of fundamental questions remain unanswered. What is the counterpart of the endogenous development requirement at the economic level? Do these principles suffice to make a development strategy? On a more modest scale, for the purposes of this study, can the concept of endogenous development be readily set over against the principles governing the action of the TNCs, so as to make it possible (a) to understand by what means the effects which they transmit come about and (b) to suggest guidelines for reducing their adverse consequences to a minimum?

The operational status of the concept of endogenous development

In view of the uses to which the concept is currently being put and the frequency with which it is invoked, on both the national and the international planes, endogenous development is, in the first instance, in the process of becoming an ideology. Readers who have followed the political and theoretical stages by virtue of which it has become part of the everyday language of the United Nations will recognize at once that the main definitions used by philosophers and sociologists to characterize an ideology are applicable to it.[38] We should first emphasize that, in this case, the term ideology is construed in its neutral meaning, i.e. as the shaping of an attitude to social reality and not in the pejorative sense of a false idea or a justification for passions. From that point of view, the concept of endogenous development is, clearly, at one and the same time: (a) a system of representations endowed with a historical existence and role, whose function is to guide social practice rather than give added depth to our knowledge; (b) a distillate of concrete experience which in part conceals the true situation and exerts a constraining effect on individuals, whose function it is to lay down guidelines for individual and collective action; and (c) the historically determined intellectual expression of a situation where interests come into play.

As an ideology, this concept performs the quite considerable function of explicitly recognizing the importance of national reality in an outward-looking context. It thereby contributes to providing officials responsible for government policy with a direction for the action they take.

However, the concept of endogenous development also seeks to project an image of itself as a norm or ideal to be attained in successive stages. While such an image can clearly serve as a point of reference for the international community to assess progress achieved, it hardly appears operational enough for taking specific action. Since it is too general, it does not take into account the particular constraints bearing on the developing countries, such as their geographical or political situation, their *de facto* economic dependence, certain forms of corruption, and so on. Thus, while the ideal significance of endogenous development should be kept in mind, it would appear more practical, for operational purposes, to use its content as a minimum, rather than as a maximum, yardstick. This implies that, instead of asking the question, 'How should one set about ensuring endogenous development?' we ought preferably to ask, 'Having regard to the constraints of the environment, what action should be undertaken to ensure that socio-cultural dependence does not become irreversible?' This second question would accordingly entail, in the first place, identifying in each case: (a) the historical heritage peculiar to the nation in question in the socio-cultural domain; (b) the heritage imported by colonial, neo-colonial or other practices; and (c) the existing combination of these two forms of heritage, giving rise to societal patterns of coherence, or incoherence.

It may then be asked whether the external impulses can, in certain fields, lead to situations where the breakdown in structure is such that the resulting patterns of dependence can be regarded as having a serious effect on the societal characteristics of the nation and being accordingly irreversible in nature.

Naturally, the problem of evaluating the threshold of reversibility then arises; but it does seem that, in certain sectors, this could provide a way of identifying behaviour patterns whose effects could scarcely be disputed from this point of view. In any event, even though the idea of endogenous development with maximum content has a significant role to play in enabling the developing countries to see how far they still have to go, it has to be supplemented by something less abstract, and hence more pragmatic and differentiated.

It remains to be seen whether the concept of endogenous development can be used as an operational concept and whether, in that regard, it can form the basis for an empirical approach. From that standpoint, the concept poses two fundamental problems: the first entails filling out the definition, while the second is bound up with the principle of unity in diversity on which its logic is founded.

As the foregoing discussion has shown, the notion of endogenous development is the outcome of a process in which a conception of development and a conception of culture converge. At the same time as the conception of development was broadened in scope by adding social and cultural aspects to the economic dimension, the concept of culture was correspondingly enlarged by addition of the socio-economic dimensions. The development of mankind, or total development, could be said to have a corresponding social culture characterizing a civilization as a whole. Hence, endogenous development has become a dual concept —both cultural and socio-economic—and it has been possible to define it in terms of the demand for cultural identity, which is likewise a dual cultural and socio-economic concept. This convergence has significantly broadened the standpoint by making it mandatory to deal simultaneously with several spheres that are usually claimed for their own by specific disciplines. Even so, as the concept broadens its image of development, it loses its operative features and its ability to produce an empirical analysis. Hence, it is only by going deeper into the question of how the different spheres are to be integrated, in other words by creating suitable intermediate categories, that such an analysis can be developed.

The second problem, which is directly connected with the first, arises out of the relationship existing between endogenous development and the world outside it. The idea of unity in diversity introduces a paradox, which is highlighted most clearly when the argument switches from the abstract to the concrete.

It is natural for the problem of the relations between nation-states and a world system to be posed in terms of unity and diversity when the purpose is to reconcile the need for universalist principles while maintaining certain forms of national identity. When the argument is confined to a single sphere, say, the cultural sphere in the narrow sense, certain universal tenets of behaviour (such as respect for individual freedom, the right to knowledge and so on) and the maintenance of endogenous cultural patterns can be readily advocated simultaneously. Scarcely any problem will be involved if the universal principles governing the whole do not conflict with the diversity which it is wished to see preserved in the parts. The reason why worldwide agreement on such points is feasible is because there is a difference in the level of concerns. However, the question assumes quite a different dimension when the argument is being conducted in the context of a system in which the economic and socio-cultural spheres are conjoined. In that case, cultural identity is liable to be subject to the full determining force of economic factors, which will exert their effects through the intermediary of the world system. If the argument is taken to the extreme, reference can be made to the fact that economic modernism is still a virtual monopoly of the dominant societies which give the world economy its structure. Where cultural differentiation comes up against the impossibility of economic differentiation, therefore, the economic factors are decisive and the remaining elements of differentiation conserve only a very specific functional significance. The laws of evolution then apply with all their force. As Arthur Koestler said, there are 'two complementary aspects of the evolutionary process: differentiation of structure and integration of function'.[39] If the economic functions destroy the structures, differentiation will then have only a limited significance bound up with the rationality of the world system or, at most, a residual character. This is the very heart of the problem posed by the TNCs, their mass and the quickened pace they impart to the evolution of the world system. There are grounds for believing in fact that (a) by integrating the world economy they increasingly tend to mould nation-states in accordance with the functions necessary for their own growth and that (b) when nation-states seek differentiation, it is, more often than not, 'in response' to the disturbances thus caused to the environment.

The important thing, therefore, is to pose in more explicit terms the problem as to the nature of the rationality of the complex system and of the power relationship accompanying it. If the analysis reveals that the system components are increasingly integrated, a real qualitative diversity will clearly be maintained and created only by: (a) according a central place to national rationality and (b) ensuring that it has a power of initiative at least equivalent to the world system's power of integration.

Section 3

Assessing the effects of TNCs on endogenous development: the search for national ways of transforming external impulses

The method used in the ensuing study will hinge on the nation-state and its overall sphere of action. While, as we have seen above, the nation is the undisputed basis for the socio-cultural concept of endogenous development, it is increasingly disregarded in economic theories. Such theories tend to make their analyses universal in application, by dint of formalizing individual behaviour patterns or else making play with a worldwide rationality based on internationalization of the capitalist mode of production. Since we wish to assess the effects of the TNCs on cultural identity, we shall start out from the assumption that each nation has a specific way or ways of transforming external impulses. This point of view, which may appear optimistic having regard to what we said earlier, is in any event the only one consistent with the idea of endogenous development, inasmuch as it situates the analysis at the level of the rationality of the nation-state. Its main advantage is that it does not prejudge the outcome as far as the homogenizing capacity of the world system is concerned, and makes it possible to assess the prospects of reaction at national level. Hence the effects of the TNCs can be investigated in greater depth by studying the various ways in which external impulses are transformed by national reaction. It should be pointed out that, although the nation is thereby viewed as the seat of rationality, each nation-state is nevertheless regarded as open to a greater or lesser extent to the outside world and consequently integrated in the world system. These points can be spelt out in the following four working hypotheses.

Four working hypotheses

1. Every nation can be characterized at a given moment in time by a state of society corresponding to specific ways of integrating values, patterns of socialization and forms of productive organization

In a completely abstract approach, we shall consider a society's ability to bring together into a coherent system the different internal vectors that socialize the individuals of which it is composed. In a nation that is observed at a given period in time and is assumed to be completely shut off from outside influences, it is difficult to ensure compatibility between the patterns of socialization which that society has produced through a conscious act of will, the heritage of its history and the outcome of the crises that it may experience. When these three elements are successfully combined in a coherent societal field, it is possible to speak of the national integration of society. The quest for integration is therefore the subject of a permanent struggle between the will to modernize and the weight of the cultural heritage. When we also take into account the random discontinuities that may characterize certain forms of conflict between the classes, the social norms connected with them and their institutional consequences at the level of the nation, we begin to appreciate the complexity of the processes that can lead to such integration. It seems reasonable to suppose that a key feature of these processes will be a system of relationships that can be built up from abstract categories and from the relations between social agents.

In the first place, the concept of the national integration of society will be defined in terms of whatever cohesion has been found in the society in question between a system of values, patterns of socialization and a form of productive organization. The term 'system of values' is taken as meaning the dominant choices of a society as shaped by its history. The system of values is represented by the preferences of individuals or groups, the norms of a society and the symbolic objects that it produces. It defines a way of life, because it is at the root of demands and criteria of choice. In a given situation, these demands and criteria will produce behaviour patterns, particularly as far as consumption is concerned. The patterns of socialization will be concerned more especially with the mechanisms of social stratification, production of skills, social and occupational mobility, social relationships and the insertion of individuals into the environment. These modes of socialization are largely conditioned by the class relationships (hierarchical relationships and the power relationships connected with them), the forms of labour and the way in which space and time are used. As to the form of productive organization, this will be defined by reference to division of labour and the technique and organization of the production units (chiefly the scale of production), all of which are factors largely dependent in the case of developing countries on the natural resource endowment. Culture, construed in the broad sense given above, is characterized by the ability to create coherent configurations embracing these different factors. For instance, forms of division of labour and given technical options exist alongside patterns of social segmentation and insertion into the physical environment, together with a particular system of values. It is not our purpose here to express an opinion on the determining sphere, level or instance, since there are probably significant differences between the developing countries in that respect. Moreover, to express such an opinion, asserting, for example, that the economic sphere, and hence the form of productive organization, is the decisive factor would impart to our preliminary analysis a bias such as seriously to influence the conclusions.

'Education', 'communications' and 'science and technology' are all concerned with one or more of those spheres and, in that regard, participate in the integration of society. The educational system, for example, can be considered as being a key integrating mechanism, in that it helps produce the national coherence of society by its action on each of the areas involved. It exerts an influence on the system of values by the knowledge that it contributes to transmitting and transforming through its critical thinking. It socializes individuals, since it produces qualifications, with their attendant consequences in regard to people's conception of the hierarchical organization and the whole range of social relationships. It is involved in productive organization, since it contributes, through research, to the discovery and application of new techniques, and it guides the insertion of school- and college-leavers into productive organization through the manner in which it deals with the training-employment relationship. The system of communications is linked more particularly to the sphere of values because, at one and the same time, it influences perception, conceptions, demands and behaviour patterns. The action it exerts on perception is due to the nature of information and the coding it conveys: the codes transmitted largely condition the codes of the individuals or groups receiving them. The action it exerts on conceptions and demands depends on the extent to which the codes transmitted are suited to the population's decoding capacity (as in the case of advertising, for example). Its influence on behaviour patterns and ways of life derives, in particular, from the ranking order of suggested choices and from the perception of the environment accompanying it. Lastly, 'science and technology', which generate technical knowlege and forms, socialize individuals through work; although their effect at the level of values is not negligible, we shall regard their main impact as deriving from the division of labour and its social consequences.

The intensification of relations between the social agents involved points the way to an understanding of the relations linking the state and the institutions, enterprises, social groups or communities taking part in social life. These relations are permeated by complex class conflicts, with managers playing a role that cannot be readily reduced to that of exclusive servants of the middle classes. Like the governing class as a whole, they are subject to a large number of determining factors, and this is a particularly pronuonced feature in developing societies because of the role of the family, the clan and the home village community. In any event, a given way of integrating system of values, pattern of socialization and form of productive organization will be matched by a particular type of system governing the relations between social agents.

From a more concrete point of view, it should be stressed that in the developing countries there is not just one form of integration between the above three areas but several, and each of these corresponds to a specific culture. It is clear, in fact, that the central characteristic of these countries is precisely the jutxaposition of cultures linked to specifics ocio-economic strata. Yet this does not necessarily mean that these societies are evolving in a manner in which there is no coherence in society. In fact, the objective of cultural identity is to co-ordinate these different cultures while ensuring their reproduction. It is accordingly the duty of the nation-state to avoid three forms of disruption in the fabric of society:

The first would consist in letting a particular sphere get too much out of step with the others. For example, in a traditional society, the widespread introduction of an object-centred system of values of the cosmopolitan productivist type will create serious disturbances in cognitive codes, distort conceptions and culminate in 'anti-social' forms of behaviour.

The second could result from a lack of communication between the different spheres. For example, a modern type of productive organization not accompanied by any carefully thought-out changes in the patterns of socialization and the system of values would split the personality of the individuals concerned as between their work and their domestic life.

The third, and probably the most common, form would result from the lack of communication between different ways of integrating the three spheres coherently. This would in fact give rise to incoherence marking the society as a whole, characterized by a dominant culture, controlled by the governing classes, alongside several 'marginal' cultures (in the sense that these cultures would not be represented in either the norms or the powers of the society).

The nation-states must, therefore, first of all take care to ensure that the factors making for society's incoherence do not reach thresholds from which it would be difficult to go into reverse and, secondly, set up institutions that are capable of maintaining a cultural identity founded on respect for the diversity of cultures and participation of the population. With regard to the latter point, we quote the lucid *a posteriori* judgement that Henry Kissinger made on the situation in Iran:

In underdeveloped countries economic growth . . . compounds political unrest. Established institutions are undermined, and if it happens before new ones are put in their place upheaval is inevitable. The mass migration from the countryside into the cities separates the workers from traditional patterns of life before new relationships can take their place. Precisely when economic development gains its greatest momentum, the existing political and social structures grow most fragile and the accepted values of tradition are most threatened. Fortunate is the country that can manage a transition to new political forms without turmoil. Wise is the ruler who understands that economic development, far from strengthening his position, carries with it the imperative of building new political institutions to accommodate the growing complexity of his society.[40]

2. Every nation is subject to external impulses
channelled through the transnational corporations, which tend to incorporate
it into an international division of labour

This second hypothesis is based, in the first place, on the idea that national production systems are progressively incorporated into a world production system. Without going so far as to say that there are no longer any goods circulating between countries through the intermediary of the world market (in accordance with the view propounded by neo-classical theory, which argues in terms of international specialization), but only the circulation of goods between the affiliates of the TNCs,[41] this appears to offer the most promising approach:

Because the fact that the international division of labour is conceived in terms of the world production system makes it possible to account for the shifts in the structure of production on a worldwide basis and, in particular, to study the nature of the production segments actually established in each country as part of a broader chain of production.

Because it is through the intermediary of the structural pattern formed by the world production system that the TNCs exert a major part of their socio-cultural effects. To approach the subject from the standpoint of this pattern is therefore more rewarding for our purpose than to view it exclusively in terms of the circulation of goods. Furthermore, the former approach has the merit of not ruling out the second, whereas the converse is not generally true.

In the second place, this hypothesis bears out the massive and ever-accelerating character of the TNC phenomenon, which makes it the central feature of the world system. The TNCs are, in this respect, the source of the main external impulses that affect the state of society of a given nation, in the first place through an indirect process of osmosis; second, through impulses that have a more immediate impact on the actual mechanisms of societal integration.

The indirect process concerns all the impulses accompanying the effects on productive organization and consumption. The establishment of one or more TNC affiliates in a developing country will, in all likelihood, tend to alter the scale of production and the nature of certain activities, as well as increasing specialization and changing the shape of industry and, in particular, the capital/labour ratio. Through its repercussions on work modalities, this may transform the patterns of socialization, the structure of skills, the conception of hierarchical relations, social and occupational mobility, work relations, the salary structure, and so on. The sphere of values may record these changes by adopting new standards of behaviour, language and signs and symbols tailored to the aforementioned changes. Similarly, the TNCs, which frequently use the territories of the developing countries as markets, are led to modify ways of life so as to make it easier for them to sell their products. New consumption patterns emerge, and are clear evidence of deep-seated changes in behaviour patterns, changes that are often questionable in view of the system of dominant values of the people concerned and of the real-life situations in which they live.

Furthermore, the TNCs will also influence the first two spheres more directly. As we have seen, any action at the level of the communications system will affect the sphere of values without passing through an intermediary. Similarly, TNCs providing training facilities help to determine the direction taken by society by making a direct contribution to construction of the cognitive codes of individuals and by preparing their socialization. Although, as a rule, those effects are closely bound up with changes in the form of productive organization, since the TNCs serve in fact to transmit a culture —in other words a way of integrating the three spheres—the mechanisms involved can be identified more clearly if they are considered separately.

3. There is a national way of transforming external impulses which governs the socio-economic evolution of the developing countries

This hypothesis amounts to basing the analysis of the social change occurring in developing countries on the dialectic between, on the one hand, a particular form of societal integration—in part inherited, in part newly created—and, on the other, external impulses transmitted by the TNCs. It implies that the economic and socio-cultural domains will attempt to assimilate those impulses and that they will transform them while transforming themselves at the same time. The overall movement can be conceived as one in which the structure of the three spheres selected to characterize the state of society will be simultaneously dismantled and reassembled. By way of a theoretical hypothesis, it might be said that the external effect consequent on the TNCs' action will increase the multipolarity of the influences and will act selectively in placing the points of impact in ranking order. As these changes are observed in the course of the structural dismantling and reassembling process, they will cause new kinds of social segmentation to emerge. A good example of a process of this type was given by Daniel Bell in connection with the division of labour:

The high degree of specialization—both in the fields of knowledge and in the structure of organizations—inevitably creates an almost unbearable strain between the culture and the social structure. In fact, it becomes quite difficult to speak even of 'the' culture, for not only do specializations create 'sub-cultures', or private worlds—in the anthropological sense—but these in turn create private languages and private signs and symbols which often . . . infiltrate the 'public' world of culture. Today, the culture can hardly, if at all, reflect the society in which people live. The system of social relations is so complex and differentiated and experiences are so specialized, complicated and incomprehensible that it is difficult to find common symbols to relate one experience to another.[42]

Accordingly, this hypothesis clearly entails acknowledging from the outset that every nation should be able to transform these external impulses in accordance with its own specific features. This consequently rules out in this regard any *a priori* universalist view such as: 'The TNCs produce a better allocation of the factors of worldwide production and even out social conditions nationally', or 'The TNCs disseminate, on a international scale, and generalize the dominant social relations of production to the point where they generate new world social relations'. Even without in any way intending to do so, a nation may transform the external impulses on the basis of a form of societal integration which characterizes it.[43] Between the two extremes consisting, on the one hand, of a transformation completely determined by the nature of the external impulse and, on the other, one in which the impulse is assimilated by the pre-existing structures, there are many middle-of-the-road situations that depend on the purely physical characteristics of the nations concerned, the degree of societal integration achieved, the weight of religious tradition, the nature of the education system (general, vocational, formal or non-formal), work modalities and so on.

To view the question from the standpoint of state policy, it is the end-purpose which the state attributes to social development that will influence the way in which national transformation will come about. Here again, any generalization would be out of place, since states' strategy and organization differ significantly from country to country. At this level, the opposing elements in the dialectic on which the argument presented here is based are simply two end-purposes: that of the TNC, interested in improving the worldwide integration of its component parts from the standpoint of its growth, and that of the state, which seeks the increased integration of society in the context of a development effort. We shall see further below in what terms that strategic conflict is posed and how the way in which it is resolved colours social change in the developing countries.

4. The establishment of the world system is itself the outcome of these transformations

This hypothesis is mentioned for reference only, in that, although it falls outside the scope of this study, it does round off the logical argument. Every national differentiation, which is now visualized as a difference in kind rather than in function, plays its part in establishment of the world system, whose coherence rests upon the coherence of the national responses. The world system can no longer be said to impose its own rationality as a matter of course and its organization can no longer be said to derive its effectiveness exclusively from its ability to fit every nation-state into a precise functional slot. Yet it would be meaningless to deny its existence: the world system exists, but its rationality is now visualized, at least partly, as a summation of national rationalities.

To summarize at this stage, we can see, therefore, how important it is to look deeper into existing forms of national transformation. The way in which the different nations have responded to the external impulses generated by the action of the TNCs provides an image of the tangible consequences of that action. It also makes it possible to contemplate suitable control measures, and indeed the mobilization of counterforces. Yet it does not purport to prejudge the outcome. It is quite possible that we shall be led to conclude that the external impulse transmitted by the TNCs is so powerful that all forms of national transformation converge towards a small number of common, and hence universal, types. It is also possible that, through procedures adapted for the purpose, some nations may have been able to control those effects in order to assimilate them into the former cultures, or indeed to use them for laying the groundwork for a new cultural identity. However that may be, the analysis conducted below will tell whether the concept of endogenous development is still meaningful when nations host TNCs, or whether the dominant features of the impulse are so pronounced that worldwide methods of regulation will have to be devised to oppose it.

NOTES

1. United Nations Department of Economic and Social Affairs, *Multinational Corporations in World Development*, Annex II, pp. 4–6, 1973 (Sales No. E. 73. II. A. II).
2. Affiliates will be taken as meaning all forms of association abroad involving at least 25 per cent capital ownership.
3. R. J. Barnet and R. E. Muller, *Global Reach: The Power of the Multinational Corporations*, New York, Simon & Schuster, 1974.

4. Commission of the European Communities, *Survey on Multinational Enterprises*, July 1976.
5. United Nations, *Transnational Corporations in World Development. A Re-examination* (doc. E/C.10/38), 20 March 1978, p. 91. The figure for the assets of firms in the EEC countries was obtained in respect of 329 firms and that for United States firms in respect of 87 firms (cf. Commission of the European Communities, op. cit.). Moreover, the differences in the sectors in which the affiliates are established have probably played an important role in the relatively small numbers employed in TNCs based in the United States.
6. L. T. Wells, Jr., 'The internationalization of firms from developing countries', in T. Agmon and C. P. Kindleberger (eds.), *Multinationalization from Small Countries*, Cambridge, Mass., MIT Press, 1977.
7. United Nations, op. cit., Tables III.70 and III.71.
8. G. Modelski, 'International Content and Performance among the World's Largest Corporations', in G. Modelski (ed.), *Transnational Corporations and World Order*, London, Freeman, 1979.
9. United Nations, op. cit., p. 36.
10. Ibid., p. 38.
11. Commission of the European Communities, op. cit., p. 34.
12. United Nations, op. cit., Table III.54, p. 263.
13. K. P. Wong, 'The Cultural Impact of Multinational Corporations in Singapore', Paris, Unesco, Division for the Study of Development, 1980. (Unesco Working Paper.)
14. United Nations, op. cit., Table III.63, p. 273.
15. P. J. Buckley and Mark Carson, *The Future of the Multinational Enterprise*, London, Macmillan, 1976.
16. Ibid.
17. United Nations, op. cit., Table III.23, p. 227.
18. On the subject of disinvestment, see R. Tornedeu, *Foreign Disinvestment by US Multinational Corporations*, New York, Praeger, 1975.
19. Preface to the work by Neil Hood and Stephen Young, *The Economics of Multinational Enterprises*, London, Longman, 1979.
20. United Nations, op. cit., p. 9. See also Tables III.16, p. 220, and III.17, p. 221.
21. R. Vernon, 'International Investment and International Trade in the Product Cycle', *Quarterly Journal of Economics*. May 1966, p. 67.
22. For a very good background account of this question, see F. H. Cardoso, 'The Consumption of Dependency Theory in the United States', *Latin American Research Review*, Vol. II, No. 3, 1977; P. O'Brien, 'A Critique of Latin American Theories of Dependency', in I. Oxaal et al., *Beyond the Sociology of Development*, London, Routledge & Kegan Paul, 1975; J. J. Villamil, *Transnational Capitalism and National Development*, Brighton, Sussex, Harvester Press, 1979.
23. F. H. Cardoso, *Dependencia y desarrollo en América Latina*, Mexico City, Siglo XXI, 1969; O. Sunkel and P. Paz, *El subdesarrollo latinoamericano y la teoria del desarrollo*, Mexico City, Siglo XXI, 1970; T. Dos Santos, *El menor caracter de la dependencia*, Santiago, Centro de Estudios Socio-Economicos, 1966; A. G. Frank and S. Amin, *L'accumulation dépendante*, Paris, Anthropos, 1978.
24. Villamil, op. cit.
25. O. Sunkel, 'Transnationalization and its National Consquence', in Villamil, op. cit.
26. R. Faben, 'Studying Latin American Politics: Some Implications of a Dependency Approach', *Latin American Research Review*, Vol. XII, No. 2; F. H. Cardoso, quoted in Villamil, op. cit.
27. J. Samuel Valenzuela and Arturo Valenzuela, 'Modernization and Dependence: Alternative Perspective in the Study of Latin American Underdevelopment', in Villamil, op. cit., p. 46.
28. A. G. Frank and S. Amin, *L'accumulation dépendante*, Paris, Anthropos, 1978.

29. D. Lerner, 'Modernization: Social Aspects', in *International Encyclopaedia of the Social Sciences*, 1968.
30. Valenzuela and Valenzuela, op. cit.
31. J. Lesourne, *Les systèmes du destin*, p. 393, Paris, Dalloz, 1976.
32. This group, set up by the Director-General, met between April and June 1975. Its report was published in *Moving Towards Change, Reflections on the New International Economic Order*, pp. 109-10, Paris, Unesco, 1975.
33. For more details, see *Encyclopedia Universalis*, Vol. V., p. 226, Paris, 1968.
34. OECD, *Facing the Future*, pp. 99 et seq., Paris, OECD, 1979.
35. M. Kaplun, 'La comunicación de masas en América Latina' *Educación hoy*, (Bogotá, Asociación de Publicaciones Educativas), No. 5, 1973.
36. Unesco, *Thinking Ahead*, op. cit., p. 19.
37. Ibid., p. 29.
38. J. Gabel, 'L'idéologie', *Encyclopaedia Universalis*, (Paris), 1968.
39. A. Koestler, *The Act of Creation*, p. 416, London, Hutchinson, 1964, quoted in J. L. Le Moigne, *La théorie du système général*, p. 187, Paris, Presses Universitaires de France, 1976.
40. H. Kissinger, *The White House Years, 1968-1973*, p. 1260, London, Weidenfeld & Nicolson, 1979.
41. This hypothesis was developed and spelt out in C. A. Michalet, *Le capitalisme mondial*, Paris, Presses Universitaires de France, 1976.
42. D. Bell, *The Cultural Contradictions of Capitalism*, p. 95, New York, Basic Books, 1976.
43. What has been shown in the case of nations as close to each other as France and the Federal Republic of Germany is even truer for all the |developing countries. See Annick Lebahar and J. L. Reiffers, 'Division internationale du travail et qualifications: une comparaison France–Allemagne', Symposium on International Relations and Employment, École des Sciences Politiques, Paris, 29-30 November 1979.

Chapter 2

The strategic conflict between TNCs and nation-states*

The TNCs, in their pursuit of growth, and nation-states, in their bid to uphold their cultural identity, are in a conflict situation. This does not mean that the TNCs deliberately set out to homogenize cultures or indeed to dominate nations, nor does it mean that many nation-states do not subscribe to the goals proposed by the major corporations. The fact is rather that there is a fundamental incompatibility between, on the one hand, the aims of the TNCs and the rationale underlying their conception of growth and, on the other, the aspiration for cultural identity, on which the concept of endogenous development is based. In this chapter we shall attempt to understand the causes of that incompatibility, outline the relationship between the contending forces, and identify the main lines of potential conflict.

Section 1

Endogenous development in practice

The situation has scarcely changed since C. P. Kindelberger pointed to the lack of theory of the state suited to the developing countries.[1] While there are now a good many more or less successful transpositions of theories based on observation of what the state means in industrialized countries, there has been no widespread or systematic attempt to construct such a theory in the development field. In point of fact, the only scattered elements that can be brought together are chiefly concerned with coping with economic constraints, but hardly ever with cultural development. This situation should come as no surprise when the variety of the developing countries from the standpoint of their physical and historical circumstances is borne in mind.

---

* This chapter was written in close collaboration with Mrs Nathalie Roux, Research Assistant at the CEFI.

While some of them are very richly endowed with natural resources, others want for virtually everything and have to provide a livelihood for what are sometimes large populations spread over a vast land mass. Some, like Singapore and Hong Kong, have very dense populations packed into a tiny area. While some countries have a highly developed public sector and a rich national tradition, others—especially the countries of Central America—became independent after their cultures had been almost completely destroyed as a result of colonization. Moreover, observation of the actual workings of the state in these countries reveals the range of possible conceptions: parliamentary systems may exist side by side with military dictatorships, monarchical regimes enlist the support of the industrial middle class, parliamentary regimes draw their strength from chiefdoms and village-style feudal systems, a westernized administrative bureaucracy sometimes joins forces with traditional rural élites against the urban middle class, or a particular cultural or racial minority may succeed in controlling the entire apparatus of the state. State intervention takes on new forms: in some instances the state controls the tertiary sector and construction industry and itself siphons off agricultural surpluses, in others it assumes responsibility for industrialization, and so on.

In short, these disparities and the ambiguous nature of the situations encountered make it difficult to formulate a general theory of the state calculated to promote development. Even so, despite this variety, most of these states have in common the feeling of representing newly fledged nations, and a corresponding desire to conceive a deliberate and conscious development process. It is this sense of awareness that is most instrumental in bringing them together and provides the key to considering what type of action the authorities should take. From this point of view, the central feature is the practical conduct of development: how the evolution of national society is directed in practice. On the way this is organized depends the extent to which the developing countries retain independence in regard to decision-making. Hence, the prime objective at the heart of the ensuing discussion on the strategy for endogenous development can be expressed in the following terms: to make it possible for the nation to choose its own path of development, in other words consciously devise ways of transforming external impulses in a manner consistent with the aspiration for cultural identity. If that objective is to be attained, the way in which the evolution of society is guided must: (a) strengthen the existing mechanisms for preservation and transmission of the cultural heritage; (b) promote national identity while paying due regard to the differences, bringing them within a co-ordinated, clearly envisaged whole; and (c) develop the social system's adaptability and creative capacity.

But this way of presenting the matter must not conceal the fact that the different elements involved have to be linked to one another in an organizational unity. If the political will displayed by the developing countries dictates such an approach, it entails recognizing, therefore, that the state can and must play an organizational role which has no counterpart in historical or functionalist determinism, recourse to history no longer being of any use, as M. Crozier says, for understanding how the present is determined, but for considering 'how change takes place on the basis of a quite different understanding of the operating mechanisms, whose transformation is much more important than the supplanting of the visible forms'.[2]

Establishing a viable memory-storage, information and communication system consonant with the historical heritage

The first feature essential to the operation of a social system is its memory, which links it to its past and which, by a process of successive enrichment, enables it to disseminate information that will serve to ensure its coherence. This memory cannot be confined to one or other of the spheres that we have singled out above. The memories of social systems have a value component, in the same way as they have an economic component and a specifically social component, bound up in particular with the actual experience of class relations. Their state is therefore the outcome of the lengthy process of social evolution that the developing countries have undergone, and especially of the role played by colonialism. From that point of view, the colonial heritage has been stored in the developing countries' memories in one form or another. In most cases, two memory-storage subsystems have been superimposed and, though there is initially little exchange between them, they tend to develop in such a way as to move progressively towards intermingling. The process by which memory-storage takes place is extremely complex. In the first place, it uses a coding system, in other words a language, that enables the inherited information to be compiled. It then goes through procedures for selecting and legitimating the data to be kept. Lastly, it makes use of all kinds of entities to deposit that information in specific areas. Individuals by virtue of their personality, social groups through their collective consciousness and institutions are all among a society's memory-storage centres.

Acculturation, meaning the sum of processes accompanying the contact between two or more cultures, can be identified at each memory-storage stage. As far as the coding of inherited information is concerned, it would be a commonplace to emphasize the role played by language and the problems arising from the lack of linguistic unity in a number of developing countries. In addition, there are all the different forms taken by rites and other symbolic practices, which are likewise carriers of specific codes. Economic information itself has to be analysed in those terms. In that respect, the manner in which national accounts are kept offers a good example of acculturation: since they were originally based on the accounting models of the industrialized countries, they are quite incapable of giving an adequate picture of the country's true position. In fact, they use unsuitable codes in regard to data that it is imperative to store if one is to control the course of development: production for own use, social data, economic sectors (currently based on the way production is organized in the industrialized countries) and so on. While the codes used are clearly not the fruit of pure abstraction (the cybernetic standpoint) but are largely the product of social life and hence of the tangible forms of social relations (relations between ethnocultural groups and class relations), this is even more true of the procedures that legitimate the selection of the information for storage. For instance, the split in the middle classes in favour of an export-oriented bourgeoisie (at the expense of the local bourgeoisie and landowners), which is bound up with the outward-looking choice made by many developing countries, especially in Latin America,[3] has given rise to 'modernist' tendencies that aim at discrediting the pre-existing norms, values and taboos.

In Africa, Samir Amin[4] rightly stresses the considerable relative influence wielded by a national bureaucracy which, in many cases, has contributed to transforming the forms of legitimation of the national culture. In that regard, the abnormal growth of the tertiary sector generally, and especially the growth of tourism, lead to cultural and artistic works being selected in accordance with mechanisms that bear little relation to traditional procedures (such as the enhanced legitimation of the hotel industry to the detriment of the traditional market for crafts). The same phenomenon is encountered in the selection of economic information, since the governing classes, regardless of their common ideological origin, always tend to store economic information that is least likely to cast doubt on their management. Thus, like the developed countries, they give prominence to flow patterns and almost always disregard the distribution aspect, whence the lack of data on income distribution, capital structure, and so on. The memory-storage centres have to contend with the same acculturation phenomenon. There have been a large number of studies showing how, as they have developed, individual personalities have recorded and assimilated the culture shock.[5] Within one and the same individual's personality forms of identification with colonial culture exist side by side with forms of reaction. Torn between an often formal Western education and a traditional, informal family upbringing which are markedly different from one another in terms of norms and values, attitudes to objects, interpersonal relationships or the choice of reference groups, the individual undergoes an identity crisis which is resolved on specific terms that are also largely dependent on the class to which the individual belongs. Thus, D. C. Gordon[6] was able to identify three main categories: the 'futurists', who subscribe to an advanced technological society and reject history; the 'apologists', who advocate a return to the past; and the 'reconstructionalists', who would like to update old values capable of being applied in the present day. Although this kind of typology is extremely rudimentary, it clearly points to the contradictory quality of the memory-storage process of a population who have been subjected to external influences, and particularly to colonization. This contradiction is plainly found again in the institutions that are more formally responsible for the memory-storage system at national level, such as the education system, as we shall see below, but also the whole range of administrative structures. In the latter respect, the Tangier Symposium stressed the fact that there are several administrative subsystems that are still marked by specific cultures, and the effects of this can be seen in regard to organizational practices as well as human potentialities and the actual procedures governing relations with the public.[7]

The main points to bear in mind, then, are the complexity and gradual nature of the processes that will enable the developing countries to evolve a national memory-storage system. This is a long-drawn-out task, and doubt as to the final outcome can only be increased by the fact that in these countries the memory-storage system is still seen in a sharply polarized and segmented fashion. This is due both to the control which certain socal classes exercise over the memory-storage process and to the differing rates at which items are stored, depending on the sphere to which they belong (e.g. the 'scientific and technical' sphere or the 'norms and values' sphere).

However, the form taken by the memory-storage processes and the role which the national memory plays in the practical conduct of development also largely depend on the way in which information and communications are organized. If we were to follow Edgar Morin, we might be tempted to draw a distinction between 'generative' information, which feeds the national memory with facts, images, models and reminders of historical events, and 'circulating' information, which brings together and co-ordinates the different elements composing a social system through a process of communication.[8] It is through contact with these two modes of information that the population and decision-makers will receive and emit a set of meaningful data. Their ability to perceive information that is meaningful to the action they take will depend on their information situation,[9] defined in those terms. This is where a good many difficulties crop up. How can a host of differentiated means of sensing, perceiving and recognizing information be maintained when a colonial past has given rise to a marked tendency to homogenize the modes of representation through the 'extroversion of information'.[10] How, in such a context, is it possible to link together the different levels at which the information is read, its associations registered and its meaning sought? What can be done to bridge the gap occurring more and more frequently between people's information situation in their private and social lives and that in their working lives? How, lastly, can a balance be struck between the information flow and the cognitive capacity of the population?[11] Moreover, while it has to be admitted that the development of a national mass-communication system has only seldom been regarded as being a priority step on the road to development,[12] there can be no doubt that it is an essential staging-point along the way to endogenous development. Permitting as they do the circulation of coded schemata for action, in other words procedures and ways of going about things that take into account all the legitimated cultural qualities, communications fulfil a uniquely important co-ordinating and unifying role. Forgoing control of communications means divesting ourselves of one of the main responsibilities involved in the search for the national coherence of society. It means washing our hands of the choice of signs or symbols, relinquishing control over the information carrier and finally, taking no interest in whether the meaning received will be consonant with the behaviour required, having regard to the direction chosen. From this point of view, control of the education and communication systems is an essential requirement. For our present purposes, we shall merely call attention to the importance of establishing a viable national memory-storage, information and communication system as a prerequisite for conducting a deliberate and conscious development process.

Promoting a co-ordinated vision of society, in terms of its identity and differences

The next step should be to define, in a deliberate and conscious act of will, what makes up the identity of the society in question, in such a way as not to gloss over the differences, but to bring them within a co-ordinated whole. This is a considerable undertaking if we bear in mind all the evidence pointing to the dualism of structures in developing countries. Although the term does not really reflect the fact that there are often a large number of cultural subsystems, it does convey the idea of the compartmentalization. In fact, dualism signifies difference without communication, hence without real unity. It has been possible to discern this in virtually all the areas forming the image of society in the developing countries. Although there is no need to repeat a point that figures so prominently in the literature or to express an opinion at this juncture on the reasons for this dualism (i.e. whether it is caused by the development of the dominant countries or is of internal origin), it should be emphasized that the plurality of subcultures goes hand in hand with plurality of socio-economic subsystems. Society as a whole is thus segmented not only between a modern area and a traditional area (corresponding to the town–country duality), but the urban area itself encompasses 'upper' and 'lower' levels.[13] Compounding the sectoral segmentations are the social stratifications which can be identified both in rural society (the haves and the have-nots) and in urban society (the primacy of employment in the tertiary sector over employment in industry).

A striking and instructive illustration of the global nature of the cultural phenomenon with which the developing countries are thus having to contend has been given by E. F. Schumacher,[14] when he contrasts the 'modern' economy with the 'Buddhist' economy. After rightly stressing that the desire to lead a Buddhist way of life calls for a Buddhist conception of economics, in the same way as a materialist life-style requires a modern economy, he goes on to ask in respect of which fundamentals the two cultures differ. In the modern economy, work is a necessary evil that stands in the way of leisure. From the point of view of the employer, it is an item in the cost of production, to be reduced to a minimum through a division of labour which will tend to make the workers increasingly remote from the final product and turn them into mere appendages of the machine. From the point of view of the workman, it is a disutility, where wages are a compensation for the sacrifice made. At the limit, 'the ideal from the point of view of the employer [is] to have output without employees, and the ideal from the point of view of the employee is to have income without employment'. In the Buddhist economy, on the other hand, work offers man a means of utilizing and developing his faculties, overcoming his 'egocentredness' by joining with other people in a common task, and providing the wherewithal for survival. Hence, to organize work in such a manner that it leads to the worker's loss of his sense of responsibility, to nervous fatigue, and to submission to the machine and to a formal hierarchy, indicates a greater concern with goods than with people. Equally, regarding leisure as an alternative to work would amount, in the Buddhist's view, to dissociating the living process which is, in fact, based on their complementarity. Since the Buddhist does not see the essence of civilization in a multiplication of wants, work must first improve the highest human faculties.

This example shows how difficult it is to visualize unity in difference when integrated cultures (in the sense that they link together a system of values, patterns of socialization and a form of productive organization) exist side by side on one and the same national territory. If the social system is to become progressively more coherent, communication must be allowed to flow between these cultures, so that it will result in their being linked together; hence a decision must be taken as to how, basically, the different cultures are to be brought within the system as a whole. This means defining forms of complementarity which make it possible to confer consistency on the whole, in other words on the nation. Many different forms of complementarity can be envisaged. In the first place, complementarity can be sought through improved communication of information. In that case, unity can be gradually achieved by using a common code. Complementarity can also be sought by the introduction of functional specialization which, as a rule, tends to be grounded in economic factors and is no doubt the key element in the organization of social systems. When such specialization is imposed, it tends to reduce the diversity of society inasmuch as it blurs many cultural differences. Making Buddhist culture specialized would amount to confining a very large proportion of the population to productive activities which would be integrated into the production system as a whole but would be characterized by work patterns that would be acceptable in terms of the values represented by that culture. In that case, however, the fundamental qualities of the culture would clearly be subject to pressure from a dominant type of rationality, and this would, in the first place, invariably tend to relegate it to marginal status and eventually to phase it out altogether.

Other forms of interaction can also be envisaged, some for example concerning areas where cultures intersect, others arising out of processes where a dominant culture influences others within its gravitational field. It can be seen from the foregoing that the unity of society in the midst of differentiation cannot come about without creating dissociation and exclusion mechanisms which, as Edgar Morin points out, will result in 'the pellucid, daylight aspect of society, the aspect which goes with association, organization and functionality' being matched by 'its mirror image, a nocturnal, blurred aspect enveloped in shadow'. Hence, awareness of the existing mechanisms, suggestions for devising other mechanisms, the rehabilitation of differences that have already been marginalized, and the protection of threatened cultures by other forms of organization are all essential factors in mapping out a deliberately, consciously chosen path to development.

Adaptability, creativity and the state's search for coherence

In the case of a developing country's social system, there can be no question of devising processes that adjust automatically to external disturbances created by changes in the international environment. Given the need for adaptation and creativity, failing which the system is bound to mark time, attention must be paid to the mechanisms underlying those two concepts. Neither flexibility, in other words the speed of adaptation, nor creativity (whether through the power of imagination or through learning) can be ends in themselves. The most adaptable individual agents are probably slaves, inasmuch as they react to the slightest whim of their masters. Whenever a social system internalizes the international environment to the point where it surrenders part of its national memory to it, and whenever the communication networks are handed over to it and the information situations thus created only reproduce those obtaining in the environment, then the question of the flexibility and creativity of the national social system no longer arises. The latter, in fact, closely follows the forms of adaptation of the environment, and that combination of convergence and submission is more the result of a power relationship than of development. On the other hand, when the national social system follows the path of endogenous development, it protects its memory, constructs its own differentiation, ensures its own coherence, sets up its own learning processes and is then confronted with much more weighty problems of adaptation: adaptability has in fact to be defined in terms of the goals which the social system has set itself. The question is then one of knowing whether the developing countries are capable of adapting to the changing environment while pursuing a goal geared to endogenous development. The overall dimension of the problem

TABLE 8. External public debt as a percentage of GNP

Country	1970	1977
Low-income countries	20.3	25.0
Bangladesh	—	41.8
Mali	88.1	67.5
Somalia	41.1	92.6
Zaire	17.1	52.8
Afghanistan	58.0	34.9
Pakistan	30.5	44.9
Guinea	65.2	66.5
Mauritania	16.8	111.7
Middle-income countries	14.7	18.6
Egypt	23.7	69.7
Yemen	0.3	50.3
Liberia	52.5	37.6
Zambia	34.2	59.5
Ivory Coast	18.2	34.6
Nicaragua	19.3	40.3
Peru	14.0	38.4
Algeria	18.5	42.5
Panama	19.0	60.9
Israel	41.4	46.9

Source: World Bank, World Development Report, 1979, p. 154.

and the weight of the economic constraint can be gauged from observing the situation created by the current world crisis. In Table 8, the widespread increase in external debt and the level at which it currently stands in several countries can be noted.

In some of the situations presented in Table 8, the economic constraint clearly represents so considerable a burden that it is liable to polarize the entire capabilities of the countries concerned.

The creativity of the developing countries poses a similar problem. Generating knowledge, introducing new technologies or elaborating alternative development strategies do not only entail maintaining and organizing cultural differentiation, with public participation. They also entail laying down long-term procedures, which in most instances require a considerable volume of investment. When it is borne in mind that the industrialized countries are responsible for 95 per cent of world expenditure on research and development, it becomes clear that the socio-economic systems of the developing countries will have to continue looking to transfers for a substantial proportion of their creativity. Although some countries, such as Argentina, Colombia, India, the Republic of Korea and Mexico have been successful in setting up agencies responsible for promoting national technology,[15] the situation generally is one where technology that can be said to be appropriate to varying degrees is imported, the task of defining whether the content of the technology is appropriate or not being left to the external environment.

These different factors give an idea of the tasks devolving upon the state as the main centre in charge of this deliberate, conscious development process. Its ability to organize and control the situation largely dictates the nature of the adaptation to the international environment. With its fourfold power—to generate social rules, define strategic courses of action (by elaborating and deciding on the policies to be followed), intervene directly (by subsidies and public enterprises), and command and control—the state has the task of establishing the processes that will make it possible to direct endogenous development. However, the state should not be defined exclusively in terms of those functions. It also constitutes a set of institutions endowed with a history and their own goals and dynamic. It is formed through the support it receives from different social groups.[16] As a social system, it is bound to crystallize the relations of domination existing between classes and fractions of classes. As a human community, it cannot be reduced to a disembodied function, and it reproduces within itself the general conditions of society and the power relationships at work. These power relationships can be observed through the system of personal or social pressures which it undergoes, through the forms assumed by the process of ideological unification which it initiates and through the way in which its authority is legitimated.[17] Moreover, there are many different forms of mediation between the state and other socio-economic agents (such as firms) and these depend on how the state elects to act, or the nature of the other party in the mediation. The net result of them all is to bring these other agents, on a selective basis, into the overall direction of the social system. The importance of this role is now widely acknowledged in that, whereas the state's legitimacy formerly rested on the fact that it was the custodian of the law, it now derives from the overall effectiveness of its action.

A good many difficulties have been raised regarding the effective (or ineffective) organization of the state in developing countries. Without going so far as to concur with Gunnar Myrdal[18] that the state does not fulfil its role in that regard, it must be conceded that the governments of these countries have the utmost difficulty in ensuring the proper conduct of development. This is due to the complex pattern of social relations they present, the ever recurring gulf between the results obtained and the aims laid down by the government, its ignorance of its own system, the multiplicity of personal strategies and the prevalence of corruption, a problem that has now been officially taken up by the United Nations under the heading of 'illicit practices'. Colonialism and the colonial heritage have also left a deep imprint on the structures of the state and its workings. The result of all this has been to leave little variety in regard to the system for directing the development of national society. Since that system has to contend both with the extremely complex problem of recasting its internal structure and with the considerable pressures exerted by the international environment, it often has only a limited spectrum of suitable courses of action and changes in structure from which to choose.

Section 2

TNC growth in practice and the conflicts to which it gives rise

The foregoing remarks have shown that, unless a state responsible for directing the course of development in practice is to accept lock, stock and barrel the modernist goals offered by its external environment, it is faced with a difficult problem of consolidation and adaptation, and to solve this it must embark on long and complex processes, and also ensure a large measure of autonomy in decision-making. It is in this context that we must consider the growing transnationalization of capital, a phenomenon marked by its scale, rapidity and flexibility, and the strong power of attraction it exerts. It is readily understandable, therefore, that, following a *laissez-faire* phase in the 1950s and 1960s, the current situation can be termed a restrictive phase in which the legitimacy of the TNCs' action is being questioned on a number of counts.[19] There can be no doubt that the roots of this mistrust lie in the power displayed by these organizations, their taste for secrecy, and their ability to move collectively in response to co-ordinated reactions on the part of states. People need little convincing that the practical conduct of endogenous development is not made any easier by the intrusion of this new economic agent, which interferes to a considerable degree with the key elements in the process, namely the triple combination formed by memory-storage, information and communication, the pattern of differentiation, and adaptibility and creativity.

The fact remains that, when the debate is confined to considerations as intuitive as these, it soon gives rise to polemics that are not conducive to a deep understanding of the conflict. From the point of view concerning us here, this leads more often than not to the demand for cultural identity being idealized, and to its losing its essential organizational and material counterpart. This is why the arguments developed below set out to draw a detailed contrast between the TNCs' organization and goals and the organization of endogenous development as outlined above. Even though there is no suggestion that the TNCs have the slightest intention of controlling the development process of nations, their organizational qualities, coupled with the high degree of concentration they have attained, make for asymmetrical relations between them and states. The contrast between the two organizational structures highlights the way in which the TNCs restrict the state's capacity for independent decision-making. Since, by definition, their aims are essentially economic, their strategies herald distortions in the coherence of society, and while these are no doubt less patent and less violent than those that accompanied colonialism, they may be no less perceptible.

TNCs and the effort to accede to a higher level of capability: the organizational shock

What distinguishes a TNC most from an ordinary firm is the fact that it is not content with exporting its output: it seeks to go beyond the framework of international relations by drawing some of the elements of its environment into its own system and hence into its own logical scheme of things. In doing this, it creates new forms of association and new combinations that endow it with qualities and properties that national firms cannot possess. It is the recasting of these elements within the firm's system that enables it to accede to a higher level of capability in the sense of being able to aggregate existing potentialities in such a way as to obtain a bonus, more than the sum of the parts. This search is going on all the time in growing TNCs: it means using the natural resources of the developing countries, and also absorbing their human resources and indeed integrating whole processes (such as production processes and processes for purchasing agricultural surpluses) into the firm's system. In the process, the TNCs decide on goals, set up organizational structures and employ adaptation mechanisms which differ from those of the states and are often unsuited to the practical conduct of a consciously directed development process.

Conflicting goals: the down-grading of the socio-cultural element

In economic terms, the debate is inconclusive. If the considerations bound up with the national or foreign ownership of capital are disregarded, it is not possible to give a clear-cut answer to the question as to whether the TNCs improve the situation of the developing countries by the effect they have on the balance of payments (after some time, the profits repatriated offset the increase in export earnings and the monetary counterpart of long-term capital flows), by the jobs they create and by all the economic potential they reveal (the mobilization of untapped natural resources, increases in productivity, and so on). In point of fact, if many countries call out for direct foreign investment, they clearly do so for economic reasons. When problems arise in this respect, the countries in question introduce procedures to regulate the modes of establishment, the repatriation of profits, disinvestment and transfer of technology, but these do not necessarily inhibit the growth of the TNCs. In a recent publication, the United Nations has conducted a survey of these regulations,[20] from which it emerges that, while the way in which the economic surplus generated by the TNCs is divided may result in being more favourable to the host countries, in no case are the actual principles underlying the process called into question.

The situation is quite different from the socio-cultural standpoint. As H. V. Perlmutter[21] stresses, the TNCs seldom ask themselves what the socio-cultural consequences of their actions will be; still less do they put forward any solutions, whereas this is an essential problem for the developing countries. Since the goals of the TNCs are essentially economic, they incorporate the more specifically cultural elements only if these contribute to the achievement of their aims, such as maximizing profits or growth. At best, the developing countries' demands for cultural identity are treated as constraints imposed by the environment. It would be no exaggeration to say, therefore, that the goals of the TNCs come into conflict with the endogenous development objective because they are based on a downgrading of the socio-cultural sphere. The following three reasons can be cited as proof of this. In the first place, the TNCs foster a system of values that is determined by their rationality. Secondly, they transform the personality of their employees so as to prevail upon them to subscribe to the objectives of the organization. Thirdly, in some sectors, the TNCs actually downgrade culture so as to generate a monetary surplus.

The first way of downgrading what has previously been called the sphere of values is by determining its configuration on the basis of strictly economic considerations. In that regard, there can be no doubt that the values which the TNCs serve to propagate are essentially materialistic values that have become widespread in the developed countries and are accentuated by them as they pass them on. The quest for profit is accompanied by an individual moral code of efficiency and mobility. The technological thrust pushes the demand for rationality to extremes 'which can only be described as a distortion of human cognitive processes. That which is non-rational is labelled irrational and equated with neurosis, primitivism and inferior, effeminate thinking.'[22] At the limit, it could be asserted that the TNCs are the present-day vehicles of a hyperclassicism in which cultures are excluded in favour of the organizational rationale of the firm. Instances are sometimes even found of attitudes reminiscent of Pascal, in that it is considered preferable to despise all reason rather than acknowledge that specific cultural contents have a rational significance. This is a far cry from the anticlassicism that underlies many national demands for cultural identity, at least unconsciously, and which is interested more in meaning than in truth and in human attitudes as a whole rather than in a rationale. Although the opposite tendency can be perceived in some cases, it may be acknowledged as a general rule that the functioning of an organization suffers when part of its effectiveness is devoted to pursuing other aims. This point will be developed below in connection with the business ethic, which is one of the key features of the cultural package delivered by the TNCs. At this point, we need only stress that a not inconsiderable and growing part of the training programme for future TNC executives consists in instilling in them an awareness of the difficulties they will encounter in the developing countries as a result of the 'archaic' and 'traditional' values predominating there. There is no question of integrating those values into the memory of the affiliate, in order to come up with technical solutions that will accord them an appropriate place; the idea is rather to make a virtue of necessity by using the constraint they place on the growth of the company to adapt its structure to changed circumtances, or else to set about transforming the value system in question, a reaction that has tended to become widespread in recent years as the TNCs' control over the world communication system has grown.

The second way of downgrading the socio-cultural element is more specifically concerned with the TNCs' employees. Geocentric man discards part of his original personality to take on a personality whose reference locus becomes the TNC. Firms are constantly concerned with getting the people comprising the workforce to move beyond their national terms of reference, and some of them even make this a priority objective. More and more studies are being carried out to relate the reactions of wage-earners to forms of management organization and to their original nationality. D. L. Schaupp, for instance, has conducted a survey of a large TNC—its name is not given— on the basis of a population of 16,000 employees spread over its affiliates in eight countries (Argentina, Canada, France, the Federal Republic of Germany, India, Japan, the Netherlands and the United Kingdom).[23] The employees replied in more or less the same way to the questionnaire on the factors which they regarded as being important in an ideal job, hence without taking their current job into account. However, India and Argentina, the two developing countries in the sample, stand out from the others, in that they 'did not place much importance on a challenging work environment'. Aspirations towards a better collective life at work were no longer discriminating factors, and this prompts the author to say, like many before him, that the test is sufficient to bear out the 'cultural convergence' hypothesis, the basis for that hypothesis being that all countries of the world have common economic motivations generating forces sufficient to cause the philosophy and practice of management to converge. We interpret this rather as being symptomatic of the ability of the TNCs to reshape the personalities of individuals in terms of their own objectives. In fact, this clearly emerges from other research, and especially from a study carried out on 13,000 IBM employees. The author concludes that there is a remarkable similarity of aims among the firm's employees throughout the world and goes on to say that this finding 'has an extremely important policy implication: since the goals of employees are similar internationally, the firm's corporate policy decisions, to the extent that they are based on assumptions about employee goals, can also be international in scope'.[24] It is quite plain, therefore, that cultural unity within the firm is a necessity if it is to be able to fulfil its ambitions. There are grounds for thinking that, in the longer run, the very large TNCs will be led to strengthen the procedures for bringing this about, thus giving rise to genuinely 'transnational' and 'supranational' companies: Types E and F in the classification proposed by R. D. Robinson.[25]

In Type E, transnational firms, resources are appropriated and managed on a multinational basis. The decision-making process is centralized but not subject to any national bias, apart from that imposed on it by law. In Robinson's words, the firm develops loyalty of a sort that transcends national identity and may accordingly come into conflict with the government of the parent country, and, we would add, to an even greater extent that of the host country.

In Type F, supranational firms, the decision-making process is free, from the structural as well as from the psychological or legal points of view, and this enables them to allocate their resources on a global basis in conformity with the corporate goals, so long as they do not enter into conflict with the international political set-up controlling the firm.

This is an eventuality which should not be underestimated and which shows, in any event, that the TNCs will tend to promote a worldwide cultural fabric paralleling the world economic fabric. This is, in fact, the objective assigned to the management-training programmes established by the TNCs, as we shall see below. They appear, in the words of one study,

designed to create an élite cadre of men who all know one another and who share operating experiences in different types of managerial activity. The purpose of creating these élites is to foster an environment in which men who are physically distant at any one time can communicate easily and informally. If men share common experience and perceive themselves as having similar status in the hierarchy, they generally co-operate more readily than they would in other circumstances.[26]

The specificity of the TNCs compared with any other form of industrial entity lies in the fact that a universal model is applied to individuals situated in socio-cultural environments that are infinitely more diversified than they are in the national arena. The resulting homogenization phenomenon plainly leads to a general downgrading of the socio-cultural element, in that it does away with the main feature of cultural creativity, namely its diversity.

There is a third form of downgrading the socio-cultural, bound up with the methods by which some TNCs seek to generate a surplus. This point can be illustrated by an example from tourism. The idea in this case is to profit from a land rent for tourism purposes by limiting the maximum price enabling a site and its human environment to be developed. As a result of the quasi-monopoly they hold over the development of such sites, some TNCs engaging in tourism minimize the cultural scarcity value when they negotiate the development, and then recover the rent in the tourist proceeds.[27] More generally, the downgrading of the cultural heritage or the failure to value it at its true worth enables natural resources to be exploited intensively in a number of ways, and offers a way round the safeguards which the industrialized countries now impose for the protection of the environment, and illustrates in the most flagrant possible way the contradiction between culture and profit.

The ambiguity of decentralized forms of TNC organization

It is tempting to imagine that the actual impact of cultural downgrading will be reduced to a minimum in instances where firms opt in favour of a decentralized form of organization. Many authors have considered that, in such cases, decentralized affiliates or subsidiaries would enable the socio-cultural demands of the host countries to be taken into account. Firms that are organized on a worldwide basis would then have diversified decision-making procedures adapted to local conditions to set against the added power they gain.

If we adhere to H. V. Perlmutter's classification, we shall in fact be led to say that the geocentric (world-oriented) or polycentric (host-country-

TABLE 9. Orientation of the TNC headquarters command structure in the classification developed by H. V. Perlmutter

Organization design	Ethnocentric	Polycentric	Geocentric
Complexity of organization	Complex in home country, simple in subsidiaries	Varied and independent	Increasingly complex and interdependent
Authority; decision-making	High in headquarters	Relatively low in headquarters	Aim for a collaborative approach between headquarters and subsidiaries
Evaluation and control	Home standards applied for persons and performance	Determined locally	Find standards which are universal and local
Rewards and punishments; incentives	High in headquarters; low in subsidiaries	Wide variation; can be high or low rewards for subsidiary performance	International and local executives rewarded for reaching local and worldwide objectives
Communication and information flow	High volume to subsidiaries orders, commands, advice	Little to and from headquarters. Little between subsidiaries	Both ways and between subsidiaries. Heads of subsidiaries part of management team
Identification	Nationality of owner	Nationality of host country	Truly international company but identifying with national interests
Perpetuation (recruiting, staffing, development)	Recruit and develop people of home country for key positions everywhere in in the world	Develop people of local nationality for key positions in their own country	Develop best men everywhere in the world for key positions everywhere in the world

Source: H. V. Perlmutter, *Transnational Corporations and World Order*, p. 37, San Francisco, Freeman, 1979.

oriented) type of organizational design for a TNC will be better able to take account of the goals of the developing countries than an ethnocentric (home-country oriented) company. Although Table 9 is very open to question, it does provide an illustration of the decision-making context in the three cases. If the firm is ethnocentric, the criteria of success used for both manpower and products are national criteria:

We have found that a salesman should make twelve calls a day in Hoboken, New Jersey (the headquarters location), and therefore we apply these criteria everywhere in the world. The salesman in Brazzaville is naturally lazy, unmotivated. He shows little drive because he makes only two calls per day (despite the Congolese salesman's explanation that it takes time to reach consumers by boat).[28]

As a rule, the ethnocentric firm is characterized by its home-country nationality and this gives the locals the feeling that they represent an inferior group compared with the home-country nationals. If the firm is polycentric, the initial assumption is that the host-country cultures are different and that foreigners have difficulty in understanding them. The aim would be to make the affiliate as integral a part of the host-country scene as possible, and this would often entail entrusting top management posts to local personnel. The fact remains that genuinely polycentric attitudes only start to become common in instances where affiliates are established in the industrialized countries, whereas they correspond much less closely to the image conveyed when the affiliates are located in the developing countries. As regards geocentric firms we can summarize the situation by saying that their ultimate objective is to institute a worldwide approach at both headquarters and affiliate levels. However, quite apart from the fact that the above classification is now out of date, it has the disadvantage of concealing the link between the firm's organization and strategy, which are essential items for understanding the nature of the organizational conflict between firms and states. It is plain, in fact, that even polycentric firms will differ in their ability to merge with the systems which states use for conducting their development in practice, depending on their growth stage and strategy, and the activity in which they engage.

Closer study of the way in which TNCs are organized (such as has been carried out by R. D. Robinson,[29] and D. F. Channon and M. J. Jalland[30] makes it possible to identify six forms of organization.

The first corresponds to the setting up of a foreign department, followed by the creation of an international division. In the first stage, therefore, the foreign-market potential is not systematically investigated and the international character of the firm is warranted only by the existence of an export service. In that case, the firm has an operational strategy in the sense that the aim is to sell products on developing-country markets. As a general rule, firms opting for this form of organization are not very diversified. They are content for their foreign links to be handled through agents established in the countries themselves. They subsequently go on to set up an international division integrated into the structure of the organization at the same level as the divisions engaged in domestic business. In cases where the international division grows in importance, its structure is broken down into more specialized subdivisions on a country or product basis. It should be noted that, in firms organized on this model, transnationalization is very slight, since it is chiefly concerned with creating trading affiliates, and this means, first, that the co-ordination of the entire organization is a matter for headquarters (since the affiliates are only foreign offshoots of the parent company) and, secondly, that the products sold on the developing-country markets differ only slightly from those traded on the domestic market. However, as the firm grows, it runs the risk of seeing its decision-making process biased in favour of export business at the expense of licence sales and international investment. To avoid this, it has to have personnel whose careers do not depend on export performance alone, but also on familiarity with production. These internal conflicts, coupled with the need to be able to control foreign operations by means of skilled personnel, are the factors that prompt the firm to change its structure.

The second organizational type marks an authentic switch to a multinational activity, inasmuch as it arises out of an awareness that an optimum penetration strategy can only be brought about through direct investment. Firms belonging to this category integrate the international aspect into their functional organization. However, they confine their opening moves on the international scene to two main functions, i.e. to production and marketing. The strategy of such firms is both one of absorption, in that they have a foreign production activity using local natural resources and productive factors, and one of performance, through its marketing department. These TNCs are usually not very diversified, and functional co-ordination is vested in the higher hierarchical level. Consequently, this first form of functional organization means that the affiliates have limited freedom of action and only have access to production or distribution. This form is to be found in several European transnationals while, in the United States, a perfect illustration of the type can be seen in John Deere & Company, the

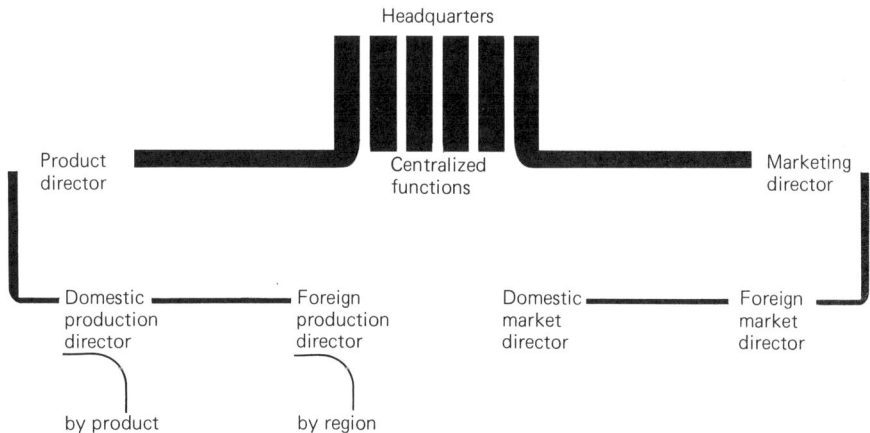

FIG. 2. Organization integrating international activities into its structure.

manufacturers of agricultural machinery. The choice of this structure has prompted the firm to integrate its R&D, and planning and finance, and to set up regional production and sales divisions.

The third form of organization is based on the production process and is representative of TNCs with vertically-integrated production activities. This is notably the case of specialist firms in the extractive industries, such as oil- and metal-processing companies. In this case, each production stage is organized globally from a central base. As a result, headquarters has considerable co-ordinating powers and the communication and transport system plays a key role. The different units have little freedom of action and, until recently at least, the product diversification of the firms involved was limited (except in the case of certain oil companies). In a situation such as this, it is plain that the logic of the firm's organization is, to a very large extent, incompatible with adaptation to the local situation. The inflexibility of the integrated production chain is such that it dictates a uniform linked pattern of organization, as can be seen in Figure 3.

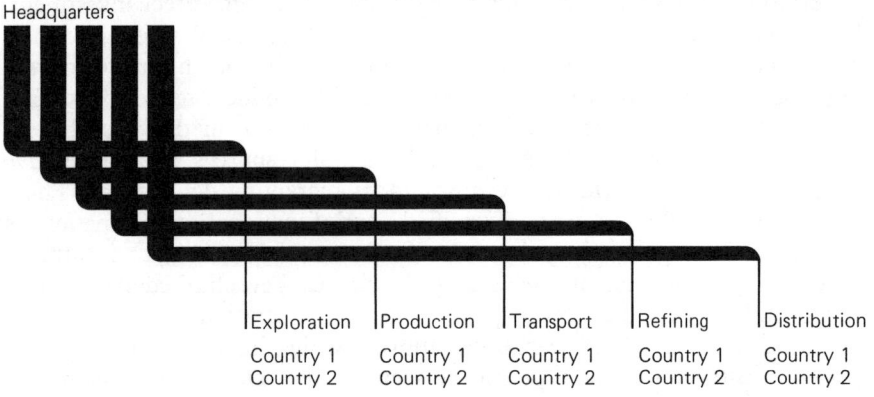

FIG. 3. Organization based on the production process.

The fourth organizational type is worldwide organization by product line. The main reason for choosing this structure stems from the need to integrate research, marketing and production activities within each division (Fig. 4).

This is clearly a form of organization, polycentric in character, and indeed even geocentric in the case of very large firms. Each product division has a functional subdivision for each country. Since co-ordination at the central level is chiefly concerned with planning and certain financial aspects, this is one of the types of organization which theoretically leaves the affiliate with most freedom of action. This structure tends to be chosen by many firms operating in several markets. In this type of organization, each division is responsible for the production and sale of its products on a worldwide basis, although most of the firms involved tend to focus on the domestic market and to deal with international operations separately. As a rule, the firms are diversified, after the manner of RCA, which organized its electronics and

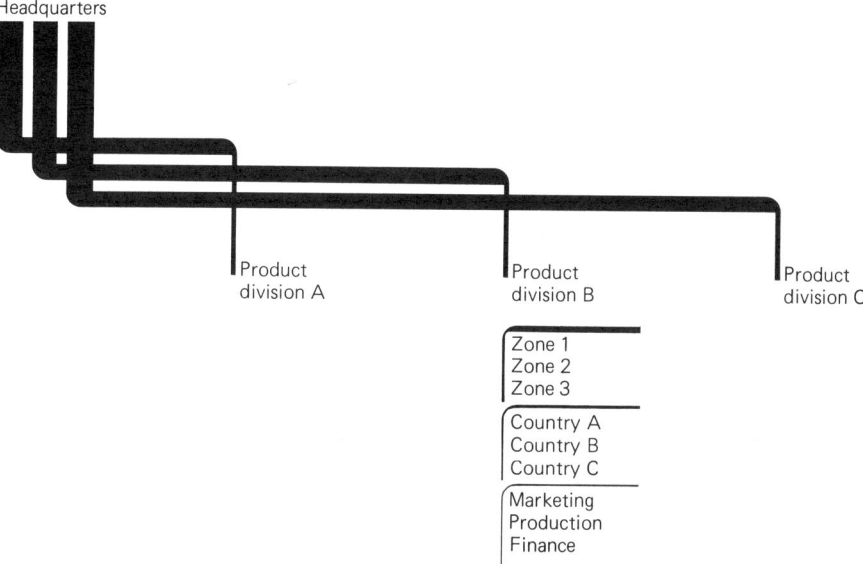

FIG. 4. Worldwide organization by product line.

data-processing activities on this system in 1967, and of the Celanese Corporation, which was one of the first transnationals in the United States to adopt this structure, setting up three separate product divisions, for fibres and timber products, chemicals and plastics, and consumer goods. It should be stressed that, offsetting decentralization in such cases, co-ordination becomes more difficult. This is what prompted the recasting of this type of organization to produce the variant known as the 'umbrella' structure, the main feature of which is the creation of a local holding company for each country or zone. The structure is designed to ensure that, in its dealings with local governments, the firm adopts a single approach as far as co-ordination and representation are concerned. This practice accordingly again increases the specific gravity of the TNC, at the same time making it more difficult to adapt to the local environment. Taking the firm's standpoint, D. F. Channon and M. J. Jalland put forward the following points in justification for this structure: (a) it presents a unified corporate face to governments and local markets; (b) it provides a channel of communication in regard to operations necessary for divisional co-ordination and for maintaining relations with the parent company; (c) it helps resolve local interdivisional differences; (d) it provides an overall corporate perspective on local business opportunities; (e) tax advantages become available by writing off losses in one division against profits in another; (f) consistent personnel policies can be introduced which also aid negotiations with trade unions and facilitate inter-divisional transfers; (g) the consolidation of divisional funds tends to permit more local borrowing; (h) the parent company has more scope for centralized international money management.

From the standpoint of the developing countries, it is clear that almost every term of the argument is reversed, in that most of the main criticisms

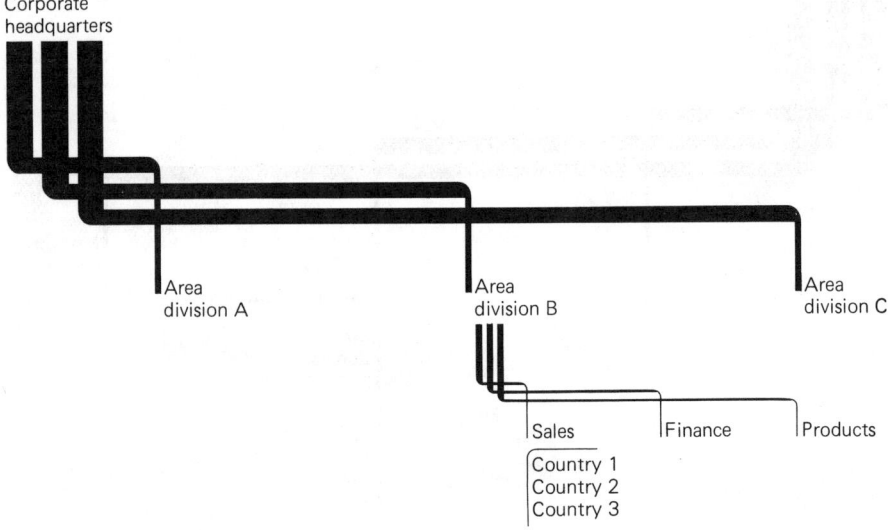

FIG. 5. Decentralization by geographical areas—first case (after D. F. Channon and M. J. Jalland, *Multinational Strategic Planning*, London, Macmillan, 1979).

which those countries level against the TNCs are to be found in the reasons given above.

The fifth type of organization is that systematizing decentralization by geographical areas, in the form of a geographical breakdown either by functions or by products. In the first case (Fig. 5) the firms involved are not very diversified in terms of products but are highly diversified by countries. A typical example is that provided by the Ford Motor Company, which decentralized its European production and sales activities to the United Kingdom in 1967. The upshot of this was that it prompted the firm to review its model designs in a bid to adapt them more closely to the European market. However, this type of organization, which is still highly centralized and embraces a considerable area, is often combined with a situation where certain countries specialize in segments of production. Mention can also be made of the case of Unilever, which has specialized divisions for Europe, Africa and the rest of the world, and has, at the same level, a specific division for managing its plantation activities in Belgium, the United Republic of Cameroon, Malaysia, Nigeria, the Solomon Islands and Zaire. However, as a general rule, it is not common with this type of organization for the head office of the area divisions to be located in the developing countries (in the case of Unilever, the overseas division or 'Overseas Committee' and the African division, the 'United Africa Group', both have their headquarters in London.[31]

In the second case (Fig. 6), the firms are usually very large and are diversified by both products and areas. This gives rise to a complex organizational pattern reflecting the desire to co-ordinate activities generating a substantial volume of trade between affiliates within the same area. The

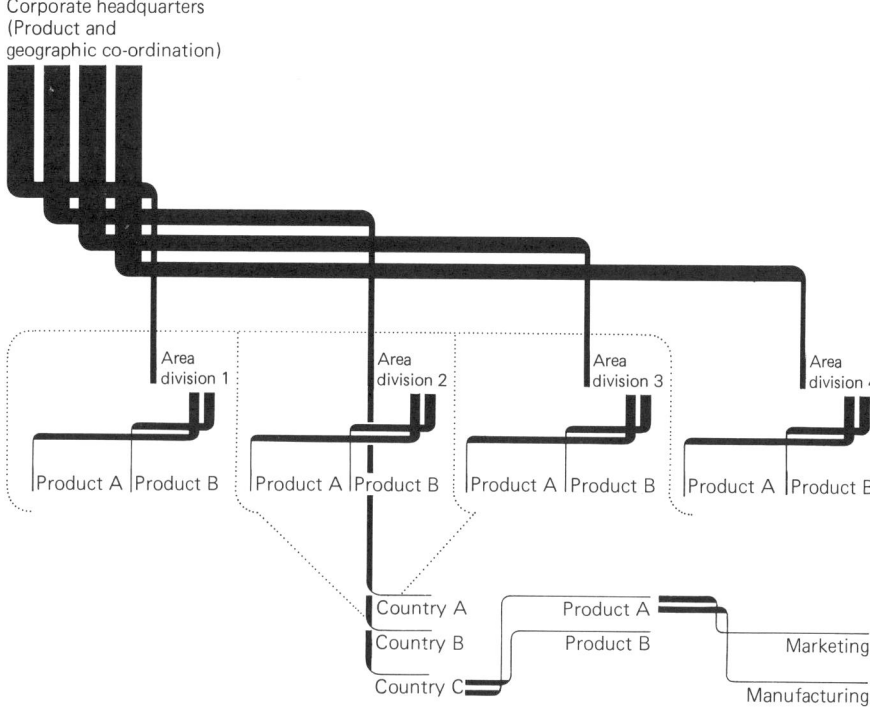

FIG. 6. Decentralization by geographical areas—second case (after D. F. Channon and M. J. Jalland, *Multinational Strategic Planning*, p. 38, London, Macmillan, 1979).

purpose of the co-ordination is to control both the many product levels and the regions. Such control is usually carried as far as the central level, as in the case of the American firm, Corning Glass, which adopted this structure in 1965. Theoretically, however, it is one of the organizational types most resembling the polycentric and geocentric models.

The sixth type is the 'mother and daughter' model (Fig 7), which splits operations in the home country or region from foreign operations. Whereas domestic operations are organized by products, foreign operations are organized by countries. This type of organization is to be found in many European TNCs, which set up affiliates in the developing countries when they first began to expand. In such cases, the affiliates have a fairly broad measure of freedom, while the parent company functions as a holding company. Philips is the most pertinent example of this type of organization, and its existence is accounted for by the fact that the parent company was cut off from its affiliates during the Nazi occupation. However, the freedom of action of the affiliates does not extend to the point where research activities are decentralized to the countries.

There are also various distinctive mixed formulae combining two or more of these six main types. The Japanese TNCs have centralized their infor-

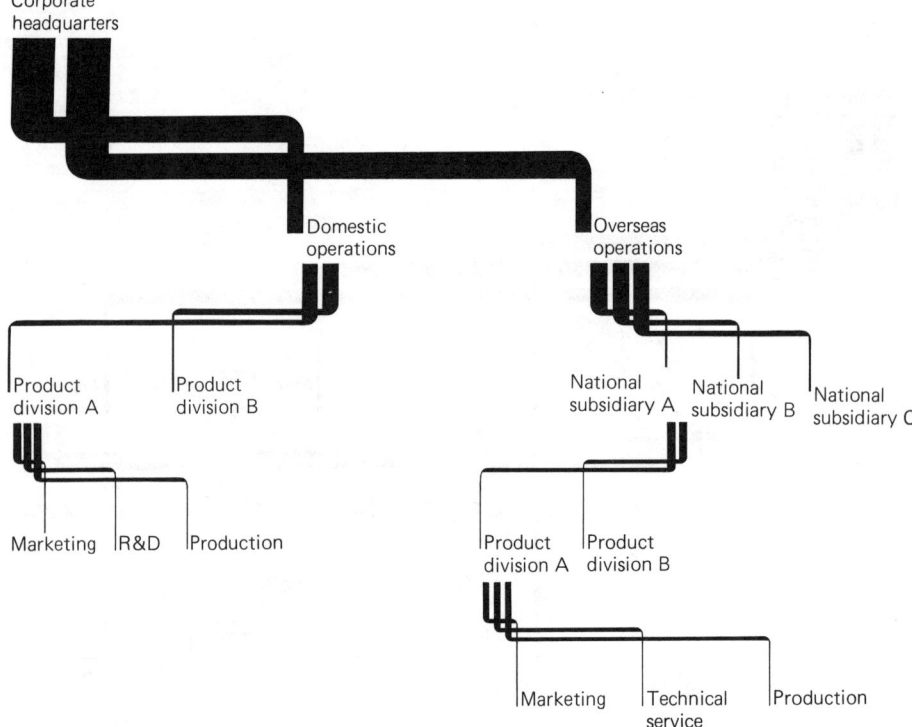

FIG. 7. The 'mother and daughter' structure (after D. F. Channon and M. J. Jalland, *Mutlinational Strategic Planning*, p, 41, London, Macmillan, 1979).

mation network, while many firms have combined a structure based on an international division (Type 1) with a product-line structure (Type 4) (such as the American pharmaceutical companies and Uniroyal). ITT makes use of several forms of organization, depending on whether it is involved in telecommunications, electrical equipment, hotel chains or insurance.

This brief overview of the international structure of the TNCs calls for several comments. In the first place, while there are indeed forms of organization that are better able to take account of the host-country environment, that ability appears to depend to a large extent on the manner of decentralization. In cases where decentralization functions on the basis of the processing chain (Type 3), the actual specialization of the production process involved leaves little scope for adapting the decentralized units. Similarly, organization by geographical zones (Type 5) has to be viewed with caution, inasmuch as the zone level may still be quite remote from the actual situation obtaining in the country, especially when the headquarters of zone divisions are situated in one of the major industrialized countries. To judge solely on the basis of the capabilities for potential integration embodied in the firm's operational structure, the 'product line' (Type 4) and 'mother and daughter' (Type 6) structures appear most suited to the polycentric model. Secondly, a permanent conflict goes on within the firm between decentralization and co-ordination. Wyverne unite his in danger of being upset, an additional co-ordination level is introduced. This further co-ordination can plainly be seen in the case of the 'umbrella structure', but it also takes less immediately visible forms in the other organizational types, mainly through staff policy, finance, and research and development, all of which are functions with a markedly centralized content. Thirdly, although genuine decentralization occurs in some developed countries, this is seldom the case in the developing countries. In that regard, polycentric and geocentric models are more a fact of life in relations between developed countries than between North and South.

By way of conclusion, let us stress the fact that, whatever form of organization is chosen by the TNCs, there is no guarantee that it will be well suited to the objectives of endogenous development. While some forms of organization virtually rule out any progress in that direction, the more decentralized forms are always visualized in terms of the firm's unity and growth and they are recast when they develop along lines that are regarded as divergent from that point of view. In fact, the evolution of the firm towards a polycentric or geocentric form of organization raises a difficult problem. It always gives rise to a considerable increase in the relative importance of the firm, and the influence it exerts, even if it often brings in a more decentralized pattern of operation, i.e. in theory one better able to take account of the socio-cultural demands of the host countries. We can thus understand why, when they look at matters from the standpoint of those countries, some authors, like C. A. Michalet, point out that:

while the adoption of a worldwide structure is bound to be accompanied by a measure of deconcentration of responsibilities in favour of regional or product managements, that transfer of responsibilities is chiefly concerned with matters relating to routine production management. It does not mean, as is sometimes made out, that there is a genuine decentralization culminating in increased integration of the affiliates into the host economy.[32]

The opposition between the TNCs' operational system and the conduct of endogenous development by the nation-state

Concealed behind the TNCs' formal organizational structure is a series of organized procedures, which enable them to set themselves up internationally and keep on expanding in accordance with their goals. The large transnational corporations have carried their analysis of the optimum procedures for this purpose as far as the present state of the art will permit, affording a constant temptation for the application of cybernetic theories; this in itself almost suffices to prove their considerable powers of adjustment and the coherent, self-contained way in which they are organized. The corollary of these two properties, which make it possible for them to change their range of action and their structure without calling their goals into question, is their increased power in relation to the governments of the developing countries, which are in an infinitely more delicate situation. The asymmetrical influence of the TNCs perhaps stems more from the relative coherence of their organizational system than from deliberate intent. Since the developing countries' concern for cultural identity makes it impossible for them to subscribe to the TNCs' goals, they will have no choice but to establish an organizational system of a different kind, and also guard it against interference. Hence, a confrontation occurs between two types of organization —one of them coherent, the other less so—based on different principles. If the TNCs' organizational system is examined more closely, this confrontation can be characterized as follows: (a) the TNCs store the information and communicate it in accordance with the goals of their own system; (b) the TNCs use control and adjustment procedures which lead to internalization and exclusion of the environment; and (c) the TNCs have a much greater potential for variety than that of the nation-states.

First, one of the essential components of the corporate organization is its memory-storage system. The way in which this system is geared to the operational system as a whole and whether the two run smoothly together largely determine how the organizational structure will develop. In addition, it is essential to examine the memory-storage procedures in order fully to appreciate how the TNCs adjust in response to the demands of the developing countries. This adjustment is quite different, both in its principles and in the results it produces, depending on whether the demands of the developing countries find an echo in the firm's memory or take the form of environmental 'noise'. The dividing-line between these two situations depends on the way in which the firm's memory is loaded with international information. In fact, the contents of the firm's memory can be regarded as being double. The memory draws a large part of its items from all the information that was collected and deposited in the firm's original storage capacity. This 'old' memory is built up on the basis of the coding and data-selection procedures specific to the 'home' cultural system. However, since the decision 'to go international' has been followed by a significant extension in the range of data stored on a worldwide scale, the fundamental problem for our purposes here is knowing whether this extension of the memory-storage field has been accompanied by any change in the actual process involved in grasping the information. Depending on the flexibility of the rules for coding the different kinds of information collected by the firm, it may or may not interiorize the new data. If the data are interiorized, the consequence will be an adaptive change in the structure of the memory. The firm would thus enrich its old memory by feeding it with new values based on different cultures, a process that could even go so far as to call into question its goals and its strategy. On the other hand, if the information is not really interiorized, it plays quite a different role, in that it provides the firm with paradigms for control or adjustment (by taking action or altering its structure), without any change in its goals and strategies.

In fact, all the evidence is that the TNCs tend to reduce the wealth of information on the developing countries to a set of norms which they regard as being significant from the narrow standpoint of their own growth and profit-making targets. The TNCs' sources of information may take several forms: affiliates, local agents or distributors, and members of the organization who travel all take part in a very pragmatic information-gathering exercise. It is becoming increasingly common for large firms to have access to a considerable volume of information on the developing countries, either directly (cf. the Japanese type of organization in particular) or else through semi-public institutions such as world trade centres or other intermediaries. Probably the most striking phenomenon at the present time is the growth of data banks, which now represent a virtually limitless data-storage capacity. Many TNCs participate in or own international data networks for their own use, such as Telenet, Cybernet, Mark III, Satellite Business System, etc. Specialized networks exist, such as SITA for air carriers, in which 200 companies participate, SWIFT for banks, etc. However, the data are usually coded in accordance with Western procedures, meaning that they are of an economic character and are quantifiable. They embody subjective elements with a twofold view to detecting, in the environment of the developing countries, both the potential capable of being exploited and the reactions of hostility or attraction liable to be aroused. The manuals used in the management training of future TNC executives abound in examples illustrating the fact that the TNCs primarily regard the developing countries as terrain for business operations.[33] An example of this manner of representing the reality of the developing countries is given in the study by J. N. Sheth and R. J. Lutz.[34] The authors distinguish six weighted environmental factors—political stability, economic development and peformance, cultural unity, legal barriers, physiographic barriers and geocultural distance (including the degree of westernization, which is given the highest weighting)—and go on to classify the countries on a 'hot–cold gradient' from the standpoint of their receptivity to direct investments.

Although this example resembles a caricature, it does appear to epitomize in broad fashion the way in which the concrete reality of the developing countries is deposited in the TNCs' memory-store.

However, this image of the developing countries will not only be disseminated widely within the TNCs; it will also colour the way in which the national memory is built up. There are clearly a large number of interconnections between the TNCs' memory and the national memory. Local employees of the TNCs will transmit, in part at least, their employers' images of national reality, while the TNCs themselves will serve as models for national firms, which will come to depend on the same information as soon as they become large enough. Since national statistical agencies are not very reliable, it may well become common practice for international organizations, and indeed even for states, to turn to worldwide data banks promoted and fed more or less directly by the TNCs. It is quite plain, therefore, that this memory-storage process conflicts with the need to build up a satisfactory national memory. As a rapid, uniform process based on a Western system of representation, it stands in opposition to the slow, diversified process which should lead to the reconstitution of national memories by tapping the potentialities of traditional cultures.

On the other hand, it makes the TNCs' organizational system highly coherent, in that it reconstitutes and unifies the data input, 'filleting' all that pertains to the national cultures. In this regard, the internal system for communicating information must be designed as an essential adjunct to organizational coherence. It is this system which must make it possible for data to circulate and so keep the firm's personnel fully informed. In the case of the TNCs, the system is generally recognized as being most effective. The conventional modes of formal communication, such as the telephone, telex, notes, etc., are highly developed in all instances, as all the studies point out. In addition to these conventional modes, some firms also introduce more specific procedures, again for the purpose of strengthening organizational coherence. At ITT, for example, direct participation in round-table discussions and weekly meetings has at times been considered preferable to more formal relations. Generally speaking, the firm's internal communication procedures are a testing-ground for new communication techniques, which are subsequently disseminated outside the firm's sphere of action by other transnational corporations. The 'communications revolution', originally connected with the development of computers, which led to the replacement of analog electronics by digital electronics and then to the link-up of data-processing and telecommunications systems, cannot be dissociated from the communications needs of the TNCs. The latter have made a significant contribution to the development of analog forms of communication and to communication based on binary language, perhaps at the expense of interpersonal relations. More basically, distance is no longer an obstacle to communication for firms, and without going as far as to claim that the TNCs are the only element that enables it to be said that the world has become synchronous, we have to acknowledge their decisive role in that respect. From the point of view of their impact on

TABLE 10. Growth of domestic and international mail

Country	Millions of units		Percentage variation 1955–74
	1955	1974	
Argentina			
Domestic	1 253	870	—31
International	68	147	+116
Brazil			
Domestic	2 475	627	—75
International	133	80	—40
Egypt			
Domestic	175	119	—32
International	58	99	+71
India			
Domestic	3 378[1]	6 746	+100
Indonesia			
Domestic	169	149	—12
International	19	38	+100
Mexico			
Domestic	531	1 032	+94
International	102	341	+78
Venezuela			
Domestic	72[2]	202	+181
International	38[2]	145	+202

1. 1959 figures. 2. 1953 figures.
Source: United Nations, Transnational Corporations in World Development, 1978, p. 204.

the internal communication system of the developing countries, they have played a twofold role: on the one hand they have modified it as a result of the control which they now wield over the entire world communication system, but on the other hand, this being a point that is generally overlooked, they have in some cases harnessed a communication potential within the country itself. A pointer to this is the change in the volume of domestic mail flows compared with international flows. In several developing countries, it can be seen that, between 1955 and 1974, there was even an absolute decrease in this form of internal communication (Table 10).

Second, two concepts can be used to analyse the way in which the TNCs are able to maintain their coherence in a dynamic perspective. These are, first, control and, second, adjustment. The term control is taken as meaning all the corrective and compensatory devices that make it possible for firms to ensure that their structure remains stable by neutralizing disturbances and departures from the norm. These include not only error-rectifying mechanisms but also the interplay of mutually supporting actions within the firm. The entire arrangement is based on the formalization of the activities of the organization's staff-members through standardized procedures, the introduction of a system of rewards or penalties, and the 'socialization' of new members. Most authors concur in stressing the sophisticated nature of this arrangement, and especially the role played by the performance-evaluation system, which enable headquarters to ascertain the variations from the targets laid down for each division or affiliate. It can be seen from an examination of the forms taken by performance evaluation that, in principle, control is carried out without taking into account the environment, since firms seek to pursue their course without their activities or structure being jeopardized by external disturbances. This clearly emerges from the performance identification variables habitually used,[35] namely: (a) conformity to decisions by higher authority; (b) local profit; (c) contribution to consolidated profit; (d) rate of return on investment; (e) turnover (dollar volume); (f) cash flows; (g) physical volumes; (h) efficiency (measured by input-output ratios); (i) cost per unit of output; (j) dollar flows; and (k) market share. The same factors appear in respect of financial control, and it has been noted that most of the TNCs are making an effort to standardize their accounting methods.

This calls for two comments. In the first place, it is clear that the control system is highly developed in the TNCs compared with what it is likely to be in even a well-organized nation-state. This means that the TNCs can fulfil their objectives more effectively and have the means to rectify errors, which is something that the developing nation-state can scarcely manage to achieve. This disparity can be accounted for by the fact that, though the social field of the TNCs is subject to tensions, it is much less liable to conflict than that of the nation-state. In addition, this disparity in respect of control capability introduces a further disparity in regard to the ability to exclude the environment. Whereas the control mechanisms enable the firm to offset, through its structure, some effects of action taken by states, the converse is not usually true. The relative situation of the two systems could be compared to that of two ships, one with stabilizers, the other without. While the former can pursue its course (its action) through a storm in the desired direction (its goal), without the need to contemplate changing its rigging (its structure), the latter may sometimes have to take other routes and indeed may even require a complete refit. In the present case, the problem is compounded by the fact that the two objects (the firm and the state) form each other's environment. Hence, the action and structure of the object with the less sophisticated control system will be subject to the impulses or disturbances caused by the other.

What in fact makes it possible to pose this problem is the concept of adjustment. The term 'adjustment' is taken as meaning the changes in the range of action or structure which an organization makes in pursuing its goals. Thus, the controlled reaction of the TNCs to external, or even internal, disturbances will involve adjustment processes, which may or may not be structural but which, in any event, will not entail changes in their goals. These adjustment processes may be interpreted differently when they are viewed from the standpoint of the developing countries. Some authors claim that the impact on the developing countries is less because the TNCs have the capacity to adjust, and do adjust, whereas others emphasize that the reason why the TNCs to some extent adjust to the developing countries is so they can more readily achieve their goals.

The fact that the firm adjusts without changing its structure is tantamount to saying that it changes some of its activities, and this requires the mobilization of specific resources and will entail additional costs. A typical case of a firm adjusting through the action it takes is that where an affiliate adopts new production processes that do not imply any far-reaching changes in organization. Similarly, all the firm's cultural activities consisting in financing foundations, contributing to university training programmes or participating in a developing country's education budget (cf. Part Two below) correspond to this form of adjustment. Whenever oil companies finance an agricultural high school in Nigeria, build a town in Peru or breed salmon in Norway in order to obtain an exploration licence, the logic of the process becomes crystal clear. The additional cost is the price they pay to make the firm's goals and form of organization acceptable. At best, cultural ventures serve as an alibi or a negotiated *quid pro quo*. In many cases, too, cultural activities are selected carefully so as to ensure that the firm's goals sink into the country's memory.

Whenever firms adapt by changing their structure, the situation is either one where the (internal and external) tensions and disturbances are more difficult to control through existing mechanisms, or else one where the firms have no longer any doubts about their power and decide voluntarily to modify their goals and their dealings with their environment. When the problem is posed in these terms, it is possible to highlight what we shall call the paradox of structural adjustment. This paradox arises out of the fact that TNCs modify their structure both in order to take advantage of the potentialities which the developing countries offer them and so as to withstand the constraints which the latter impose on them. The adjustment therefore embodies both an acquisitive mechanism and a defence mechanism. It is not very easy, in concrete terms, to situate the dividing line between the two motives, since they are obviously combined in some of the visible changes in organization. For instance, when a TNC introduces a new product line into a developing country through a 100-per-cent-owned affiliate, it is clearly changing its structure so that it can lay hands on a potential existing in that country. On the other hand, all modern forms of establishment involving joint ventures, licensing contracts, franchise and management agreements and so on are undoubtedly a result of the pressures which states exert on the firms. Even so, the idea of capturing a market is still there. As a result, these structural adjustment mechanisms are paralleled by mechanisms for assimilating and excluding the environment. Since the TNCs are prepared to adjust their structure only to those disturbances in the environment that do not jeopardize their goals, the rest will be rejected. As far as the effect on the developing countries' overall sphere of operation is concerned, this means that functional specialization will take place in those areas where the firm has been assimilated, whereas endogenous development, which is often conservative and limited in its horizons, keeps to areas where the firm has excluded the environment or refused to adjust. This situation is probably not very conducive to building a coherent society whose unity and differentiation have been carefully thought out. It will perpetuate and accentuate the polarization of the system, or else cause the social system to develop on a co-ordinated economic basis consistent with the firm's objectives.

The third and last factor distinguishing TNCs and states in respect of their ability to conduct a deliberate, consciously conceived development process is the potential for variety, by which we mean their ability in general to cope with the constraints of the environment. This is an essential factor in assessing their relative adjustment capacities. The number of possible forms a firm or state may take depends on its organization, the constraints imposed on it, its capacity for innovation and its ability to explore the potentialities offered by the world outside and take advantage of them quickly (or alternatively, appreciate the nature of the constraints and forestall them). It has become almost a commonplace to observe, as H. Schamm does, that the firm's overall capacity to adapt to constraints is greater than that of the nation-state:

It is pointless to purport to situate the activities of a multinational enterprise geographically, in other words to apportion them between territories, nations or regional groupings, since they are based on function rather than location. Its ability to choose and its flexibility appear as an overwhelming advantage to those having to deal with it. Asymmetry characterizes its relations with them. The game between the recipient country and the enterprise is one-sided.[36]

The explanation for this disproportion lies in the wealth of sources of variety available to the TNC. The first of these sources is internal and stems from the firm's qualities of initiative and innovation which, as J. A. March and H. A. Simon (*Organizations*, 1958, p. 174) stress, emerge 'when change requires the devising and evaluation of new performance programmes that have not previously been a part of the organization's repertory and cannot be introduced by a simple application of programmed switching rules'.

The firm possesses the ability to generate new programmes because it has resources for innovation in reserve which enable it to create variety at each hierarchical level. This also accounts for the interest that firms take in forms of organization that enable that capacity to be increased (and this is the significance that has to be attached to some of the efforts made to relax control over the affiliates). Secondly, the firm draws its variety from its environment. Its worldwide structure allows of an extremely wide-ranging combination of programmes, to be put into effect where it chooses. In point of fact, it is the great range of possible responses compared with those available to the state that has led to the idea that national control needs to be supplemented by an international code of conduct.

The control which the developing countries exert through their national legislation is not sufficient, since it does not enable them to grasp the full dimensions of the phenomenon of international direct investment. Although each unit of a TNC is necessarily subject to the laws of the country or region in which it is established, there is currently no single authority which can exercise control over the entire multinational network and all its operations. In order to prevent the TNCs from pitting one country against another so as to benefit from more favourable terms—since there are significant differences between national laws—the developing countries argue that it is essential to lay down rules of conduct specifically for those companies. The only institutional framework within which such an international instrument can be drawn up is the United Nations.[37]

To summarize these points, it should be emphasized:
First, that the TNCs' constant endeavour to rise to a higher level of capability results in a conflict of goals in regard to the very conception of culture, since their conception runs counter to the notion of cultural identity based on the diversity of cultures and willingness to recognize cultures not founded on economic or materialist considerations.
Second, that the TNCs' greater organizational coherence is due to and explained by their downgrading of the notion of culture.
Third, that the forms taken by the memory-storage, information and communication system, which are closely attuned to the firm's goals, result in interiorization and in the dissemination of an image of the real-life situation in the developing countries that is consistent with the cultural values of the firms' home countries but usually conflicts with those images that are compatible with local cultural values.
Fourth, that the procedures for control and adjustment (through action or through a change in structure) provide the organization with ways and means of coping with disturbances in the environment while continuing to expand in conformity with its own goals.
Fifth, that the TNCs' system for directing the course of development is much more coherent than that of states, as a result of which the former exerts an asymmetrical influence on the latter.
Sixth, that unless cultural control is imposed at a suitable level, the differing potential for variety that exists between states and TNCs will generate

adaptive mechanisms that can only enhance the cultural downgrading process triggered off by the worldwide growth of the TNCs.

The main lines of socio-cultural conflict from the standpoint of the TNCs' strategies

A clearer picture of the socio-cultural consequences of the growth of the TNCs can be obtained from observing their main strategies or, in other words, the principal courses of action they pursue. What is it about their action that very often leads them into conflict with states intent on preserving their cultural identity? To determine this we shall distinguish three main types of strategy, though we should make it clear that the TNCs usually develop through a combination of the three:

Absorption strategies, i.e. essentially those aimed at laying hold on a resource that is available or latent in the country, but without further local processing of the resulting commodity.

Realization strategies, where a sales potential is realized thanks to local processing of commodities into marketable goods.

Consolidation strategies, the aim of which is to stabilize a number of external relations through a variety of approaches, such as establishing links with international organizations, exercising pressures on states, forming alliances with certain social classes, seeking geographical mobility, and so on.[38]

The socio-cultural effects of 'absorption strategies'

In this case, the TNCs set out to make use of the country's raw material and labour resources. Although it has often been stressed that large firms also participate in the mobilization of national savings, this phenomenon will be disregarded, since its relative importance is by no means on the same scale as the other two.

The mobilization of natural resources. Although agriculture, mining and oil production all derive from specific techniques, they nevertheless have a number of features in common.

In the first place, they represent activities that cannot be broken down very easily, and consequently entail the state's surrendering a substantial part of its potential in respect of each venture. The extensive land concessions of the colonial period—in 1938 Unilever owned 350,000 hectares in the Belgian Congo and, from 1907 onwards, its plantation concession rights in the Solomon Islands amounted to 150,000 hectares; at the end of the nineteenth century, the mineral rights granted in respect of the whole of the Congo covered 231 million hectares, out of which Forminière owned 140 million hectares, the Comité Spécial du Katanga 38 million, the Compagnie des Grands Lacs 21 million, and the Union Minière 7 million—have given way to more flexible arrangements which have gradually enabled the states concerned to recover part-control of these activities. However, the fact that they cannot be readily divided is still plain to see (even in agriculture), since the TNCs still own very considerable concessions. For example, although the

Union Minière de Haut-Katanga suffered a loss when Zaire became independent, Unilever still has 350,000 hectares in that country and a very large concession in the Solomon Islands; United Fruit has a considerable estate in Central America; Gulf Western have 50,000 hectares of sugar-cane plantations in Colombia; Brascan has secured a 225,000-hectare mining concession in Brazil; and Meneg—an affiliate of Gulf Oil—still has a 700,000-hectare concession in Venezuela which does not expire until 1984. Moreover, the new arrangements introduced have scarcely altered the nature of the system, since it has been fairly common practice for states to subscribe to the new production techniques being used in these sectors. As a result, the primary industries in which the TNCs play an important part are still conducted over vast expanses and utilize standardized production processes. Even so, a distinction has to be drawn between such commodities as oil, copper and bauxite, and agricultural produce like coffee, cocoa, sugar and cotton. Commodities in the first category all involve the use of very capital-intensive production processes and a generally high level of organization and skills, and their value is increased by interaffiliate sales (a typical feature of a vertical integration strategy), whereas those in the second category can be produced in a variety of ways, and are largely sold on the open market, so that the technical constraints play a much greater role in the case of the first category of commodities, and it is also much more difficult for competitors to enter on the scene.

Secondly, the production sites for agriculture, mining and oil production are usually situated far from urban centres, very often in underpopulated regions, where they act as poles of attraction.

Thirdly, these sectors operate as intermediate consumers though their distribution-side processing chains, which are quite highly developed in some instances. This has two consequences: the income counterpart is based more on rent factors than on labour (the labour value added is usually low in this type of activity) and the price is contingent on world prices. The last point to be noted, in order to round off this brief but, for our purposes, adequate description of the general features of these forms of activity, is that working conditions in them are harsh (whether this be the cause or the outcome of the foregoing observation is open to question).

An attempt can now be made to identify the socio-cultural consequences of this absorption strategy on the basis of four particularly representative factors.

In the first place, activities mobilizing natural resources turn peasants into wage-earners. The outcome of that tendency, initially very marked, was to change the population's value system, destroy pre-capitalist modes of production and efface a good many ethnic differences. These activities also brought about far-reaching changes in social structure, with the endogenous feudal classes being replaced by a *comprador* middle class, which itself gradually gave way to what Samir Amin has called the state bureaucracy. It is difficult to determine exactly what specific role the TNCs have played in this process. They appear to have given a new lease of life to colonialist tendencies (in many cases, in fact, we find the same firms after independence as before) and to have contributed more specifically to the shift of the population towards urban areas by using more capital-intensive production processes. Here again, however, it is important to draw a distinction between extractive and mining industries, which represent a low volume of direct employment (Yves Sabolo and R. Trajtenberg[39] consider that it is seldom higher than 2 per cent of all employment), and agriculture, where the labour force is much greater (in 1968, the same authors estimated the number of jobs created by the main agricultural TNCs operating in Zaire at 230,000 directly employed and 200,000 employed by independent contractors, making altogether 10 per cent of the working population). Moreover, all the authors stress that employment in agriculture is often of a seasonal and precarious nature, that it is largely in the hands of underskilled migrant labour and that the work offered is sometimes harsh. It is the resulting unrest among the labour force, echoed by the local authorities, that has contributed to the changing situation in that sector; for example, D. K. Fieldhouse[40] shows clearly how, faced with these difficulties in the Pacific islands, Unilever was led to switch to lumbering as a substitute for its plantation activities. On the other hand, to judge from an ILO study on the oil-producing TNCs, working conditions overall in that sector appear to be relatively more favourable.[41]

Secondly, developing the production of these commodities wields sociocultural effects through income distribution. Since the proceeds earned from agriculture and mining depend on world price trends, the total volume of wages paid out is probably linked to the random fluctuations in those prices (more through the impact they have on employment than through the actual per capita wage). In point of fact, wages are held down by two requirements which are themselves contradictory. The first of these is the country's need to draw off a surplus from those activities so as to give impetus to industrial development, which is one way of saying that wages in the primary sector cannot be governed by the law of productivity. The second originates in the integrated TNC, which is always tempted to lower the transfer prices for primary intermediate-consumption products so as to generate additional profit margins for its downstream (distribution-side) activities using those products. Even in cases where the TNC has decentralized the primary activity, it will often prefer to record profits in its processing affiliates than in those exploiting the natural resources. In many cases, states have succeeded in improving their position, first, by themselves laying hands on part of the agricultural surplus through the agency of produce marketing boards (particularly for coffee and cocoa) and, second, in the case of mineral commodities, by arranging with the TNCs for them to set up processing industries in the country itself. Even so, while that evolution no doubt helps the state to exercise economic control over the process, it has not arrested the relative deterioration in the situation of agricultural wage-earners. These latter, attracted by the consumption of manufactured goods, have seen their relative purchasing power decline, as a result of the changing price of industrial goods compared with agricultural produce. This, and the abandonment of traditional rural values in favour of the attractions of city life, suffices to explain the massive flight from the countryside that can be observed even in countries where such primary activities have been extensively developed.

Thirdly, at least in mining and the petroleum industry, where the phenomenon is particularly visible, the TNCs now tend to transfer a complete technical package comprising production methods, machinery, skills and even, in some cases (that of oil exploration), a large part of the labour force. As a result, they contribute to the dissemination of an integrated culture with which the inhabitants of often sparsely populated regions will have to cope.

Fourthly, it should be stressed that direct cultural and social activities are very largely carried out by TNCs which base their growth on that strategy. It is probably the oil companies that have made the largest contribution to setting up infrastructural, health and education amenities. While such operations are clearly connected with the firm's determination to adjust through taking action, it seems reasonable to suppose that they are beneficial to the country, particularly since they are increasingly requested by states, which look upon them as a way of making up for the resources absorbed by the firm and of prevailing on the population to accept its 'visibility'. Until very recently, many of these investments served the firm's immediate interests. Louis Turner,[42] for example, has stressed the key role which United Fruit managed to play in Central America because of its control of the railways and the Tropical Radio Telegraph Company, the leading communications network in the region. This kind of operation now seems to be less common and firms are apparently trying to become genuinely involved in improving the welfare of the population. We shall have occasion at a later stage to make a tentative evaluation of these activities, chiefly in the educational field. For our present purposes, however, we should stress that in many instances operations such as these, where culture is a dominant factor, are badly received because they are regarded as bogus compensation offered by firms. Furthermore, firms appear to have the utmost difficulty in countering the effects inherent in the nature of their activities and in the actual forms that these take. To illustrate this point let us consider the misadventures of the Peruvian affiliate of Standard Oil of New Jersey, when it set out 'to build a city' in the north-east of the country.[43]

In the belief that it would be possible to solve labour problems by raising living standards through higher wages, improved housing and the provision of medical facilities, the firm changed the structure of the townships used for housing its workers. It accordingly embarked on a large-scale construction programme comprising brick houses, half a dozen schools, a modern multipurpose clinic, a large supermarket, a church, theatres, a civic centre and a social club. Since 1946, this complex has become a town by the name of Talara, and is now even a provincial capital. However, all this expenditure of time, money and effort met with a less than enthusiastic reception. In the first place, the workers were reluctant to move into their new homes. Then they had difficulty in becoming accustomed to the floor, since the houses they had left were made of wood, and they also tried to turn some of the dwellings into '*chicharas*', a kind of bar serving beer, but the firm refused to allow this. Altogether, it soon became clear that the workers' expectations were not the same as those which the firm had worked out rationally in their stead. In addition, the trade-union representatives pointed to the gap between the situation of the inhabitants of Talara and that of the surrounding population. In 1958, when new contracts were being negotiated, the trade unions pressed for substantial wage increases, amounting to 40 per cent for the lower-wage categories and 20 per cent for the higher ones. Availing themselves of their constitutional rights, they called a strike, but these rights were suspended when the police also went on strike for higher pay. According to R. D. Robinson's account of the events, it was clear that the workers' feeling that they were in a difficult economic situation lay more in the nature of the Talara township than in the number of goods that the workers could purchase and bring home every week. In 1945, the firm employed 5,000 people in the region, and these provided a livelihood for 20,000 townspeople, but twelve years later the firm, which was virtually the only source of jobs, employed only 3,587 workers, while the urban population had risen to 43,000 inhabitants. This case-history clearly epitomizes the futility of attempts at adjustment which do not completely rethink the organization's structure or goals and which disregard the innermost nature of the developing countries where they are applied. It was because the firm was incapable of fitting into the broader context of economic development that an enclave came into being. The change in situation, which at the outset was badly received, subsequently led to a population shift to the town of Talara at the very same time that the firm was using labour-saving techniques and was becoming increasingly powerless to provide a livelihood for the population involved. We should add that the problem in this case is primarily a cultural rather than an economic one. The firm can cite a good many economic and humanitarian reasons to justify its behaviour. The only reproach with which it can be taxed in the case in point is that it projected an external rationality that was alien to the environment in which it was applied, and that it developed a production activity that was scarcely susceptible to real adjustment.

The mobilization of human resources. The issues discussed under this heading will be narrowly confined to the socio-cultural effects transmitted through the dissemination in developing countries of forms of work organization based on the use of an abundant labour force. Hence, no account will be taken of any of the considerations pertaining to the activities of ILO and involving such matters as agreements on the freedom to form trade unions and the protection of trade-union rights, the right of association and collective bargaining, workers' representation, employment policy and, generally speaking, the whole range of labour relations. Firms basing their worldwide growth on the mobilization of human resources are chiefly engaged in textiles, clothing, footwear, mechanical and electrical engineering, and electronics. As Sabolo and Trajtenberg point out, they undoubtedly make a significant contribution to the growth of employment in the developing countries. They are mainly located in Asia, where they use labour-intensive production techniques. For instance, G. K. Helleinert[44] observes that in the Republic of Korea these firms use an organic labour component twice as high as in industry as a whole. In point of fact, the key motive prompting transnational corporations engaging in these activities to set up establishments in developing countries is to enable them to take advantage of a labour-cost differential so that they can export to the developed countries. In this regard, a distinction has to be made between the textile, clothing and footwear industries and the mechanical and electrical engineering and electronics industries.

The former are not highly integrated and sell most of the goods produced in the developing countries on the open market. By contrast, the latter are often highly integrated and the goods they manufacture circulate through intracompany flows. These observations suggest that the economic effects differ according to the industry involved: as far as the textile, clothing and footwear industries are concerned, the obstacles to entering the market are slight and local firms can therefore gain a foothold by imitating the TNCs' affiliates, whereas, in the case of the mechanical and electrical engineering and electronics industries, the degree of vertical integration and the obstacles to market access are such that the establishments set up in developing countries are very often mere window-dressing, offering local firms little by way of a model or example. Even so, these activities are very much in demand in the developing countries because they create employment in urban areas and contribute to improving the balance-of-payments situation.

The main lines of potential conflict with the developing countries therefore pertain narrowly to the cultural consequences stemming from the forms of work organization introduced, and primarily those deriving from the way in which production is organized and the attendant modes of socialization. It is through this bias that the establishment of such industries is able to alter the coherence of national society.

The feature that such activities have in common is that they break down the work involved by installing assembly-lines or comparable production processes, as in the case of textiles. It is the textile industry that has been most affected by the compartmentalization and impoverishment of work as a result of mechanization and, increasingly, the use of automated equipment.[45] It is recognized that, in such cases, the workers perform simple and repetitive tasks and that they participate in the manufacture of the product more as components in a collective work-force than as individuals. On the other hand, as the production or assembly work becomes more straightforward, the design factor grows more complex. M. Freyssenet and C. Palloix[46] have spoken of this as being a process where the skills of workers are downgraded, while those of professional and research staff are enhanced. This shift in skills goes hand in hand with several types of internal organization within the affiliates, such as the establishment of a ranking order by status or function, or varying degrees of decentralized organization, all of which are expected to give rise to forms of control that are adequate to cope with the compartmentalization of the technical work. In order to promote appropriate technical skills it is accordingly necessary to give corresponding training in organizational skills, and here again the result will be to enhance the skills of some and downgrade those of others. Nevertheless, an important proviso must be made at this point. Although there can be no denying that the skills of higher-grade personnel in the technical and administrative hierarchy are enhanced, the downgrading of skills may be more debatable, first, because it involves a de facto downgrading that does not feature in the statistics (since these are not capable of reflecting the change in the scope of the work) and, second, because this observation is based on a comparison of the current jobs of workers employed in the relevant industries in the developed countries with their previous jobs, and such a comparison is not very meaningful in the developing countries, where workers have come from initial jobs that very often do not correspond to a higher level of skills. However, it is almost generally agreed that technical developments in the industries concerned have added to the complexity of the work involved in technical design, control and supervision, and have improverished the actual execution (compared with the situation of workers in the developed countries in the past).

The role played by the TNCs emerges more clearly when it is borne in mind that it is the production segments requiring least skills that are set up in the developing countries. In other words, the execution is moved to the developing countries, while design and control and a large part of the supervision remain in the home country. This phenomenon is particularly marked in the electronics industry, in which growth is one and a half times that of the rest of industry (while growth in the semiconductor-manufacturing branch exceeds that in the electronics industry by the same proportion). As a rule, assembly operations are established in the developing countries, while the two high-technology features in the production process—mask-making (the manufacture of printed circuits) and wafer-fabrication (the laying-out of the components on the printed circuits)—are left in the home country. Hence the only benefits the developing countries might conceivably derive in terms of know-how or the force of example pertain to skills acquired in assembly work, and these are skills that are acknowledged as not being very important because of the low technical demands of the operation. As Mark Lester points out the simplicity and specialization of the work at the assembly level depend entirely on a set of technical, managerial and control skills; the division of labour that is at the heart of any industrial process stems from a rationalization of the industrial technology combined with the management skill needed to operate the system where such rationalization has taken place.[47] In the case in point, the tasks transferred are so unimaginative that they can be performed after one week's occupational training. On the other hand, they seldom become of a routine nature, owing to the pace at which innovations are introduced, and this is why it has not been possible to automate these tasks. The cultural conflict proper will arise when the mass mobilization of this unskilled labour force becomes too patently incompatible with the expectations of the population. If we accept the idea that skills are not only an expression of a particular state in the relationship between man and the machine, but are also a reflection of man's qualities and abilities, and the outcome of a process of social evolution, then we can perceive the socio-cultural consequences with which states would have to contend if they were to centre their development on extending this form of impoverished technical skill. In fact, it is this concern that is now prompting governments which have in the past subscribed to this form of development to devise national means enabling them to consolidate their cultural diversity.

The socio-cultural effects of 'realization strategies'

The decisions accompanying this strategy are concerned more particularly with the TNCs' customer markets. In this regard, the company will attempt to realize enhanced sales potential for its products, so as to safeguard its stability and also ensure its growth. R. Vernon[48] has emphasized the competitive aspect of the TNCs' strategic decisions: a company occupying the leading place on a market is always faced with the risk of seeing other TNCs usurp its place. From the defensive standpoint, this constant threat, linked to the growing imbalances between competing firms, prompts them to look to new market openings. In an attacking strategy, they also attempt to broaden their potential markets, so as to generate a higher rate of return on their competitive edge and reduce their costs. There are two types of activity corresponding to the 'realization strategy'. The first is concerned with the sale of capital goods and poses the problem of the transfer of technology in very direct terms, while the second is bound up with the sale of consumer goods and services. In view of the considerable range of these two issues, we shall confine ourselves at this stage to analysing the main general features of the cultural effects induced by these activities.

In the first place, the sale of capital goods (plant) means that the work processes and patterns of socialization accompanying introduction of the plant are transported to the developing countries. We need not emphasize again the consequences of the new forms of the division of labour accompanying automated production lines and machinery, and all the comments already made on the strategy for absorbing human resources accordingly apply in this instance, with the one difference that these activities create fewer jobs. OECD has made a protracted study of the consequences of the transfer of technology and, in particular, has shown how important it is to consider the technical system and the social system both at the same time.[49] The important factor is that the TNC's aim will always be to standardize its machinery, whereas the developing countries will want equipment suited to their social goals. Quite apart from the difficulties inherent in gaining access to and controlling technology, it is clear that, unless the developing countries can design and produce the capital goods they need, they will often be compelled to sacrifice important elements of cultural diversity for the sake of their bid to industrialize. This point, which reveals a number of incompatibilities between endogenous development (with its cultural dimension) and auto-centred development (with its emphasis on the economic aspect), is readily illustrated by the new approach taken to selling capital goods. The TNCs now increasingly deliver turnkey factories and production-ready industrial complexes. This means that they supply a complete range of services comprising installation, training, commissioning and even management, and implies that the technical and work systems and the related social system all penetrate the institutions of the developing country in accordance with an integration pattern conceived in the developing countries. However, the difference between this approach and the 'absorption strategy' lies in the fact that, in this case, processes requiring the lowest skills are not the only ones to be established in the developing countries. While those countries are liable to see skills downgraded as tasks at the execution level evolve, the possibility of their sharing in the enhancement of tasks at the design level cannot be entirely ruled out, provided they have the technical and administrative management adequate to the purpose. D. Germidis[50] has shown, in fact, how a country like Algeria has endeavoured to combat the cultural-dependence phenomena inherent in these practices and how it has sought to become involved in the design process. This deliberate policy largely accounts for Algeria's practice of calling on a number of countries in connection with the construction of industrial complexes and for the role played in some projects by industrial-design consultants, who are highly skilled in the actual setting-up of large integrated units, notably in the steel industry.

The dual aim of the Algerian companies, which is to acquire the physical and technological production capability and to gain access to know-how—in other words, to imitate before being able to innovate directly—can be perceived in their selection policy and in the fact that they conclude separate agreements with engineering consultants and equipment suppliers. For instance, the industrial design consultants are not necessarily recruited on a one-time basis for a particular project, like the equipment suppliers. The Algerian national companies are free to engage such consultants on a long-term contract, under which they are required to provide all the technical assistance needed to improve and develop production, offer the Algerian company the benefit of their technology and patents, and allow any employees of their Algerian partners access to their factories or offices for the purpose of instructing them in their methods and processes.[51]

The role of occupational training is of capital importance, therefore, and this explains why, in the opinion of the contractors, the services proposed for training operating personnel have become a decisive factor in the client's choice and often take precedence over the price factor. Along with such training, which is written into 'production-ready' contracts, co-operation agreements are demanded for training technicians in the host country. This type of occupational training is provided either by the contractor or by specialized companies, or else through technical co-operation between governments.[52] Occupational training can thus be seen as being a key factor in enabling the host country to understand the technology involved and then adapt and select it: 'bursting the technological package', in the words of Germidis. Light will still have to be shed at a later stage on the way in which such training and technological enclaves can be integrated into the education system and the social system as a whole. However, the problem then takes on a quite different dimension, in that it raises the broader issue of the applications of science in traditional societies.

Secondly, the 'realization strategy' will be concerned with the goods and services intended for the final consumer. From the standpoint of the TNCs, the aim is to sell the goods they produce on a wider scale, and this aim is accompanied by product standardization. The big problem for the company is then to reconcile that requirement with the differences in people's tastes, which merely reflect socio-cultural differences. The company's marketing strategy will consist in adapting both the product and the customer so as to ensure that tastes and standardization converge. Marketing-strategy literature is full of recommendations aimed at bringing about this adaptation without questioning the actual nature of the product involved. The company begins by adjusting its attitude to the target market, and this often prompts it to set up trading affiliates that are better placed to provide the information needed, since they are closer to the potential clientele. As W. D. Dymsa points out,[53] companies can make grave mistakes in transplanting a marketing strategy that has been effective in one country to another country without taking into account the differences in social, cultural and customary models and trading institutions. Many firms have been led by such fairly obvious considerations to modify the appearance of their products. Singer, for instance, has a marketing strategy which differs from country to country and it manages to sell a standard product by changing the colour of the light bulbs and certain accessories. It even uses training as a promotion procedure and the main purpose of its sewing centres is to familiarize dressmakers with its equipment. Very many examples of this type could be quoted.

Next, through advertising, the TNCs change the customer by creating expectations by means of visual or verbal symbols geared to the particular context. For example, the use of animals as symbols has been the subject of studies which have shown that the reaction to them differed significantly from one culture to another. One of the most widespread advertising slogans in recent years was Esso's 'Put a tiger in your tank!'. After being highly successful in the United States and Europe (in France, the term 'engine' was preferred to 'tank'), the slogan was tried out in Asia and succeeded in conveying the message in countries where the tiger was a symbol of strength and beauty. On the other hand, the company recorded a complete failure in Thailand, where the tiger does not symbolize power. It is also a well-known fact that Coca-Cola's advertising campaigns seek to create an undifferentiated worldwide need through the similarity of the messages conveyed and the visual aspect. Here again, many other examples could be described at length.[54]

We shall examine in detail below the extent to which sales of consumer goods and the procedures accompanying them can have an influence on a country's culture. We merely wish to stress here that this form of 'realization strategy' will cause far-reaching changes in the system of values of traditional societies, because it literally fosters an object cult. In most instances, new needs will emerge at the same time as a risk of latent dissatisfaction occurs as a result of the disproportion existing between the aspirations of the people affected by those needs and their tight budgets. Since the quality of individual and community life is measured in terms of the quantity of goods consumed, a phenomenon will occur whereby the poorest members of society will be attracted by the consumption patterns of those higher up the social scale. Since those patterns are, in fact, beyond their reach, the lower classes will often have to content themselves with a symbolic participation in the world of consumption: 'Coca-Cola, the baby's bottle and cigarettes serve less to satisfy immediate needs than they do to symbolize the hope of gaining entry to an inaccessible world.'[55]

As Jean Ziegler has shown in a scathing pamphlet,[56] market rationality not only destroys cultural identity, but gives rise to a semiotic system in which man plays no part. It is this dehumanizing feature of market rationality that is at the root of the unity and coherence of the system of values transmitted by the TNCs. It is the reproducibility and transmissivity of that system of values that enables it to spread worldwide. Nation-states have no means of coping with this self-reproduction of consumer goods which, once they have been introduced into the social system, tend to generate their own demand.[57] Besides the changes they make to the sphere of values, sales of consumer goods and services cause far-reaching alterations in the consumption models of the population. We shall see in greater detail in Chapter 4 what place the TNCs occupy in this restructuring of consumption. What needs to be stressed here is the fact that, in many instances, the new consumption models proposed are often unsuited to the social systems of the developing countries, conforming as they do to the social features of the home country. As a result, the harmful effects may sometimes be considerable. Some nations or groups of people, for instance, have not grasped the true properties of some products, and have replaced them with other substances that have turned out to be dangerous. In recent years, there have been some notorious cases connected with foodstuffs and pharmaceutical products. As a rule, they reveal a combination of two factors: the firm's garbled memory-storage of the real socio-cultural situation in the developing country and the consumers' lack of information on the true qualities of the product. In conclusion, it should also be stressed that the dissemination of standardized products by the TNCs is accompanied by a like dissemination of modern distribution circuits and that these are taking over from the traditional markets which play so important a role in interpersonal communication in the developing countries.

The socio-cultural effects of 'consolidation strategies'

In order to keep on growing, the TNCs, especially when they are very large, tend to consolidate their position, so as to limit the scale of their adjustment. Speaking very generally, this prompts them, in the first place, to rely in many instances on the international agencies for project financing.[58] Furthermore, the TNCs are engaging increasingly in concerted action and may coalesce whenever they feel that the situation warrants it. For example, R. J. Barnet and R. E. Müller[59] point out that, in response to growing co-operation among trade unions, a group of nine very large corporations, including Singer, Michelin and General Electric, have set up an information pool aimed at facilitating their negotiations with trade unions. Mention can also be made of the orchestrated response of the major oil companies to the OPEC countries in 1971. In what, according to Anthony Sampson, these countries described as a 'poisoned letter', the 'Seven Sisters'—i.e. the oil companies—put forward joint proposals and indicated that, in future, they would present a united front.[60] More relevant to our purpose here are the consolidation moves whereby the TNCs exert direct pressure on states. Apart from the more glaring revelations to which the press gave considerable prominence after the hearings before one of the Committees of the United States Senate, mention should also be made of the more discreet representations which have the effect either of corrupting senior officials in the developing countries or of drafting them indirectly into the TNCs' strategy. There are grounds for believing that this phenomenon plays a considerable part in the decision-making mechanism of the developing countries. By the subtle manipulation of financial counterparts, training fellowships, assignments and positions of responsibility, the TNCs alter the roles of large numbers of administrative officials in the host countries. Even if these officials are not corrupted, they are often placed in an ambivalent position, in that they are responsible for their country's interests yet at the same time have a vested interest in the TNCs' results. Whenever the designs of the two protagonists are not absolutely compatible, they find themselves in a conflict situation that is prejudicial to the exercise of their responsibility to the nation.

To sum up, there are a host of possible conflicts between the TNCs' strategies and the need for endogenous development. We cannot say that some of those conflicts are more important than others, or how they relate to each other, since the action that firms take to adjust often succeeds in circumscribing or even concealing them, with the support of local administrators. If we are to obtain some idea of how in general the process is developing, we must therefore change our time-scale and take a long-term view of the way in which these different elements are recombining. *A priori* it seems probable that the state of the relationship existing between the contending forces will tend to result in the socio-cultural field evolving in a manner that will be significantly influenced by the TNCs' goals.

NOTES

1. C. P. Kindelberger, *Economic Development*, New York, McGraw-Hill, 1965.
2. M. Crozier, 'Sentiments, organisations et systèmes', *Revue française de sociologie*, No. XI/XII, 1970–71, p. 143. (Special number.)
3. On class relations in Latin America, cf. F. H. Cardoso and E. Faletto, *Dépendance et développement en Amérique Latine*, Paris, Presses Universitaires de France, 1978.
4. S. Amin, *Le développement inégal*, Paris, Éditions de Minuit, 1973.
5. H. Abdilahi Bulhan, 'Reactive Identification and the Formation of an African Intelligentsia', *International Social Science Journal*, Vol. XXIX, No. 1, 1977, p. 149.
6. D. C. Gordon, *Self-Determination and History in the Third World*, Princeton, N.J., Princeton University Press, 1971.
7. Tangiers Symposium, Unesco, 26–30 September 1977.
8. E. Morin, *La méthode I. La nature de la nature*, pp. 325 et seq., Paris, Seuil, 1977.
9. For an explanation of this concept, see Jacques Melesse, *Approaches systématiques des organisations*, Paris, Hommes et Techniques, 1979.
10. In the case of Africa, for example, see Babakar Sine, *Impérialisme et théories sociologiques du développement*, pp. 180 et seq., Paris, Anthropos, IDEP, 1975.
11. J. L. Le Moigne, *Les systèmes de décision dans les organisations*, p. 150, Paris, Presses Universitaires de France, 1974.

12. I. de Sola Pool, 'Factors Contributing towards Modernization and Socio-economic Performance: V. Communication', *Approaches to the Science of Socio-economic Development*, pp. 191 et seq., Paris, Unesco, 1971.
13. Milton Santos, *L'Espace partagé*, Paris, Éditions Génin, 1975.
14. E. F. Schumacher, *Small is Beautiful*, London, Blond & Briggs, 1973.
15. World Bank, *World Development Report*, 1979, p. 66.
16. G. Myrdal, *The Challenge of World Poverty*, pp. 214-15, Harmondsworth, Allen Lane, The Penguin Press, 1970.
17. For a general and very elaborate analysis of these issues, see Liliane Sardais, 'L'État et l'internationalisation du capital', University of Paris-X, 1977. (Doctorate thesis.)
18. Myrdal, op. cit.
19. H. V. Perlmutter, 'The Perplexing Routes to Legitimacy: Codes of Conduct for Multinational Corporations regarding Technology Transfer and Development', *Codes of Conduct for the Transfer of Technology: A Critique*, New York, Council of the Americas, June 1976.
20. United Nations, Centre on Transnational Corporations, *National Legislation and Regulations Relating to Transnational Corporations*, New York, 1978. (ST.CTC.6.)
21. Perlmutter, op. cit.
22. Maureen Leblanc, *The Psychodynamic Side-effects of Technology Transfer. Present and Future Perspectives*, Cambridge, Mass, Fletcher School of Law and Diplomacy, April-May 1976. (Mimeo.)
23. D. L. Schaupp, *A Cross-cultural Study of a Multinational Company*, New York, Praeger, 1978.
24. D. Sirota and J. M. Greenwood, 'Understand Your Overseas Workforce', in T. D. Weinshall (ed.), *Culture and Management*, Harmondsworth, Penguin, 1977.
25. R. D. Robinson, *International Business Management*, Cambridge, Mass., MIT Press, 1973.
26. G. G. Sanberg, 'The Organization of Multinational Corporations', pp. 52-5, Sloane School of Management Science, MIT, 1972. (Unpublished thesis.)
27. J. F. Cristofini and A. Latz, *Aspects socio-culturels du dévelopment d'une branche d'économie nationale sur la base d'une participation déterminante des S.T.N. : l'exemple de l'industrie touristique dans les pays en voie de développement*, p. 25, Paris, Unesco, August 1979. (Mimeo.)
28. Quoted in H. V. Perlmutter, 'The Tortuous Evolution of the Multinational Corporation', *Transnational Corporations and the World Order*, p. 37, San Francisco, W. H. Freeman & Co., 1979.
29. Robinson, op. cit.
30. D. F. Channon and M. Jalland, *Multinational Strategic Planning*, London, Macmillan, 1979.
31. D. K. Fieldhouse, *Unilever Overseas. The Anatomy of a Multinational*, London, Croom Helm, 1978.
32. C. A. Michalet, *Le capitalisme mondial*, p. 170, Paris, Presses Universitaires de France, 1978.
33. M. Hermitte and N. Roux, 'Systèmes externes et développement: le choix de projet, la multinationale', Aix-en-Provence, CEFI, 1980. (Mimeographed thesis.)
34. J. N. Sheth and R. J. Lutz, 'A Multivariate Model of Multinational Business Expansion', in S. P. Sethi and J. M. Sheth (eds.), *Multinational Business Operations*, p. 96, Santa Monica, Calif., Goodyear Publishing Co., 1973.
35. Robinson, op. cit.
36. Henri Schamm, *Entreprises multinationales, les codes de conduite*, Geneva, Institut Universitaire d'Études Européennes, 1977.
37. Ibid., p. 2.
38. The so-called renewal strategies, which are concerned with research and development, are not discussed here, but will form the subject of another chapter.
39. Y. Sabolo, R. Trajtenberg, and J. P. Sajhau, *The Impact of Transnational*

Enterprises on Employment in the Developing Countries, Geneva, ILO, 1976. (Working paper.)
40. Fieldhouse, op. cit.
41. ILO, Social and Labour Practices of Multinational Enterprises in the Petroleum Industry, Geneva, ILO, 1977.
42. Louis Turner, Multinational Companies and the Third World, p. 23, New York, Hill & Wang, 1973.
43. Robinson, op. cit, p. 214.
44. G. K. Helleinert, Transnational Enterprises, Manufactured Exports and Employment in the Less Developed Countries, Geneva, ILO, June 1975.
45. As a rule, automated machines are much less widely used in affiliates established in the developing countries. In Brazil, for example, the proportion of non-automated machines in the electrical-equipment industry stands at 62.91 per cent compared with 30.85 per cent in the same industry in the United States; S. A. Morley and G. W. Smith, 'The Choice of Technology: Multinational Firms in Brazil', Economic Development and Cultural Change, Vol. 25, January 1977, p. 249.
46. M. Freyssenet, La division capitaliste du travail, Paris, Savelli, 1977; C. Palloix, Procès de production et crise du capitalisme, Paris, Maspéro/Presses Universitaires de Grenoble, 1977.
47. M. Lester, The Transfer of Technological and Managerial Skills through Multinational Corporations: A Case Study of the Vertically-Integrated Electronics Industry in Export-Processing Zones, p. 7, Honolulu, East-West Center, 15 October 1979. (Mimeo.)
48. R. Vernon, Storm over the Multinationals, Cambridge, Mass., Harvard University Press, 1971.
49. OECD, Methodological Principles for the Social Evaluation of Technology, Paris, OECD, 1975.
50. D. Germidis, Le Maghreb, la France et l'enjeu technologique, Paris, Cujas, 1976.
51. Ibid., p. 92.
52. Danielle Decourt, La dépendance technologique des pays du bassin méditerranéen, Aix-en-Provence, CEFI, 1975, 78 pp.; D. Germidis, Multinational Firms and Vocational Training in Developing Countries, Paris, Unesco. (Doc. SHC-76/CONF.635/11.)
53. Cf. W. D. Dymsa, Multinational Business Strategy, p. 111, New York, McGraw-Hill, 1972.
54. G. E. Miracle, 'International Advertising Principles and Strategies', in Sethi and Sheth, op. cit, Vol. 3.
55. Groupe de Berne, Nestlé contre les bébés, p. 40. Paris, Maspero/Presses Universitaires de Grenoble, 1978. (Cahiers libres, No. 348.)
56. Jean Ziegler, Main basse sur l'Afrique, Paris, Seuil, 1978.
57. Krishna Kumar, A Working Paper on the Social and Cultural Impacts of Transnational Enterprises, p. 110, Honolulu, East-West Center, August 1979.
58. Robinson (op. cit., p. 442), underscores the importance of the international financing on which the TNCs can base their operations. In particular, USAID contributes to many of the projects involving the participation of TNCs.
59. R. J. Barnet and R. E. Müller, Global Reach, p. 319, New York, Simon & Schuster, 1974.
60. Anthony Sampson, The Seven Sisters, p. 215, New York, Viking Press, 1975.

Chapter 3

The changing system of interactions: the role of cultural values and of communication, education, science and technology

In this chapter we shall explore the major trends in the conflictual system described above and the ways open for voluntarist action. Our inquiry will be conducted from the standpoint of the different types of change that may be brought about by the effects transmitted by TNCs in a particular national context. By extending the time range of the study we can even point to a number of universal determining factors which will guide social change in the developing countries open to TNCs. There is no contradiction between this type of approach and the method hitherto used for the study. To present as a synchronic pattern the system of manifold and often conflictual connections linking TNCs to nations in their quest for cultural identity does not prejudge the diachronic path chosen by history. As pointed out by M. Serres:

The single path followed by theory, by decision-making, by history, or by any given change in a mobile situation, is chosen from among other possible paths, which may constitute the entire set of such paths or merely a random selection among them. On the chess-board we have the struggle of two differentiated and different networks involving their intricate dovetailing and interlocking. In the space-time of the game each network alters, each for itself, and each according to the way the other alters. The overall situation is therefore one of highly complex mobility and of such fluidity that it is practically impossible to foresee what will happen after two moves.... Over a certain time cycle one network slowly adapts to the other, in probabilistic fashion, where chance plays a greater part than the strict laws of causality; it might even be said that in some games it makes not the slightest difference (has no causal or 'determining' effect) whether a particular pawn is moved forward before another. As time goes on, the area of interpenetration of the two networks becomes more and more firmly structured, and the whole picture is of a system of increasing causality or determination. Some moves will take place that are of medium determining effect so far as the system as a whole is concerned, then others of increasingly strong determining effect until the absolutely decisive move resulting, within a principal subsystem, in a position of checkmate, with which the game ends. In the same way that the opening move was completely without determining effect, with this last move the effect is rigidly determined, for more than one reason, by what has gone before.[1]

The metaphor of the game of chess seems particularly appropriate to the question with which we are concerned here. As TNCs become established worldwide, the ways in which the relationship between them and nation-states changes come into sharper focus. The years following on the post-war period have brought a progressively clearer awareness of the causal factors at work; and the process has now being going on long enough to afford a glimpse of some of the long-term trends that will go to shape the future world system. There nevertheless still remains a considerable area of obscurity (where strict causality furnishes relatively little help) and what eventually emerges will depend on the contingencies of history and the extent to which states are resolved to direct and control their development.

This chapter's brief venture into futurology is intended, first, to examine the major trends discernible from an exploratory analysis of the present, working on the assumption that there will be no major voluntarist attempt to modify the way in which the system evolves and subsequently to analyse why cultural values, communication, education, science and technology are central to any normative action designed to promote endogenous national development. The first part of this analysis corresponds in fact to a deterministic scenario of the probable, while the second introduces us to a libertarian scenario in terms of what is desirable.

Section 1

The scenario based on extrapolation: spontaneous national responses to the worldwide dissemination of socio-cultural characteristics transmitted by TNCs

The central assumption underlying this scenario is that TNCs—and thus the values they convey, and the attendant patterns of socialization and forms of production—will spread throughout the whole world. This implies that the economic constraints facing the developing countries will still be such that greater economic efficiency will be sought, in D. Bell's words, in 'the economizing mode',[2] namely through improved productivity, a technique serving the prime aim of social systems, which is to increase the volume of goods produced. It also looks forward to means and ends continuing to be associated in the institutional framework of the very large companies whose emergence is a signal feature of the most developed contemporary societies. Our assumption therefore tallies with the school of thought that sees in the centralization, concentration and internationalization of capital an unavoidable stage in the development of market economies. It also implies that changes in the forms assumed by TNCs will do little to alter their present characteristics, and that any restructuring they undergo will be designed to facilitate adaptation and will not call into question their ultimate purposes. Even if new forms of relationship with states are established, they will have little effect, so the assumption goes, on the asymmetrical power relations enjoyed by the TNCs on account of their dominant position; they will even be looked to additionally to structure the world system and lead it on towards economic efficiency. It is noteworthy that this assumption corresponds to the two main patterns of thought at present underlying economic analyses of the world system. Although one is favourable to TNCs while the other adopts a critical attitude, they tend to converge on this central point. The TNCs shape the world system along economic lines, which may of course be differently appreciated according to whether they are seen as a new form of extension of the capitalist mode of production or as a means of improving the world distribution of production factors. The convergence of these two points of view on the question appears still more marked when it is seen that they hold cultural, human and social factors to be largely determined by economic considerations: in the first, social relations hinge on the level of development of productive forces, and values and institutional structures are largely determined by this 'material infrastructure'; while in the second, social rationality is guided by a universal-type individual economic rationality.

The scenario based on the extrapolation of present trends is therefore necessarily coupled with the view that economic factors play a largely determining role with the corollary that the socio-cultural characteristics of the developing countries will tend to converge in line with the TNC-inspired process of economic unification of the world system and that such differences as subsist between individual countries will be exclusively functional in character.

Pointers to the socio-cultural characteristics of the future world system

From all the elements that might serve to project into the future the components of the present situation, we have selected three factors making for socio-cultural convergence: the first is linked to the worldwide application of a uniform pattern of organizational management; the second stems from the dissemination of a particular type of interface between technology and consumption; and the third is a mode of social control.

The counterpart to the process of downgrading the social and cultural field implicit in the TNCs' ultimate aims will be the worldwide dissemination of managerial culture. Taught first in North American business schools and applied in the main TNCs, it is spreading in Eastern Europe, and now very extensively in the developing countries, through the agency of the TNCs themselves, by means of local institutions or even through the medium of particular international organizations. This managerial culture, which must on the strength of this scenario be regarded as set for dominance in the near future, brings with it a process of human moulding which is perceptible in outline today. Its ambition is nevertheless to be ideologically neutral and so to become a universal technique for organizational management, regardless of the social or religious backgrounds of the individuals who have acquired it. It would constitute an additional qualification overlying the other qualities of individuals without affecting them. There is, however, an immediately apparent contradiction between this ambition, with its underlying reasons, and the communication function tagged on to it. The reason behind the worldwide spread of this culture is, as we have seen, the need to raise the economic efficiency of a type of organization whose ultimate aim is profit and growth. Since one of its main functions is to permit communication between individuals with differing socio-cultural characteristics, it will tend to recombine them and hence to efface or damp down these characteristics, an aim that is moreover explicitly assigned to it by the leaders of the major TNCs in countless statements. Another point is that the widespread dissemination of this culture, its special features and the self-awareness it brings with it means that those possessing it constitute a distinct class which tends gradually to become the ruling class in industrial societies. We can therefore join K. P. Sauvant in considering that, far from being neutral, managerial culture is both a set of attitudes, values and behaviour models, and a set of forms and models of organization.[3] As a philosophy and a mode of management simultaneously, managerial culture is based upon the connection between a general ideological attitude and more specific types of behaviour.

We may attempt to identify the ingredients of this philosophy by emphasizing that it is cosmopolitan and individualistic. Cosmopolitanism is no doubt the feature that has developed in the closest conjunction with TNCs. This is put very clearly by J. Maisonrouge of IBM:

For business purposes the boundaries that separate one nation from another are no more real than the equator. They are merely convenient demarcations of ethnic, linguistic and cultural entities. They do not define business requirements or consumer trends. Once management understands and accepts this world economy, its view of the market-place—and its planning—necessarily expand. The world outside the home country is no longer viewed as a series of disconnected customers and prospects for its products, but as an extension of a single market.[4]

Enhanced by the standardization of attitudes, this cosmopolitanism will loosen the ties of national identity. The observation made by M. Gloor, director of the Nestlé food company, on himself and his colleagues may then be generally applicable:

It will not be possible to regard us as purely Swiss, or purely multinational, namely belonging to the whole world, if there could be such a thing. We are probably something in between, a race apart. In a word, we hold a special nationality, 'Nestlé nationality'.[5]

Seen in this way, the cosmopolitan aspect of managerial culture goes well beyond the universalist pretensions of the Age of Enlightenment, which sought to substitute a humanitarian patriotism for the restrictive nationalism that kindles passions and wars. The aim in fact is to permit a worldwide mobilization of labour serving the major enterprises.

This scenario considers that, internationally speaking, there will be the same kind of severing of the organic link between a man's trade and his hearth as that noted by J. P. de Gaudemar within the national context during the Industrial Revolution.[6] We shall then see productive space and business space becoming generally independent of geographical space. It may furthermore be supposed that the social hierarchy within the TNCs will largely hinge upon the ability of employees to reflect this growing separation in their lives, the leading strata finding justification for their status in their ability to break away from their national roots and the others paying the price of remaining attached to them.

The individualistic character of the philosophy underlying managerial culture stems from a similar function. The aim of personal fulfilment and individual freedom is bound up with the desire both to play down the importance of group referents and to encourage competitiveness among employees in order to make the organization more efficient. These virtues are contrasted with the unwieldiness of state machinery, which is readily dubbed bureaucratic.

The idea that the unity of society takes shape not in the group but in the individual does nevertheless overlook the fact that, over and above formal freedom, there is a real freedom which cannot be conceived otherwise than within the framework of the relations which man enters into with his fellows. In this respect, the group is conducive to freedom by virtues of its 'conviviality', a phenomenon attested in detail in a great many anthropological studies showing ways in which the individual can be taken care of in traditional communities. For instance, Africans are in some ways rather less fearful than others of unemployment because they have a kind of insurance to fall back on in the form of aid from their collaterals, affording them the means of subsistence. This 'conviviality' is even in many cases very strictly codified. An example of this is provided by S. B. Kouyaté who, in a very revealing study, describes the closeness of community links within the Bambara population of Mali, where the young 'pupils' of the '*flanton*' owe assistance to all the village elders and to all the disabled.[7] The freedom attaching to general prevalence of the individualistic point of view may therefore be more than offset by loss of real freedom as a result of the loosening of community ties, which is virtually inevitable after prolonged contact of some members of the group with international affairs. In the concrete practice of managerial philosophy the group inevitably re-emerges. But progressively it is the collectivity represented by the firm or collective subsets peculiar to it in which the individual becomes incorporated. The present aim of the TNCs is to hasten this process while leaving the ambition of personal fulfilment enough scope for the individual efficiency of employees to be maintained. There is room for conjecture as to whether, in the long run, the individualistic content of managerial philosophy, at present indispensable in disengaging the employee from his previous background, will not gradually give way to a conception of the organization as the focal point for socialization. The present phase of disengagement from the determining influence of one's national background will, in that event, be followed by a phase of societal recomposition under TNC auspices. This is probably the direction in which managerial culture will move in the near future. However that may be, individualism is at present still an all-important ingredient of it, as attested by all cross-cultural surveys. From Table 11 below, which appears in one of the most quoted studies (D. Sirota and J. M. Greenwood),[8] it is obvious that the end-purposes of employees are essentially marked by considerations of individual fulfilment with an eye to efficiency and gain. Opportunities for higher qualifications, competitiveness of work, an independent approach to work and financial gain overshadow goals connected with working conditions, group life and the growth potential of the firms to which the employees belong.

TABLE 11. Goal ranking by occupation

Occupation goal	Average rank		
	Salesmen	Technical personnel	Service personnel
Training	2	1	1
Challenge	1	2	2.5
Autonomy	3	3	7
Earnings	4	4.5	4
Advancement	5	6	5
Recognition	6	4.5	9
Security	10	11	2.5
Friendly department	9	8	8
Personal time	11	7	6
Company contribution	7.5	9.5	10
Efficient department	7.5	9.5	11
Benefits	13	13	12
Physical conditions	14	12	13
Successful company	12	14	14

Source: D. Sirota and J. M. Greenwood, 'Understand Your Overseas Workforce', in T. O. Weinshall (ed.), *Culture and Management*, p. 266, Harmondsworth, Penguin Books, 1977.

This result, which is amply borne out by studies of the same type, seems in any case to reveal that the individualist element in managerial philosophy gives rise to egocentric behaviour patterns. Even if one accepts J. Fayerweather's distinction between the term 'individualism' as describing the independent, liberalistic attitude of a man who feels the need for a considerable degree of freedom in his personal life, and the word 'individualist' applied rather to someone who is reserved and unsociable by nature,[9] it must be admitted that the individualism of managerial philosophy leads to a perception of life at work focused solely on personal aims, which clearly runs counter to several philisophical conceptions embodied in traditional cultures.

Hand in hand with the spread of this managerial philosophy goes the general adoption of a uniform type of behaviour in the management of organizations. This behaviour is based primarily on a pragmatic attitude. As has been emphasized by Ross A. Weber, 'hindering ideologies, beliefs and dogmas surrender to economic pragmatism'.[10]

This pragmatism of the managers of large organizations implies a fairly independent attitude to the public authorities and even to the owners of the capital. It is accompanied by a considerable degree of mental flexibility and indeed a keen sense of opportunity. Noteworthy too is a marked capability for strategy and long-term planning. Within the general framework of a mode of reasoning in terms of ends and means, this capability enables executives to refer their short-term decisions to a distant future. Furthermore, the individual marked by managerial culture is very much predisposed to occupational mobility, dissociates work, leisure and domestic life almost completely, and commands a large array of technical tools and procedures enabling him to pilot his sector of responsibility in the organization.

Such, in outline, is the image of the managerial behaviour whose dissemination by the TNCs is here assumed. Many components of this new management technique do of course represent an advance that few can contest. What is more, it would clearly be absurd to ascribe its advent to the TNCs alone. Its future forms will nevertheless be transmitted by them, with an accentuation of some specific features. It seems to be at the level of philosophical content rather than at that of technique as such that the TNCs make themselves most felt. Management techniques themselves will, however, in the long run inevitably be influenced by the more marked cosmopolitan character of the general ideology.

Technique and consumption are very often treated as two barely connected phenomena reproducing themselves in accordance with parallel processes. This tendency is further accentuated when it is emphasized that technical development concerns the sphere of production, or indeed of socialization through the organization of labour, while consumption characterizes a way of life and constitutes, in fact, one of the possible expressions of a society's dominant values. When economists address themselves to the issue, they link up these two factors by reducing the concept of consumption to the materialization of a purchase. They thereupon incorporate technique and consumption in a relationship (dialectical or otherwise) between production and increased value. The viewpoint we shall adopt here is quite different. Technical forms and consumption patterns are integrated into a culture. In a long-term outlook, it is utterly unrealistic to think that a form of technical development may not be accompanied by a specific mode of consumption. Whether one initially gives pride of place to a 'push' model of development, on the basis of prior industrialization, or sees industrialization rather as induced by the 'pull' of final demand, these two factors will ultimately tend to be bonded together in a particular way. It is even reasonable to suppose that the way in which they are bonded together will largely determine the nature of the society. However, the development of techniques through science and technology, taken as a form of mediation between a tool, a machine and scientific production, is no doubt in a dominant position in relation to consumption, owing to its more autonomous status. Technical development may be considered to take place largely in accordance with its own laws, which, unlike those of nature, may culminate in explosive processes. As pointed out by E. F. Schumacher, where the laws of technical change differ from those of nature is that the former possesses no self-regulatory devices for avoiding such processes.[11] This does not mean that there is no reciprocal relationship running from consumption to technique. However, this relationship leads to the choice of a technique from a range of alternatives determined *a priori* by scientific production and technology. It should also be noted that unless a country possesses specific natural resources, it will not be able to renew installed technical facilities if its market cannot absorb at least part of their output. The problem of relations between technique and consumption should in fact be set in the context of what has come to be called the technology-based civilization. As Herbert Marcuse recalls in this connection, the point about the technology-based civilization is that it has caused the ends to become suffused by the means. Traditionally there had been virtually general agreement on the desirability of distinguishing cultural ends from the means applied in order to attain them; and the distinction between culture and civilization was habitually based on the non-coincidence of these two factors. Culture was seen as 'lying at a higher level of human autonomy and accomplishment, with civilization characterizing the realm of necessity, labour and behaviour as dictated by society'.[12] What the technology-based civilization has achieved is submission of higher ends to daily life and to work, thereby rendering the foregoing distinction obsolete. It is in this context that we can regard the bonding of technical system and consumption as one of the key factors enabling us to understand the integrating effects of the technology-based civilization. It is not our purpose here to give an account of the considerable body of literature by means of which a bridge can be constructed between, on the one hand, the general application of a technical model, with its accompanying dethronement of the object of production and the productive subject, and, on the other, the fetishism of commodities, now spilling over into the sphere of needs.[13] Let us however remember that it is the division of labour, including its technical forms, that makes individual work dependent on the organization of production. The greater the advance of techniques, the greater the submission of the worker to the machine and the distance separating him from the product. As observed by A. Touraine, 'in losing his occupational autonomy, the worker has also lost one of the principles of his cultural autonomy'.[14] It is that loss which probably explains the general incursion of the world of objects into individual life, the transition from a 'possession of conquest' to a 'possession of enjoyment' and the general relinquishment of the sense of work and necessity pointed to by the critics of the technology-based civilization.

The question then arising is whether the TNCs will extrapolate on a worldwide scale the present characteristics of this civilization and whether they will determine how its forms gradually change. The answer to the first part of the question leaves little room for doubt after what has previously been said about the role now devolving upon the TNCs in the structuring of the world system. The second point, on the other hand, presents a more awkward problem since, in order to prove the specific nature of the TNCs, it would be necessary to describe the anti-world corresponding to their world. We shall nevertheless venture the assertion that the TNCs will play a special role in the way the forms of this civilization evolve. Without going so far as to claim that they themselves create these forms, they do none the less constitute the principal pre-condition for them. The first reason for this statement is that the general characteristics of transnational enterprises (size, organization, geographical coverage) are the only ones compatible with the modern features of technological development. To understand this, it has to be recognized that, contrary to general belief, technological progress is increasingly hard to achieve. We would even be ready to state, like O. Giarini and H. Louberge, that technological progress now lies in the area of diminishing returns. As is pointed out by these authors, whereas in the social and cultural fields there is an accelerating capability to derive public and commercial benefit from an invention, the opposite process is taking place in regard to technology. The more scientifically based a technology is, the longer it takes to develop:

Physicists confirm that nowadays any discovery at the fundamental research level has very little chance of becoming usable within twenty years. Furthermore, a discovery is seldom the outcome of illumination; it usually lies at the end of a long haul, which by fits and starts takes decades to accomplish.[15]

Only the very large enterprises will be able to establish the necessary research facilities and bear the financial burden. The second reason concerns the actual machinery for reproduction of the technology-based civilization. In the first place this implies a worldwide extension of the value-enhancement base, an extension foreseen by Karl Marx nearly 100 years ago. Secondly, the new forms this reproduction takes have been very largely invented by the TNCs and are assuming dimensions that only such enterprises can lend it. For example, the standardization of methods and products, the shortening of the life of products (a way of reconstituting the market), formal differentiation by means of presentation or altered labelling, and the accelerated depreciation of plant (which is particularly pronounced in the case of computerization) are all mechanisms that only the TNCs can really command. The third reason concerns the phasing of technological production and of consumption. In the past two centuries there has often been a marked lag between a technological discovery and its finalization, meaning the point at which the market becomes able to absorb the resulting products. Because they are very often integrated and have a high level of mutual knowledge, the TNCs can attune technological modification to market conditions. When the market seems open or likely to be rendered receptive, technological discoveries are put to use almost immediately; otherwise they will be kept in abeyance. Considering too that the TNCs are better placed than any other enterprises to influence directly the expectations of end-users (producers for capital goods, individuals for consumer goods), it is no doubt through them alone that the technology-based civilization will be able to reproduce itself in new forms. It may reasonably be supposed that these forms will bring about an even closer bonding between technology and consumption, that each succeeding type of bonding will be shorter lived than the last, and that all will be of a still more marked materialistic character.

As has been pointed out by F. Perroux, the class struggle observed in the developing countries has not confirmed the Marxian schema.

The diversification of wage-earners, clashes of interest and ideology among the divers types of wage-earner, the growing schism between those strata favoured by industry and the rest of the labour force and the widespread movement of protest in the multi-class mass, all show that we are here far removed from the ordinary dichotomy.[16]

In other words, the distinction between bourgeoisie and proletariat is ill-fitted to reflect the consequences of the extension of TNCs at the level of social relationships, inasmuch as it is too inclined to analyse social structure in terms identical with those used in the industrialized countries, fails to take account of the very great diversity of classes in the developing countries and in the final analysis views the process of social control solely in regard to the apparatus of state, which is deemed to be wholly subject to the dominant class. The first question then is whether the word 'class' can be used without caveat to describe the social reality of the developing countries. Trite as this may sound, the understanding of social relations has more to gain from examination of social practice than from the adaptation of historically obsolete conceptions and notions. If we follow A. Touraine, we will recognize that a social structure is primarily characterized by

social environments socially and culturally distant from one another. This distance has to do with the slowness of transformation of cultural heritages. A specific culture is transmitted from generation to generation within community units where institutional relations are not separable from personal relations.

While analysis in terms of class places social organization on an abstract and general principle qualifying one or more types of class relations,

cultural heritages on the other hand are concrete and particular; they are systems of order defining and regulating all social relations within a unit whose limits are those of family, territory or traditional environment and hence of 'transmitted' rather than 'acquired' situations.[17]

In traditional societies, if there is a dominant class the fact is very often linked more to heritage factors than to a definite economic function or any real power of domination. Furthermore, to explain social relations in the developing countries solely in terms of proletarianization resulting from industrialization is to give short shrift to the peasantry and to sub-proletarianized urban strata left outside the mainstream of production. In fact,

identification of society with the class struggle presupposes a combination of three factors: an internal occupational and community principle of self-defence; awareness of contradictions between conflicting economic and social interests; and reference to the general interests of a society.[18]

None of these factors is present in the general social structure of developing societies. Consequently, if we recognize that there can be no class conflict without awareness both of a social distance and of a higher social contradiction, it follows that neither conflict between different strata nor the recognition of inequality in respect of social participation suffices in order to characterize social relations in terms of class opposition. And the second observation is that while there are undoubtedly social environments that may be regarded as classes in the sense of the foregoing definition, many others, either because they are better defined by their cultural sedimentation or because they have no clear awareness of their relative situation, are not directly involved in the class struggle. There is accordingly a third preliminary observation to be made: the institutionalization of social conflicts and the various forms of social control assume characteristics that are quite distinct from those to be found in industrial societies. Here, more than elsewhere, N. Poulantzas's remarks concerning the plural character of the apparatus of state are applicable, not only, as that author points out, because the power bloc is made up of several fractions of the dominant class or classes, but also because the power bloc builds class awareness on economic and ideological bases that are very often in opposition.[19]

With these preliminary considerations in mind, how are we to conceive the role of TNCs in social organization?

We shall consider three main characteristics of the activity of TNCs in this respect. First, virtually all studies on the question emphasize that TNCs profoundly modify the social structure and the political system by appropriation. In so doing, they have allegedly disrupted the process of training a group of local entrepreneurs, absorbed the best talent and left national independent entrepreneurs with secondary subcontracting activities or hazardous associations eventually giving TNCs room for further expansion.[20] As has been observed by O. Sunkel, not only a large part of the international bourgeoisie but also part of the middle class, the workers and some of those previously relegated to the sidelines of national life, or 'marginalized', are in this way becoming a private transnational technocracy.[21]

Secondly, the TNCs help to modify the entire social hierarchy through the changes they introduce in its economic base. In a noteworthy study on the non-Hispanic Caribbean, S. Hall highlights this process.[22] It will be seen from Figure 8 how the advent of the TNCs has contributed to the emergence of a national commercial and administrative bourgeoisie linked to their activities, to the detriment of the local planter class. This is a phenomenon to be found in different forms in all the developing countries, which reflects greater participation of the middle strata in power to the extent that they are involved in TNC activity.

Thirdly, the TNCs rely on a national technocratic bureaucracy which is extensively represented in the apparatus of state and tends gradually to become the dominant class. This is indeed a new social class in that its economic base is generally a common one, it is clearly aware of its own interests and it is open to the general interest. Originating in the middle bourgeoisie, it brings together the fractions of the middle class around some of the cultural values transmitted by the TNCs. It is nevertheless in an ambiguous position, for though its economic base is directly or indirectly the TNC, it often looks to its nationalism for its legitimation and its class ideology. This explains why in many cases this ruling class may display a fair variety of behaviour patterns in regard to development issues and even in regard to the TNCs. The direction in which the consciousness of this class moves is decisive for the future. Either it will without any undue effort of adaptation transmit the managerial philosophy, or it will revert to its national roots and may curb the type of development produced by the TNCs.

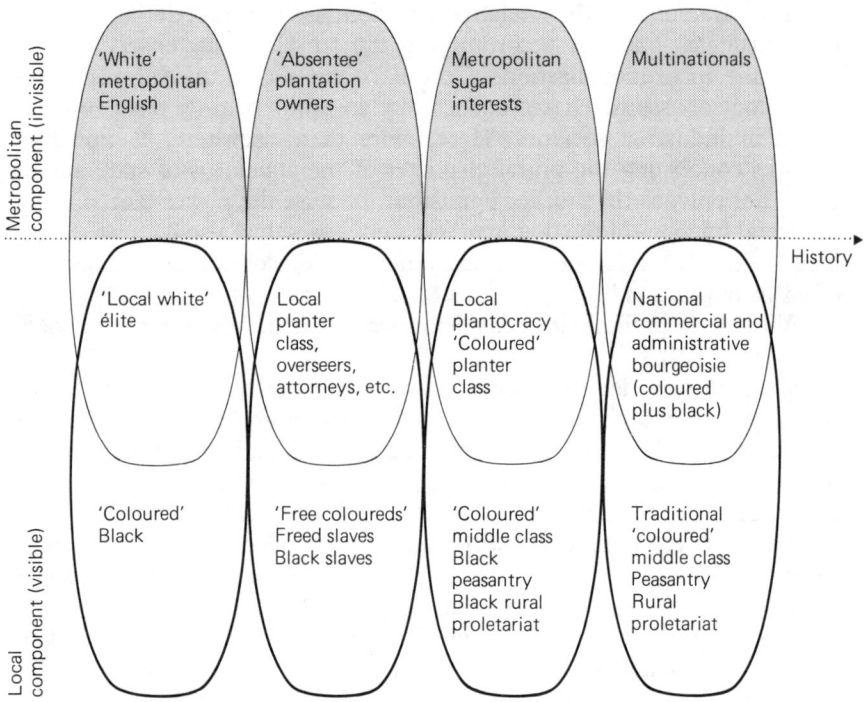

FIG. 8. The 'invisible' component in metropolitan/Caribbean economic and legitimation system (after S. Hall, *Pluralism, Race and Class in Caribbean Society*).

What is to be observed, however, is that this new social structuring presents a considerable problem of social control. In the present phase the advent of the TNCs has disrupted the previous forms of social control and made them very much less varied. Selecting certain vectors of dissemination (the best ones) for their own rationality, they have left the nation-states the onus of disseminating control under probably more awkward circumstances. This explains why it is very difficult in some national entities to effect social control of the silent majority of development, namely the peasantry and the urban sub-proletariat. These social strata, which often form a clear majority, can hardly be termed classes since they possess an increasingly ill-defined economic base and, in many cases, a blurred class consciousness. They nevertheless frequently become politically aware and take sides in respect of major policy issues. Not being represented in any recognized power structure and commanding no institutional means of making themselves heard, they constitute a particularly fluid mass. It is probably this fact, coupled with the bureaucratic trend, making as it does for remoteness of the decision-making centres from those responsible for implementation, that explains why some states have established 'apparatus of constraint'[23] containing by military or police artifice the phenomena of tension inherent in this unstable situation.

Unconscious national responses

It would be an over-simplification to assert that the aforementioned major trends towards socio-cultural convergence of the world system are going to propagate homogeneously throughout the nations. Each nation, if only because of its special physical characteristics, will 'respond' to the external disturbances caused by TNCs. We shall nevertheless suppose, for the purposes of this scenario, that it will do so quite unconsciously through its structures and not out of any political will to assimilate the external stimulus so as to subject it to specific and intentional national development objectives. In that case two phases should be distinguished. The first is the destructuring phase, very much under way at present, which accompanies internal propagation of the external stimulus. The second is the restructuring phase—that of putting back into order—which in the context of this scenario will correspond to the reorganization of social systems around the rationale of the TNCs.

There is no dearth of terms to describe the mechanisms that go with the destructuring brought about by the establishment of major firms. The words, polarization, enclaving, stratification and disintegration are commonly used as metaphors for these processes. They all reflect the same idea: the TNCs, having the power to select elements of the developing country's system for integration within their own system, ensure the rapid reproduction of those elements which set them apart, and so cut them off from the rest of society. The socio-economic system is consequently split in two, one part superior to the other, on the basis of the selectivity brought into play by the TNCs. To illustrate this point we shall refer to the examples given by F. Perroux, I. A. Egorov and others, and O. Sunkel in regard, respectively to polarization effects, the structure of consumption and social mobility. In a short but interesting article the originator of the notion of development poles speculates as to whether the TNCs are going to act on the system by development of poles or whether they will form development poles capable of reconstituting the system indirectly at a later stage, through the impetus they impart to it. The importance of this debate is quite considerable. First, because it corresponds to a substantive issue regarding the very conception of development, the standpoint in terms of poles possibly seeming in many respects to conflict with the communication and participation requirements which tend to underlie our point of view on the matter. Secondly, because concrete attempts to establish development poles have often been accompanied by polarization of the system by overdevelopment of some components and the marginalization and excessive underdevelopment of others.

But let us hear what F. Perroux himself has to say.[24] In a given territory the TNC carries on an exchange with the interior, which in accordance with its rationale necessarily develops in the direction of built-up regions, marked as they are by denser economic activities and relatively higher incomes.

If nothing corrects this trend inherent in large firms, the relative development of the built-up area will continue cumulatively, from period to period, without the rest of the population necessarily benefiting from a development process of their own.

A transport route established between the large firm and the built-up area 'stimulates and increases activity at the extremities, extends the horizon of small units in the built-up area and brings in more customers for the large firm'. The author then recommends that to this 'itinerary of solvency' be added 'itineraries of intraversion' which, leading off from the large firm, will spread within the system (an idea which is currently being explored in depth by the United Nations under the name of 'backward linkages').[25] But 'inevitably there will emerge along these routes influences, dominances and possibly partial dominances' according to how the TNC's action is directed. Where therefore such action follows a 'territorialized itinerary' (with which Perroux contrasts the 'non-territorialized itinerary' not tied to a particular location), it has a polarizing effect which can only lead to 'backward linkages' if it is complemented by action on the part of the public authorities. Any 'backward linkage', which will be effected in the framework of an asymmetric relationship governed by the nature of the TNC's action, will moreover be preceded by an extension of space at the extremities and the destruction of many former patterns of communication.

I. A. Egorov and his colleagues lay emphasis for their part on the foreseeable consequences as regards the stratification of consumption.[26] While most of the population will continue to consume agricultural produce and craft products, the rapidly growing urban population will demand cheap manufacturing goods and the most sophisticated consumer goods (expensive cars, stereo equipment, television sets, household appliances) beginning to appear in small quantities. A very specific 'demand pyramid' is then formed, with a very broad base of cheap mass consumption goods, overlaid by the urban-consumption stratum, and an extremely limited peak representing trade in the consumer goods of the most advanced industrial societies.

O. Sunkel for his part dwells on the consequences of the disintegration of each social class following the incorporation of some of its members within the system of the firm.[27] Under the theme of mobility we find again the aforementioned phenomenon of the extension of space. Such mobility will be in the downward direction both for the marginalized entrepreneurs, who will switch to small-scale industry or crafts or become employees, and for the marginalized sectors of the middle class, who 'will form a group of disappointed people in the lower middle class trying to give the impression of belonging to the middle class, but having little prospect of moving upwards and terrified by the danger of proletarianization'. As to the marginalized workers, 'they will surely swell the ranks of absolute marginality'. Lastly, there will be 'selective and discriminatory' mobility in an upward direction in that 'some people previously in an absolutely marginal position will become members of the working class, some workers will join the lower categories of the middle class, and some sections of the middle class will produce small- and medium-scale entrepreneurs'.

Many examples could be given of this type of destructuring. Generally speaking, the impetus conveyed by the TNCs will affect the societal consistency of the nation as a whole and will in this initial phase act as a disorganizing principle. If the original assumption of this work is accepted, to the effect that a culture integrates a system of values, patterns of socialization and a form of productive organization, it may seem plausible to distinguish two main situations.

The first situation corresponds to an impetus focused initially on the sphere of values (Fig. 9).

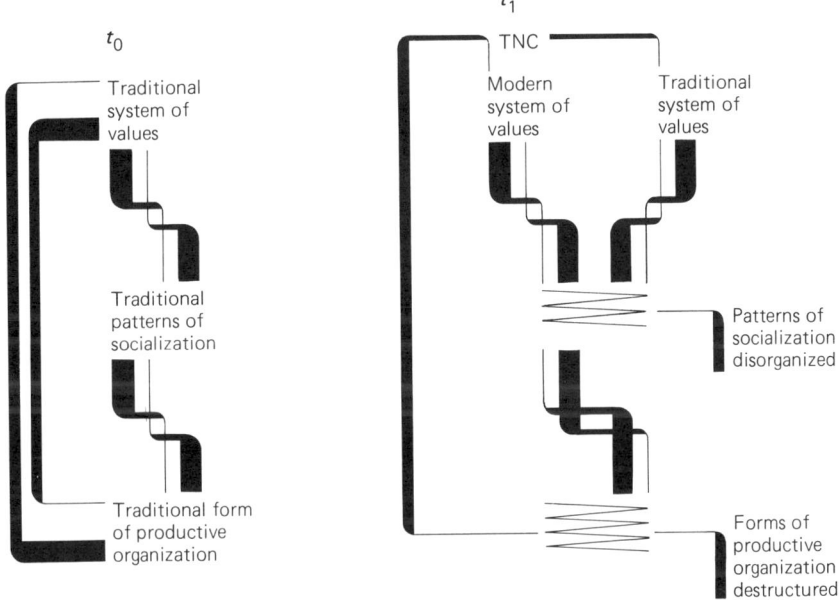

FIG. 9.

From an initial state assumed to be marked by strong bonding between the three spheres, the TNCs, by introducing into the sphere of values a set of modern values, will weaken the bonds between this sphere and the other two spheres, which will in consequence be affected also. This situation corresponds, it will be noted, to a direct strategy on the part of the firm, involving deliberate action. It will therefore chiefly concern countries with large populations which host TNCs whose activities result in imparting an artificial value to consumer goods on the domestic market.

The second situation could be outlined diagrammatically on the basis of entry into the productive sphere following the application of an indirect strategy of absorption, this case applying rather to agricultural countries or to countries possessing a specific natural resource or a large labour force. Here it is a

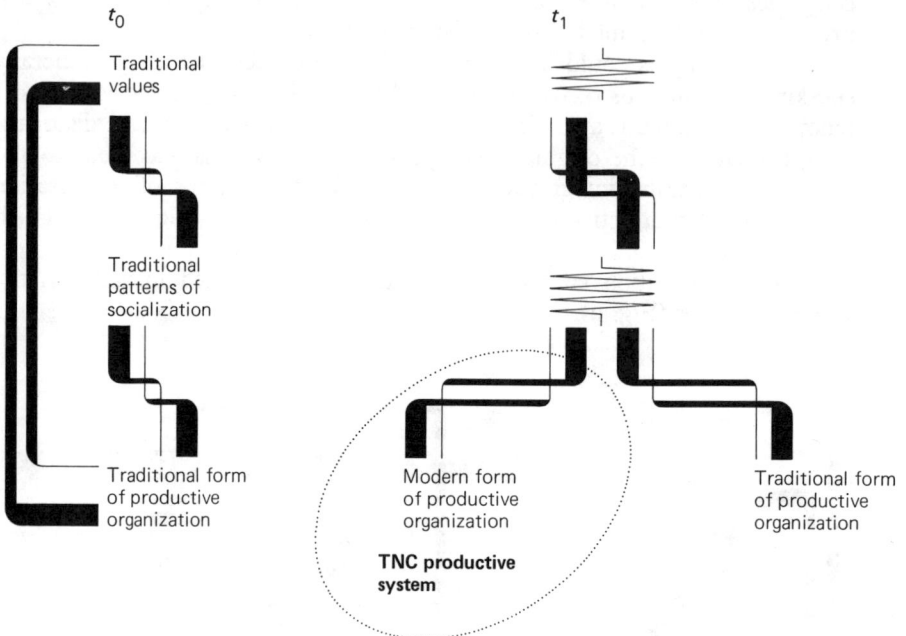

Fig. 10.

'mounting' process which will set off the destructuring of society (Fig. 10).

The two types of process will finally give a segmented image of societal reality marked by the coexistence of a TNC culture and one or more national cultures (the simplifield schema represented in Figure 11 is of course excessively 'dualistic'; a concrete study would ultimately distinguish numerous subcultures), these being in a state of opposition to the culture implanted by TNCs. It is the forms taken by this conflict—dominated by the asymmetric action of firms—which will show themselves in the various spheres in ways consonant with those described above, in regard to the particular cases of polarization effects, the structure of consumption and social stratification.

The destructuring period will nevertheless inevitably be succeeded in the long run by a restructuring and reorganizing phase. The situation most favourable to the scenario we are here considering is that where the national cohesion of society is redefined around the TNCs' activity. In this case the TNC culture spreads in all spheres and in the end gradually incorporates the other cultures. Singapore may be regarded as an almost perfect example of what such a new society could be. That country's acceptance of Western values is stressed unequivocally by Dr Goh Keng Swee, one of the builders of the state. Observing that the developing countries have all too often been loath to apply technical knowledge systematically to production, which has left much of the rural world out of the modernization process, Dr Goh Keng Swee adds:

The result has been economic stagnation and a continuation of the traditional cultures which, however charming when read in the accounts of anthropologists, serve as a hindrance to the absorption of new values which are necessary in the efficient management of a modern economy. In Singapore we are not handicapped by problems of this kind. The impact of modernization on us is less painful because many of the values of traditional societies have long been abandoned.[28]

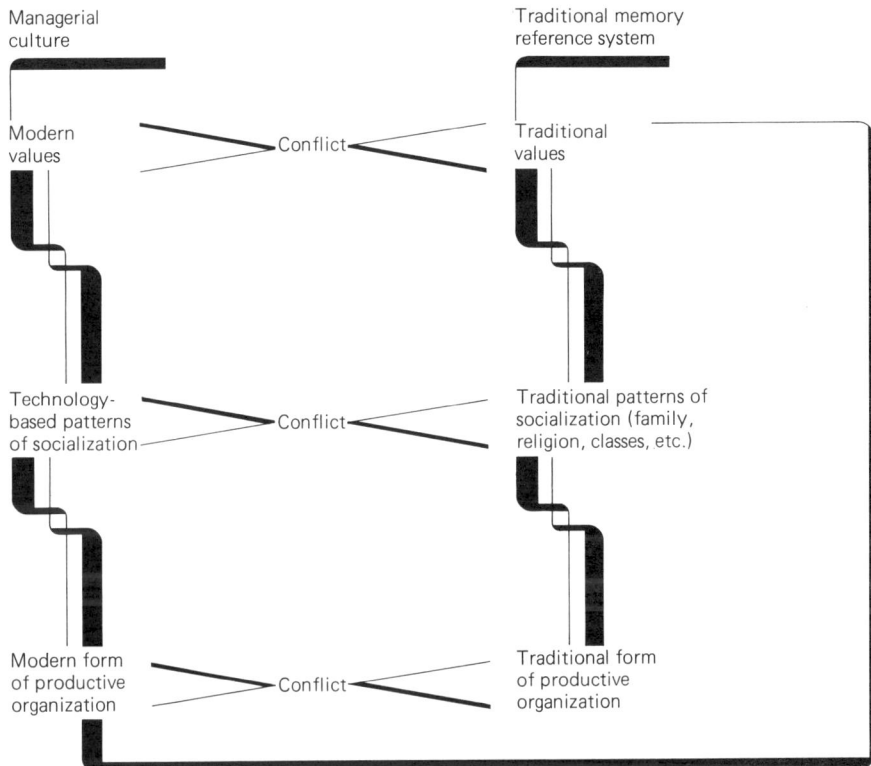

FIG. 11.

This acceptance of modern values is furthermore matched by the virtually complete fusion of technology and consumption, in that 'relocation' of the TNCs' productive subsidiaries is accompanied by dissemination of the Western way of life on an incomparable scale (indirectly via department stores) and a powerful organization of social control, reflected in a large measure of convergence between the trade-union movement and the authorities. Singapore thus represents the very paradigm of acceptance of the technology-based civilization by a Third World country, a paradigm which cannot however be generalized, even for the purposes of the present hypothesis. In many societies this restructuring will clearly be slower, even if accepted by the states concerned. In many cases traditional cultures are so firmly rooted that when other cultures are absorbed they will merely overlay them, with little or no communication between their components. Even if the TNC can one day 'realize its moral responsibilities, which are akin to those of a service in the general interest taking the form of a private enterprise,[29] the major agricultural and mining countries will have the utmost difficulty in ensuring the general spread of development. Sparse population over a large territory is also a major obstacle to the process. Lastly there remains a big unknown in this scenario on which we have not chosen to dwell here, namely in regard to the prospects for perpetuation of the technology-based civilization, both in the industrialized and in the developing countries, having regard to the internal contradictions affecting it.

Section 2

The controlled scenario: consciously planned national responses through the maintenance of cultural values and the control of communications, education, science and technology

This scenario assumes that, because they represent living systems, nations will defend their capability to determine ultimate aims of their own and to direct their development towards those aims. It will therefore be assumed that the social systems of developing countries will remain autonomous entities, that is, they will not gradually become inferior subsystems of the transnational system. The immediate consequence will be that the major trends towards the worldwide convergence of societies on which the previous scenario was based will lose their weight and undergo a radical change of nature. From this it will be inferred that, if a coherent world system is to be constituted in the future, it will rest more upon a system of communication between real national entities than upon any functional economic specialization decreed by the transnational system. Stated thus, these assumptions can be seen to have a very marked Utopian character when the importance already acquired by the TNCs is borne in mind. It is accordingly necessary to spell out the completely different methodological approach implied by this scenario, compared with the previous one, and again view the precise scope of voluntarist action from the only realistic standpoint, i.e. in conjunction with the continuing effects, doubtless in modified forms, of the advent and growth of transnational corporations.

The need for a completely different methodological approach

The most suitable framework for tracing the possible configurations of autonomy is that of a general systems theory. If we accept that the developing country is a living system capable of self-reproduction, we can imagine courses of action that are relatively free and hence less determined by the major trends which formed our starting-point for analysing the first scenario.

The system of the developing countries is a complex system

Taken as a complex system, the developing country first of all possesses the property of emergence, which means that, through organization of the interrelations of its constituent parts, new qualities emerge which cause the unit as a whole to possess something more than its component elements. Being incorporated into an environment (here the international environment), it must contemplate a number of adaptations to be able to pursue its aims. In no case will it relinquish its aims, and any changes it makes in them will stem from an internal, endogenous process. There will be no substitution of aims (as there was in the previous scenario) in favour of those of the environment, but a conscious recomposition. Interrelations are organized through a system of conduct hinging on the state but also involving a good many social agents. This system of conduct, which rests, as we have seen, on the memory–communication–information trio, must determine differentiation and modes of adaptation and give rise to creativity. The life of this system depends on its complexity since it is that which enables it to select a suitable state from a sufficiently broad spectrum of possible states. And its complexity is expressed by its variability, defined as the number of states among which a choice may be made in response to a disturbance from the environment. The more an organized system develops, the more differentiated and variable it becomes. But perpetuation of the system depends also on its having surplus capacity, in the sense of different means of carrying out the same function if, for one reason or another, one of them can no longer fulfil its role. Variability and surplus capacity are therefore two requisite properties for evolution of the system. The problem is, however, that in many cases they are contradictory. As the system evolves, its components become differentiated and its variability increases, which may result in the elimination of equivalent means of functioning, and hence in diminished surplus capacity. As A. Wilden puts it:

In biological terms the simpler an organism is, or the less complex the level of organization of a system, the greater will be the preponderance of the structure and reproduction over the system and evolution. And the more complex an ecosystem is, and the more 'technologically' efficient (that is, the less dependent on surplus capacity to avoid the effect of errors), the more sensitive it will be to error.[30]

In the case of social systems the situation most clearly illustrating this contradictory phenomenon is that in which the complexity of the system increases solely through functional specialization. Yet situations can be imagined in which increased variety would stem from new relations between the components of one and the same structure, or from a change in the number of the system's components accompanied by a change in structure. However that may be, what needs remembering is that efficient organization must strike a compromise between surplus capacity and variability. If there is too much surplus capacity the system's development will be obstructed by the lack of variability; while excessive variability as a result of functional specialization will halt development by the fact that there is no relay mechanisms.

Lastly, a distinction must be made in regard to the processes governing the system between those enabling it to maintain its steady state, those allowing it to select paths from among preordained alternatives, and those permitting the establishment of new programmes and new aims. The first correspond to all the phenomena of regulation and adaptation through action; their operation calls for no structural changes. The second accompany 'a process of selection and combination within the given norms of the system';[31] any changes in structure are compatible with the preordained aims and system of norms. (For a biological system it would be said that new structures are programmed in the system's instructions.) The third type of processes concern not only the achievement of preordained aims but the modification of aims. They are linked to the accumulating contradictions of the system and to random disturbances from the system's environment (what systems theorists call noise). These give rise to 'morphogenesis', in the sense of the creation of new structures as a result of the functioning of the system.

Indeterminacy and autonomy: the role of consciously planned action in relation to the TNCs

If the developing countries wish to remain in control of their evolving structure and aims, they must retain a large area of autonomy in which to engage in voluntarist action. In speaking of autonomy we necessarily have to consider whether it is possible to describe the configurations of a sphere of relative indeterminacy. Although systems theorists shrink from this type of question, the nature of the problem raised here involves speaking of the relations between norms and values (the 'superstructure') and the material

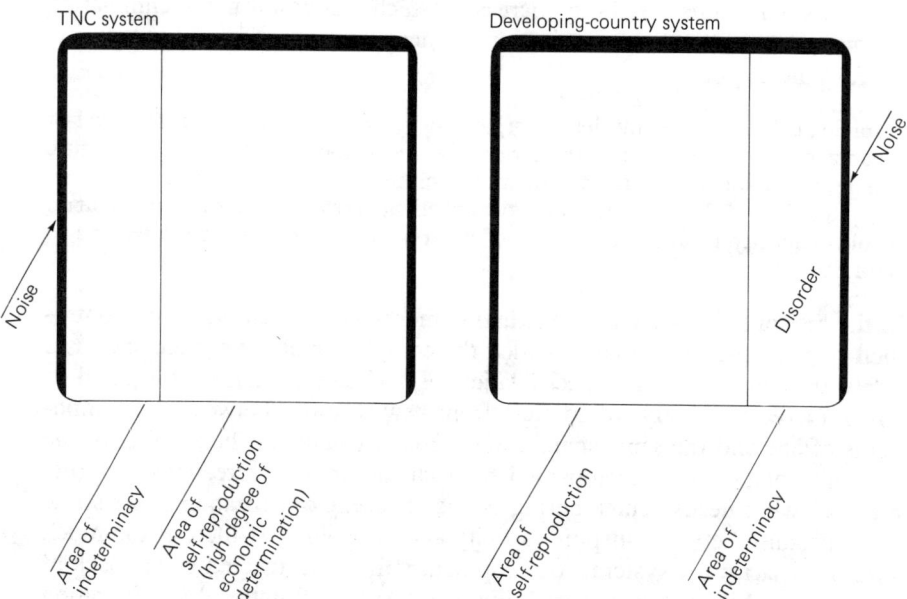

FIG. 12.

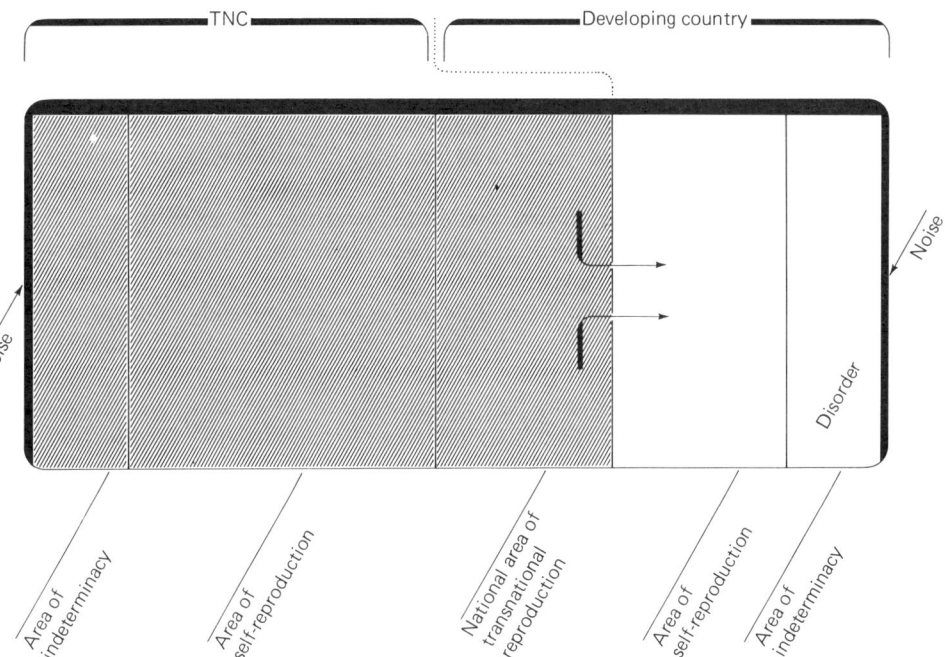

FIG. 13.

base or 'infrastructure'. The figures below represent (again in an over-dualistic manner) the two systems (TNC, developing country) first separately (Fig. 12) and then in the context of the present situation (Fig. 13). The TNC system is represented in such a way as to distinguish, first, an area of self-reproduction marked by a high degree of economic determination—what has been said about managerial culture and technology-based civilization amply justifying the subordination of the sphere of values to the material infrastructure—and, secondly, an area of relative indeterminacy, where the random element of noise comes into operation. It has to be acknowledged that the TNC system is powerful enough to absorb noise because it is so well organized. Furthermore, this area of indeterminacy is necessary, as stated by H. Atlan, 'beginning at a certain degree of complexity, to enable the system to adapt to a certain noise level'.[32]

Representation of the developing-country system taken on its own will also show up an area of self-reproduction to which the notion of economic determination will not be applied, in view of the character of traditional cultures, and an area of indeterminacy which will be the theatre of random effects from the environment. From the point of view of relative organizational capacities, we know that the developing country will find it harder to assimilate external disturbances owing to a relatively smaller variability (more through lack of communication than through lack of complexity). On the other hand, it possesses greater surplus capacity, i.e. more numerous stand-by mechanisms, because of its lesser degree of specialization. This is obvious when one thinks of the diversification and autonomy of small social entities such as African villages. It is clear from the present situation that, from the standpoint of the developing-country system, the TNCs' advent and growth cannot be treated simply as noise that the developing country could easily absorb by virtue of the way it is organized. First because the TNC phenomenon is a lasting, not a random, event, and secondly because it represents a considerable mass. The TNC takes over for its own use a national area of self-reproduction and tends gradually to structure the entire developing-country system. Most efforts made to spread the effects of the TNC phenomenon more evenly can be regarded as equivalent to a desire to integrate the country into the TNC system. In so doing, the TNC increases its own variability, and possibly (though by no means certainly) that of the country through functional economic specialization; in any case, it progressively eliminates its surplus capacity. There are thus four levels on which conscious adaptive responses may be focused:

The first concerns that part of the national area of transnational reproduction subject to a high degree of economic determination, which includes all negotiations concerning forms of control of subsidiaries and support for projects with a multiplier or knock-on effect. We would be tempted to say that it is hard to see how consciously planned action confined to this level will be able to avoid the consequences presented in the previous scenario, the logic of such action usually consisting in selecting processes preprogrammed by the TNC.

The second concerns the autonomous area of reproduction of the system. Consciously planned action with reference to this area should ultimately make it more coherent and tie it in more closely with history, in particular by amplifying the inherent links between values, patterns of socialization and the economic field. This action will concern values at least as much as the material infrastructure since the reproduction of this area rests broadly on development mechanisms that pertain properly to the superstructure.

The third concerns the area of indeterminacy on which are based the capacities for renewal and breaking off in a new direction. It is at this undetermined level that the voluntarist action envisaged in the controlled scenario will perhaps be the most valuable. It will pertain in large measure to the superstructure in that it will concern components of the system which, while often preponderant, are little integrated into either transnational reproduction or autonomous reproduction. The reactions of this area are essential in the life of the system, for they determine its ability to reformulate norms and aims in an intrinsic endogenous fashion.

The fourth and last possible level of response concerns overall organization. This should be based on the establishment of manifold connections between the components of the system, ensure autonomy and permit increased complexity consistent with a suitable balance between variability and surplus capacity.

Such is the general framework of the controlled scenario, which differs markedly from the extrapolatory scenario marked by functional specialization and seems to involve paying very special attention to values, to ideology and hence to superstructure.

Consciously planned action: the protection of cultural values, and action in regard to communications, education, science and technology

It is of course in keeping with this scenario to acknowledge that the consciously planned action of developing countries will anyway include a certain economic content. Protecting natural resources, giving the entire socio-economic system a greater stake in the effects of the TNCs and strengthening autonomous patterns of economic reproduction are essential activities. Yet these albeit necessary activities are in themselves of a relatively limited character because, at best, in the event of success: (a) they afford the socio-economic system protection against massive proliferation of the 'programmes' set up by the TNCs and as it were seal the system off by excluding everything they do not themselves select; (b) they ensure better distribution of the effects of the 'programmes' thus chosen; and (c) they consolidate previous national processes by ensuring their reproduction.

On the other hand, it is hard to see how such activities will lead to establishment of the new programmes needed for further development of the socio-economic system and, above all, how they will enable the system to produce them itself, which is a condition of its autonomy. That is where action at the level of the superstructure plays a fundamental complementary role.

The unity of Unesco's field of competence in the pursuit of a consciously planned process of development

We are too often in the habit of dissociating the protection of cultural values, communications, education, and science and technology. These various domains are in fact closely interlocked by virtue of the function they perform in the life of social systems. Since the various chapters in Part Two study each of them in detail, we shall confine ourselves here to a number of general observations. It will be affirmed that national control of these fields is essential to ensure the identity, cohesion and autonomous evolution of developing countries.

First, they underpin the identity of the social system inasmuch as they link it to its historical heritage and ensure the production of ideas. Protecting the diversity of cultures must not be regarded as a foible of anthropologists. It is necessary for two reasons, first because it maintains the complexity of the system of inherited values and hence protects the memory of the social systems and, secondly, because this complexity is a pledge of future creativity. Clearly, however, protection of the diversity of cultural values is inconceivable unless the subcultures enter into communication. These communications must preserve the unity of the social system, give rise to reciprocal information and involve broad participation. In this respect, progressive adaptation of the means of communication is essential. It is probably not desirable to think in terms of keeping traditional forms of communication as they are. It has often been observed that, in primitive societies without writing, memory is literally localized in each home and in each individual who spreads a ritual or transmits a myth. As A. Wilden puts it:

the objective memory of such a culture—the layout of the village, tools, cultural objects—is relatively small. This mnemonic system contributes to the survival of the structural pattern of the culture from generation to generation, but for the most part the significant distinction of such a culture must be maintained, reconstructed, represented—in a word, reinvented—in the very flesh of each generation.[33]

While it is clear, however, that modern means of communication constitute objective forms of memory, permit greater variability of the system, reduce its surplus capacity and facilitate its adaptation, they must themselves be selected so as not to throw out the multiplicity of cultures for the sake of the means. As is well known in information theory, 'the more different components there are to a system the greater is its quantity of information, for the less likely it is to be constituted through random assemblage of its constituent parts'.[34] Education presents a similar problem. As a process of transmission of knowledge, it links the system to its history; as a learning process, it gives it a considerable part of its self-reproduction faculties; as a factor in communication between people, it enables them to 'recognize' one another and so to exchange and debate. These are the reasons why it is inconceivable to separate educational action from the protection of cultural values. It seems reasonable to suppose, like Unesco, that:

If the majority's means of access to culture are identical with its means of access to knowledge, a community cultural project will have no meaning and no chance of succeeding except in so far as it is linked with a project for enabling people at large to have access to knowledge. Education must be open both to the contemporary cultural situation and to life in general. Teaching methods and even the content of education will have to be adapted, so as to allow not only for 'real life', but also for 'life of the imagination'. For this purpose, education needs to undergo a transformation from within, affecting both its content and its spirit. In addition, it must awaken in the pupils an awareness that they are rooted in their cultural traditions, so as to establish unifying ties in times and space which will determine the distinctive nature of the culture they have inherited.[35]

The tie between science and technology, education, cultural values and communication from the standpoint of the identity of the system needs no further demonstration. This tie is even so decisive at present that it has been thought that the abstract representation of reality, which is science, and the manner of doing, which is technology, are in a rank-ordered position in relation to the other fields. Scientific production and the technology indissolubly linked to it seem to take universal forms out of all proportion to the empirical production of knowledge found in traditional societies. It is very difficult to control the different fields with a view to promoting societal identity because basically all one will be able to do is select from a spectrum of alternatives offered as having universal validity. The fact remains that to recognize that it is the social system which must furnish science with its ultimate aims would in itself be an attitude very favourable to the controlled scenario. To accept that science and technology are only means would make it possible to lay down a national science policy that could provide a basis for weighing the pros and cons of decisions in the scientific and technological fields, with the result that science and technology would no longer be regarded as an autonomous structuring element but as a system interacting with the socio-cultural system. It must nevertheless be stressed that the developing countries' almost total lack of a science–technology–tool chain, and the fact that there is thus no reasonable possibility of envisaging its autonomous reproduction, is a considerable limit to efforts to promote their identity.

Secondly, these various fields contribute to the societal cohesion of the nation in that, to different degrees, they help to integrate the three spheres of values, patterns of socialization and forms of productive organization. Communications bring about a horizontal cohesion between cultures; education has the same property, plus that of providing communication between the various spheres composing them—transmitting norms, giving individuals general training and instruction in social relations so as to equip them as members of society, and contributing to productive organization through vocational training. As we have seen, science and technology have an identical role inasmuch as they link the generalization of a particular representation of nature to a production technique and a mode of work.

Thirdly, these three fields are essential to the autonomous evolution of the system and, in particular, to the ability of the social system to renew itself through modification of goals (morphogenesis). The point here is not to lay down a cut-and-dried goal for the social system and discuss ways of achieving it, but to enable it to reproduce itself, assign its own goals and fix own organizational structure. From this point of view, Unesco's field of competence is essential inasmuch as, confined *per se* to the immaterial sphere, it is more sensitive to conflict, contradiction, disorder or noise. To show this, let us imagine the morphogenesis of a national system conquered by TNCs and the materialistic type of rationality associated with them. If there is an accumulation of contradictions causing a break, this break will occur only in the economic infrastructure and will be confined to the area of what are referred to as the countries of the centre. Modification of the goals and structure of the system will therefore occur outside the developing countries (as is also predicted in the Marxist analysis) and will take the form of an extremely brutal break.

On the other hand, the relatively less materialistic character of developing societies means that they can look forward to a no doubt more continuous morphogenic evolution, provided they establish and defend an area of creative freedom. In this respect, special attention should be paid to informal forms of education, which permit non-directed adaptive learning: general education, which imparts the ability to recognize and to select, and adult education, which fosters desirable attitudes (by force of example) and at the same time helps people to arrive independently at their decisions. Similarly, it is important to preserve debate and confrontation in the different spheres making up the superstructure if their creative evolution is to be promoted. If, on the other hand, these spheres were to become polarized around a cleavage between the modern and the traditional, the capacity for autonomous development and hence reformulation of the 'programme' would be much impaired.

Machinery

Rather than attempt to forecast the future societal state of the developing countries seeking to follow this voluntarist path—an appreciation that would moreover be contrary to the very method of our reasoning, which implies that they will be largely responsible for transforming themselves and fixing their own ultimate aims—we shall consider the foregoing fields not on the basis of their essential functions but through the institutional forms into which they merge. Just as there is a social system, there is also a cultural system, a communications system, an education system, and a science and technology system, each characterized by a form of institutional organization and forms of social relationships between the members composing it. Seen like this, each of these systems will reflect to a greater or lesser degree the general features of the society and will, in its social practice, possess an additional function which will be that of reproducing them. These matters are too well known, particularly in the field of education, for it to be necessary to dwell on them. We shall simply observe that account must be taken of what we shall call a 'rematerialization' of the fields concerned in the machinery vested with practical responsibility for organizing them. This point will restrict the field of national voluntarism in that the action of the TNCs will be transmitted by society when not directly making itself felt on the structures underlying them. This is in fact the heart of the issue: if the TNCs also control a large portion of cultural values, of education, of communications and of science and technology, and if they apply to them their own conceptions, the controlled scenario of endogenous development becomes a mere culturalist Utopia without the slightest chance of ever materializing.

To emphasize the probabilistic character of this scenario, let us conclude with a particularly eloquent case as related by the person in charge of the operation concerned. Here is how the project manager for a large foundation describes the case of the island of Samoa.

The island of Samoa was the trial site for one of the three major tele-education projects financed by this foundation. The aim of the project was to study the reactions of an undereducated public to tele-education plans. The result was as follows: the educational shock reverberated over the entire socio-cultural life of the population of the island, thereby modifying social relationships, consumption patterns, life-styles, and so on. After conducting anthropological studies, the foundation introduced six television channels and equipped all classrooms with television sets, thinking that it was the right way to give the island the best education system. The television service put out educational programmes during the day and films and serials in the evening, mainly Disney and *Bonanza* chosen as being the 'purest' programmes'. In the words of Robert Dahl, who was the director of the study, 'initially nothing was imported into the island, but the inhabitants are now beginning to complete their diets with foodstuffs from outside: one cannot live eternally on coconuts, pawpaws and bananas'. According to him, the Samoans are starting to realize that there are things which make their lives easier, like washing machines, mopeds and cars; they are beginning to enjoy modern amenities and their life-style is to some extent changing. Previously they had to hand over their money to the chief, who gave them no amenities in exchange. Now they need money to acquire the amenities and forsake their ancient customs. They say: 'You see, I earn money. I want money so as to be able to buy a car and get about, go from one end of the island to the other the same day.' His foundation, in Dahl's words, has brought change to Samoa, a higher standard of living, better health facilities, including a hospital. He also expresses the view that the inhabitants of Samoa are better disposed than they used to be towards the United States and concludes by saying that the Samoan system has been hailed as the most successful educational television system in the world.[36]

NOTES

1. Michel Serres, *La communication, Hermes 1*, pp. 17–19, Paris, Éditions de Minuit, 1968.
2. Daniel Bell, *The Coming of Post-industrial Society*, p. 274, New York, Basic Books, 1973.
3. K. P. Sauvant and B. Mennis, 'Socio-cultural Investments within the International Political Economy of North–South Relations: The Role of Transnational Enterprises', Symposium organized by the Association Française pour l'Étude du Tiers-Monde, 30 May–1 June 1979, Dijon, France.
4. Cited by R. J. Barnet and R. E. Müller, *Global Reach. The Power of the Multinational Corporations*, p. 14, New York, Simon and Schuster, 1974.
5. Cited by N. Chomski, Y. Fitt, A. Fahri and J. P. Vigier, *La crise de l'impérialisme et la troisième guerre mondiale*, p. 73, Paris, Maspero, 1976.
6. J. Paul de Gaudemar, *La mobilisation générale*, p. 108, Paris, Éditions du Champ Urbain, 1979.
7. B. Kouyaté, *Composantes de pauvreté et valeurs socio-culturelles des populations bambara dans la région de Ségou, Mali*, Paris, Unesco, Division of Study and Development, 1977.
8. David Sirota and J. M. Greenwood, 'Understand your Overseas Workforce', in T. D. Weinshall (ed.), *Culture and Management*, p. 261, Harmondsworth, Penguin, 1977.
9. John Fayerweather, *Personal Relations, Management of International Operations*, pp. 14–36, New York, McGraw-Hill, 1960.
10. Ross A. Weber, 'Convergence or Divergence', in Weinshall, op. cit., p. 45.
11. E. F. Schumacher, *Small is Beautiful*, p. 122, London, Blond & Briggs, 1973.
12. Herbert Marcuse, *Culture et société*, p. 313, Paris, Éditions de Minuit, 1970.
13. See for example H. Bartoli, 'Économie et création collective', *Economica*, 1977, pp. 62 et seq.
14. Alain Touraine, *La société post-industrielle*, p. 264, Paris, Denoël, 1969.
15. Orio Giarini and Henri Louberge, *La civilisation technicienne à la dérive*, p. 69, Paris, Dunod, 1979.
16. F. Perroux, 'Firmes transnationales et développement', *Mondes en développement*, No. 12, 1975, p. 660.
17. Touraine, op. cit., p. 50.
18. Ibid, p. 5.
19. Nicos Poulantzas, *L'état, le pouvoir, le socialisme*, p. 138, Paris, Presses Universitaires de France, 1978.
20. Celso Furtado, 'La concentración del poder económico en los Estados Unidos y sus proyecciones en América Latina', *Estudios Internacionales* (Santiago), Vol. I, No. 3/4, 1968.

21. O. Sunkel, 'Big Business and Dependence', in G. Modelski (ed.), *Transnational Corporations and World Order*, p. 222, London, Freeman, 1979.
22. S. Hall, 'Pluralism, Race and Class in Caribbean Society', *Race and Class in Post-colonial Society*, p. 174, Paris, Unesco, 1977.
23. J. Ziegler, *Main basse sur l'Afrique*, p. 30, Paris, Seuil, 1978.
24. F. Perroux, 'Transnationales et pôles de développement', *Forum du développement*, November 1978, p. 4.
25. United Nations, *Transnational Corporations: Linkages in Developing Countries*, March 1980. (Economic and Social Council Document, E/C. 10/71.)
26. I. A. Egorov et al., 'The Impact of the Scientific and Technological Revolution', in G. E. Skorov (ed.) *Science, Technology and Economic Growth in Developing Countries*, p. 49, Oxford, Pergamon Press, 1978.
27. O. Sunkel, 'L'âge du néo-mercantisme', *Symposium on Multinational Corporations in Africa*, Dakar, 1974, pp. 27 et seq.
28. Goh Keng Swee, *The Practice of Economic Growth*, p. 190, Singapore, Federal Publications, 1977.
29. Perroux, op. cit.
30. A. Wilden, 'L'écriture et le bruit dans la morphogenèse du système ouvert', *Communications*, 1972, p. 48.
31. H. Atlan, 'L'intégration de l'événement: l'événement transformateur et organisateur', *Communications*, 1972, p. 23.
32. Ibid.
33. Wilden, op. cit., p. 68.
34. Atlan, op. cit., p. 26.
35. Unesco, *Thinking Ahead*, p. 127, Paris, Unesco, 1977.
36. Interview with Robert Dahl, *Performance* (New York), September/October 1972, cited by Armand Mattelart, *Multinationales et systèmes de communication*, pp. 202–4, Paris, Anthropos, 1976.

PART TWO

The impact of TNCs on cultural values and communication, education, science and technology

A thorough analysis of the consequences of TNCs' activities for endogenous development necessarily entails, therefore, a detailed examination of their impact on cultural values, communication, education, science and technology. Since TNCs are themselves the product of a civilization, it would be surprising if they were to forgo control over the main areas that go to make up a nation. Possibly because that control will enable them to ensure the stability and reproduction of their economic base. Probably because economic activities always have more specifically cultural activities as a corollary. And certainly because in a world in which the tertiary sector is growing more and more rapidly, such activities are in response to a swiftly expanding demand and hence market. They affect a sphere which is perhaps more fundamental than the economic sector, for they are liable to lay hold on a series of processes which make up the very meaning of life for the human beings concerned—in the first place, at the societal level, the transformation of the framework of socio-mental cohesion, that is to say the learning codes which validate and legitimate a social structure, secondly the actual pattern of interhuman relationships or what are commonly known as social relations, and lastly the relationship between man and nature, i.e. the deep-rooted sense of man's place in the ecosystem. The non-industrialized nations may not be fully aware of the type of civilization offered them, and it may well be that the people at the head of TNCs, obsessed by their mercantile rationalism, have in a way lost their sense of a life less attached to material things. Above and beyond the goal of endogenous development, a contribution can undoubtedly be made to the understanding and acceptance of the future world order by pinpointing the impact of TNCs on these areas and suggesting alternatives so as to minimize some of their more disastrous consequences.

Chapter 4

The influence of TNCs on cultural values and communication in the developing countries

The impact of TNCs on cultural values, communication media and patterns of consumption will be dealt with together in this chapter inasmuch as these constitute what has previously been called the sphere of values of a society. To be more precise, the object is to assess the impact of TNCs on such metasystems as ideologies, systems of representation, standards and criteria of choice. These are all areas or components of the societal state that are essential to the autonomy of developing countries. In concrete terms, cultural values are structured through a great many transmission channels, as much by the introduction of new modes of labour organization and the disciplines attaching to them as through the interplay of educational influences. But whatever the way in which the socio-cultural realm is entered, the initial effects on values spread and become the dynamic factors of social change, for example through the exemplary effects of the prestige enjoyed by TNCs in many countries.[1] Among other phenomena, it is found that the spread of advertising and the tourist trade in Third World countries plays an active part in developing the business aspects of life in society, so that in social relations an increasingly preponderant role is assigned to consumption patterns designed to satisfy new needs that have been created or induced.[2] Outward signs of success progressively take on the form of material goods, tokens of access to the civilized way of life, that of the TNCs' countries of origin.[3] From this point of view, the communication systems and modes of consumption characteristic of these countries today lie at the heart of cultural dependency and constitute the two themes that will enable us to adduce evidence in support of our hypothesis that there is a divergence between national cultural values and the activities of TNCs.[4] It should be noted, however, that our analysis of the role of TNCs in shaping communication, that complex system linking a collective memory-store to its various forms of expression in social life as a whole, will be confined here to the ways in which their influence is exerted over the concrete forms in which signs and images are exchanged, in other words to modes of communication and their effect on cultural values.

The first step will be to identify in outline the culture shock produced by the irruption of TNCs into a socio-mental territory that is not their own. Then a more thorough scrutiny will be made of the cultural and informational dependency brought about by the presence of TNCs and the key role that presence plays in structuring social consumption patterns in Third World nations. Lastly, we shall propose some guidelines for action designed to preserve the cultural values of developing countries from undue external influence.

Section 1

National cultural values and TNCs: the terms of a contradiction

The social and mental basis of cultural values

It has already been pointed out that, as a complex aggregate of social norms, values, customs, frames of reference and modes of thought, culture is akin to the notion of civilization, to the extent that it is held by some to be what distinguishes man from the realm of nature and, in particular, marks off what is human from the general characteristics innate in any living species.[5] This takes us back to the conscious and unconscious or voluntary and involuntary patterns of behaviour in social life as a whole.[6] Seen in this global perspective, culture determines the way in which individuals identify and recognize one another within their own social sphere of action.

From this point of view, setting up a TNC poses a threat to national identity and cultural authenticity, as it changes certain outlooks or attitudes, for instance by strengthening individualism and business-oriented utilitarianism.[7] But all the artistic or intellectual creative work that constitutes the cultural heritage of an ethnic group, a nation or a country must not be overlooked. Written and oral language, graphic signs, images or acoustic signs and, more generally speaking, the essential kernel of communications are all symbolic productions expressing the specific character of a social entity, even in the deviant manifestations due to the very forms which artistic creation takes. But our attention must first and foremost be focused on values and mentalities, for the nineteenth-century view of culture as synonymous with fine arts and literature to the exclusion of all else appears to be obsolete.[8] The hypothesis of transnational shock must therefore be postulated from the standpoint of traditions, ways of life and prevailing representations in a society.

We may therefore concur with J. Ladrière[9] in considering that a society's culture is primarily comprised of sets of concepts and symbols derived partly from the realm of the imagination, by means of which individuals and groups of individuals interpret the world and themselves ('systems of representation'). These mental representations, images or knowledge signify a selective manner of perceiving reality, thanks to a filtering of information or messages, reflecting in particular inherited priorities. These modes of representation, deriving from the combined effect of socialization procedures, are therefore closely bound up with education in the widest sense, or communication. But culture is also made up of aims and ultimate purposes which constitute 'systems of standards' laying down the fundamental rules of behaviour for life in society as a whole and providing the basis for a codification of representations. Social norms are thus evolved, justified and rank-ordered.[10] These systems of standards or norms are interiorized to a great extent and therefore reveal themselves to the unconscious mind as what is termed 'normal'. At the same time, systems of expression can be discerned, in other words 'the material and formal modes whereby representations and standards find concrete expression, in terms of feeling, enabling what is deeper . . . to be externalized into meaningful forms, made available for endless interpretation'.[11] It is here that demands for consumer goods emerge, expressing the specific preferences of individuals as a product of the representations and norms which prevail in society. The diversity of modes of expression is reflected in the types of communication and in the everyday or symbolic languages employed and is embodied in the actions and behaviour ('systems of action') which constitute social relations, and which include consumption.

In fact, cultural values, as categories of human existence, can be seen to possess both a cognitive and a social dimension, determining their social and mental basis and sphere of action. For the individual, 'his feelings, his will, his thinking, his language, his perception of reality and therefore his very conception of what reality is are to a great extent determined by his society's system of values and attitudes'.[12] Cultural specificity, then, is no more than a multi-faceted code for evaluating reality amounting, in synthesis, to the 'social code', which may be defined as the sum total of associations between the ideas prevalent in society and their outward form.[13] It is in the cultural arena that the manifold significations of social life come into being and that existence takes on, or rather is given, its full meaning. It is in the realm of culture that personalities are formed and that the patterns of life determining the actual course of a human existence are mapped out in advance.[14] The cognitive and ethical dimensions of culture appear, therefore, to be decisive, for it is their components which 'govern the norms of action and therefore give final shape to patterns of behaviour, selection principles, evaluation criteria and the motivations on which short-term and long-term concrete objectives are based'.[15]

Communication: different forms but the same issue

If the notion of communication indeed refers to all relations between individuals, it may be regarded as being cosubstantial with life in society since any human group, whatever its level of historical development, establishes interpersonal relationships which imply a minimum of mutual comprehension. Whether or not the interpersonal relationship comes about by means of stockable material media (books or newspapers, for example), communication is above all an exchange of ideas which are evaluated or deciphered according to a set of norms or representations. In its outward forms as well as in its substance, communication thus lies at the heart of the cultural identity of a nation since it is cultural values which create the symbolic bonds and ensure and preserve the cohesion of a society.[16]

Admittedly, as mankind has evolved, and life in society has become more organized, modes of communication have changed radically, partly as a result of scientific and technological progress, but the actual nature of the communication process has remained unchanged: the individual was and is still today the pivotal point of all communication. The now virtually infinite mass of transmitted messages, the vast capacity for storing information, the increasingly rapid renewal of techniques and devices for transmitting signals and messages and the whole change of scale in delivering information must not obscure the fact that the individual is still the subject of communication, which continues to fulfil long-standing functions, namely to inform, educate, transmit the cultural heritage, socialize while ensuring societal cohesion, or even persuade.

But, if communication is logically connected with cultural identity, to the extent of its being apparently necessary that there should be coherence between the two concepts, we can expect an analysis of modes of communication to show how cultural identity comes into being, in other words to give some idea of how representations and norms evolve. In fact, the 'systems of expression' referred to earlier are also the vectors of the perpetually changing combination of images and values, the main reason for this being that the codes and reference frames determining an individual's perception of society are engendered by the messages or representations produced by interpersonal or mass communication themselves.

This explains why communication has always been seen as a key issue in power, as well as an instrument of domination. Witch-doctors, sorcerers, mandarins or tribal chiefs were, and in some cases still are, the keystones of a mode of communication largely subjected to traditions or rites which also provided the basis for a system of social organization they helped to legitimize. This is not always explicitly evident, for instance because of the latent character of many of the significations conveyed (imaginary or subconscious factors, for example). But communication may also be instrumental in challenging the established order, which may in some cases lead the representatives of that order to resort to censorship.

Going back now to the actual situation in the developing countries as regards communication, we find disruption due to two causes: changes in the forms of communication, and the markedly transnational character those forms have come to acquire. Mass communications, impersonal by nature, are steadily ousting interpersonal modes of communication by diminishing their status,[17] and their development has contributed to making the whole business of exchanging signs very much more the preserve of professionals. A valuable industry for the production and dissemination of messages is taking shape before our eyes, which not only exerts a dehumanizing influence in many instances but also results in the development of vertical communication to the detriment of horizontal relations, which are important since they alone assign a preponderant role to inter-individual relationships. The process of a one-way flow of messages, transmitted directly by professionals, is replacing two-way exchanges, which alone can ensure true communication or dialogue. That communications are now referred to as a 'sector' clearly indicates that this is another branch of economic activity and hence that business interests are now closely bound up with the choice of vectors and messages.

At the same time, communication is an activity which is becoming transnationalized and is contributing to ever greater socio-mental dependency among Third World peoples by affecting people's attitudes and society's norms. Transnationalism admittedly has historical precedents, as attested by the spread of the major religions and the messages of Christ or Muhammad. But the fact remains that communication as it stands in many developing countries can be seen more and more as the output of TNCs, whose messages, codes or value systems are naturally those of Western societies with market economies, as will be clearly seen in the section that follows. However that may be, communications in developing countries are already to a large extent ruled by submission to private interests and preponderant foreign influence. Imported cultural values are likely to clash with national social patterns and codes and as a result may well jeopardize the extension of a form of development consistent with local values and cultures.[18] Finally, communication is central to a fundamental issue, that of the freedom of peoples to determine for themselves their systems of representation and values, and hence also their systems of action. Is it not to be feared that the Third World peoples will be increasingly confronted by images and shadows cast, as in Plato's allegory, on the walls of a cave in which they are prisoners, and in lending credence and currency to these images will at the same time be propagating a flame of distinctly Western aspect?

Culture shock

It has become clear that a process of economic development must necessarily be seen as part of a blueprint for society with underlying socio-cultural connotations and this is due to the fact that the components of the economic system have a role and a power enabling them to exert some influence outside the economic sphere. From this standpoint, TNCs cannot be regarded as agents whose function is confined to allocating the productive factors as rationally as they can in order to produce goods and services, themselves aimed at satisfying predetermined or revealed needs. On the contrary, transnational corporations are 'active entities' structuring economic and social space. It is difficult to see how value systems which might form the basis of policies of autonomous development resting on national cultural identity can be compatible with the rationale governing TNC behaviour and strategies. This warrants the supposition of a clash between the two systems of values and at the same time points to the need to analyse the consequences of this culture shock for the developing countries.

The dominant position of the TNCs and the risk of the developing countries' cultural dependence are enhanced by the fact that these corporations have now become one of the foremost structuring agents of the world economic system.[19] Our purpose here is to inquire into the nature of their overall impact on cultural values in addition to their widespread influence in many spheres. In other words, in what way or ways do the socio-cultural systems of the developing countries absorb the culture shock? Should these transnational influences be seen as resulting in total socio-cultural homogenization, or are they not rather conducive to an accentuation of cultural heterogeneity which, in a sense, poses a threat to the national identity of countries with a significant TNC presence?

Although it is true that TNCs tend to produce in Third World countries a uniform socio-cultural pattern modelled on that of the country of origin, all the evidence suggests that, as we have already assumed when considering 'the extrapolatory scenario', this process is instrumental in bringing about some degree of modernization. The groups and individuals who are incorporated into new formal or informal structures connected directly or indirectly with TNC operations find themselves adopting new ways of integrating into society, at the same time that other individuals and groups are unable to adapt to this evolution.[20]

As a result, if one accepts this schema, individuals belonging to certain social groups in the developing countries might well find themselves increasingly incorporated into a socio-mental system based on the rationality and ethic of TNCs, and hence more and more remote from other groups in their own country. Taking this to an extreme, there would be a tendency for social groups in developed and developing countries to share a common culture, that is to say identical life-styles and modes of behaviour which would be reflected in the same demands, the same concerns, the same books, the same films, the same aesthetic standards and above all similar consumption patterns. Despite language and territorial barriers, such groups or classes might have a greater capacity for communicating among themselves than exists between 'marginal' and 'integrated' individuals in the same country. This would mean that there would be a 'transversal effect', linked with the process of transnationalization, cutting across social and mental structures and modelled on the TNCs which penetrate and restructure the productive systems in the host countries. But in that case the culture shock becomes indissociable from a new type of social stratification, which, coupled with a form of socio-cultural dependence, mirrors the dualism and economic dependence of the Third World nations.[21]

Among the individuals affected by TNC rationality, such a process very often gives rise to a sense of belonging to two socio-mental camps: on the one side to the traditional world and, on the other, to the 'modernized universe' spearheaded by the TNC. This sense of divided loyalties, which was also to be found during the colonial era, causes individuals to be torn between two systems of representation and social norms. In some African countries, for instance, the individual is involved at one and the same time in a primary system of relations in which the group is preponderant, giving him the benefits of brotherly dependence and in a second system stemming from transnational influences in which the norms of autonomy restrict dependence to the point of isolation.[22] This is another of the disruptive effects of the culture shock. One of the basic ideas of Western modernity, namely that the unity of society is not embodied in the group but in the individual, or rather man in his attainment of freedom,[23] overlooks the fact that a person can only assert his autonomy or freedom within his relationships with others. This being so, it is no longer in the group, with its many qualities of companionship or 'conviviality', but in society that the individual marks out his territory and forges his links, chiefly through consumption.

Finally, it must not be forgotten that the nation-states of the developing world are culturally extremely heterogeneous.[24] This means that various 'subcultures', different systems of collective beliefs and different patterns coexist within one and the same society, which was by no means true of traditional societies. J. Ziegler[25] even goes as far as to use the term 'protonation' (from the Greek *protos*, meaning primitive or rudimentary) to describe those national entities which are to a great extent subjected to external needs and norms, in particular as a result of the construction of symbolic images that can seldom be taken at face value.[26]

At any rate, it seems difficult to dispute the fact that a process of cultural destructuration is under way, the main form it takes being the establishment, on a worldwide scale, of a consumer society which, in Herbert Marcuse's terms, makes for a 'repressive satisfaction of needs'. Today, TNCs ply the world's peoples with the same products, the same images and the same standards for living, and are active in substituting exchange values for use values. It is perhaps appropriate then to speak of a risk of 'ethnocide', i.e. a destruction of cultures.[27] What gives TNCs their strength and structuring power is that, with the shortages and poverty that prevail in the countries of the Third World, there is the danger that before long any personal development of the individual in his work and in his leisure will automatically involve participation in activities dominated and controlled by TNCs. For the impoverished masses there is often only one way out of unemployment and that is to join the transnational sector. In those circumstances, the fact of securing employment, consuming goods and services, and gaining access to certain media leads people to relinquish their cultural heritage and adopt imported socio-cultural models. As a result extroversion and deculturation become voluntary processes even if they are in fact logically and socially imposed by the transnational system.[28]

These relatively general considerations must now be supplemented by an in-depth examination of the concrete mechanisms through which TNCs influence value systems in Third World countries, on both the 'supply' side (communications) and the 'distribution' side (consumption patterns).

Section 2

Communication media and cultural dependence

Although it is true to say that the notion of communication refers to all relations between individuals and is expressed outwardly in the exchange of signs or objects endowed with a sense or meaning that is open to a variety of interpretations, any communication process conveys messages and exerts an effect on the socio-cultural plane. From this point of view, developing as it has done on a worldwide scale, the mass-communications sector has become one of the principal vectors of cross-cultural exchanges, especially in the direction of the Third World. The influence of the TNCs that dominate this sector must therefore be examined in depth since the internationalization of information and the communication media plays a part in the process of socio-cultural destructuration and extroversion of norms and values, and in so doing hinders endogenous cultural development. Our analysis will bear on the following different media: radio, television, records, tape-recordings, cassettes, films, newspapers, books, magazines, advertising, news-agency networks and satellite communications.

The TNCs' dominant position *vis-à-vis* the developing countries in regard to control over the media

The media sector is highly concentrated and predominantly American. Of the TNCs of various origins operating in this sector (advanced technology, tertiary sector, advertising) some are quite new to the branch. It is, then, a sector with a future, much in favour with TNCs, but giving rise to marked cultural dependence of the developing countries in that the flow of information goes mainly one way, i.e. towards the Third World countries.

A market characterized by concentration and TNC domination

As has already been noted, the mass media comprise television, radio, films, the press and publishing. TNCs operating in this sector are concerned both with actual equipment (professional equipment, domestic apparatus) and with content (radio and television programmes, films). To these may be added educational material and certain educational activities (educational television, for instance) but this aspect will be dealt with later under 'education'.

As industry has become increasingly concentrated and multinationalized, the TNCs operating in the field of advanced technology have assumed an ever more significant role both in the manufacture of heavy equipment and the establishment of management systems and techniques, and in the preparation of programme material.[29] TNCs are therefore concerned as much with software as with hardware in producing and disseminating 'information' and messages. Historically speaking, the internationalization of the media industry has affected news-agencies, publishing, the production of newspapers and magazines, film production, television and radio. The TNCs operate at three levels:

TNC owns or controls media industry (publishing house, radio station, etc.) abroad;
TNC owns or controls marketing network (distribution system, offices, etc.) abroad and;
TNC controls the foreign sales of media products (is in dominating position in world markets).[30]

Today, international sales and distribution operations are preponderant in this sector and 'the dominating role of the TNCs in world marketing and distribution is much higher than their proportion in the field of production of media material would give them'.[31]

Furthermore, TNCs operating in the communication sector are often part of large conglomerates. For example, the production and distribution of films in the United States are increasingly a minor activity of a parent company whose subsidiaries operate in several branches. For instance, since 1966 Paramount Pictures has been owned by Gulf & Western (tobacco, insurance, raw materials), and United Artists was acquired by Transamerica Corporation (banking, air transport, building) in 1967.[32] There are many other similar cases. In 1972, the managing director of RCA stated that over 70 per cent of the company's business was still in electronics, but that RCA was by then to a great extent more than an electronics company.[33] It is in fact also Hertz, the car-hire firm, Random House publishers, a building firm, a carpet-manufacturing business and a frozen-foods concern.

A highly concentrated market dominated by United States-based TNCs
Leaving aside American companies, which lead the field, the main media firms are based in the Federal Republic of Germany, the United Kingdom, Japan, France, Sweden, the Netherlands and Italy. But the communication sector is undisputedly controlled primarily by the American TNCs, particularly the transnational electronics corporations. In this connection, the development of the electronics sector in the United States is characterized by two features. First, this sector as a whole and the media technology it involves (telecommunications, satellite communications) have been affected, like other sectors, by the financial restructuring of American industry, and is today almost entirely controlled by three major banking groups, Morgan Guaranty Trust, Chase Manhattan Bank–Chemical Bank N.Y. Trust and First National City Bank.[34] The second point is that alongside its financial reorganization the sector has considerably expanded its operations abroad, especially in the 1960s,[35] and today an average of over 40 per cent of its income comes from foreign earnings. It may be remembered that expansion of communication firms in the developing world began with the 1929 crisis and carried on during the Second World War, when the Latin American countries entered a phase of import substitution. RCA, for instance, commenced operations in Brazil in 1940, and a subsidiary of ITT has been manufacturing radio and telecommunications equipment in Santiago de Chile since 1942.

Radio and television
Although British and French firms have a firm foothold in the countries of their former colonial empires (the Commonwealth as regards the British and French-speaking West Africa as regards the French), three American corporations—CBS, NBC and ABC—play a major role throughout most of the Third World. For example NBC made its first foreign investment in 1953, supplying technical assistance to Portugal, Peru and Saudi Arabia, and in 1959 invested in Mexican television. In 1960 it built the first Egyptian

station, invested in Argentina and then in Mexico and distributed programmes. Its African operations began in 1961 with Nigeria, in particular, after which it set up the radio network in Sierra Leone and Sudan in 1963 and introduced television to Uganda.[36] It may be noted that NBC is an affiliate of RCA which operates virtually the world over, whereas ABC concentrates mainly on Central and Latin America.

Very often, transnational radio and television corporations operate through direct sales of technology (equipment and programmes) and technical assistance to stations in the developing countries which may be state or privately owned (as in the developed countries):

Television has developed primarily as a commercial medium . . . in the United States and a few other countries, notably in Latin America. . . . Elsewhere, however, broadcasting was a State monopoly without commercial connections. . . . At present, television systems in over fifty countries are controlled, in whole or in part, by private interests.[37]

With regard to radio and television programmes, world distribution is largely dominated by a handful of United States-based TNCs. The big television programme producers for the developing countries are: MCA-TV, Time-Life Television, Paramount, CBS, Twentieth Century Fox and MGM. Although the main income from exported American television programmes is earned in the developed countries, the share of developing countries is substantial in terms of programme hours, for in many cases 'whole packages of equipment and programmes have been offered to new television stations'.[38] In Latin America, commercials account for a very high proportion of earnings.[39]

Films

'The complex of less than a dozen important production and distribution companies of "Hollywood" keeps half of the theatres in the non-socialist world supplied with films'.[40] These companies are part of big conglomerates. The American film industry has been transnational since the beginning of the century. Today, half of its income comes from abroad (Table 12).

Since 1946, film exports of the major Hollywood motion-picture companies have been dealt with by a pool, the Motion Picture Export of America (MPEA).

TABLE 12. Turnover of the American Film industry

Year	Foreign sales		United States sales		Total
	$ millions	%	$ millions	%	
1963	293.0	49.9	293.4	50.1	586.4
1968	339.0	47.6	372.3	52.4	711.3
1973	415.5	51.5	390.5	48.5	806.0

Source: *Variety*, 15 May 1974.

In 1973, the percentage breakdown of the foreign turnover of the major American film companies was as follows: United Artists (22.5), Twentieth Century Fox (16), Paramount (14), MGM (14), Warner Bros (12.5), Universal (10.5), Columbia (10.5).[41] The developing countries accounted for 23 per cent of foreign turnover in 1973, two-thirds of which came from Latin America.[42] Columbia Pictures Industries, for instance, has subsidiaries in Iran, Brazil, Mexico, Panama, Colombia, Bolivia, Kenya, Venezuela, Hong Kong, Thailand and Malaysia.[43] Generally speaking, as shown in Table 13, the number of films produced by the developing countries is negligible compared with imported full-length films.

The African film-distribution market is to a very great extent in the hands of SOPACCA (Société de Participations Cinématographiques Africaines) which comes under the Institut Français de Développement Industriel and through nine African companies, is represented in Ivory Coast, Mali, Togo, Niger, Benin, Chad, Cameroon, Senegal, Mauritania, Congo and the Central African Republic. The major American companies set up a pool in these same countries in 1971, AFRAM Films, with sole rights over the distribution of Hollywood films in Africa. It is the French-speaking countries' version of AMPEC which was set up in 1961 to distribute American films in Ghana, Gambia, Sierra Leone, Liberia and Nigeria. It is clear that the films to be distributed in Africa are selected abroad.[44]

Their dependence on imported films in fact prompted a number of African countries to set up an Inter-African Film Distribution Consortium (CIDC) and an Inter-African Film Production Centre (CIPROFILM) at the Ouagadougou Pan-African Film Festival.

It may also be noted that there is a tendency among the major companies operating in this sector to diversify their range of activities or to join conglomerates. An example already quoted is Paramount, but this also applies to Walt Disney Productions, Columbia Pictures and Twentieth Century Fox.

News-agencies
As early as the end of the nineteenth century, three news agencies, the Reuters (United Kingdom), Havas (France) and Wolff (Germany), divided up the world. After the Second World War, their expansion which had been the result of the European countries' colonial power gave way to the influence of the American news agencies. With the rise of United States political power on the international scene, these agencies launched a campaign for 'freedom of information', thereby restricting the scope of their European counterparts. The three great international news agencies today are Associated Press (AP) and United Press International (UPI), both based in the United States, and Reuters (United Kingdom), although Tass (USSR), AFP (France) and Kyodo (Japan) play a not insignificant role. For example in 1970, UPI, which employs 10,000 people in 238 offices (62 countries), supplied 40 per cent of the news reproduced in the 14 main Latin American newspapers; similarly, Associated Press sends 90,000 words a day to Asia, but receives only 19,000 words from New York concerning Asia for world distribution. Four major TNCs have, then, a virtual monopoly over the flow of information throughout the world

TABLE 13. Full-length feature films

Country	Date	Number of imported films	Number of films produced
Africa			
Algeria	1974	436	
	1975	210	6
Benin	1976	331	
Botswana	1975	208	
Burundi	1975	40	
Egypt	—[1]	—[1]	45
Ethiopia	1974	333	
Ghana	1975	36	1
Ivory Coast	1976	372	
Kenya	1974	165	
	1976	337	
Libyan Arab Jamahiriya	1975	201	2
Mauritius	1974	660	
	1975	393	1
Morocco	1974	831	
	1976	473	
Senegal	1976	248	
Seychelles	1974	221	
	1975	283	
Swaziland	1975	319	
Uganda	1976	200	
United Republic of Cameroon	1974	760	
	1975	387	2
United Republic of Tanzania	1976	176	1
Latin America and the Caribbean			
Argentina	1974	381	
	1975	215	34
Brazil	1975	595	90
Ecuador	1974	2 184	
Jamaica	1974	150	
Mexico	1975	514	162
Peru	1975	307	1
Venezuela	1974	795	
	1975	680	9
Asia			
Hong Kong	1974	465	
	1975	517	112
India	1974	26	
	1975	28	475
Indonesia	1975	400	41
Iran	1974	563	
	1975	400	68
Iraq	1974	543	
	1975	129	
Jordan	1974	560	
	1976	738	
Republic of Korea	1974	37	
	1975	34	99
Malaysia	1974	844	
	1975	909	5
Pakistan	1975	110	120
Philippines	1974	589	
Singapore	1974	889	4
	1975	1 468	
Sri Lanka	1974	39	
	1975	83	31

1. Not known.
Source: *Statistical Yearbook*, Paris, Unesco, 1977, pp. 971–85.

(Associated Press, United Press International, Reuters and Agence France-Presse), and the situation is practically the same as regards newsreels, with a quasi-monopoly by three major agencies, Visnews (United Kingdom), UPITN News (United Kingdom and United States), and CBS News (United States), to which must be added DPA-Etes (Federal Republic of Germany) and ABC News (United States). These agencies alone supply all the developing countries' newsfilms, and half of those of the Western world.[45]

Publishing
The first transnational publishers were British: (a) Macmillan, which is well established in India, for example; (b) Longman, which today is part of the veritable empire formed by the Pearson group which controls, among others, Penguin Books and the Financial Times; and (c) Oxford University Press.

These firms are dominant today in English-speaking Africa and India. The French publisher, Hachette, has consolidated its position throughout French-speaking Africa, where it is represented in thirty-three countries, and has also expanded into Latin America (Argentina, Brazil). Books account for a third of its gross export earnings and periodicals two-thirds. Hachette controls printing firms in the developing countries and also exports books to those countries. But the largest exporter of books in the world today is the American publisher McGraw-Hill.[46]

As shown in Table 14, the developing countries import a very substantial proportion of their 'scholarly' literature.

There are, then, relatively few transnational publishers and their main revenue is derived from scientific and technical publications. The American publishers are preponderant in this field.

With regard to newspapers and magazines, 18 million tonnes of newspapers and news magazines are printed in the developed countries, as opposed to 3.1 million in the developing countries, i.e. a per capita ratio of 16.3 to 1.1 kilograms. This means that the consumption of newsprint in the industrialzed countries is fifteen times greater than in the other countries.[47] The two leading news magazines are *Time* and *Newsweek*. In 1972,

TABLE 14. World book production and various indicators of educational level

	1950	1970
Percentage of developing countries in world book production	24	19
Developing countries' percentage of world's literate adults	37	50
Developing countries' percentage of school-going population	42	63

Source: K. Smith, *The Impact of Transnational Book Publishing on Intellectual Knowledge in Less Developed Countries*, p. 3, Paris, Unesco, 1976.

TABLE 15. World estimate of number of titles published

	1955	1965	1975
World total	269 000	396 000	568 000
Africa	3 000	7 000	11 000
Americas	25 000	77 000	121 000
Asia	54 000	61 000	88 000
Europe	131 000	200 000	264 000
Oceania	1 000	5 000	5 000
USSR	55 000	76 000	79 000
Developed countries	225 000	336 000	480 000
Developing countries	44 000	60 000	88 000
Africa (excluding Arab States)	1 600	4 300	8 300
North America	14 000	58 000	92 000
Latin America	11 000	19 000	29 000
Asia (excluding Arab States)	53 200	69 700	85 800
Arab States	2 200	4 000	4 900

Source: International Commission for the Study of Communication Problems, Unesco.

for instance, Time had a circulation of 300 million and was distributed in 180 countries.

Gramophone records
The mass production of gramophone records today is in the hands of a few major TNCs.[48] From as early as the beginning of the century four large companies dominated the record industry: Grammophon (Germany, United States); Columbia (United States); Victor Records (United States); Pathé (France). RCA took over Victor Records in 1929 and Columbia was bought up by CBS in 1937.

The British firm EMI was set up in 1931 as a result of a merger between Columbia Europe, Pathé and the Gramophone Co. (United Kingdom).[49] After the Second World War, Deutsche Grammophon was taken over by Siemens, while its French affiliate became part of the Philips group. Since 1962 Phonogram (Philips) and Polydor (Siemens) have had technical co-operation agreements as part of the holding company, Polygram. In 1975,

TABLE 16. Record-producing firms

Company	Country	Share of world market in 1975 (%)
CBS	United States	17
EMI	United Kingdom	16
Phonogram (Philips)	Netherlands	—[1]
Warner	United States	8
RCA	United States	7
Polydor (Siemens)	Fed. Rep. of Germany	—[1]
MCA	United States	4
Decca	United Kingdom	4

1. Polygram (Phonogram and Polydor) = 18 per cent.

eight firms controlled three-quarters of the world record market (see Table 16).[50]

It may be noted that EMI owns record-producing companies in some thirty countries and markets its musical publications under the following brand names: EMI Records; His Master's Voice; Music for Pleasure; Capitol (in the United States).

Communication technologies

The transnational 'hardware' corporations play a considerable role in the acquisition of new communications technology by the developing countries.[51] Examples are General Electric, IBM, ITT, Western Electric, Westinghouse, General Telephone and Electronics, and RCA. But other major electronics firms such as Control Data, Digital Equipments, Xerox, Texas Instruments and Hewlett Packard, and, in Europe, Philips, Siemens, AEG, Telefunken, Thomson and Erickson have turned their attention to the sector, as shown in Table 17.

Noteworthy in this respect is the development of space technology for communications. In Latin America, LATINO (Latin American Television International Network Organization) was established in 1968 by the American Broadcasting Company (ABC) of New York to provide a single organization for satellite broadcast of Channels 9 and 13 from Buenos Aires; 9 from Bogota; 7 from San José, Costa Rica; 7 from Santo Domingo; 3 from Ecuador 2 from San Salvador, 2 from the Dutch West Indies; 1 from Panama; 1 from Uruguay; Channels 2 and 4 from Caracas; 3 from Guatemala; 4 from Mexico; and 13 and 14 from Chile.

In India, where television is not very widespread, it was decided in 1979 to invest $500 million in the construction and launching of a direct-broadcasting satellite, INSAT I (Indian Satellite System), to be constructed by Ford Aerospace Communications, a subsidiary of the transnational motor company. There is also Cable & Wireless, an unobstrusive TNC but in fact the leading firm in telecommunications by cable with an important base in Hong Kong.

There is a marked tendency among the TNCs operating in this sector to diversify their activities and particularly to branch out into software, in other words the content conveyed by the mass media. RCA for instance now controls Random House and its publishing subsidiaries (A. Knapft, Pantheon Books and Vintage) and, more recently, Ballantine Books, which specializes in paperbacks.[52] ITT has likewise purchased two publishing firms (Bobbs-Merrill and Howard-Sams), while Hughes Aircraft, which manufactures satellites and equipment for cable-television systems, now has a hand in operating cable and programme-production systems (Teleprompter Corporation).

TNCs are also tending to take an ever-greater interest in the education market. This applies to ITT, General Electric and Control Data. This latter organization, for instance, has founded an Institute for Advanced Technology and offers seminars on communication theory, but also on the role of the individual and the place of private life in the face of organizational needs.[53]

TABLE 17. Leading world firms in the audio-visual field

Position	Name of company	Country	Consolidated turnover 1975 ($ millions)	Percentage share of audio-visual	Main activities
1	General Electric	United States	13 399	5*[1]	Electricity and electronics
2	ITT	United States	11 368	3*	Telecommunications
3	Philips	Netherlands	10 746	33	Electronics (general public)
4	BASF	Fed. Rep. of Germany	8 152	4	Chemicals
5	Siemens	Fed. Rep. of Germany	7 760	6*	Electricity and telecommunications
6	GTE Sylvania	United States	5 948[2]	7*	Telecommunications
7	Hitachi	Japan	5 916	11*	Electricity and electronics (trade)
8	Westinghouse	United States	5 863	6	Electricity
9	AEG Telefunken	Fed. Rep. of Germany	5 187	12	Electronics (general public)
10	Eastman Kodak	United States	4 959	80	Photography and film
11	Rockwell International	United States	4 943	5	Aerospace and automobile
12	RCA	United States	4 790	46	Electronics
13	Matsushita	Japan	4 677	47	Electronics (general public)
14	Toshiba	Japan	4 201		Electronics (general public)
15	Rhône-Poulenc	France	4 174	0.3	Chemicals
16	CGE	France	4 072	ε	Electromechanics and telecommunications
17	Ciba-Geigy	Switzerland	3 498	6	Chemicals
18	3M	United States	3 127	14*	Chemicals
19	Robert Bosch	Fed. Rep. of Germany	2 966	4*	Automobile accessories
20	Thomson-Brandt	France	2 932	16*	Electronics
21	Gulf & Western	United States	2 602	14	Conglomerate
22	CBS	United States	1 939	75	Radio-TV network
23	Thorn Electrical	United Kingdom	1 702	41	Electronics (general public)
24	Nippon Electric	Japan	1 676	10*	Telecommunications
25	Schlumberger	United States/France	1 588[2]	0.4	Oil prospecting, core drilling

Position	Name of company	Country	Consolidated turnover 1975 ($ millions)	Percentage share of audio-visual	Main activities
26	Sanyo	Japan	1 432	50	Electronics (general public)
27	Sony	Japan	1 385	90	Audio-visual electronics (general public)
28	EMI	United Kingdom	1 182	80	Records and electronics (trade)
29	Agfa Gevaert	Fed. Rep. of Germany/Belgium	1 137[2]	58	Emulsion coatings and photographic equipment
30	Hachette	France	967		Books
31	Time	United States	911	3	Magazine and paper pulp
32	Zenith	United States	901	96	Audio-visual electronics (general public)
33	Grundig	Fed. Rep. of Germany	831	98	Audio-visual electronics (general public)
34	Polaroid	United States	813	100	Photography
35	MCA	United States	811	80	Cinema and television
36	Fuji Photo Film	Japan	739	100	Photography and cinema
37	Rank Organization	United Kingdom	734	62	Cinema and audio-visual electronics
38	Warner Communications	United States	670	88	Records and cinema
39	AVCO	United States	651	6	Aeronautics
40	Sharp	Japan	625		Electronics
41	Havas	France	560[2]	ε	Advertising
42	Harris	United States	501		Electronics
43	GBS	France	465[2]	ε	Telecommunications
44	Bell & Howell	United States	455	41	Office and audio-visual equipment
45	Pioneer Electronic	Japan	434	96	Audio electronics
46	General Instrument	United States	420	48	Electronics
47	Canon	Japan	401		Cameras
48	Publicis	France	372	ε	Advertising
49	Decca	United Kingdom	365	54	Records and electronics
50	Twentieth Century Fox	United States	341	100	Cinema

TABLE 17 (continued)

Position	Name of company	Country	Consolidated turnover 1975 ($ millions)	Percentage share of audio-visual	Main activites
51	Columbia	United States	332	100	Cinema
52	Fairchild	United States	291	7*	Semiconductors
53	Konrshiroku Photo Industry	Japan	269	62	Emulsion coatings
54	Ampex	United States	245	67	Magnetic recording

1. Asterisk denotes approximate figure.
2. 1974 turnover.
Source: P. Flichy, *Contribution à une étude des industries de l'audio-visuel*, Paris, Ministère de la Culture et de l'Environnement, 1978.

With regard to data banks (references) and data bases (statistics, files), TNC control is decisive. While the first data systems were established by United States Government agencies, under the auspices of the Rand Corporation in particular, data banks are nowadays private and, here again, marked by high concentration. The three leaders in this field are Lockheed (System Development Corporation), Control Data and General Electric. Specialized private data systems have been set up by TNCs. With 450 data banks and data bases, the United States holds 90 per cent of the world stock of data.

A one-way flow

Although the proportion of television programmes imported by the developing countries varies considerably from one to the other, it is on average very high. Such countries are in fact not alone here, since only the United States, the People's Republic of China, Japan and the USSR can be regarded as self-sufficient in this respect. Table 18 covering the 1970/71 period gives an idea of both the extent and the unevenness of the phenomenon. While the developing countries as a whole import at least 30 per cent of their television programmes, some of them (like Guatemala, 84, Malaysia 71 and Zambia 64 per cent respectively) are particularly dependent on imports. This also applies to Nigeria and Uruguay 66 per cent, Costa Rica 80 to 90 per cent, and Ecuador 75 per cent. On the other hand, Argentina is tending to pull out of importing foreign programmes. This is what emerges from a survey of programmes broadcast on Channel 13 in Buenos Aires. The proportion of foreign programmes, which accounted for 46.88 per cent of television time in 1960, had dropped sharply to 32.88 per cent in 1970 and 28.35 per cent in 1972.

On average, half the television programmes of Latin American and African countries originate abroad. Furthermore, in Latin American countries (except Colombia and Cuba) most programmes centre very much on light entertainment, series and films. A very considerable proportion of the programmes imported into Latin America come in fact from the United States, and this type of broadcast accounts for nearly 30 per cent of total television time. In Argentina 80 per cent of imported television programmes come from the United States, which is also the main exporter to Asia and the Pacific (e.g. Republic of Korea), Africa and, in particular, the Middle East.[54] The African continent, however, is the least developed in regard to television.

Table 18 gives figures for selected countries showing the proportion of total television time taken up by imported programming material.[55]

TABLE 18. Imported programming material as a percentage of total television time, 1970

Country and channel	Imported material as percentage of whole	Method of calculation
Argentina (Channel 9 B.A.)	10	A[1]
Argentina (Channel 11 B.A.)	30	A
Chile	55	W[2]
Colombia	34	W
Dominican Republic (Channel 3/9)	50	A
Guatemala	84	W
Mexico (Telesistema)	39	A
Uruguay	62	W
China	1	W
Taiwan (Enterprise)	22	A
Hong Kong (RTV & HK-TVB) English	40	W
Hong Kong (RTV & HK-TVB) Chinese	31	W
Republic of Korea	31	A
Malaysia	71	A
Pakistan	35	A
Philippines (ABC-CBV)	29	A
Singapore	78	W
Thailand (Army TV)	18	W
Dubai	72	A
Iraq	52	A
Israel	55	A
Kuwait	56	A
Lebanon (Telibor)	40	A
Saudi Arabia (Riyadh TV)	31	W
Saudi Arabia (Aramco TV)	100	W
United Arab Republic	41	A
People's Republic of Yemen	57	W
Ghana	27	W
Uganda	19	W
Zambia	64	W

1. A = annual figures. 2. W = data based on sample weeks.
Source: Krishna Kumar, 'Imported Programming as a Percentage of Television Time, 1970-71', *A Working Paper on the Social and Cultural Impacts of Transnational Enterprises*, Honolulu, East-West Center, 1978.

It has been noted that the main American corporations exporting television programmes have formed a pool, the MPEA (Motion Picture Export Association of America), whose members account for some 80 per cent of American programme sales abroad, which indicates high concentration. The company, Screen Gems, for instance, has had a great deal of export success with its series *Rin-Tin-Tin* and *Bewitched*. The same applies to MCA with *Ironside*, *The Virginian* and *Men from Shiloh*, and for Twentieth Century Fox, whose distributions included *Peyton Place* and *Bonanza*: the adventures of the Cartwright family were seen each week by almost 400 million viewers.[56] The American Broadcasting Company (ABC), one of the companies operating the television network in the United States, has established an international programme-distribution network (World Vision) enabling it to reach 60 per cent of non-American sets. For its part NBC, an extension of the transnational electronics company RCA, was selling to over 115 countries in 1972.

Most imported programme material is consequently of American origin. A study of television broadcasts in eighteen Latin American cities in 1970 shows that the share of American programmes averages 31.4 per cent. It is as high as 92.7 per cent in Panama.[57] A similar survey in Thailand reveals that at least 50 per cent of imported programmes originate in the United States.

Also noteworthy is the case, which will be studied in detail at a later stage, of the *Sesame Street* television programmes, featuring entertainment with an educational element, which have been produced and distributed the world over with the backing of a great many TNCs (see Chapter 3).[58]

The amount of programme material imported by the developing countries is largely due to high production costs. Quality programmes call for sophisticated technical equipment. What is more, major producers offer programmes at attractively low prices, for in order to secure the market of the developing countries they often bill at marginal cost. Ralph Frankin, vice-president of MCA-TV, ascribes the enormous expansion of American programmes abroad to price factors: Hollywood techniques and producers, in his words, are still the best in the world, so at the present time it is less costly, in any country, to buy programmes from the United States than to try producing ones of equal quality.[59]

Latin America is a particularly large importer of films from the West. In 1970 Argentina, for instance, imported 391 films, 88 per cent of which were from the United States, Italy, France, the United Kingdom and the Federal Republic of Germany, while the domestic output was only twenty-eight films. In the developing world, however, Hong Kong is an important film-making centre with two companies, Shaw Brothers and Golden Harvest, of international repute. Golden Harvest produces most of its films in English, which facilitates their international distribution. In general, these productions are intended for the South-East Asian market.

With regard to news-agencies, while Associated Press circulates 17 million words a day on average, a national agency like Antara (Indonesia) puts out 69,000 in Indonesian Bahasa and 27,000 in English, and the national agency of the Philippines 15,000, UPI circulates 11 million words and Reuters

1.5 million. Tanjug (Yugoslavia) issues between 75,000 and 120,000. These gaps show the preponderance of the major international news agencies when it comes to world information. It is hardly to be wondered at then that the newspapers of developing countries contain news which is often not locally relevant and does not always arouse much interest on the part of their readers.[60]

In the publishing and press world it is to be noted that *Time*, for instance, is published abroad in four editions. In 1972 the print run per issue was 180,000 for Asia, 115,000 for Latin America and 155,000 for the South Pacific. As the Spanish edition for Latin America came to grief, all issues of *Time* are in English. *Newsweek* similarly offers an international edition in English with about 50 per cent of the content different from the American edition.

On the other hand, *Reader's Digest* started foreign-language editions as far back as 1940 and is now published in fourteen languages in over 100 countries.

The language probelm is important and very often hinders international circulation. Some countries make it a condition that the language of publication should be their own. In most countries the number of books translated is nearly always less than 30 per cent of total output, but market trends are inclining companies towards translation. The international publications division of CBS, for example, adapts and translates publications for professional or educational use in the health, science, technology and business fields. McGraw-Hill translates works and tape recordings into Afrikaans, Bantu, Chinese, Malay, Nyanja and Tonga.

The transnational advertising agencies

Comparison of the world's fifty largest advertising agencies with the fifty largest TNCs points to the domination of transnational advertising agencies of American origin. While the fifty largest TNCs included nineteen based in the United States, the fifty largest advertising agencies included thirty-six. It is to be noted that the Japanese agency, Dentsu, has recently ousted J. Walter Thompson from first place (see Table 19). Another feature of the world industry is the existence of groups of companies linking up the major advertising agencies (see Table 20).

Furthermore, these transnational agencies have a dominant share of the market in the developing countries, as can be seen from Tables 21 and 22, so that their impact in those countries is very great. A survey of forty-five developing countries in 1973 showed that five American agencies controlled two-thirds of the advertising agencies.[61] In Latin America, at least three of the five largest advertising agencies are American, and McCann-Erickson plays a dominant role (in Argentina, Brazil and Venezuela). In Ghana, Sierra Leone and Nigeria, Lintas is on top, while in Kenya the leaders are McCann-Erickson and Ogilvy & Mather. In Asia, Lintas comes into the lead again.[62]

A survey of forty-six developing countries confirms the preponderance of foreign advertising agencies, for they regularly feature among the country's

TABLE 19. The leading advertising agencies in 1977

Position	Agency¹	Country of origin	Gross earnings ($ millions)
1	Dentsu Inc.	Japan	212.6
2	J. Walter Thompson	United States	189.0
3	Young & Rubicam	United States	164.7
4	McCann-Erickson	United States	162.6
5	Ogilvy & Mather International	United States	127.9
6	BBDO International	United States	118.6
7	Leo Burnett	United States	116.0
8	SSC & B Inc.	United States	100.5
9	Ted Bates & Co.	United States	98.8
10	Grey Advertising	United States	97.2
11	Foote, Cone & Belding	United States	89.1
12	D'Arcy-MacManus & Masius	United States	81.4
13	Doyle Dane Bernbach	United States	74.8
14	Dancer-Fitzgerald-Sample	United States	72.0
15	Benton & Bowles	United States	70.7
16	Hakuhodo Inc.	Japan	70.1
17	Campbell-Ewald	United States	61.2
18	N. W. Ayer ABH International	United States	57.4
19	Kenyon & Eckhardt	United States	45.6
20	Needham, Harper & Steers	United States	41.2
21	Norman, Craig & Kummel	United States	40.8
22	Wells, Rich, Greene	United States	39.1
23	Compton Advertising	United States	38.7
24	Marsteller Inc.	United States	36.0
25	Eurocom	France	35.2
26	William Esty Co.	United States	33.0
27	Daiko Advertising	Japan	32.4
28	Ketchum, MacLeod & Grove	United States	29.9
29	Bozell & Jacobs International	United States	27.3
30	Ross Roy	United States	21.9
31	Cunningham & Walsh	United States	20.7
32	Dai-Ichi Kikaku	Japan	20.0
33	Campbell-Mithun	United States	18.0
34	Tokyu Advertising	Japan	17.0
35	Yomiko Advertising	Japan	16.0
36	Dai-Ichi Advertising	Japan	14.5
37	Publicis Conseil	France	13.7
38	Asahi Kokoku-Sha	Japan	13.4
39	William Wilkens & Co.	Fed. Rep. of Germany	12.8
40	Marschalk Co.	United States	12.1
41	Leber Katz Partners	United States	11.8
42	Asahi Tsushin Advertising	Japan	11.5
43	Keller-Crescent Co.	United States	11.4
44	McCaffrey & McCall	United States	11.3
45	Orikomi Advertising	Japan	11.2
46	Doremus & Co.	United States	11.2
47	Della Femina, Travisano & Partners	United States	11.1
48	Tracy-Locke	United States	10.9
49	Warwick, Welsh & Miller	United States	10.9
50	John Clemenger	Australia	10.7

Source: *Advertising Age*, 17 April 1978.

TABLE 20. World groupings of advertising agencies

Group	Country of origin	Gross earnings 1977 ($ millions)
Interpublic Group of Cos.[1]	United States	222.5
SSC and B—Lintas International	United States/ United Kingdom	100.5
D'Arcy-MacManus and Masius	United States/ United Kingdom	81.4
DFS Dorland Fortune	United States/ United Kingdom/ Fed. Rep. of Germany	73.0
Ayer Barker Hegemann	United States/ United Kingdom/ Fed. Rep. of Germany	57.4
Univas Network	France	47.1
Group Publicis-Intermarco-Farner	France/Netherlands/ Switzerland	45.4

1. The group comprises McCann-Erickson Worldwide, Campbell-Ewald Worldwide, Erwin Wasey Inc., and Marschalk Company Inc.
Source: *Advertising Age*, 17 April 1978.

TABLE 21. Gross earnings of main TNCs and other major agencies by geographical region, in selected countries, 1977

	Transnational agencies		Others		Total	
	$ millions	%	$ millions	%	$ millions	%
Developed countries	779.9	86.7	811.4	91.0	1 591.3	88.8
Southern Europe	16.7	1.8	11.4	1.3	28.1	1.6
Developing countries	104.5	11.5	67.9	7.7	172.4	9.6
Africa	4.0	0.4	0.8	0.1	4.8	0.3
Latin America	71.9	7.9	51.5	5.8	123.4	6.8
Caribbean	3.5	0.3	0.3	0.03	3.8	0.2
Middle East	2.6	0.3	4.5	0.5	7.1	0.4
Asia and others	22.4	2.5	10.8	1.2	33.2	1.8
TOTAL	901.1	100	890.7	100	1 791.8	100

Source: United Nations, Centre on Transnational Corporations, *Transnational Corporations in Advertising*, New York, 1979. (Technical Paper, ST/CTC/8.)

top three agencies, with a few exceptions.[63] A virtual foreign monopoly is patently the case in the Dominican Republic, Ecuador, Egypt, El Salvador, Ghana, Indonesia, Malaysia, Nigeria, Peru, Singapore and Uruguay.[64]

At the same time, the material forms of advertising have changed with the spread of new media. A study on Argentina covering the period 1959–72 shows that newspapers and radio have surrendered some of their share of advertising expenditure to television.[65] In Thailand 25 per cent of publicity

TABLE 22. Market share of the Nain transnational agencies in their operations outside their countries of origin, and for selected countries, 1977 (percentages)

	Transnational agencies	Others
Developed countries	49.8	50.2
Southern Europe	59.4	40.6
Developing countries	60.6	39.4
Africa	83.3	16.7
Latin America	58.2	41.8
Caribbean	91.8	8.2
Middle East	36.6	63.4
Asia and others	67.4	32.6

Source: See Table 21.

TABLE 23. Breakdown of advertising expenditure by medium and by region, 1978

Region	Media					
	Printed material		Radio		Television	
	$ millions	%	$ millions	%	$ millions	%
United States and Canada	13 751	38	2 599	7	7 090	20
Western Europe	7 906	64	423	3	1 724	14
Asia	2 145	37	324	6	1 914	33
Latin America	865	29	480	16	1 214	41
Austrialia and New Zealand	621	50	119	10	350	28
Middle East and Africa	453	41	85	8	147	13
TOTAL	25 741	43	4 030	7	12 439	21

Source: See Table 21.

spending in 1975 went to television,[66] which devoted 16 per cent (Bangkok region) and 18 per cent (provinces) of its broadcasting time to advertising.[67]

Comparison of advertising expenditure for the different media (Table 23) shows that the press is the main medium in Africa, the Middle East and Asia, but that television is increasingly given preference in Latin America.

With the generally high cost of television advertising, only TNCs can avail themselves of it. In Indonesia, for instance, only large foreign companies or joint concerns, like Unilever, Toyota and Benjer, can so advertise. Consequently, all the publicity goes to their products (detergents, soap, beverages, cars, etc.).[68] The same phenomenon is to be found in Thailand, where advertising focuses on foreign consumer items. In October 1976, advertising on the HSA/TV channel was for Pepsi-Cola, Seiko, Ford Galant and Toyota, Nescafé, Bear Brand Milk, Ovaltine, and so on. For Argentina the advertisers were Molinos, Río de la Plata, Compañía Nestlé de Alimentos, Lever (Unilever), Colgate Palmolive, Crush, Coca-Cola, Cinzano, Ika, Renault,

Ford, General Motors, Fiat and others.[69] In Kenya 75 per cent of newspaper advertising was inserted by TNCs.[70]

The underlying rift between transnational communication corporations and the cultural identity of developing countries

These mass-communication media transmit messages and symbols which initiate a process of socialization of individuals and cross-cultural transmission. The systems of values and norms and the systems of representation of developing countries are therefore directly affected by the control exerted by TNCs in this sector. To use the expression of Professor Kekkonen, President of the Republic of Finland, 'communication imperialism'[71] is such that it modifies the images formed by individuals of the world and of themselves and, at the same time, what they would like 'themselves' to be. It consequently reaches into people's awareness and plays an active part in the process of socio-cultural destructuring referred to earlier. At the same time, the dependence of the Third World countries on the major information media places them in a situation with some inevitable political repercussions. Clearly then, there is a deep rift between the activities of transnational communication corporations and the cultural identity of developing countries, and this rift comes to the surface in regard to intellectual products and their dissemination.

'Asymmetric communication' and socio-cultural destructuring

During the General Conference of Unesco at its nineteenth session (Nairobi, 1976), there was considerable discussion of the question whether the socio-cultural effects of information items produced and put out by TNCs were not altering endogenous creativity and cultural values, and exerting a powerful influence on the formation of socio-cultural values and attitudes in the host countries.[72] There is no longer any room for doubt on the matter: TNCs do have a hand in structuring ways of life and systems of norms and values in a direction that does not appear to be that of endogenous and autonomous development. Whether we take a look at the messages put out by radio, television or film, or examine the models offered by the transnational advertising corporations, the type and nature of the influence is identical: what is involved is the mere importing of the patterns of thought and value systems of the West, and more particularly of the transnational system.

The television programmes of TNCs that are imported and broadcast on a large scale in the Third World are initially designed to appeal to viewers in the United States or Europe and have therefore been produced for Western eyes, or rather minds.[73] These items, far from being neutral, convey images and values likely in many cases to substitute prejudice for ignorance. In other words, these cultural products and processes help to establish certain structures which legitimize political relations and political values, in the noble sense of the term, prevalent in other socio-cultural systems.

A. Dorfman and A. Mattelart have shown, for instance, how Walt Disney cartoons, particularly Donald Duck, convey prejudices and norms quite in keeping with the Western rationale of TNCs, and help to shape people's attitudes, including those of children in the Third World.[74] These cartoon films, which are viewed all over Latin America and in the rest of the world, lend very marked legitimacy to economic 'jungle law' and reflect a mercantile morality which acknowledges only one ultimate value, the dollar, and is embodied in the aptly named Uncle Scrooge. Likewise, the heavily caricatured revolutions of Latin America always take the incomprehensible or reprehensible form of person-to-person conflicts with no real justification. In this type of cartoon most of the objects are sold but are never, or virtually never, produced. The sphere of consumption is therefore given clear pride of place without anyone wondering where the items of wealth come from and who creates them. The symbolism of the object is already present and no doubt serves to guide the motivations and aspirations of children and adults alike. As to the workless person, when he makes his appearance, usually in the shape of Donald Duck, his situation is explained by individual or psychological considerations (aversion to work and to effort) and not blamed on pressure of the economic and social system.

Television programmes, in the same way as cinema film for that matter, thus form highly ideological stereotypes and clichés.[75] A study by E. Santoro, a Venezuelan psychologist, on stereotypes induced in children by television programmes imported into Venezeula[76] points out that for young Venezuelans the 'hero' is a North American in 86 per cent of cases, or at least speaks English, and that the Chinese are 'bad' and whites are 'better' than blacks. The rich for their part are 'good' in 72 per cent of cases and the poor 'bad' in 41 per cent of cases. Television therefore has a very marked role in coding the mental representations of children and transplants into the developing countries the bases, in particular the racialist bases, of certain social stratifications. In the words of M. Ordóñez,

> radio and television convey to our societies [Latin America] values which alienate real needs. The social myths and the false heroes created and the excessive importance attaching to entertainment and violence are instruments of alienation and cultural disorientation.[77]

The power of television and of the programmes it puts out can also be seen in the reluctance of some governments to introduce it. The example of South Africa is striking in this respect. Until 1974 that country had no television, the contention being that its introduction was liable to upset the national economy. But did not the real reason lie rather in South Africa's policy of apartheid and racial discrimination? A South African television service would very probably have been obliged, at least in the initial period, to use imported programme material which might well have been at variance with such a policy.[78]

From this point of view, the content of television engenders specific models of representation, attitudes and values amounting to nothing less than progaganda[79] and may lead to an idealization of the images of others or even to transformed structures of authority.[80]

Dependence where television or film is concerned hinges, it is true, on economic limitations. It is both more convenient and above all more economical to buy serial programmes from American TNCs than to produce such material on the spot, expressing local values and sensibilities. However that may be, the importing of television programmes or films into the developing countries must be perceived as a factor in 'cultural extraversion',[81] for what we have here is a 'daily infiltration of norms'[82] that are very largely North American, whose archetype is of course the American serial (*Bewitched* or *Peyton Place*, to mention just two that have been broadcast all over the world), and which, for instance, justify the confinement of women to the home and to entertainment of the family and children. In a way, these serials have a 'subliminal' effect which enlists public sympathy and support. This only makes their socio-cultural influence all the stronger.[83]

Amadou-Mathar M'Bow sums up the situation perfectly when he says that the messages transmitted in programmes sold by TNCs to Third World countries

reflect the thinking, the ideas, the values, in short, the vision of the world of those who use them. When they serve as the channel for transmitting to a given region value systems or ways of life which are foreign to the peoples of that region, thay cannot be prevented in the end from wiping out the specific values of those peoples, thus becoming, even if unintentionally, instruments of cultural alienation.[84]

What is really at risk in this audio-visual dependence is the cultural identity rooted in the age-old traditions of peoples and hence the maintenance of mankind's heritage of cultural pluralism.[85] The cultural control exerted by TNCs cannot therefore be seen as the aberrant, localized and time-situated effect of their worldwide growth, but as the objective means whereby people are brought to accept a particular model for living, and therefore ideological in scope.[86] In this respect, and contrary to what is affirmed by Z. Brzezinski when he speaks of a 'technetronic society', cultural levels are determined and minds shaped, not according to communications or other technology or electronics, but according to the values such technical media convey, namely Western values. Cultural dependence goes hand in glove with economic dependence. There is in fact an intimate link between the two processes since the former predisposes people to the pattern of production and consumption of wealth introduced by TNCs into the Third World.[87]

An identical process of acculturation is clearly to be found in the influences of the transnational advertising firms, whose activity in the Third World is very largely devoted to promoting the sales of TNC products. As pointed out by R. Vernon in 1971, this is due primarily to the general expansion of TNCs and also to the fact that they make greater use of advertising than national enterprises. In Colombia, for instance, TNCs spend an amount on television advertising equal to four times the country's own budget provision for television. In addition to its impact on consumption patterns, which we shall be considering in detail in due course, the advertising put out by the TNCs assigns distinct roles to men and to women and creates a need for social recognition of a status. The main key to status for women, in particular, at any rate from the image provided of them in advertising, lies in their beauty or their appearance.[88] In the guise of ensuring a maximum range of economic choices, and hence the freedom of the consumer, the sole objective of advertising in the developing countries, as elsewhere, is to sell the products of TNCs whether or not they are suited to the basic needs of the public in question. Travel advertising, for its part, serves as a channel for the ideology of 'transnational exoticism'[89] which arouses new needs and is therefore liable to contribute to new frustrations. On this subject, M. Brigaud-Robert cites the case of a village of settled Fulani forty kilometres from Dakar, beside Lake Retba, where travel advertising and tourism itself have made people business-minded to the point of venality since everything now has a price-tag, from the snapshot to the visit to the family hut (entry 450 CFA francs).[90] This helps to develop a mercantile logic and largely transforms social relations into consumption relations.

Generally speaking, the various 'information items' transmitted by TNCs via audio-visual programmes or through advertising are marked by the fact that the 'receivers', namely individuals, are very often incapable of linking up the characters or the situations portrayed with their own lives and therefore tend to have an incomplete perception of the images transmitted, particularly when they concern the Western world.[91] From this point of view, television becomes a particularly potent means of escaping everyday reality, chiefly through self-identification with the hero, who usually reflects the values, consumption patterns and habits of the most privileged social strata.[92] The main point, however, is that the mass media, which are very extensively controlled by TNCs and belie their name, are not instruments of reciprocal exchange but vectors for a one-way distribution of culture, models and images or, in short, social codes. They accordingly have a hand in the deculturation of the peoples of the developing countries, that is, strictly speaking, in a process of deprival of memory.[93] The transnational communication and information concerns, which transmit new 'knowledge and memories',[94] give rise to a full-scale socio-cultural destructuration a particular form of which is extroversion of the prevailing 'social code'.[95] The Samoan experience is a perfect illustration of the power of TNCs, via television in that particular case, to abolish traditional community ties. Modern communication media tend increasingly to dismiss traditional modes by discrediting them or relegating them to the realm of folklore.[96]

What it all amounts to is that the media fulfil a key function in the continued expansion of TNCs by stepping up the processes of destructuration of traditional attitude and behaviour models and by enlisting mass public support for whatever is conducive to dependent industrialization or development.[97] The rift between this and what is necessary for autonomous, endogenous development is total. This seems to have been the feeling of G. Valdés, Deputy Administrator of UNDP for Latin America and the Caribbean, when he said in a moving statement to the Bogotá Conference in 1978:

The influence of transnational corporations is gaining strength from day to day, and there is a growing dependence on the information which the irresistible technological media thrust into people's hearts and minds, spreading ideas which are alien to the character of our nation and of the whole continent, and distorting the truths on which our activities are based.[98]

Informational dependence

The transnational news-agencies are often considered veritable arbiters regarding knowledge of the current state and operation of the economic, political and diplomatic world. It is they who bear the responsibility for deciding which social, economic and political events should be related, and they display a marked tendency in this connection to encourage the economic and political status quo, and implicitly to base their 'news'-selection criteria on the interests of the transnational system.[99]

Whereas Salvador Allende was 'the Marxist President of Chile', his successors are, simply, presidents. The fact of not using and of using a qualifier stems from the value system of the transnational news agencies and hence from their view of what is normal or pathological.[100] That has nothing to do with false information. But with an accumulation of facts isolated from their context and of distortions by unstated implication, the 'facts' become preconditioned. Let us examine in this light an item of information put out by UPI in 1974. Under the dateline, 'New York, 27 February 1974', UPI had reported that the meeting of several of the chief bauxite-producing countries, included despite some hesitation in the programme for 5 March in Conakry (Guinea), had caused a degree of 'dismay' in Washington. 'Some experts', according to the agency, feared that the conference might take the lead in establishing a series of international cartels designed to control the raw materials essential to the industrialized nations, which could set the American economy back forty years.[101]

Through an item of information, both the interests of the industrialized economies and TNC control of supplies are defended. Noteworthy is the proximity of the 'dismay', implicitly presented as comprehensible, and the 'experts', namely the norm.

The same process is found in the way in which the transnational news-agencies present the successive increases in the price of oil, which always precede and never follow a jump in inflation in the West.[102] What is at stake here may be more than informational independence and access to knowledge of others and of the world. According to some authors, TNCs have not hesitated to use their financial resources, and their advertising contracts in particular, to induce sections of the press to oppose the constitutional governments of particular Latin American or Central American countries.[103] Furthermore, the emphasis is placed on 'events' rather than on deep-lying processes and mechanisms. The daily round, however steeped in hardship, is forgotten. The Third World countries are well aware of this problem, and specifically brought it up at the Conference of Non-aligned Countries held at Algiers (1973) and Colombo (1975), where agreement was reached to set up a pool of Third World news-agencies.

The control of TNCs over data banks, those veritable reservoirs of thought and memory, quite apart from the strategic and political issue involved, constitutes an obstacle to autonomous scientific or cultural development. This activity has turned into a thoroughgoing industry, that of statistical, technical or scientific information which is necessarily commanded by micro-economic management criteria.[104] What is more, English is patently predominant; it is the top documentary language, being used for 60 per cent of articles on chemistry and 55 per cent of those on biology and medicine. This is also true in economics, where the dominance is very marked and incidentally is prompting a growing number of countries (e.g. India and Pakistan) to publish their own reviews in English. Another factor which ought never to be overlooked is the risk of retention or sifting introduced by such a situation.

In this respect, J. B. Brzezinski has advanced certain views in favour of establishing a world information system which would facilitate mutual intellectual influences, permit the pooling of knowledge and, above all, result in the formation of international professional élites and the emergence of a common scientific language.[105] This is precisely what is to be feared, for it must not be forgotten that the fundamental motives underlying the activity of transnational agencies or the 'managerial culture' that characterizes them are merely logics, among other possible logics, which take shape in specific languages and exert socio-cultural effects outside the field of information. The general public has but very scant means of voicing its preferences or or engaging in a dialogue. The images, words and thoughts poured out by television, radio, international news-agencies and the transnational press itself manipulate people's thinking and ultimately apportion only a marginal place to national identity. Here again, the uniformization of minds is the central issue as attested by the following:

Operating on a worldwide scale, some information agencies—most of which have their headquarters in one of the industrialized countries—have, by reason of their equipment and capital, acquired a position of strength which probably enables them to offer better services but also leads them to convey one-way information reflecting the point of view of those countries, and which, above all, allows them to dominate the information market to an extent that borders on cultural aggression. Only a few powerful countries and—what is more serious—a few transnational companies are in a position to control both the production of infrastructures and the transmission of programmes. This *de facto* monopoly is opposed to the establishment of a new international economic order.[106]

Obstacles to endogenous cultural development: the example of intellectual products and their dissemination

In publishing, especially of scholarly literature, transnationalism is 'metropolitan oriented' and 'transnational book publishing, international languages and transnational intelligentsias are closely linked together'.[107]

This undoubtedly affects the whole area of book production, for it is probable, to say the least, that authors in the developing countries of necessity accept, implicitly or explicitly, the constraints of transnational publishing and the fact that their manuscripts, whatever their originality or specific nature, will be judged in terms of a market which must in most cases be transnational. True, the possibility of gaining an international audience for one's works is an undoubted advantage. But only a minority of intellectuals will be concerned.

What is more, the production and dissemination of intellectual works depends on the headquarters of the transnational publishers, most of which are located in the Western countries. The decision to publish or not to publish a manuscript depends, therefore, on outside advisers and hence on opinions reflecting the criteria, tastes and modes of evaluation of the transnational élite. This provides a 'safety net' for Third World academics and dissuades them from giving open expression to the transnational constraints which govern publication of their works.[108]

Then there is the problem of the virtual necessity to operate via English, or, to a lesser extent, French. These languages subject the content of cultural products in general, and of books in particular, to the demands of a logic peculiar to a certain culture. Only local languages, from this point of view, express in their diversity and fullness the centres of interest that go to make up local outlooks and customs.[109]

The predominance of the transnational publishing language builds itself up by accentuating the intellectual cleavage between those who have had the benefit of a so-called 'classic', but in fact exogenous, education (involving foreign languages in particular) and those able to read only the very few works published in local languages. This consequently adds to the already glaring cultural and social differences in which illiteracy is so marked a feature.[110]

Here again, such a state of affairs originates in economic constraints. Publishing, whether transnational or national, is in most cases a profit-seeking activity and hence needs a sufficiently large market, which is something of a scarcity in the Third World, at least as regards scientific or scholarly publications. In this connection, D. Smith has shown that while the unit cost of a work drops considerably with an increase in the number of copies produced, the phenomenon is less marked than in the industrialized countries as can be seen from Table 24.

The break-even point lies somewhere around print-runs of 5,000 copies, which is relatively high for Third World intellectuals or academics seeking national publishers. There is every reason for authors to turn to the *métropole* for publication of their works, and to present them in a transnational language—that of their publishers—which is usually English and sometimes French or Spanish.[111] This again betokens very clear cultural and intellectual dependence, which helps to accentuate social and cultural cleavages.

In these circumstances, the rift between the activities and influence of the TNCs and endogenous cultural development is plain for all to see.

To sum up, we would endorse the view expressed at the Accra conference that the capacity of TNCs to spread foreign models via the communication networks they control was all the greater because

TABLE 24. Declining manufacturing cost per copy (in local currency units)

	Per 1,000 copies	Per 5,000 copies	Per 10,000 copies
Non-industrialized countries (all regions)	100	51	44
Highly industrialized countries	100	29	21

Source: D. Smith, *The Economics of Book Publishing in Developing Countries*, Paris, Unesco, 1977. (Reports and Papers on Mass Communication, 79.)

the fascination of the radio and cinema, especially for peoples who were particularly sensitive to the power of words and pictures, affected the audience to the deepest part of their consciousness, influencing not only their ideas but their inclinations, life-styles and behaviour as well.[112]

Socio-mental destructuring occurs with reference as much to the 'information items' and images which pour out towards these people as to the social codes which give them a meaning. The importing of norms and values and the structuring of modes of representation strike at the innermost self of individuals, at their cultural identity and at the way in which they envisage the potentialities of life. The messages put out by TNCs help to steer behaviour in directions which are profitable to them, for instance by imposing a particular pattern of consumption, but which hardly seem to tally with the autonomous, national development of Third World economies.

Section 3

Extroversion of tastes:
TNCs and consumer patterns—an overview

The structuring of social consumption patterns by TNCs is a particularly revealing example of their socio-cultural influence. The fact is that TNCs are conducive to the introduction into the developing countries of a 'consumer logic' such as already prevails in Western societies. The symbolic character attached to the consumption of certain goods results in their performing a function of social integration and differentiation, and brings considerations of social stratification to bear on the consumption sphere. At the same time, the structure of consumption is very largely dependent on TNCs' activities and on their effects, either deliberate (advertising) or rather more involuntary (by force of example). From this point of view, consumer patterns are a particularly relevant frame of reference for the overall process of extroversion prompted by the TNCs' own interests: a process which tends to accentuate the cultural destructuring of the Third World nations

Consumer patterns and cultural identity

Consumer patterns cannot be dissociated from the systems of values and norms, whether social or individual or both, that characterize consumer profiles. Although they may be channelled and guided by influences from various sources, especially foreign, the consumption choices of Third World peoples undoubtedly reflect their representation of an order of priority and hence their mentality. While there is no denying that processes of social consumption may be seen as having a utilitarian dimension (satisfaction of physiological needs), they also clearly have a symbolic function, i.e. social significance. Quite apart from their intrinsic properties, goods and services convey a semiotic content and are both indicative of and agents in social stratification. This is why it is worth examining in detail how TNCs shape consumer structures.

The consumption of goods and services is in fact also the consumption of signs charged with meaning by codes inherent in the societies in which individuals live, whatever their degree of economic and social development. In this respect, consumption is a crucial area for the shaping of attitudes and values brought about by TNC activities, since the symbolic implications of consumption or the code implicit in the object consumed are one among other possible expressions of a cultural state or a cultural identity.[113] By their access to particular commodities, individuals identify their position not only in society, according to its criteria and standards, but also in relation to themselves. The object becomes a comment on oneself and on other individuals, fulfilling a social distinguishing and discriminating function, for a distinction based on objects serves to establish or reflect social differences which classify individuals and imply a social hierarchy. This symbolic dimension is to be found at all levels in society, albeit according to different codes, and is by no means confined to any particular social class (Veblen's 'leisure class', for instance).[114] Consumption also involves the imaginary, for the object also becomes a means of escape, a fetish whereby the world can be seen in terms of magic. Desires are channelled towards needs and satisfied, if at all, by commodities. This all goes to explain why advertisers are constantly trying to discover the image consumers have of themselves, the ever-present, ever-sought-after 'ideal ego'. The self-image into which the individual projects his desires, fantasies or fears is no more than a behaviour model, such as that of Western man, seen within a social context, in other words in relation to the other individuals who combine to make up the socio-cultural reference group, usually the nation. The interplay between self and self-image, that is to say between motivations and values, is revealed and enacted in consumption and, where the developing countries are concerned, very often also in the frustration caused by altogether inadequate consumption. In other words, what the individual is trying to find in consumption is a way of overcoming his sense of inadequacy or meeting his desire for full social involvement and advancement.

In his desire to assert his existence, define his ego and identify his status and role in relation to others, he looks for products or brands, images that are compatible with his own conception of what he is, what he should be and what by magic, he will become.[115]

The forms, in particular the symbolic forms, of the model with which the individual identifies himself are, then, the expression of a particular mode of socialization bound up with the messages and information a person receives from society as a whole but also derived from his social position, which depends, for example, on his occupation and the social status it confers. Whatever the case may be, consumption patterns must be closely associated with the cultural identity of a society, taking into consideration, of course, distinct patterns of consumption that may differ to a greater or lesser degree according to the heterogeneity of the socio-cultural system and the extent of socio-economic stratification. In the developing countries, social differentiation based on consumption is not just reflected in a socio-cultural hierarchy and the social dynamics arising therefrom, but also takes the form of a cross-cultural clash and a conflict between tradition and modernity. The introduction and development of modern ways makes for a social dynamics of consumption through a process of decoding and recoding of aspirations and needs. Within that framework, the consumption pattern is intricately bound up with the communication pattern. On the one hand, it is the result of a set of messages and signs which shape people's attitudes and are embodied in consumer behaviour. On the other, consumption is a means of communication between man and society and between man and himself. But, as J. Attali so aptly puts it, 'Man falls silent and leaves it to the object to provide the vehicle for his culture, the code which determines his hierarchical system, the substitute for a dialogue.'[116]

Consumption patterns consequently reflect outlooks and aspirational models, traditional and/or modern, inherited and/or imported.[117] If in fact TNCs have the means to structure consumption patterns in the developing countries—and we shall see shortly that this is indeed the case—then they also exert their influence over the innermost recesses of man's mind, over his aspirations. In that sense the structuring of consumption patterns is all part of an acculturation process which it brings to light.

The structuring of patterns of consumption and acculturation

The influence of TNCs on consumption pattern is twofold. In the first place, TNCs help to develop in the Third World countries the consumer patterns already prevalent in the 'rich countries', the symbolic content of which was sufficiently stressed above. Secondly, TNCs seek to substitute new products, some more sophisticated than others, for the traditional ones. In doing so, their commercial success affects the whole structure of consumption in the developing countries.

It has already been said that TNCs transmit and propagate systems of representation and standards and systems of expression (needs, behaviour patterns), the main feature of which is the idea that a person's efforts, for instance in his work, are rewarded by access to consumer goods and therefore that increased consumption is a sound indicator of economic development. The spread of this type of approach and the quest for increased consumption thus acquire special significance in the dynamics of social change. This means that, because of the nature of their own rationale, TNCs are instrumental in drawing the Third World nations increasingly into a mercantile economic system in which personal status depends to a great extent on the goods and services the individual has access to, and on the social status attached to them. This type of rationale is introduced in various ways. Where communication is concerned, the messages disseminated by the media (television, cinema, advertising) play a significant part by 'displaying' the advantages of the consumer society and structuring both forms of representation and systems of norms. The spectrum of what is possible widens, encompassing a large number of goods that had never been heard of before, or had never been thought or even imagined to be useful. At the same time, there is a growing tendency to imitate Western life-styles and the goods that go with them, and individuals' motivations increasingly revolve around access to mercantile consumption. To a great extent traditional values are discredited and this alters individuals' representations of their own society and of their role in it. This destructuring process carries within it the seeds of new structures and new social codes which cause the individual to direct his attention outside his own society, and turn him into the epitome of *Homo consumens*, to use H. Schiller's expression. Dependence where communication is concerned and the development of an economic and social system based on a dynamics of material needs are clearly to be seen as related phenomena, since the life-styles shown up in a favourable light by the media, and especially by advertising, are in the last analysis mere window-dressing for a system of objects. The degree of acculturation is enhanced by the fact that the messages conveyed very often represent 'tradition' as synonymous with 'backwardness', and 'modernity' with 'progress'.

TNC employees also play a significant part in this process, whatever their position in the firm, by transmitting the firm's ethic. As has already been pointed out, employment with a TNC implies adopting its rules and norms. Consumption of TNCs' products and the example this sets also play a part in establishing the ethic of material consumption.

A final point is that TNCs tend to shape consumer habits in a manner that will be to their own advantage and therefore to see to it that their products replace traditional ones, or again seek to induce a regular commercial demand for certain goods or services (their own) for which there was none before. The TNCs thus channel certain needs or wants towards particular brands. More broadly speaking, there is evidence of a process of extraversion whereby tastes are redirected outside the individual's own society; and this process, directly connected with the TNCs' business interests, justifies us in seeing them as active agents in a veritable reorientation of choice.

Extroversion: the mechanisms and some examples

Advertising and sales-promotion policies are undoubtedly one of the most effective channels of TNC influence and are instrumental in modifying individuals' basic needs and directing them towards particular products or brands. Clearly such transfers of tastes are the result of massive-scale marketing policies and their influence on representations and standards. According to M. Godfrey and S. Langdon,[118] in 1973 80 per cent of the commercials on Swahili radio in Kenya were produced by TNCs, which included Brooke Bond, Nestlé, Colgate-Palmolive, Coca-Cola, Unilever, Glaxo and Sterling Winthrop.

These commercials were clearly aimed at needs, and hence products capable of satisfying them, which could in practice only be produced by the TNCs. Unilever, for instance, relies for its sales on ambitious, worldwide advertising campaigns, which very often make people lose all interest in local products; thus in India it is in the process of ousting the local butter product, ghee, with its rival margarine, Vanapasti, and the likelihood is that ghee will disappear altogether as a result.[119] The same corporation has succeeded in creating a need and subsequently a market for chemical washing powder and detergents in Indonesia,[120] and has also developed its sales of ice cream, sausages and frozen foods in the inland regions of Sierra Leone and Liberia, which can scarcely be described as places where 'discretionary incomes' are the rule, and where supplies often have to be brought in by air.[121]

In Central and Latin America, the power of advertising is such that even very poor people in rural areas feel practically compelled to drink beverages like Coca-Cola or Pepsi-Cola, even if it means selling their own natural products.[122] R. Ledogar has demonstrated, with particular reference to Mexico and Brazil, how TNCs have been so successful in creating a need for soft drinks that in Mexico for example the annual consumption of these beverages has reached the incredible figure of 14,000 million bottles, i.e. nearly five bottles a week per person. (It may be noted that Coca-Cola's share of the market in Mexico amounts to some 40 per cent.) Commercial 'brainwashing' is so effective that the inhabitants of some Mexican villages, for all their low incomes, are convinced that they cannot do without such drinks which have to be drunk every day.[123] In June 1974, a Mexican priest wrote in this connection:

I have heard some people say they can't live one day without drinking a soft drink. Other people, in order to display social status, must have soft drinks with every meal, especially if there are guests. . . . The great majority of people feel they have to be consumed every day. This is mainly due to extensive advertising especially on the radio which is so widespread in the mountains. . . . In the meantime, in these same villages, natural products such as fruit are consumed less, in some families just once a week.[124]

The object of these advertising campaigns is to convince people that traditional eating habits (millet, rice, beans, maize, water) are inferior to Western products, which are more sophisticated (fancy packaging, artificial distinctions through different brands). What it comes down to is a social symbolization of products. The impact is all the greater since these people are the more vulnerable for being less educated. To take the example of Kenya already referred to, the advertising costs of marketing the soap manufactured by affiliates of foreign TNCs amounts to 6 per cent of its price as against 1 per cent for comparable products from local firms.[125] This clearly reflects a policy of channelling local demand towards sophisticated products (toilet soap, detergents), drawing attention, for instance, to the outward appearance of the soap or the attractiveness of the packaging. To give a more general idea of the amount of money involved, TNC subsidiaries in Kenya spend some 12 million Kenyan shillings on advertising, compared with the sum of 7.5 million set aside in Kenya's latest development plan for the construction of rural health centres over the next five years, considered by the government to be the key component of the health service in rural areas, where 90 per cent of the population live.[126]

One of the best known examples of foreign influence on consumer patterns is Nestlé with its policy to develop its sales of powdered milk for babies.[127] Nestlé launched an energetic campaign to promote its food products as a substitute for breast-feeding. The methods used included:

Free, often door-to-door distribution of feeding bottles and milk products (Lactogen).

Promotion campaigns in hospitals and maternity homes (where they used for their campaigns special envoys called 'milk-nurses', who were dressed in white uniforms, with the result that they could be mistaken for hospital staff).

Free distribution of weight charts for new-born babies with an advertisement for Lactogen and also a word of encouragement to mothers to breast-feed their babies as long as possible; but in fact how many of them were able to read it?

Tendentious advertising in hospitals and on the radio, stressing the strength and vigour the product could impart (in Nigeria for example, where these are all-important notions). In Jamaica, advertising for Lactogen revolved around the themes of strength and health, or again energy and vigour.

The consumption of formula milk was thus associated with certain symbols: 'modern', 'better' and so on. Commenting in 1974 on a commercial that had been broadcast over the radio in Sierra Leone two years previously, in which a mother could be heard to ask her baby whether he liked Lactogen, to be met by a chuckle and a delighted 'mm', Doctor T. N. Maletnlema said that a mother hearing this slogan would be led to believe that Lactogen was better for her baby than her own milk. She would not know that it was in fact a sound montage. She would not know that the question could be recorded first and some time later the baby's laughter and chuckles, quite likely induced by some entirely different reason, in all probability its mother's milk.[128] Powdered milk is now widely used in many Third World countries.

Transnational business can thus lead to a full-scale transfer of consumer patterns and, in the process, needs are redefined in terms of brands and sophisticated and often expensive products substituted for simple, cheap ones. At the same time, advertising by TNCs causes their products to become rapidly obsolete, since it makes artificial distinctions between them and encourages their constant renewal.[129] Examples of extroversion abound, and the consequences are regrettable, to say the least.

In Mexico, more and more people in rural areas are buying white bread instead of their traditional bread, even though the latter is cheaper and richer in protein.[130] In Jamaica, it used to be customary for people to have fish and bananas for breakfast, which was both cheap and very nourishing, but, through advertising, the idea was put out and firmly lodged in people's minds that it was better to eat breakfast cereals, and now people eat Kellogg's products while the bananas rot in the market places for want of buyers.[131] In Mexico, the arrival in 1973 of Danone S.A. and Chambourcy, subsidiaries of the BSN–Gervais-Danone group and the Nestlé group respectively, and the large-scale advertising campaigns they launched resulted in a 350 per cent increase in the overall demand for yoghurt in Mexico.[132]

The process of substituting TNC's products for local ones has also been very marked in cigarette consumption. It is a highly concentrated sector[133] and the world market is dominated by eight TNCs, including: British American Tobacco (BAT), a firm of British origin and the world's leading manufacturer of cigarettes, selling one in every five cigarettes sold in the capitalist world; Imperial Group Ltd (United Kingdom); American Brands Inc. (United States); Philip Morris Inc. (United States); (Rothmans, Rembrand-Rupert the South African group). These TNCs are responsible for making people turn to foreign cigarettes, preferring the industrial variety to the ones made locally by small-scale producers. As tastes have changed, so locally produced black tobacco has declined in many countries such as India, Pakistan, the Republic of Korea, the Philippines, Argentina or Brazil. The Indonesian *kretch*, the Sri Lankan *delti* or the Indian *beedies* are being dislodged by mild, Virginia-type cigarettes. Vast advertising campaigns are largely responsible for this. The campaigns run by the transnational tobacco corporations are moreover altogether typical of the general 'tone' of TNC marketing, with heavy emphasis on Americanized stereotypes and constant references to luxury, status, high standards of living or the image of the 'freedom-loving cowboy'.

New markets are sometimes created to provide outlets for by-products manufactured by certain TNCs. F. M. Lappe and J. Collins quote the example of Ralston-Purina which developed the poultry industry in Colombia not for the purpose of introducing chicken as a staple item of the Colombian diet but so as to create a demand for animal-feed concentrates, its main product.[134] Special facilities were accordingly given to chicken farmers with the result that between 1967 and 1971 the annual production of roasting chickens in Colombia doubled, from 11 to 22 million.

Children are an ideal target for TNCs, mainly because they are so easy to influence as potential buyers. In Central and Latin America, certain firms producing soft drinks supply drinks and refrigerators for school celebrations free of charge in exchange for permission to sell their drinks in the schools themselves. Another sales gimmick used for instance by General Foods in Mexico are small figurines, representing Walt Disney characters for example, that come free with the product. A great many products (e.g. Coca-Cola or Pepsi-Cola) have in this way become symbols of belonging to the modern world, and this is used to the full by advertisers. In an article in the very reputable *Columbia Journal of World Business* on marketing policies in developing countries, we find H. Walter, for example, arguing that people need a small luxury like a soft drink or a fragrant cigarette.[135]

The societal impact of TNCs where consumer behaviour is concerned emerges clearly from the arguments put forward by the person in charge of Pepsi-Cola advertising in Brazil, to the effect that in Brazil there is nothing to channel the young people's spirit of revolt: the present generation has received no civic or political education. We, he says, provide them with a mechanism of protest channelled in consumption. Pepsi is a new, young image. People are happy because they are young, and because the young drink Pepsi.[136]

The advent of transnationalism thus coincides exactly with the upheaval in consumer patterns, some of which had remained unchanged for centuries. But the structures are altered by other, less intentional processes as well. Because of their intrinsic properties (refinement, novelty) but also on account of the social symbolism they convey, the products sold by TNCs find their readiest adepts in local élites who are particularly attracted to Western life-styles and products.[137] The compelling example they set causes the influence of these needs and commodities to percolate right down through society.[138] What we have in fact is a mimetic effect: TNCs introduce products which are soon adopted by the local élites, and their example is in turn followed by the rest of the population after the time it takes to become familiar with the new products. This is the sort of process R. Nurkse was referring to when he said that consumption in the developing countries did of course depend on level of income, but also on the difference between that level and the level of those in the highest income bracket. Social attraction has the effect of prompting the least well-off sectors of the population to imitate the highest income groups and hence, in particular, members of TNCs.[139]

The clear overall pattern, then, is for the TNCs to introduce new products into the developing countries and then channel consumer needs towards these products. TNCs exert their influence in a variety of ways (intentionally through advertising, relatively unintentionally through the force of example) but the aggregate effect is to direct consumer patterns towards the goods and services produced by the TNCs: the structure of supply is largely responsible for determining demand. The fact is that such products are put on to the market regardless of the basic needs of the population concerned, not because the TNCs have no social consciousness, but because it is 'their normal way of doing business.'[140] This type of approach and its consequences are yet another illustration of the clash between two types of rationale, for it is so much easier for a multinational to adapt to another language an advertising campaign already tried and tested than to develop new products to meet specific local needs.[141]

By and large it may be said in conclusion that by introducing Western consumer habits into developing countries, TNCs contribute to a global process of cultural extroversion, for

> eating habits also reflect the manner in which each people manages and creates its own ways of thinking and acting, assimilates and revitalizes its traditions and blends and combines its *mores* with those transmitted to it by other cultures.[142]

From this point of view, the proliferation and worldwide success of fast-food restaurants of the McDonald's type can largely be explained, not by the actual products sold, but by the life-style and symbols that go with them.[143] It may be added that apart from the socio-cultural significance of the TNCs' impact in structuring consumer patterns, their influence produces distortions in other areas as well. The shift of consumption patterns in Third World countries towards new crops, notably as a result of pesticides, in which TNCs played so great a part, has largely contributed to increasing these countries' economic and technological dependence.[144] But its most significant corollary has been unsatisfactory allocation of scarce resources. With the transformation of agricultural products, their prices rise in proportion with their diminishing nutritional value as a result of the addition of fats and chemicals.[145] In this respect, the new emphasis on animal products in production and consumption constitutes a major waste of plant crop resources.[146] In Colombia, for instance, the shift from the cultivation of leguminous plants to fodder crops not only replaced a cheap source of protein by a more expensive one but also actually decreased the protein supply, since animal protein sources yield less than vegetable sources. To go back to an example referred to earlier, it has been demonstrated that in the region of Valle, an acre of fodder crops for chicken-rearing provides man with only a third of the protein it would produce if it were planted with maize or beans. If it were planted with soya beans, that acre of land would yield sixteen times more protein than it produces by being used for chicken fodder. And the fact that chickens are being produced is, as we have seen, in the first place due to action taken by a TNC specializing in animal feeds with a view to serving its own interests.[147] To take another example, surely it is paradoxical that in Mexico, one of the largest exporters of oranges, the percentage of fresh orange juice in the soft drinks Fanta and Orange Crush was nil until 1974. Then, the government ordered that there should be a minimum of 10 per cent. A final example is that of CAPRAL, a Nestlé subsidiary in the Ivory Coast, which promoted the consumption of Maggi stock cubes there to the point where the annual average consumption now totals 700 cubes per household, roughly two cubes a day for each household.[148] Maggi stock cubes can be said to have become a significant feature of Ivorian diets, particularly among the poorest sectors of the population. Used as a condiment in the rich countries, it is however altogether inadequate as a staple food. The product is composed of vegetable protein, and its use in a diet in which there is already a severe lack of animal protein accentuates nutritional deficiencies among Ivory Coast peoples, especially the lack of amino acids.

There is little doubt, then, that TNCs have the power to channel people's wants and needs towards their own products or services. Consumer patterns reflect attitudes and, to a great extent, individual aspirations, and by the same token the structuring of consumer patterns epitomizes the socio-cultural extroversion of Third World peoples, severing them from their roots and their traditional ways of thinking. In this way TNCs may be regarded as contributing actively to a form of social change which causes deculturation and pays little heed to what is necessary to bring about an autonomous, national transformation in the poorer countries.

Section 4

How to preserve cultural values from the influence of TNCs: guidelines for action

The fact must be faced that the TNCs' influence on cultural values seriously jeopardizes Third World countries' capacity to control their own economic and social development. If endogenous development is the object, then the transformation of economic and social structures must be backed by a blueprint for society rooted in the actual cultural life of a nation. It is culture 'that determines the goals of an endogenous form of development which the people can understand and adopt and which, as a result, will have the benefit of their active, conscious participation'.[149] International action is needed as well as national policies, and they must be commensurate with the significant issues at stake, namely the ability of peoples in the developing world to interpret their past, organize their present lives and decide on their future as they see it.[150]

In any scheme to regulate the conflict between nation-states and TNCs as far as cultural values are concerned, there are two pitfalls to be avoided. In the first place it must not be forgotten that the standards, values and aims of a society stem from everything which goes to make it what it is and therefore as much from the mode of socialization through education as from the structuring of life-styles and the behaviour patterns arising from the system of production, especially technology. Even so, since communication plays a central part in the socio-mental influence exerted by TNCs, it is not irrelevant to examine possible strategies in this particular sector before going on to the others. Secondly, one must at all costs avoid falling into the trap of ethnocentrism and so being guilty of 'cultural arrogance' by laying down precise rules for action or making specific proposals.[151] In our view, only the peoples concerned, through their political representatives, or the international community gathered together in the forums specifically designed for that purpose, are entitled to decide what course of action should be followed. Besides which, the variety of ways in which TNCs operate in the developing countries and the diversity of local situations make it difficult, to say the least, to specify measures of universal relevance. There is, however, nothing to prevent us from making some contribution to the deliberations on what such action should entail by giving some general guidelines that might help in working out a policy. The approach adopted is accordingly intended to provide some food for thought on the broad principles to be borne in mind in preserving the cultural values of developing countries from adverse influence by TNCs.[152]

Some general principles

Three types of approach to TNC development may be considered, in particular with regard to their impact on standards and values: (a) inaction, which might also be described as dependent assimilation of TNC influence; (b) withdrawal; and (c) bringing about a change in TNCs' influence through national assimilation. The first approach, which consists in making no attempt to counteract the power of TNCs to make and break local structures and the extroversion of cultural aims and values that implies, must be ruled out if the perspective is one of endogenous, autonomous change. The second approach, which recognizes the need for political action, can be put into effect through direct, assertive measures or through more indirect arrangements. TNCs can be prohibited outright from operating within a nation's territorial boundaries, but there is another way of tackling the problem and that is progressively to take away all the various advantages (concerning tax, wages, tariffs, legislation and so on) which the TNCs have an eye to in setting up operations in the poorer countries and doing business with them. They could be prohibited from developing their activities in the service sector and from advertising, and could be required to alter their material products (goods) or 'symbolic' products (films, television programmes, books or newspapers) so that they are genuinely suited to local conditions. In more specifically economic terms, they could also be compelled to re-invest all their profits in the countries concerned or employ only nationals in their subsidiaries' headquarters.

In our view, this approach should also be discarded, for at least two reasons. The first is prompted by realism. In the present state of affairs, especially in the light of geopolitical and diplomatic considerations, and the reactions to which such a step could give rise, it seems unthinkable to close the frontiers of developing countries to TNCs. Furthermore, economic shortages in these countries (employment, financial resources, technology, investment) are such that this cannot be regarded as a feasible solution except in a few isolated cases and certainly not on a wide scale. The other reason has to do with the dangers of such a policy for those very cultural values that are under discussion. Isolationism causes cultures to withdraw into themselves, become impoverished and ultimately even condemns them to death. This, in fact, was the view which emerged from the Yogyakarta Conference on Cultural Policies in Asia, in the course of which it was reaffirmed that

> the quest for cultural identity was in all cases combined with sympathetic receptivity to the other cultures of the region and of the world, and, ultimately, to all that is universally human, which ruled out cultural isolationism and entailed the disavowal of chauvinistic assertions of distinctive nationhood.[153]

This, then, leaves the alternative of national assimilation as a basis for discussion. The first point that springs to mind is to devise safeguards, largely of a defensive nature, to be established both as part of national policies or legislation and by the international community as a whole. We shall come back to these shortly; for the time being it is sufficient to point out that they include: (a) establishing means whereby information put out by transnational news agencies can be given a national or regional interpretation; (b) resisting the widespread use of foreign languages; (c) controlling consumer products manufactured by TNCs and adopting various measures to bring supply into line with demand, instead of the reverse; (d) monitoring the signs and messages transmitted by TNC communication media (advertising, films) where the contradiction between local values and imported stereotypes appears too acute; and so on.

The list could be extremely long if the disruptive effects of TNCs were to be counteracted point by point. In this respect, the countries concerned are the best judges of the areas of penetration calling for safeguards. A word of caution must be given from the outset, however, as to the danger of falling into a form of censorship that might rapidly be diverted from its original aims and might well be used to strengthen certain political regimes. The methods of control must therefore be consistent with endogenous cultural development objectives accepted by the whole population, and they must be legitimately established through democratic procedures (e.g. by setting up boards of control established by and answerable to democratically elected assemblies). The fact remains that such measures are primarily defensive in character, which seriously curbs their effectiveness when compared with the sheer volume, speed, flexibility and magnetism of the TNCs. What makes TNCs so powerful is their ability to shape economic and social structures, and also attitudes, to fit their own micro-economic rationale. They are at the heart of a dynamic process constituted by the equilibrium-in-motion of a totality of interacting economic, social and cultural forces. As a result, it is only by calling into play another set of interacting forces that states can assimilate and control the conflict. An offensive policy in regard to cultural values and communication is the only way of transforming external influences from within. Modernization must not be passive, since otherwise it will result in subservience to imported models and value systems. It must be fundamentally active and actively accepted.[154] If the commitment is to endogenous development the initiative must come from the assertion of cultural identity. Where might such a cultural counter-attack find its sources of inspiration, and what forms might it take? Again, it is up to the peoples concerned or their representatives to decide, but the evidence suggests that the cultural heritage, rituals and popular and ancestral memories or traditions may provide the wellspring from which the common ingredients for endogenous social change may be drawn, in regard to both their matter and their form. Nor is the support of certain pre-existing mental structures to be ruled out: for instance, the cultural homogeneity and the frequent persistence of inherited tradition found in the Arab world are indisputably bound up with the spiritual and hence socio-mental strength of Islam. Even so, the Third World countries must accept some modification of forms of expression of cultural values and not resist the fact that henceforth they are expressed through the modern media, for example.

The cybernetics experts have taught us that a system can only resist entropy, that is internal decay affecting its energy, by increasing its volume of information. This also applies to the socio-cultural systems of developing countries, with regard to which we cannot do better than quote J. Berque when he writes:

The real question that arises is not, therefore, which parts of the cultural identity to be protected should be safeguarded from external aggression, but what kind of change based on those elements that are authentic and specific will render such aggression powerless—I almost said pointless.[155]

Since TNCs' influence on value systems can be seen as a process of dissemination of signs, symbols and norms, it is through a counter-process of the same type that indigenous values can be safeguarded, subject, no doubt, to some changes in form. Once this is accepted, the problem of finding a truly endogenous basis for development can cease to be the object of theoretical utterances, as is so often its lot today, and become a genuine, explicitly objective of nation-states which from now on must consciously accept full responsibility for domestic social change, which includes adopting measures applicable on an international scale. Equal importance and as much emphasis must be given to cultural development policies as to economic development policies. This means, in particular, that the encroachments on cultural identity as a result of the penetration of foreign capital must no longer be seen as the perverse effects of the transformation of the productive system, but as the logical manifestation of the type of economic and social relations that have been allowed to take root, implicitly or explicitly, and therefore as one of the elements of a form of societal cohesion bound up with economic and socio-cultural factors. The nation-states must assume their own responsibilities in this respect, just as public consciousness must be aroused on the subject.[156] It is also important that peoples should be provided with the means to express ancestral values and national symbols, since the TNCs for their part have means of channelling their own forms of cohesion and their social codes. They have the instruments and vectors, especially where communication and information are concerned, to spread and legitimate their own cultural values outside the firm. One of the ways in which states can match this is by launching an offensive on the communication front, competing with the TNCs on a terrain that was long treated as their preserve. Mass media can in fact be 'a vehicle for cultural integration which denotes a process of communication concerning fundamental values in broad social demand which involves and is carried out by means of common cultural symbols'.[157]

Let us now endeavour to specify in which areas these general guidelines could be applied with the aim of safeguarding cultural values from undue influence by TNCs.

Some key areas for application

As has already been stated several times, it is out of the question here to propose specific measures. The object is rather to suggest a number of avenues to be explored if the collective memory and social codes of Third World countries are to be preserved from the influence of transnational corporations.[158] For each level of action there will be defensive measures or safeguards, and measures of a more offensive nature. These measures should be such as could be brought into a system of worldwide or regional control, owing to the TNCs' sheer size which makes it out of the question for the developing countries to compete with them. But they should leave considerable scope for nation-states to be able to express their sovereign wishes and adapt their policies to their own particular situations and to the specific form of the culture shock experienced through contact with TNCs. Three potential spheres of action deserve special emphasis: (a) mass media and advertising; (b) information; and (c) languages.

The Third World countries must regain control of their media, today largely in the hands of TNCs, in order to adapt both the substance and the form to local conditions. Consideration might be given to cutting down gradually on imported films (television or cinema), or again radio broadcasts which transmit stereotypes of the transnational system, in music for instance, even if it means reducing broadcasting time; at the same time local production centres could be developed in culturally homogeneous regions, along the lines of the African CIPROFILM. Emphasis should also be placed on the development of community or small-scale media (video cassettes, tape-recorders, local radio stations) in order to ensure greater relevance of communications to the needs of local communities, whether such groups are based on cultural, occupational, ethnic or geographical ties. Such horizontal forms of communication would be instrumental in reinstating dialogue and asserting identity; by decentralizing production and the messages broadcast, they would make it possible to replace the much decried dehumanization and uniformization of cultures by local, authentic focuses of communication. Examples abound, particularly in broadcasting, of how radio has been used to reach the general public in matters of national significance. One is Algeria, where radio was the key instrument of Arabization, and another the pilot educational broadcasting programmes in Senegal,[159] which made it possible to reach the majority of the rural population each week at a relatively low overall cost. Television was also used in Senegal for the purposes of cultural expression, notably in Wolof. It should, however, be borne in mind that programmes

are not an end in themselves, their social significance is greatly enhanced when they are part of a dialogue between specialists and the public. Both communication and education are two-way processes, programming must be matched by organized reception and the availability of economic and social services in the communities.[160]

This means that the return to horizontal and interpersonal forms of communication must not simply be equated with minaturization or the proliferation of electronic gadgets. The small-scale media are not intrinsically neutral, and 'contrary to a still common fallacy, no technology is freedom-giving *per se*. The only important things are how it is used and how it enables genuine communication to be established.'[161] In other words, the development of the small-scale made is a significant factor in changing the nature of communications provided that it goes hand in hand with deprofessionalization of broadcasts and message transmission and therefore with the establishment of a genuinely interpersonal communication system so that the individual is not totally swanped.[162]

The international community and nation-states should make a concerted effort to provide the Third World peoples with the means of expressing their own cultural values so that they can compete with the foreign-controlled media. There is evidence of the need for this in book publishing, for example, in sound products (records, cassettes), and in television or radio. It is doubtless at the regional level that international institutions could be made responsible for this type of work, which should of course be carried out in such a way as to promote the greatest possible measure of cultural pluralism.

However, the formidable problem remains of what attitude should be adopted with regard to heavy technology and the latest developments in the marriage between electronics and communications (information technology, data systems and data banks, satellite communications, domestic computerization, and so on).

Can we discuss a movement which all the evidence suggests is worldwide and irrevocable? Are we entitled to think that defending the monopoly on television, the radio and transmission networks is the ultimate weapon against multinational imperialism? In what way does computerization actually spell progress? All these are fundamental questions ignored by many professional futurologists who confine their predictions to 'when and how'.[163]

Although these remarks were written about France, the authors would no doubt have no objection to their being made to refer by extension to the Third World.

The question is how the developing countries can be expected *not* to seize the opportunities afforded by the new technology, so as to avoid lagging behind the developed countries to a point that may well prove irrevocable. But in that case do they not run the risk of encouraging the dehumanization and mental destructuration discussed in detail above? The problem is all the more delicate in that it often calls for huge investments which most of the developing countries, taken individually, will probably not be able to afford in the near future. Clearly these problems call for some fresh research of the kind entrusted to the International Commission for the Study of Communication Problems, but focusing attention on the relationship between medium of communication and endogenous change in developing countries. Whatever the case may be, specific measures (establishment of networks and data banks, transmission and reception of satellite communications, etc.) can only be decided on at the international level, for such questions evidently transcend the present scope of Third World countries and would seem to be more a matter for 'cultural areas' having 'transnational' institutions which could alone counterbalance the TNCs.

Advertising, one of the most insidious and powerful agents in shaping cultural values according to the TNCs' rationale, should be brought under stricter control and should be used as one of the vectors of a cultural counter-attack. A war must be waged on the unadulterated transfer of advertising stereotypes and clichés which occurs in transnational agencies. One way of doing this might be for the international community to draw up a code of ethics. But it is by employing the same methods that nation-states can offset the adverse effects of advertising campaigns. An idea might be to develop national advertising concerning the values, traditions and rituals of the country concerned but using the publicity man's device of snappy spot commercials, for instance. This type of operation could be financed by a special tax on TNC advertising in the developing countries. It has in fact been demonstrated that information systems of this kind, which amount to a form of counter-publicity, can be relatively effective in non-formal education. An example is Ecuador's National Institute of Nutrition which had recourse to a New York advertising firm as part of their social policy to develop better nutrition and campaign against early departure from breast-feeding and the practice of drinking impure water.[164] The results were encouraging on a number of points and there is apparently no reason why this aspect of the media should not be used to spread endogenous cultural values and further their development.

As to the monitoring and channelling of information, recent initiatives have shown the way to the establishment of a new balance of information flows and ought to be encouraged. The setting up and expansion of regional or subregional news-agencies should be further developed and promoted. As far back as 1975, the English-speaking Caribbean countries set up the Caribbean News Agency (CANA) with the assistance of the United Nations Development Programme (UNDP) and Unesco, and today it comprises seventeen public or private information agencies. An African News Agency (PANA) is currently being set up, under the auspices, more particularly, of the Organization of African Unity (OAU), with its headquarters in Dakar. On a broader scale, the Group of 77 decided in 1975, for the purpose of countering 'one-way information', to organize a pool of news-agencies comprising more than fifty countries, encompassing the regional agencies and based on the national agencies which serve as local liaison offices, such as TANJUG (Yugoslavia), TAP (Tunisia), MAP (Morocco), INA (Iraq), Press Trust (India) or Prensa Latina (Cuba). But these agencies will not be able to offset the power of the 'great' news-agencies unless they, too, set up offices and agencies in the Third World countries, as well as in the industrialized countries to collect and circulate the 'news' from the Western countries as viewed from the standpoint of the peoples, concerns and mentality of the various cultural subregions that serve as the basis or constitute the local arm of the organization. One of the effects of this would be to redirect information towards 'processes' and 'mechanisms' instead of the 'news' and events which too often have pride of place.

There remains the language problem and the best response to the tendency towards alignment on foreign TNC-favoured models. As everyone knows, English is very widely used by TNCs as their working language. The fact that instructions or documents that come with the sale of capital goods are written in English or that the installation operations are carried out in English means that it is necessarily being used increasingly by local employees, and subsequently by their children. Now, if there is one type of society in which socio-cultural dependence may become irreversible, it is that of civilizations based largely on oral traditions and speech, as is generally the case in Africa for example. From this point of view, 'the safeguarding of cultural authenticity calls for the reinstatement and promotion of African languages as the irreplaceable media of social communication and the carriers of the cultural inheritance of the various communities'.[165] But this does not only apply to Africa. In more general terms, the fact of belonging to a language area and hence to a cultural area shapes intellectual or aesthetic tastes, and is therefore clearly bound up with cultural values. Action must be taken to counter the erosion of local languages which to a certain extent has been brought about by the process of economic modernization for which the TNCs and their systems of norms and communication are largely responsible, for if it is not, ancestral dialects may gradually die out or no longer serve any practical purpose. A case in point is Singapore, where there are four national languages (Malay, Mandarin, Tamul and English) in addition to the countless local dialects. But English has been established as the working language and is officially considered to be the language and vehicle of modernization. True, the government is in favour of the existence of the three vernacular languages and provides substantial incentives for their continuing to be taught in schools, but English is seen as the only language giving access to Western technology and science, and very probably also as a key medium of communication in economic activities, in a country largely controlled by TNCs. This no doubt explains the fact that in 1977, for over 73 per cent of pupils in state and subsidized schools, English was the medium of instruction. What is more, attempts to persuade people to revert to their own languages, in particular Mandarin for the Chinese, have met with an extremely hostile response, no doubt prompted by the fear of marginalization. This may cause local traditions and ancestral forms of expression to die out, or speed their death. These languages must therefore be reinstated, both in schools and within the TNCs themselves, by enforcing multilingualism for instance instead of English.

In this connection, attention should be drawn to the tendentious character of certain arguments claiming that vernacular languages are incapable of expressing the new subtleties of the modern world.

Every language, including those that are looked upon as archaic, has as great a potential as the most complex and makes use of logico-mathematical structures which are connected with its own vision of the world while at the same time extending (or rather being capable of extension) towards the most elaborate varieties of formalism.[166]

Maintaining a large number of languages does, however, pose the problem of cultural unity in the states concerned and certainly does not facilitate the dissemination of information in developing countries. To give an example, in 1972 Radio Uganda broadcast in twenty languages, which inevitably gave rise to difficulties and even had an adverse effect on national identity:

Such multilingualism . . . divided the available air time into small parcels and limited vernacular programming essentially to news (which is translated from a common news file prepared in English). A single-language service might broadcast approximately an hour's news per day. . . . Thus, no special language group receives a continuous service, and much of the time broadcasts are unintelligible to a large portion of the national audience. This tends to drive listeners to foreign stations. For example, on the border in the far north-west of Uganda, people of Arna listen to Swahili programmes from Radio Bukavu, a regional transmitter in Zaire, when Radio Uganda is broadcasting in vernaculars they do not understand.[167]

This is a problem that can only be tackled by the governments themselves and cannot be resolved by universally applicable measures. By allowing a large number of languages a share in the media, traditional cultures are preserved, the loyalty of minority groups is assured and the widest listening public can be reached, but the risk is that it will encourage separatism or disrupt national identity. Broadcasting in a single language to expedite the process of national integration entails the danger of dooming certain local cultures to a speedy death and makes communication more difficult with the peoples whom the government probably most needs to reach, to explain what its intentions are. Here again, regional solutions might provide some answer to what must be regarded as a particularly thorny problem.

Finally, with regard to cultural values, if the nation-states—individually or as members of the international community—wish to counteract the influence of TNCs and direct their own development along a course which is not at variance with the preservation of endogenous values and standards, it must be realized that difficulties may well be encountered within the countries themselves, since the media and communication in general are closely bound up with a certain form of power which no doubt had its origins elsewhere but is now inevitably to be found in Third World countries as well.[168] However that may be, the requirements of economic development and the perpetuation of local cultural values do not appear to be incompatible. On the contrary, might it not be expected of Third World cultures that they revitalize the values and standards of a Western world which, it must not be forgotten, is in the throes of a far-reaching crisis that is not just economic? How could one forget, when it comes to symbolic forms of expression, the revival of Western art by African art or that of 'modern music' with the rhythms and folklore of Africa or Asia! An example of no great scope but singularly eloquent as to the possibility of a successful blend of the traditional and the modern (the latter being nowadays largely vested in TNCs, as far as means of cultural expression are concerned) is given us by S. B. Kouyaté when he tells of the orchestras that have grown up in Mali, composed of young Malians who import their instruments from abroad (trumpets, saxophones, clarinets), but the music they play has its roots more and more in traditional sources. Songs dating back three centuries are given modern arrangements and create an almost mystical bond between the generations. The best orchestra of the region of Ségou—and the leading orchestra of the Republic of Mali—took the name of Super Biton, in honour of the founder of the Bambara Kingdom of Ségou.[169]

The lesson is worth remembering.

NOTES

1. K. P. Sauvant, 'His Master's Voice', *CERES*, Vol. 9, September/October 1976, pp. 27–32; see also A. Pinto and J. Kuakal, who say that local entrepreneurs display a marked tendency to emulate executives of foreign firms in their behaviour and management practices ('The Centre–Periphery System, Twenty Years Ago', *Social and Economic Studies*, Vol. 22, No. 1, March 1973). For general reading on this subject, see K. P. Sauvant, 'The Potential of Multinational Enterprises as Vehicles for the Transmission of Business Culture', in K. P. Sauvant and F. Lavipour (eds), *Controlling Multinational Enterprises—Problems, Strategies, Counterstrategies*, pp. 39–78, Boulder, Colo., Westview Press, 1976; see also K. P. Sauvant, 'Multinational Enterprises and the Transmission of Culture: The International Supply of Advertising Services and Business Education', *Journal of Peace Research* (International Peace Research Center, Oslo) Vol. XIII, No. 1, 1976. K. P. Sauvant and B. Mennis, 'Socio-cultural Investments within the International Political Economy of North–South Relations: The Role of Transnational Enterprises', Symposium organized by the Association Française pour l'Étude du Tiers-Monde on 'L'Information et le Tiers-Monde', 30 May–1 June 1979, Dijon (France).
2. M. Brigaud-Robert, *Méthodologie de la mesure de l'impact de la publicité des STN du tourisme sur les valeurs socio-culturelles des pays en développement*, Paris, Unesco, Division for the Study of Development, TNC. 5, 1978. (French only.)
3. A. Mazrui, 'The African University as a Multinational Corporation: Problems of Penetration and Dependency', *Harvard Educational Review*, Vol. 45, No. 2, May 1975; and 'The Impact of Transnational Corporations on Educational and Cultural Processes: An African perspective', *Prospects, Quarterly Review of Education*, Vol. VI, No. 4, 1976.
4. This is the view expressed in an official statement by a group of Central American and Latin American countries on the dangerous effects of TNC operations on their cultural identity: 'The social institutions, cultural values, traditions, the usages and customs of a nation, are affected by the attempts of the transnational corporations to transplant to the host country their own models of social development that, in more than one case, have differed considerably from the cultural identity and social structure of the host country. That is especially true of developing countries in that the transnational corporation, when importing a culture peculiar to industrialized countries, distorts the local social and cultural character.' *Commission on Transnational Corporations, Report on the Second Session (1-12 March 1976)*, pp. 33–4, United Nations Economic and Social Council (document E/5782–E/C.10/16.) Paper submitted by the delegations of Argentina, Barbados, Brazil, Colombia, Ecuador, Jamaica, Mexico, Peru, Trinidad and Tobago, and Venezuela.
5. For a discussion of the distinctions made in the literature, see D. Kaplan and R. Manners, *Culture Theory*, Englewood Cliffs, N.J., Prentice-Hall, 1972.

6. To the American anthropologist R. Linton, culture is the set of acquired behaviour patterns and their results, the components of which are shared and transmitted by the members of a given society. Likewise, to R. Preiswerk, 'it is the values, institutions and modes of behaviour as a whole that are produced by man' ('Relations interculturelles et développement', *Le savoir et le faire, Cahier de l'Institut d' Études du Développement*, p. 16, Geneva/Paris, IUED/Presses Universitaires de France, 1975).
7. Mazrui, 'The Impact of Transnational Corporations....', op. cit.
8. This on no account means that it is an aspect to be dismissed, but merely that it should be regarded more as an outward expression of cultural values. R. Maheu sees creative artists as those who 'create the expressions and works in which we recognize, magnified and analysed, the realities and trends of our culture' (*Report of the Intergovernmental Conference on Institutional, Administrative and Financial Aspects of Cultural Policies, Venice, 24 August–2 September 1970*, p. 54, Paris, Unesco). This aspect may, however, be assigned a predominant role. For instance, in a recent work, G. Bell places considerable emphasis on the artistic aspect, while acknowledging that the cultural sphere includes forms of knowledge, philosophy and science, and describes culture as 'the arena of expressive symbolism ... painting, poetry and fiction', but also 'the religious forms of litany, liturgy and ritual which seek to ... express the meanings of human existence in some imaginative form' (*The Cultural Contradictions of Capitalism*, p. 12. New York, Basic Books, 1976). In this perspective, aesthetic considerations appear to have the upper hand over ethical considerations.
9. J. Ladrière, *The Challenge Presented to Cultures by Science and Technology*, Paris, Unesco, 1977 (see in particular pp. 9–16).
10. Such preferences might, for example, explain the distinction drawn between power, prestige, security, comfort, escape, desire for action, etc.; see on the subject J. Lesourne, *Les systèmes du destin*, Paris, Dalloz, 1976.
11. Ladrière, op. cit., pp. 12–13.
12. W. A. Weisskopf, *Aliénation, idéologie et répression*, p. 29, Paris, Presses Universitaires de France, 1976.
13. M. Guillaume, *Le capital et son double*, p. 64, Paris, Presses Universitaires de France, 1975.
14. Ladrière, op. cit., p. 57.
15. Ibid., p. 100.
16. H. Skolimowski, 'Cultural Values, Science and Technology', *Cultures*, Vol. VI, No. 1, 1979, p. 119.
17. See in this connection, the fears expressed at the Intergovernmental Conference on Communication Policies in Asia and Oceania, Kuala Lumpur, 5–14 February 1979.
18. A.-M. M'Bow, writes that 'any attempt at internal development calls for an awareness of distinctive cultural values and for continued initiatives based on the assertion of cultural identity. Although culture is what provides the individual with an awareness of himself and determines his choices and actions, it also represents his aspiration to dignity, and it is national dignity which at the state level is seen as a basic requisite for community action for development. It is their deep-rooted cultural values that enable peoples to regain the confidence and motivation necessary for the work of innovation entailed in development.' ('Preservation and Further Development of Cultural Values', Note by the Secretary-General. *Report submitted by the Director-General of Unesco*, dated 30 November 1976. United Nations General Assembly document A/33/57, 6 September 1978. Item 79 of the agenda, p. 10).
19. 'Because of their growing size, expanding areas of activities, globalization process, increasing concentration and productive factors they control, transnational enterprises have considerable power in forging the structure of national and international development', J. Tinbergen (co-ordinator), *Reshaping*

the International Order, A Report to the Club of Rome, p. 157, New York, Dutton, 1976.
20. O. Sunkel, 'Transnational Capitalism and National Disintegration in Latin America', Social and Economic Studies, 22 March 1973, pp. 132–76; O. Sunkel and E. Fuenzalida, 'Transnationalization and its National Consequences', in J. Vallamil (ed.), Transnational Capitalism and National Development, pp. 67–93, Brighton, Harvester Press, 1979; O. Sunkel, External Economic Relations and the Process of Development, Brighton, Institute of Development Studies, 1974 (Discussion Paper, No. 51); O. Sunkel and E. Fuenzalida, Transnationalization, National Disintegration and Reintegration in Contemporary Capitalism, Brighton, Institute of Development Studies, 1974 (Internal Working Paper, No. 18). For an application to the Kenyan context, see M. Godfrey and S. Langdon, 'Partners in Under-development? The Transnationalization Thesis in a Kenyan Context', in Vallamil, op. cit.
21. As M. and A. Mattelart see it, however, 'The internationalization of business will increasingly go hand in hand with a wave of cultural nationalism' (De l'usage des média en temps de crise, p. 115, Paris, Moreau, 1979). This national feeling would not therefore become any less vigorous, but it would remain theoretical. 'The more concessions of sovereignty the nation-states make under pressure from multinational firms, the more urgent it becomes for there to be a verbal expression of national sovereignty. The repatriation of ideology follows the expatriation of the centres and working of decision-making' (ibid., p. 124).
22. This goes to explain why in some respects Africans are less apprehensive of unemployment than others, because of their being 'assured' of being able to subsist with the help of their fellows. In a highly revealing study, B. Kouyaté describes the community ties and group responsibility for the individual among the Bambara peoples of Mali, where the flanton, (schoolchildren) are expected to lend a helping hand to the older and the handicapped members of the village. (The Components of Poverty and Socio-cultural Values among the Bambara Population of the Ségou Region (Mali), Paris, Unesco, Division for the Study of Development, POV. 1, 1977).
23. Bell, op. cit.
24. R. Georges, Hétérogénéité culturelle et communication, Paris, Anthropos, 1978.
25. J. Ziegler, Main-basse sur l'Afrique, Paris, Seuil, 1978; Le pouvoir africain (new ed.), Paris, Seuil, 1979.
26. Ibid., p. 26. In Ziegler's view, 'Aggression by the hegemonic capital of the centre not only determines the non-capitalist modes of production of the centre and the periphery but also dissolves local cultural bonds and motivational structures. In short, it destroys the self-identity, memory and history of the peoples it subjugates' (ibid., p. 28.) In that sense, he seems inclined to adopt the theory of homogenization—of minds in particular—as a result of the development of 'a philosophy of pure rationality which reduces man to a state of mercantile functionalism, and deprives him of any identity other than that which he derives from the system of production and reproduction of merchandise, of which he is now an interchangeable component'. (Ziegler, Le pouvoir africain, op. cit., p. 246.)
27. P. Clastres, 'De l'ethnocide', L'homme, July/December 1974.
28. In B. Sine's view, the development of foreign life-styles and the modelling of consumer structures are acts of 'diversion, extraversion and cultural rape'. (Impérialisme et théories sociologiques du développement, p. 173, Paris, Anthropos/IDEP, 1975.)
29. A. Mattelart, Multinationales et systèmes de communication, Paris, Anthropos, 1976.
30. T. Varis, The Impact of Transnational Corporations on Communication, Paris, Unesco, 1976. (Document SHC-76/CONF. 635/7.)
31. Ibid., p. 10.
32. See T. Guback, Hollywood's World Market. An Historical Anthology of the American Film Industry, 1975.

33. Radio Corporation of America (RCA), *Annual Report*, 1972.
34. Mattelart, op. cit., pp. 20–1.
35. Over 1,000 subsidiaries or branches were set up outside the United States by American-based transnational electronics corporations in the 1960s (*Business Abroad*, June 1971).
36. Varis, op. cit., p. 18.
37. W. P. Dizard, *Television, A World View*, pp. 12–13, Syracuse, N.Y., Syracuse University Press, 1966.
38. Varis, op. cit., p. 9.
39. E. Katz and G. Wedell, *Broadcasting in the Third World*, Cambridge, Mass., Harvard University Press, 1977.
40. Varis, op. cit., p. 33.
41. *Variety*, 6 August 1975.
42. *Survey of Current Business*, August 1974.
43. T. Guback and T. Varis, *Transnational film and Television*, p. 53, Paris, Unesco, 1977 (mimeo).
44. O. Inoussa, 'Vers une économie affranchie', *Le Monde diplomatique*, March 1979. On the obstacles to the African film industry, see F. Kodjo, 'Les cinéastes africains face à l'avenir du cinéma', *Revue Tiers-Monde*, Vol. XX, No. 79, July/September 1979, pp. 605–14.
45. Cf. 'La communication inégale', *Le Monde diplomatique*, January 1979.
46. K. Smith, *The Impact of Transnational Book Publishing on Intellectual Knowledge in Less Developed Countries*, Paris, Unesco, Division for the Study of Development, TNC.3, 1977.
47. Y. Mignot-Lefebvre, 'Vers une communication à sens unique? Mythes et réalités', *Revue Tiers-Monde*, op. cit., p. 510.
48. P. Gronow, *The Record Industry, Multinational Corporations and National Music Traditions*, Vienna, International Institute for Music, Dance and Theatre in the Audio-visual Media, 1975.
49. P. Flichy, *Contribution à une étude des industries de l'audio-visuel*, Paris, Ministère de la Culture et de l'Environnement, Institut National de l'Audio-visuel, 1978.
50. Ibid., p. 19.
51. Mattelart, op. cit. Generally speaking this is an extremely useful reference work on the subject.
52. Ibid., pp. 170–1.
53. Ibid., p. 170.
54. The Arabian American Oil Company (ARAMCO) station imports all its programmes from the United States.
55. Taken from K. Kumar, *A Working Paper on the Social and Cultural Impacts of Transnational Enterprises*, Honolulu, Hawaii, East-West Center, East-West Culture Learning Institute, 1978. Most of the statistics quoted are taken from K. Nordenstreng and T. Varis, *Television Traffic—A One-way Street? A Survey and Analysis of the International Flow of Television Programme Material*, Paris, Unesco, 1974. (Reports and Papers on Mass Communication, 70.) The report contains the findings of a survey carried out in 1970 by Nordenstreng and Varis.
56. A. Horowitz, 'The Global "Bonanza" of American T.V.', *More Magazine*, May 1975.
57. M. Kaplun, 'La comunicación de masas en América Latina', *Educación Hoy*, (Bogotá, Associación de Publicaciones Educativas), No. 5, 1973.
58. See also on this subject M. Jokela, *Film—T.V.: An International Comparison of National Self-Sufficiency in Three Media*, Tampere, Institute of Journalism and Mass Communication, 1975; L. Beltran and E. F. de Cardona, 'Latin America and the U.S.: Flaws in the Free Flow of Information'. Paper presented at the Conference on Fair Communication Policy for the Internal Exchange of Information, Honolulu, March/April 1976, East-West Communication Institute, East-West Center.
59. *Broadcasting*, April 1977, p. 48.

60. F. Matta, 'The Information Bedazzlement of Latin America: A Study of World News in the Region', *Development Dialogue*, No. 2, pp. 29–42.
61. Sauvant, 'His Master's Voice', op. cit., p. 31.
62. On advertising agencies in Latin America, see H. Schiller, *Communication and Cultural Domination*, White Plains, N.Y., International Art and Science Press, 1976.
63. Taken from, *Transnational Corporations in World Development: A Re-examination*', New York, United Nations, 20 March 1978. (Document E/C.10/38.)
64. Sauvant and Lavipour, op. cit., p. 39.
65. Guback and Varis, op. cit., p. 128, Table 18.
66. Ibid., Table 16.
67. G. B. Sdandlen, 'Broadcasting in Thailand', 1973 (draft), quoted in ibid.
68. A. Alfian, 'Some Observations on Television in Indonesia'. Paper presented at the Conference on Fair Communication Policy for the International Exchange of Information, Honolulu, March/April 1976, East-West Communication Institute, East-West Center.
69. Guback and Varis, op. cit., pp. 122 and 131.
70. S. Langdon, 'We've Got What She Wants ... and It's All Yours', *The New Internationalist*, 1972.
71. 'The Free Flow of Information: Towards a Reconsideration of National and International Communication Policies', in Nordenstreng and Varis, op. cit., p. 44.
72. Unesco General Conference, Nineteenth Session, Nairobi 1976, Item 16 of the Agenda, 'Proposals of the Director-General in regard to Unesco's contribution to United Nations action concerning study of the impact of the activities of transnational corporations', 19 C/76, p. 6.
73. Nordenstreng and Varis, op. cit.
74. A. Dorfman and A. Mattelart, *How to Read Donald Duck*, I.G. Editions, 1975.
75. In Western-produced films, the heroes usually belong to a well-off social milieu and seem to have no worries or cares and no restrictions on their time. An idealization of the West follows on naturally from this.
76. Quoted in Beltran and de Cardona, op. cit., 1976, p. 29. In the same vein, see also N. R. Garcia, *Tecnología, comunicación y publicidad: formas ocultas de dominación*, Caracas, Escuela de Sociología y Antropología, Facultad de Economía, 1975. See also N. Janus and R. Roncagliolo, 'Advertising, Mass Media and Dependency', *Development Dialogue*, No. 1, 1979; 'Transnational Advertising, The Media and Education in the Developing Countries', *Prospects, Quarterly Review of Education*, Vol. X, No. 1, 1980, pp. 68–74.
77. M. Ordóñez, 'El rol de la comunicación en la sociedad', Quito, *CIESPAL Paper*, 1975, p. 7.
78. Nordenstreng and Varis, op. cit., p. 29.
79. 'The words, images, conventions of expression, and themes which make up TV content embody in various ways reference to "real" groups of people and individuals. This relation of TV content to the "real" world is a dialectical one: the TV "world" reflects the "real" world on the one hand, and in turn changes the "real" world'. D. Smyth, in ibid., p. 29.
80. J. Lee, *Towards Realistic Communication Policies: Recent Trends and Ideas Compiled and Analysed*, p. 75, Paris, Unesco, 1976. (Reports and Papers on Mass Communication, 76.) Moreover, as A.-M. M'Bow, Director-General of Unesco, has said, this information or these films are 'stereotypes of a lamentable mediocrity, whose effect is to depersonalize consumers mesmerized by the power of words and images' (*Final Report of the Accra Conference*, Paris, Unesco, p. 75).
81. Regarding dependence as far as films are concerned, the backwardness of Third World countries does not seem to be due to technological or economic factors alone, but also to political factors. For a study of multinational

conglomerates in the film industry and their attempts to produce films which can be viewed the world over, see J. Phillips, 'Film Conglomerate "Blockbusters"', *Journal of Communication*, Vol. 25, No. 2, Spring 1975; Mattelart and Mattelart, op. cit., p. 353. See also M. Winn, *T.V. Drogue?*, Paris, Fleurus, 1979.
82. Mattelart, op. cit.
83. In M. Gallagher's view, the representation of women is always two-sided: good or bad, mother or whore, virgin or mistress, etc. (*The Image Reflected by Mass Media*. III: *Women* Paris, Unesco (CIC Report, No. 59).)
84. Intergovernmental Conference on Cultural Policies in Latin America and the Caribbean, Bogotá, 10–20 January 1978, *Final Report*, p. 72, Paris, Unesco.
85. See also on this subject, E. Contreras, J. Larson, J. Mayo and P. Spain, *Cross-Cultural Broadcasting*, Paris, Unesco, 1976 (Reports and Papers on Mass Communication, 77); and R. C. O'Brien, 'Domination and Dependence in Miss Communications: Implications for the Use of Broadcasting in Developing Countries', *Institute of Development Studies Bulletin*, Vol. 6, No. 4, March 1975.
86. Mattelart and Mattelart, op. cit.
87. Herbert I. Schiller rightly considers that the mass media are actively responsible for the emergence of a new type of man, *Homo consumens* (H. I. Schiller, *Mass Communications and American Empire*, New York, Beacon, 1971). See also the various contributions to the special issue of the *Journal of Communication* entitled 'Forms of Cultural Dependency' (Vol. 25, No. 2, 1975), particularly the examples of Colombia (E. de Cardona) and Lebanon (N. Dajani).
88. See S. Ewen, 'Advertising as a Way of Life', *Liberation Magazine*, January 1975; or F. Marquez, 'The Relationship of Advertising and Culture in the Philippines', *Journalism Quarterly*, Vol. 52, No. 3, 1975.
89. M. Brigaud-Robert, *Méthodologie de la mesure de l'impact de la publicité des transnationales du tourisme sur les valeurs socio-culturelles dans les pays en développement*, Unesco, Division for the Study of Development, TNC.5, 1978. (French only.)
90. Ibid., p. 17. However, Brigaud-Robert holds that travel advertising and tourism can have a positive influence by emphasizing local characteristics or age-old traditions. 'Through such publicity, the population will regain the diversity of its identity, a tenuous acquisition threatened with 'reification' or a source of conflict' (ibid., p. 19). To a certain extent, this may then strengthen the feeling of belonging to a socio-cultural, and particularly national, entity, stemming from a renewed sense of collective pride.
91. This may also lead to some misunderstanding. For instance, some films in which children were shown naked met with extremely negative reactions on the part of mothers in the United Republic of Tanzania, because it is an age-old tradition, still observed, that a child should never be seen naked and its head must always be washed first, never last.
92. M. Colomina de Rivera, *El huesped alienante: estudio de audiencia y efectos de las radiotelenovelas en Venezuela*, Maracaibo, Universidad de Zulia, 1968.
93. Mattelart and Mattelart, op. cit.
94. As described in the NORA-MINC report entitled *L'informatisation de la société*, Paris, La Documentation Française, 1978.
95. M. Guillaume defines the 'social code' as 'the totality of associations between things having a social significance (objects, services, acts, etc.) and what they signify, such associations being created or controlled by organizations so that they themselves can subsist and, if possible, develop'. (*Le capital et son double*, p. 64, Paris, Presses Universitaires de France, 1975.)
96. B. Sine, *Impérialisme et théories sociologiques du développement*, Paris, Anthropos/IDEP, 1975. From time immemorial, for instance in Africa, people spoke to one another and addressed one another through their own means of communication (drum language, tam-tams, 'palavers') which were commensurate with the scale of the communities. Above all, there was real communication, in other words two-way communication. Today, African

radio faces a serious problem of cultural extraversion (p. 189), 'over-saturated' as it is with Western music and characterized by the use of European languages on a massive scale or the predominance of foreign news which provides more information about the outside world than about Africa itself.

97. In the same vein, see C. Hamelink, *Perspectives for Public Communications*, Baarn, 1974; R. C. O'Brien, op. cit., and 'Mass communications: Social Mechanisms of Incorporation and Dependence', in J. Vallamil, op. cit., pp. 129–43. See also L. R. Beltran, 'Communication and Cultural Domination: U.S.A.-Latin American Case', *Media Asia, An Asian Mass Communication Quarterly*, Vol. 5, No. 4, 1978; and L. R. Beltran and E. F. de Cardona, 'Mass Media and Cultural Domination', *Prospects, Quarterly Review of Education*, Vol. X, No. 1, 1980, pp. 76–89.
98. Bogotá Conference, *Final Report*, op. cit., p. 79.
99. See J. Somavia, 'The Transnational Power Structure and International Information', *Development Dialogue*, No. 2, 1976.
100. R. Morris, S. Mueller and W. Jellin, 'Through the Looking-glass in Chile: Coverage of Allende's Regime', *Columbia Journalism Review*, 1974, Vol. 13, No. 4, pp. 15-26.
101. Quoted in Somavia, op. cit.
102. According to Somavia, OPEC action has been presented as being to blame for world inflation, causing the collapse of the international economic system and lacking all responsibility in the use of oil, coupled with a thoroughly inadequate description of the historical dimension and implications of OPEC decisions for the balance of world power (ibid.).
103. Varis, op. cit. See also, on this subject, G. Tuchman, 'Objectivity as Strategic Ritual: An Examination of Newsmen's Notions of Objectivity', *American Journal of Sociology*, Vol. 77, No. 4, 1972; and F. Matta, 'The Information Bedazzlement of Latin America: A Study of World News in the Region', *Development Dialogue*, No. 2, 1976, pp. 29-42.
104. A. Lefevre and M. Ronai, 'La guerre des données', *Le Monde diplomatique*, November 1979.
105. J. Brzezinski, *La révolution technétronique*, Paris, Calmann-Lévy, 1971.
106. Unesco, *Moving Towards Change, Some Thoughts on the New International Economic Order*, p. 91, Paris, Unesco, 1975.
107. Smith, op. cit., p. 3.
108. K. Smith refers to the case of the West Indies, where readership is limited for certain types of books—scholarly and academic works—and where authors almost inevitably have to write for an international public as a result (ibid.). Cf. *From: Imitation to Innovation: The Production and Distribution of Books in the Caribbean. Report on the Seminar on Regional Problems of Books and Distribution at the University of the West Indies*, St Augustine, Trinidad, The Library University of the West Indies, 1973. See also P. Altbach, 'Publishing in Developing Countries', *International Social Science Journal*, Vol. 26, No. 3, 1974; 'Literary Colonialism: Books in the Third World', *Harvard Educational Review*, Vol. 45, No. 2, May 1975.
109. See on this subject the Senegalese experiment of producing and broadcasting programmes in Wolof (H. Cassirer, *Mass Media in an African Context—An Evaluation of Senegal's Pilot Project*, Paris, Unesco, 1974. (Reports and Papers on Mass Communication, 69.))
110. Smith, op. cit., pp. 299-308.
111. 'In spite of TNCs' pluralist ideology the major influences determining the distribution of intellectual knowledge outside school-books are metropolitan editorial decisions and the metropolitan-dominated international market' (ibid., p. 304). See also on these problems, P. Altbach and S. Macvey (eds.), *Perspectives on Publishing*, Lexington, Mass., Lexington Books, 1976.
112. *Final Report of the Intergovernmental Conference on Cultural Policies in Africa*, p. 16, Accra, Unesco, 1976.
113. J. Baudrillard, *Le système des objets*, Paris, Gallimard, 1968; see also, by the same author, *La société de consommation*, Paris, Gallimard, 1970; and

Pour une critique de l'économie politique du signe, Paris, Gallimard, 1972.
114. 'Whether a house is large or small, as long as the houses surrounding it are the same size, it meets whatever can socially be expected of a dwelling. But let a palace be built next to it and it becomes no more than a hut.' (Karl Marx, *Wage Labour and Capital*).
115. B. Cathelat and A. Cadet, *Publicité et société*, p. 190, Paris, Payot, 1976.
116. J. Attali, *La parole et l'outil*, p. 178, Paris, Presses Universitaires de France, 1978.
117. Which does not mean that it is the only form of expression of that culture. It is reflected in other spheres such as metaphysical or religious behaviour and beliefs, e.g. attitudes to death. But in societies in which the social division of labour has separated man from the creation of the products he consumes, the mode of consumption is an important reflection of the psycho-social bases of a society and a culture.
118. Godfrey and Langdon, in Vallamil, op. cit., pp. 261–86.
119. See Counter Information Service (London), Soma (Amsterdam) in co-operation with the Transnational Institute, Unilever.
120. Ibid.
121. Ibid.
122. Cf. R. Ledogar, *Hungry for Profits: U.S. Food and Drug Multinationals in Latin America*, New York, IDEC North America, 1975.
123. Ibid., p. 113.
124. Ibid.
125. S. Langdon, 'Firmes transnationales, transfert de goût et sous-développement: une étude de cas au Kénya', *Options méditerranéennes*, No. 27, 1975, p. 71.
126. Ibid.
127. See Group de Travail Tiers-Monde, *Nestlé contre les bébés*, Paris/Grenoble. Maspero/Presses Universitaires de Grenoble, 1978.
128. Ibid., p. 148. This work gives ample details of the effects on infants of not being breast-fed.
129. Sauvant, 'His Master's Voice', op. cit.
130. R. J. Barnet and R. E. Müller, *Global Reach: The Power of the Multinational Corporations*, p. 183, New York, Simon & Schuster, 1974.
131. R. Girling, 'Mechanisms of Imperialism: Technology and the Dependent State', *Latin American Perspectives*, Vol. 3, No. 4, 1976, p. 59.
132. R. Montavon, M. Wionczek and F. Piquerez, *L'implantation de deux entreprises multinationales au Mexique*, p. 81, Paris, Presses Universitaires de France/CEEIM, 1979.
133. See on this subject, World Confederation of Labour, *Les entreprises multinationales du secteur tabac*, Brussels, WCL/CMT, 1977.
134. F. M. Lappe and J. Collins, *Food First: The Myth of Scarcity*, London, Souvenir Press, 1980.
135. H. Walter, 'Marketing in Developing Countries', *Columbia Journal of World Business*, Winter 1974.
136. Quoted in Lappe and Collins, op. cit., See also M. Bader, 'Breast Feeding: The Role of Multinational Corporations in Latin America', *International Journal of Health Services*, Vol. 6, No. 4, 1976, pp. 609–26, or R. Bechtos, 'International Advertisers Change Consumer Ways', *Advertising Age*, Vol. 46, No. 20, 1975, pp. 1–38.
137. According to S. George, local élites 'ape' Western life-styles. (*Comment meurt l'autre moitié du monde*, p. 78, Paris, Laffont, 1978.)
138. O. Sunkel and E. Fuenzalida, *The Effects of Transnational Corporations on Culture*, Paris, Unesco, 1976. (Document SHC-76/CONF. 635/6.)
139. R. Nurkse, *Problems of Capital Formation in Underdeveloped Countries*, Oxford, Blackwell, 1966.
140. Sunkel and Fuenzalida, *The Effects of Transnational Corporations . . .*, op. cit.
141. Ledogar, op. cit., p. 111.
142. Mattelart and Mattelart, op. cit., p. 180.

143. Ibid.
144. On the problems posed by the 'green revolution', see George, op. cit.; Lappe and Collins, op. cit.
145. A. Berg, 'Industry's Struggle with World Nutrition', *Harvard Business Review*, January 1972.
146. See in this regard B. Rosier, *Type de développement et rapports sociaux: pour une nouvelle stratégie de développement agricole et agro-industriel*, Aix-Marseille-II, CEFI, April 1979 (mimeo), (To be published in *Mondes en développement*.)
147. G. Acciarri et al., *Producción agropecuaria y desnutrición en Colombia*, Coli, Universidad del Valle, Division de Ingenieria, 1973, quoted in Lappe and Collins, op. cit.
148. Between 1974 and 1975, consumption increased by 122 per cent. Cf. J. Masini M. Ikonikoff, C. Jedlicki and M. Lanzarotti, *Les multinationales et le développement. Trois entreprises et la Côte-d'Ivoire*, Paris, Presses Universitaires de France/CEEIM, 1979.
149. R. Maheu, *Final Report of the Intergovernmental Conference on Cultural Policies in Asia*, Yogyakarta, *10–19 December 1973*, p. 61.
150. For as Herbert I. Schiller (op. cit.) points out, 'cultural patterns, once established are endlessly persistent. . . . In modern mass communications hard and inflexible laws, economic and technological, operate. If these are not taken into account in the beginning and at least partially overcome, courses of development automatically unfold that soon become unquestioned natural patterns'.
151. Unesco, *Thinking Ahead*, op. cit.
152. It is not enough, however, to fall back on blanket statements of uncertain relevance from an operational point of view, such as the following: 'The exchange of ideas, news, messages and cultural works should help to reduce existing imbalances without prejudice to the sovereignty and dignity of all peoples or to their cultural identity.' ('Towards a New World Information Order', *Interim Report on Communication Problems in Modern Society*, p. 78, Paris, Unesco, September 1978.)
153. *General Report of the Yogyakarta Intergovernmental Conference on Cultural Policies in Asia, 10–19 December 1973*, p. 8.
154. P. Fougeyrollas, 'Modernisation des hommes, l'exemple du Sénégal', quoted by J. W. Lapierre, 'Le développement et la mort des cultures', *Esprit*, May 1970.
155. J. Berque, 'Towards a Better Transfer of Knowledge and Values', *Prospects, Quarterly review of Education*, Vol. VI, No. 3, 1976, p. 335.
156. To borrow an expression of P. Freire's, although admittedly in a different context.
157. J. Ziolkowski, 'Cultural Dimension of Development', *Cultures*, Vol. VI, No. 1, 1979, p. 28.
158. According to G. Rama, for example, culture involves the provision of a code which legitimates a status. ('Education, Social Structure and Styles of Development', *Prospects, Quarterly Review of Education*, Vol. VIII, No. 3, 1978.)
159. Cassirer, op. cit.
160. Ibid., p. 53.
161. Mignot-Lefebvre, op. cit., p. 522. See also J. Jouet, 'Critique de l'utilisation des médias légers dans le Tiers-Monde', *Revue Tiers-Monde*, Vol. XX, No. 79, July/September 1979.
162. Apropos of the small-scale media, it is difficult at the present time to appreciate fully the pros and cons. For a favourable view, see A. Mattelart, 'Mozambique, communication et transition au socialisme', *Revue du Tiers-Monde*, Vol. XX, No. 79, July/September 1979, For a more reserved judgement, see Mignot-Lefebvre, op. cit.
163. J. H. Lorenzi and E. Le Boucher, *Mémoires volées, satellites, micro-ordinateurs, robots, télématique, séries TV U.S., réseaux vidéo, banques de données . . . et demain la France*, p. 18, Paris, Ramsay, 1979.

164. J. Gunter and J. Theroux, 'Developing Mass Audiences for Educational Broadcasting: Two Approaches', *Prospects, Quarterly Review of Education*, Vol. VII, No. 2, 1977.
165. *General Report of the Accra Conference*, op. cit., p. 8.
166. Berque, op. cit., p. 338.
167. E. M. Moyo (1974), quoted in *Cross-cultural Broadcasting*, p. 18, Paris, Unesco, 1976. (Reports and Papers on Mass Communication, 77.)
168. The élites have to exert some control over the flow of information if they are to preserve their power (R. Kletter, L. Hirschhorn and H. Hudson, 'Access and the Social Environment in the United States of America' in F. J. Berrigan (ed.), *Access: Some Western Models of Community Media*, Paris, Unesco, 1977).
169. Kouyaté, op. cit., p. 22.

Chapter 5

The impact of TNCs on education

TNCs are also one of the vehicles for the transmission of a new educational model, either directly by means of their action in respect of vocational training through the intermediary of their subsidiaries, or indirectly by the changes they bring about in social, economic and cultural spheres. As the propagators of a specialized education whose content is directly related to its being turned to full account under modern industrial conditions, as the holders of knowledge in branches of technology which Third World countries lack and, lastly, as the users of adaptable, decentralized educational management models, TNCs bring their full weight to bear against the cumbrousness, unsuitability and lack of any genuine cultural foundation of the education systems which often prevail in the Third World.

The way in which the countries concerned absorb the educational impact of TNCs depends in large measure on the level of development of their education systems, but above all it depends on the extent to which those systems are consistent with the tasks assigned to education in economic and social development.

Development policies have been pursued in the firm belief that progress in the general provision of education, coupled with economic growth, would be able to strengthen the national cohesion of the newly independent countries. This hope was based on a widely accepted view of the part played by education:

Education is first and foremost the means whereby a society constantly renews that which makes its own existence possible. A society can only live if its members are sufficiently homogeneous. Education perpetuates and strengthens this homogeneity by fixing in advance in the child's mind the basic similarities necessarily implied by community life.[1]

The recent history of Third World countries shows that in many cases it is difficult for them to resist the centrifugal forces influencing their development. Frequently for example economic growth tends to exacerbate the political, social, ethnic or cultural rifts within the pluralistic nations which have been produced by colonial partitions and in dualistic economies, which still bear the deep imprint of external constraints.[2]

This being the case, the view is held in some quarters that the dominant education system, by legitimating such differences, far from helping to strengthen national cohesion, parallels the various forms of inequality and may actually reinforce them.[3] This should probably be seen as one of the consequences of insufficient development, which does not equip these countries to absorb the shock of the historical heritages to which their education is still in bondage. The fact is that most of them are obliged to combine, with a system for transmitting knowledge broadly geared to ancestral customs and religious beliefs, an education system produced by the action of colonialism and copied from the Western model, as well as new forms of education determined by their situation in the internationalization process and by the need to introduce new technologies. Within national communities the traditional method of transmitting knowledge has usually been relegated to a marginal position by an education which is a product of colonialism.

At the time when these societies emerge from their isolation and adopt new life-styles and techniques, education at school progressively replaces the education by example that is a feature of illiterate societies. But this education is only too often a slavish copy of the European model, including its functions: the functions of transmitting knowledge, recognizing social hierarchies (in the colonial era formal education served to legitimate the presence of the foreigner) and creating new social divisions (it was also one of the main causes of the present contempt for manual labour and the social distance between the educated and the illiterate).[4]

The inflexibility inherent in this type of education, and the manifold pressures and requirements resulting from the need to restore the national culture to its rightful place in education and at the same time introduce the radical changes called for by the new forms of development, explain why, notwithstanding the deployment of continually increasing resources and the substantial rate of increase in school enrolment in Third World countries, finance is not available to cover the unit costs of educating entire populations.[5]

In the less developed regions, during the period between 1960 and 1975, enrolment figures doubled in primary education and trebled in secondary education, while those for higher education rose almost four and a half times (Table 25). These growth rates considerably outstrip those for the more developed countries.

However, the progress of enrolment ratios masks great differences between regions and countries. Whereas some regions will probably have attained universal primary education by 1985 for the age-group 6 to 11 years (East Asia, Latin America), this objective is unlikely to be achieved in Africa or South Asia, still less in the twenty-five least-developed countries (Table 26).

TABLE 25. Enrolment trends by level of education from 1960 to 1975

Region	Level of education	Number of students enrolled		Multiplier
		1960	1975	
More developed	Primary	126 884	134 156	1.06
regions[1]	Secondary	48 261	81 013	1.68
(MDRs)	Higher	9 701	26 262	2.71
	Total	184 846	241 431	1.31
Less developed	Primary	115 980	238 373	2.06
regions	Secondary	22 293	59 074	3.10
(LDRs)	Higher	1 955	8 536	4.37
	Total	140 228	305 983	2.25
	Primary	19 401	44 243	2.28
Africa	Secondary	1 730	7 811	4.52
	Higher	180	865	4.81
	Total	21 311	52 919	2.48
	Primary	27 588	57 213	2.07
Latin America	Secondary	3 186	12 151	3.81
	Higher	572	3 451	6.03
	Total	31 346	72 815	2.32
	Primary	68 752	136 077	1.98
South Asia	Secondary	12 276	47 128	2.73
	Higher	1 303	4 581	3.52
	Total	82 331	187 786	2.15

1. North America, the Continent of Europe and Japan.
Source: Unesco, *Trends and Projections of Enrolment by Level of Education and by Age*, September 1977. (CSRE.21.)

TABLE 26. Enrolment ratios by age-group (boys and girls) (percentages)

Region	Age-group											
	6–11 years				12–17 years				18–23 years			
	1960	1965	1970	1975	1960	1965	1970	1975	1960	1965	1970	1975
MDRs	91	92	93	94	73	79	82	84	15.2	24.6	26.5	30.0
LDRs	46	54	58	62	22	28	32	35	3.4	5.0	7.0	8.7
Africa	33	40	44	51	17	22	26	31	1.9	2.7	4.1	5.8
Latin America	59	65	73	78	36	43	50	57	6.3	9.1	13.1	19.7
East Asia[1]	95	97	98	99	68	73	75	83	7.9	11.2	14.6	19.8
South Asia	48	56	58	61	19	26	29	31	3.3	5.0	6.4	6.9
25 LDCs[2]	13	19	22	28	9	11	14	17	0.7	1.1	1.8	2.7
Sahel countries[3]	9	15	17	19	5	9	12	13	0.5	1.1	1.9	2.6

1. Includes Japan, the Republic of Korea, Mongolia and Hong Kong.
2. These 25 countries are: Afghanistan, Benin, Bhutan, Botswana, Burundi, Chad, Ethiopia, Guinea, Haiti, Laos, Lesotho, Malawi, Maldives, Mali, Nepal, Niger, Rwanda, Sikkim, Somalia, Sudan, United Republic of Tanzania, Uganda, Upper Volta, Western Samoa and the Yemen Arab Republic.
3. These countries are: Chad, Mali, Mauritania, Niger, Senegal and Upper Volta.
Source: Unesco, *Trends and Projections of Enrolment by Level of Education and by Age*, September 1977. (CSRE.21.)

The persistence of a high rate of educational wastage in the less developed regions (45 per cent of children do not complete their fifth grade of primary schooling) throws doubt on the ability of education systems to reduce endemic illiteracy, particularly in Africa and South Asia (Table 27).

TABLE 27. Out-of-school youth both sexes (millions)

Region	Age-group					
	6–11 years			12–17 years		
	1965	1975	1985	1965	1975	1985
MDRs	9	7	7	23	19	12
LDRs	110	121	130	139	173	197
Africa	30	32	34	32	37	41
Latin America	14	11	9	18	19	19
East Asia	0.5	9.1	0.1	3	3	1
South Asia	66	77	86	88	115	137

Source: Unesco, *Trends and Projections of Enrolment by Level of Education and by Age*, September 1977. (CSRE.21.)

It is thus considered that the number of young people not attending school will continue to increase in these regions, and the total number of illiterates may rise from 742 million in 1970 to 884 million in 1980.

Taking steps to make it possible to combat these forms of educational underdevelopment would probably mean interfering with the very logic which has so far governed the development of these education systems. The fact is that enrolments at the secondary and higher levels of education are increasing at a much more rapid rate that in primary education due to the pressure of demand from the more privileged social strata, who are generally town-dwelling. Education systems linked to their social contexts have an extraordinary ability to perpetuate themselves unchanged and to resist innovation. To begin with,

the persistence of a part-feudal and part-colonial class structure accounts for the relative durability of the colonial system of education. The ruling class ... has consciously or unconsciously adopted some of the life-styles and interests of the old rulers. It has a vested interest in the perpetuation of élite institutions through which their wards could pass to qualify for positions of privilege in society.[6]

At a later stage, and directly in relation with the level of economic development, the upwardly mobile groups in the lower middle and middle classes aspire to élite status and help to preserve the same educational model. Furthermore, in some cases these education systems oppose their institutional inflexibility to the economic changes and reforms which governments would like to introduce. As noted by Durkheim, educational trends are in fact characterized by the interplay between the historical causes 'which determine and control change within education systems themselves' and the educational institutions 'which stand in the way by their very nature, that is to say, by virtue of certain structural invariants'.[7] Thus the increase in enrolment, which is welcome in itself, tends to take place in forms of education which only too often are unsuited to the needs engendered by development. In a large number of Third World countries educational 'stagflation' is becoming endemic, with increasing enrolment ratios and expanding education budgets seemingly going hand-in-hand with growing under- and unemployment (probably for other reasons)—in particular among young people and in towns—coupled with a persistent shortage of skilled manpower in the countryside.[8] However, there are two reasons why this pattern is not likely to become more widespread: first, states are no longer able to finance the increase in educational expenditure caused partly by the growing proportion of enrolments in higher education (current unit costs for a student in higher education represent twenty to thirty times those for a primary-school pupil; and, secondly, the government services of these states can no longer absorb university graduates who cannot find employment. Graduate unemployment is without any doubt less important numerically, and less permanent, than the unemployment produced by dualistic development among country-dwellers and in the urban subproletariat. Nevertheless, the gap between the aspirations of the middle classes and the employment prospects afforded them by degrees is in the long term explosively dangerous for the powers that be.

Are we then still to take the view that this type of educational development can 'guide children just as efficiently towards various social roles and, by contributing towards maintaining the social order, act as a powerful stabilizer in the evolution of social system'?[9] Must we not ask ourselves whether, on the contrary, the present contradiction does not stem from the threat to established authority represented by a model of educational

TABLE 28. Average annual growth-rate of GNP and public expenditure on education, 1965–74 (percentages)

	Years	GNP	Expenditure on education
Developed countries	1965–70	8.7	10.8
	1970–74	13.7	13.8
Developing countries	1965–70	7.7	9.8
	1970–74	17.3	22.0
Africa	1965–70	8.1	11.7
	1970–74	16.7	24.0
Latin America	1965–70	9.1	11.0
	1970–74	14.8	21.0
Asia	1965–70	11.7	12.0
	1970–74	20.0	24.0

Source: G. Carceles, 'World Public Expenditure: Education and Armaments, 1965–74', Prospects, Vol. VII, No. 4, 1977.

development which has been diverted from its primary function of consolidating an élite?

It is in the light of these two questions that we must interpret the educational reforms which countries are trying to introduce, and the ways in which they are affected by the forms taken by the internationalization of capital. How then are we to analyse the encounter between two educational models characterized by differences in their underlying values, the functions they perform and the way in which they are organized? According to P. Bourdieu and J. C. Passeron:

> The way in which education develops depends not only on the force of external constraints but also on the cohesion of its structures, that is to say both the resistance it can oppose to events and its ability to select and reinterpret chance phenomena and influences according to a logic whose general principles are given from the time that the function of inculcating a culture inherited from the past is taken over by a specialized institution with a staff of specialists working for it. Thus the history of a relatively independent system is the history of the way in which it systematizes accidental constraints and innovations in accordance with the norms which define it as a system.[10]

Whatever the specific forms taken by the encounter between these two educational models—the co-existence of two separate systems, one a formal, state system, and the other informal, controlled by TNCs, or a mingling of the two systems, with enterprises taking action within the formal system or, conversely, the state adapting its system to the needs generated by the presence of TNCs—the mode or pattern according to which individuals are socialized—the nation will emerge therefrom totally changed. By 'pattern of socialization' should be understood the transmission of a culture and the assimilation of a system of values, the inculcation of a hierarchic pattern or patterns and integration within the social body; to these should be added the acquisition of a skill or qualification, and incorporation in an occupation. This transformation of education must be interpreted in terms of a logic of integration or social exclusion (marginalization).

Will the search for a new combination of education and production capable of promoting development proceed by an overhaul of curricula to produce a blend of general and vocational education for the population as a whole? Or will this process result in widening the gulf between technical education, usually short, and a long course of general education which, in countries where the social structure is highly hierarchical, favours the selection and exclusion of certain categories at particular rungs on the educational ladder? Will the reallocation of resources be carried out in such a way as to favour a type of education that will promote development in rural areas, where the greater part of the population is concentrated in many countries? Or will training be encouraged in technologies that are used only in the modern, extensively internationalized production sector, with the risk that forms of dualism will be reinforced? Will the education policy followed help to strengthen national cohesion, and with it the participation of the people at large, by an education which 'creates awareness'? Or will education be still further split up into a hierarchical, specialized system justified by a technological division of labour, thus renewing the conditions on which inequality is based? Will the education system be geared to transmission of the values stemming from the national cultural heritage, or will it be divided between a traditional, inward-looking education which is likely to become equated with social exclusion and outward-looking forms of education which encourage extroversion? Lastly, will the state retain complete control over the future of the education system, or will it have to abandon its prerogatives in whole sectors of the transmission of knowledge?

These questions, which are not exhaustive, indicate the framework within which the encounter between TNCs and the nation-state takes place, and underscore the importance of the stake involved in education and its role in development.

Section 1

The transmission of an educational model by TNCs

In their strategy of internationalization through absorption and activities, TNCs have increasingly frequent recourse to action in the educational field. In the first place, we shall consider that educational activities constitute a market in themselves. The existence of this internal market accounts for a large number of TNC activities in respect of the production of educational goods and services. Secondly, we shall assume that educational action is of a deliberate, conscious and positive nature in so far as it is basically designed to provide TNCs with the qualified personnel required for their productive activities. Thirdly, TNCs incur expenditure on education in order to justify their presence in the host country. This is a typical case of ad hoc adaptation, the educational expenditure in which they participate being designed to demonstrate their social involvement. It is not possible to draw any absolutely clear-cut distinction between these three motives. We shall however assume that the 'sale of goods and services' attests to a desire to enter the education market. We shall next assume that direct action in the educational field is a by-product of firms' economic strategies, consisting as it does of the vocational training required when a subsidiary is set up, local diversification of education activities in order to integrate the subsidiary in its environment, and the constitution of transnational education networks corresponding to the way in which TNCs organize their production. Lastly, we shall consider the general impact of TNCs on education through the training–employment relationship, an impact which is more usually described as indirect.

Firms specializing in the sale of educational goods and services

Audio-visual techniques and modern transmission technology have together transformed the market for educational products, formerly limited to the publishing of schoolbooks. This proliferation of new educational materials also corresponds to a transformation of instructional systems and methods, with two purposes in mind: (a) to improve the way in which knowledge is transmitted, and in some cases to cope with the shortage of teachers; and (b) to be able to use new educational methods for highly specialized functions (literacy work, public health and hygiene, technical training), in respect of clearly identified groups.

Thus in the Ivory Coast, a television network was set up in 1971 in order to broadcast to rural populations an out-of-school programme designed to improve the standing of agricultural work, prevent the drift of young people towards the towns and provide instruction in civics.[11] Educational television programmes were also developed in Niger, the Samoan Islands, Thailand, and particularly, in 1974, in El Salvador, where they cover all levels of secondary education.[12]

The distinction between educational and general television is not really valid in developing countries, where not only the pressing social and cultural needs of the people but also their programme preferences lead the audience to seek above all information, education and an understanding of the society in which they live.[13]

Although the book, *Learning to Be*, stressed that radio was the only advanced communication technique which had found its proper place in the Third World, and that it should more and more be recognized as a particularly suitable medium for cultures based on oral transmission and unwritten values,[14] Unesco estimates that less than 5 per cent of total radio broadcasting time in the Third World can be classified as educational.[15] Furthermore, educational radio broadcasting has a long way to go before it can be said to have reached mass audiences; many of the projects carried out in the Third World in respect of audio-visual educational techniques are still no more than trial runs of innovations which have not yet proved their efficiency. In a recent review of sixty-five development-oriented radio projects, only five involved open broadcasts to non-captive mass audiences.[16] Of the twenty projects for which audience data were supplied, only three claimed anything like mass audiences. These were the Brazilian Movimento de Educação de Base (MEB) of the 1960s (with 111,006 participants), Colombia's ACPO Radio Sutatanza schools (with 167,451 pupils in 1968) and the United Republic of Tanzania's Health Campaign of 1973 (with 2 million participants). It should however be stressed that the United Republic of Tanzania was the only one of the three countries in which the audience exceeded 1 per cent of the total population.

A renewal of educational methods is expected to result from the use of small-scale media such as recording systems, new information-storage carriers (tapes, discs, cassettes), reproduction equipment and audio-visual aids. These media are generally more suited to the decentralized and highly specialized programmes introduced in the field of out-of-school education.[17] Such small-scale media are also very well suited to meet the shortcomings of communication systems in developing countries.

Their flexibility, moderate cost and easy handling are all cited as features in their favour, given the financial resources of these countries and the shortage of skilled personnel. In addition, employed in limited geographical areas, they can use local languages and thus be adapted to the ethnic and linguistic fragmentation of each country.[18]

In this way, for J. Jouet, small-scale media are seen as corresponding to a new philosophy of development based on self-sufficiency, participation and community expression. However, when such media are introduced into the socio-political fabric of developing countries, numerous problems arise which

> emphasize the gap between a real, two-way process of communication and the practical deployment of this technology. . . . The way in which they are used as a means of social action remains limited to marginal experiments, and has little lasting impact on the living conditions of the small communities concerned.[19]

The market in small-scale audio-visual equipment is dominated by a few firms: for super-8 films and cameras, Kodak, Chinon, Bell and Howell, Beaulieu, Philips, Sony, to mention only the most important. Sanyo, Akai, JVC and Nivico share between them the market in small-scale video equipment. As is the case with any technology, small-scale media do not always play a neutral role. New small-scale systems, or microsystems, are every bit as much integrated as the mass media in the TNCs' network of economic and commercial domination. Dependence in respect of hardware and maintenance services is coupled with the impact of an exogenous culture influencing the ways in which they are used.[20] The market for educational materials (i.e. hardware) is accompanied by its own closely connected market for educational programmes and services (software). It is in fact becoming increasingly difficult to distinguish between the two as regards the marketing flow: educational games are now electronic; conversely, mini-computing equipment and the most recent types of calculator come complete with programmes for learners. This accounts for the fact that this new market has attracted firms such as publishing houses, which in this way can give a fresh slant to their range of traditional products (schoolbooks, educational games and, above all, films and mounted transparencies). Firms producing electronic, audio-visual or reproduction equipment find here a new field of application for their products and a diversification of their activities. Lastly, there are also firms specializing in large-scale communication media (film and television-programme production firms).

It seems an established fact that in electronics, communications and publishing TNCs control the future of the market for educational products, whether in regard to technology, production or distribution. However, the market is still more potential than real, and is concentrated in the most developed countries. For the time being, these new educational products are being introduced into developing countries through aid programmes provided by AID or American foundations or universities, which bring about or accompany educational reforms in these countries.[21]

A. Mattelart cites as examples Iran, Indonesia, Nigeria and El Salvador.

Less direct than the effects caused by the infiltration of technology into developing countries are those deriving from the educational programmes broadcast by media such as television. The best example of the international distribution and success of a televised educational serial is provided by *Sesame Street*, produced by a non-profit institution (Children's Television Workshop), one of whose aims is to improve the use of electronic media, and in particular television, as a means for teaching children. CTW is financed from governmental resources and by foundations, and also, more directly, by TNCs (see Table 29). Other firms helped with the translation of the serial and its distribution in developing countries, for example ABC and Xerox for Latin America, RCA, General Foods, and the Time-Life Group. The success of the programme was overwhelming, since by 1975, four years after it first appeared, ninety countries had applied to purchase it. In February 1971, the *Unesco Courier* hailed the occasion by commenting that this type of activity was a model for international television. 'As opposed to the programmes filled with violence found in so many countries, it brings to children's TV a series of wit and humour, devoid of any violence, containing the positive message that no problem can be solved without co-operation.' Two countries, the United Kingdom and Peru, turned down this children's educational serial. The BBC took the view that *Sesame Street* was the product of a still prevalent philosophy according to which television should be watched absolutely passively: American children, according to the BBC, just sat looking at television for hours on end, whereas in all the programmes it produced for British children, the BBC tried to discourage a passive attitude in front of the screen and sought to stimulate the imagination and the intelligence, and to encourage creativity and activity. In Peru, the Ministry of Education explained its refusal in 1973 chiefly on the grounds of the incompatibility between the objectives of the reform and the ideological standpoint of the American programme.[22] The distribution of this serial, intended for a pre-school public, was on such a scale that its promoters extended the experiment to a group of 7-to-10-year-old children for whom a programme *The Electric Company* was produced. ITT has also financed a children's television serial, *Blue Marble*, broadcast in fifty countries.[23]

Thus the trend seems to be towards internationalizing television production, solely with a view to increasing the profitability of serials by seeking the maximum possible distribution.

Direct TNC educational action

There are several ways of studying the different forms in which TNCs take direct action in regard to education. The first is to establish a typology of all the forms of educational action by firms and then, by evaluating their relative importance, to try to apprehend a logic of TNC behaviour in this field. A preliminary survey of the field might lead to the following classification of activities as regards the formal education system: (a) providing funds for the general national education budget, or to cover the total or partial cost of particular schools; (b) financing studies by providing grants or

TABLE 29. Sponsors and financing of the Children's Television Workshop

Institutions	Budgetary years ($ thousands)		
	1968–70	1970–71	1971–72
US Dept Health Education and Welfare (HEW)	4 000	2 900	7 000
Ford Foundation	1 538	1 000	1 000
Carnegie Foundation	1 500	600	1 000
J. and M. Markle Foundation	250	—	—
Corp. for Public Broadcasting (CPB)	750	500	2 000
Mobil Oil Corporation			250
Revenue other than from TV	126.3	259	165.7
Other TV activities	206.7	84	—
TOTAL	8 371	5 343	11 415.7

Source: *A Special Report from the Children's Television Workshop*, New York, 1972.

funds; (c) the transfer or loan of educational premises; (d) heightening teachers' awareness of problems (conferences, travel); (e) the donation or sale of educational equipment (books, instructional material, machine-tools for learners); (f) educational assistance for certain types of training in the form of paid or voluntary work by teachers from the TNC systems; (g) the assumption of responsibility for trainees coming from the formal system; (h) participation in drawing up the overall national education policy and also policy in regard to school management; and (i) participation in research conducted in university laboratories.

As regards the out-of-school system, activities would include: (a) vocational training in the enterprise; (b) the setting up or part-financing of non-formal educational activities in schools as well as in associations, clubs, trade unions, etc.; (c) courses in literacy, public health, home economics, child care, etc.; (d) technical training in industry or agriculture as part of sales services; and (e) media-based educational action (television, radio, the press, etc.).

Quite apart from the virtually insurmountable obstacles involved in the quantification of activities which do not all give rise to a monetary transaction, and the need to have a very large number of cases in order to make an exhaustive study, it is not certain that such an evaluation would yield a true picture of TNC behaviour. The fact is that this typology is only a classification of the educational resources used, which is meaningless unless these resources are studied in relation to TNC strategies or economic constraints.

The second way of considering TNC educational activities is to place them in the context of the firm's adaptation. We saw earlier that TNCs adapted themselves in order to develop their ultimate aims. The direct educational activities they conduct take on their full significance when they are seen as actions which facilitate the firm's integration in its environment. These act as a substitute for changes in the firm's internal structure, and constitute an essential prerequisite for the pursuit of its aims. In order to approach the question in these terms we have addressed our study to three types of consideration which interest firms: (a) considerations linked to the establishment of an affiliate or subsidiary company in a developing country; (b) considerations linked to the integration of their subsidiary in the society of the developing country; and (c) considerations linked to their subsidiary's operation in the framework of a transnational organization of production.

These considerations do not seem to be entirely differentiated, even chronologically, in the actual operation of a TNC subsidiary in a developing country. In fact, the reality is usually to a greater or lesser degree a combination of the three types. However, the distinction makes it possible to bring out operational categories of behaviour to which can be made to correspond different forms of action in the educational field. For example in situation (a), a predominant feature is educational activities designed to facilitate the establishment of a subsidiary by training the personnel recruited so as to adapt them as speedily as possible to the firm's productive and organizational processes. In situation (b), educational activities are mainly directed towards the firm's environment, and are designed to forge a set of links which will show the subsidiary to be completely integrated in the national community of the host country. In situation (c), on the contrary, educational activities help to impart an increasingly supranational—and, in consequence, increasingly uniform—quality to the firm's mode of operation.

The relative importance of these considerations, and the pattern into which they fall, vary depending on the sector and on whether the TNC is organized on a centralized or decentralized basis. This is not however to suggest that there will be any uniformity of behaviour on the part of one and the same TNC in all countries. Educational activities are in most cases introduced with a view to adapting the firm to what it perceives as being local constraints. Later on, we shall therefore have to compare these education policies with the conditions and policies prevailing in the developing countries.

Establishment of subsidiaries and method of training

Here we are considering the very common case in which the firm's training effort is assumed to remain narrowly confined to the needs generated by the establishment of a subsidiary in a developing country. It is for this reason that vocational training policy is always highly dependent on the policy for the recruitment and utilization of local personnel. In many cases, whatever the level of qualification, the TNC cannot find locally either the degree, or more important still, the type of technical skill it seeks. It is generally considered that the difficulties experienced by firms in recruiting in developing countries begin at the technician level, and increase the higher up one goes in the technical and administrative hierarchy.[24] There is however reportedly nothing to indicate that as regards in-service training up to the level of intermediate executives and technical personnel, TNCs encounter problems that are very different from those experienced by local enterprises in similar economic and cultural conditions and having reached a comparable degree of development.[25] Can it therefore be considered that the educational level of the population of a country or region can be regarded by the firm as a criterion in the choice of a location for a subsidiary? For R. B. Helfgott, who has carried out a survey on a sample of United States-based TNCs, the human-resources factor rarely plays a key role in decisions as regards location, though it substantially influences production efficiency.[26] The fact is that by comparison with other factors which may enter into the choice of location and which it is difficult for the firm to influence, such as the location of the market, suppliers or raw materials, the cost of labour and political stability, the human-resources factor is still the one that it is the easiest to act on. Three types of attitude can, according to Helfgott, be envisaged if one is faced with an inadequate supply of human resources: the training of local personnel, the use of expatriates and the restructuring of the technologies used.[27] A study carried out at the instigation of UNITAR on twenty-eight firms established in the Philippines and Mexico (fourteen of them subsidiaries of United States-based TNCs, and fourteen under local management) throws light on this subject.[28] Only four American firms and one local firm changed their production processes or the organization of their factories to cope with the shortage of skilled personnel. The majority of the firms preferred to train their personnel, recruit expatriates or increase their supervisory personnel. It should however be noted that out of twenty-four firms providing training, only seven organized training courses: the other seventeen introduced on-the-job training; thirteen firms had a separate training budget. On an average, the United States-based firms did not devote any more resources to training than the local firms though, on the other hand, it appears that they invested more in training their supervisory personnel.

The proportion of expatriate personnel employed by subsidiaries varies depending on the TNC's sector of activity, and also depending on prevailing employment conditions in the host country. Table 30, compiled from an ILO survey, shows clearly that the proportion of expatriates employed varies depending on the hierarchical level in the firm.

It will also be noted that firms gradually replace their expatriate personnel by local staff. This trend, which is, in varying degrees, almost general in TNC subsidiaries located in developing countries, can be accounted for by three categories of reasons:

The expatriate personnel brought in to set up the subsidiary cease to be necessary when production, marketing and management processes have installed and standards of quality and output have been reached.

Expatriate personnel cost the firm more, and it is becoming difficult to recruit staff willing to go abroad.

In replacing expatriate personnel by local personnel the firm is meeting demands which are frequently voiced by the host country.

However, the replacement of expatriates by local staff is still relatively limited at the level of higher supervisory personnel. The TNC retains a restricted number of expatriates locally so as to facilitate communication and cohesion within the group, and to provide better control over the management of the subsidiary. Thus, even in developed countries where they could

TABLE 30. Percentages of foreign personnel among higher executives and foremen (1969–73)

Country	Firm	Higher supervisory personnel		Intermediate supervisory personnel		Foremen	
		1969	1973	1969	1973	1969	1973
Brazil	L M E	50	50	60	25	20	10
	Philips	60	50	10	0	0	0
	Siemens	86	57	52	35	2	0
Colombia	L M E	100	80	30	19	50	0
	Philips	36	28	12	4	0	0
	Siemens	100	100	60	40	0.4	0
India	Philips	20.6	10	14.9	1.6	0	0
	Siemens	60	40	16	2	0	0
Malaysia	L M E	—	75	—	0	—	0
	Philips	—	100	—	33.3	—	9
Mexico	L M E	100	60	50	30	15	0
	Philips	70	54	8	5.8	0	0
	Siemens	60	50	43	33	0	0

Source: ILO, Social and Labour Practices of Multinational Enterprises in the Metal Trades, Geneva, ILO, 1976.

find the necesssary skilled personnel, the firms cited by ILO retain a percentage of expatriate professional personnel (Philips, United Kingdom, 14 per cent; Philips, Sweden, 10 per cent; Siemens, Switzerland, 16 per cent). Generally speaking, firms take a very pragmatic approach to local recruitment problems. For this reason the resources used to train personnel owe much to circumstance, as the firm can combine internal with local resources for this purpose.[29] The bulk of training is provided within the TNC, but if the educational machinery in the host country lends itself thereto, the TNC may use facilities made available by the country. From the many examples given by ILO we would cite Metal Box in India, which has recourse to national training services when these provide suitable programmes, but draws up its own programme as necessary. The firm assists in the vocational training of students in official institutions, its own professional personnel providing certain courses. In Malaysia, intensive courses in machine finishing, management, foremanship, supervision and business subjects are provided in official institutions and supplemented by specialized training in the firm. These institutions also provide trainee courses. However, it is recognized that the majority of firms prefer where possible to be responsible for the training programme. A survey carried out on sixty-one United States-based TNCs shows that with two-thirds of them, training is an integral part of the contract for technology transfer; it concerns chiefly production and management personnel, and to a much lesser extent indus-

trial scientists and engineers. In 85 per cent of cases firms remain responsible for the training programme.[30] This may be due to a variety of reasons:
- There are no local educational facilities for the firm to train its personnel under clearly defined conditions in the special fields required by a technology that is usually new to the host country.
- In most cases it is better and more efficient for the firm to train its personnel directly on the job, by strengthening its supervisory personnel or having professional staff or technicians from the home country work alongside the local personnel.
- Generally speaking, the organization, working methods and procedures introduced into the subsidiary, and the standards of productivity and quality criteria applied, tend to be modelled on previous experience so as to safeguard the efficiency and cohesion of the group. In such cases firms prefer to make use of internal training courses in other subsidiaries of the group.
- Lastly, through internal training the firm can identify with its objectives and values the professional staff which is to be responsible for managing the subsidiary. Both communication between subsidiaries, and control procedures, will be made easier as a result.

In this connection it should be noted that the tendency is for firms to strengthen training activities, and to institute a specific function of managerial responsibility for training (or for social questions separate from the traditional function of personnel management). Firms that have to establish subsidiaries abroad are now able to provide themselves with facilities for solving their specific training problems.[31] All the indications are that subsidiaries are increasingly using the training facilities made available to them by headquarters in preference to those of the host country. At a time when the developing countries are beginning to acquire a financial stake in TNC subsidiaries, and when local professional staff are replacing expatriates, internal training, particularly at headquarters, becomes a key method of exercising control over subsidiaries and integrating them more effectively in the TNC structure.

The basis for the distinction between training provided locally and that provided in countries other than the host country, which is one of the specific features of TNC vocational training, is difficult to determine, since types of training vary considerably depending on the firm, the country, the level of qualification, the type of technology and circumstances. However, the cost of training, which can be appreciably increased by the cost of travel for trainees or instructors between the host country and the parent establishment, is an important criterion in the choice of the place of training. It is for this reason that training for less skilled jobs, involving a large number of trainees, is usually provided locally by means of direct apprenticeship on the job. By contrast, the smaller number of professional staff receiving management training are more often trained at the firm's headquarters.[32] This distinction is not always so clear-cut. For example, for the training of production and factory assistants, foremen and heads of teams in its subsidiary CAPRAL, in the Ivory Coast, Nestlé combines instruction provided on the spot by a professional from the parent establishment with training courses attended by some of the participants in Switzerland or in other subsidiaries of the group in Europe. With SIEM, a subsidiary of the Carnaud group in the Ivory Coast, training is carried out at two levels: professional staff and foremen go to France to attend training courses in the group's factories. However, these training courses are designed to enable participants to learn about changes which have taken place at all levels in the group, rather than to receive training; this system is one of the key mechanisms in the flow of information. The second level of training is provided on the spot, for factory hands and maintenance staff.[33]

Local diversification of educational activities

In many cases firms established in developing countries extend their education policy to include fields not strictly related to the vocational training of their personnel. Such action is usually presented by the firms as a contribution to the development effort, or as a social responsibility.[34] It is very difficult to convey an overall view, and particularly to evaluate these highly diversified activities, since they are largely determined by the firm's local environment. On the other hand, it is possible to classify these activities roughly on the basis of cases presented by the firms themselves. These examples cannot be taken as a general rule; they nevertheless show that the educational activities of TNCs which are not directly related to their productive activity are not exceptional, but one form of response by firms to environmental constraints.

A transnational petroleum corporation in Venezuela[35]

In the case presented here, the International Chamber of Commerce seeks to show that the TNC has made a substantial contribution to the transfer of knowledge and know-how, thus facilitating the development of the country, both by educational activities linked to its commercial activities, and through the intermediary of a foundation wholly financed by the TNC. According to the authors of this study, when recruiting, the firm was faced with two major difficulties: first, the absence of even a minimum level of education as a basis for the acquisition of techniques (an illiterate population) and, second, the lack of a sufficiently wide range of skills on the labour market.

As regards vocational training, the firm estimates that it has provided training at one level or another to almost all its employees. In the last eight years considered, 2,800 operatives received basic training, 2,000 Venezuelan nationals attended courses in training institutions outside the firm, and 560 pursued studies abroad free of charge, with the result that, by the end of 1969, 96.3 per cent of all employees, and 82 per cent of the supervisory personnel were Venezuelan. As regards activities not directly related to its production activities, the firm draws attention to its establishment of a crafts centre (after fifteen years' activity, taken over by the state), co-operation with universities (grants given to students wishing to study abroad, courses given by the firm's engineers, etc.), the gift of equipment to fit up public or private university laboratories and of documentation to a university library, the establishment of a film library, etc. Stress is laid on highly satisfactory co-operation with state bodies, both in respect of the 2 per cent of the total amount of salaries paid towards technical training, and as regards participation in the work of the National Institute for Educational Co-operation (INCE), a body responsible for planning vocational training.

Through its foundation, the firm has lent its support to agricultural development, with the declared aim of reducing the country's dependence on imported products. The agricultural department, with its two experimental stations, has made a determined effort to develop new techniques: in this way 12,000 agricultural workers have been trained, courses given to their wives (hygiene, domestic work), and group clubs set up for their children—similar to the '4 H' clubs in the United States—where they receive training in market gardening, bee-keeping and chicken farming. University agricultural education is encouraged by the award of grants and the provision of new courses (attended by students from other Latin American countries). Continuing support is being given to an agricultural college set up in 1967, which trains 500 young men yearly; studies are financed in association with the Ministry of Health, and documents, newspapers, films and slides are disseminated free of charge in order to extend knowledge of certain agricultural techniques. In other fields, the foundation contributes towards the financing of forty-six vocational schools, attended by 12,000 students; it is providing finance to the amount of $300,000 towards the establishment of an institute of advanced administrative studies modelled on the Harvard Graduate School of Business Administration, and has donated laboratories to the Faculty of Medicine and equipment to the hospital at Maracaibo.

A great number of finer details should be sketched in, and additional information provided, in order to obtain a real picture of the part played by transnational petroleum corporations in Venezuela. P. Furter stresses that the oil industry forms a virtual enclave which imports its capital goods from abroad and uses a very advanced technology, employing relatively little labour, so that its direct impact on the industrialization process has been very limited.[36] On the other hand, its indirect impact is considerable, due both to the increased rate of internal migration and the flow of oil revenue, which is bringing about for the first time an integrated domestic market and, above all, to the fiscal resources made available to the public sector. However, the distribution of revenue has remained very unequal, and while there is progressive urbanization and a growing industrialized sector geared to import substitution, this sector is primarily aimed at satisfying the consumer requirements of a small privileged stratum of the population. This has brought about two consequences: first, the diversification of industry in the context of a restricted market, which has resulted in leaving a great part of production capacity under-utilized and hampering vertical integration; second, the use of an advanced technology which is essential to meet demand from the privileged classes, who expect to have products of an equivalent standard to foreign ones. The constraints imposed by this technology, bearing in mind local conditions, increase costs, put up the price to the consumer of the end product, and still further increase the restricted and selective nature of the market.

To these comments, which show that the oil sector has not provided a basis for balanced job-creating industrial growth, can be added a number of criticisms in regard to the educational activities carried out. As users of a very advanced technology, the TNCs in Venezuela very early on lost interest in their directly subordinate staff. In addition, knowing that they were going to be nationalized by 1980 at the latest, while at the same time bound by law to contribute 2 per cent of their salary costs to vocational training, oil companies invested primarily in training their higher professional staff, or in rural schools.[37] The Venezuelan Government is therefore now giving a new impetus to training in the oil industry, with a new institution, INAPET, whose facilities include training for young people, with the average age of workers being 46 years and that of professional staff 42 years.

General Motors in South Africa[38]

In this case the firm, through its vice-president, is led to defend its activities in South Africa in the face of criticism levelled by radical movements, anti-racist associations and a number of American churches. General Motors is criticized on two levels: (a) it does nothing to challenge the social order in that country; and (b) by its very presence, it sanctions the government in power.[39]

General Motors points to its labour policy ('equal pay for equal qualifications') as being free from racial discrimination (in this respect it should be noted that of 3,462 employees, 16 per cent are black Africans, 53 per cent 'Coloured', usually Indians, and 31 per cent white). Vocational training is used to raise the level of qualification of non-whites (workshop technicians and sales staff). Bursaries are granted to the children of non-white employees (500 in 1972). The firm also contributes 43 per cent of its welfare assistance to organizations concerned with the advancement of Africans and 'Coloured' people. Through the National Study Loan and Bursary Fund it finances a university for 'Coloured' people and three African universities. The limitations on these activities are stressed by the participants:

Labour legislation is centralized by white trade unions: 'a non-white cannot supervise a white'.

Racial discrimination is practised in the education system (only 1 per cent of blacks in South Africa reach the level of higher education and thus benefit from bursaries).

The firm is also obliged to go along with the government in power, and it provides finance for the South African Foundation, whose purpose is to promote the policy of apartheid.

This case is fairly representative of the social and political constraints that weigh on a firm, and of the response it can make through its education policy. Should it therefore be considered that a firm's education policy does not reflect a 'managerial ethic' or a 'social responsibility',[40] but rather that it constitutes a component, in its own right, of the firm's strategy? In that case two questions should be asked:

First, is it not a fact that the tendency of firms to become involved in socio-educational activities other than the training of their personnel, and their collaboration with the machinery of state, are primarily determined by the need to retain their footing in the host country? In this case, firms making use of raw materials, or engaged in agriculture, should be among the first to become involved.

Second, is it not a fact that the socio-educational activities of TNCs form part of a publicity strategy for improving their image so as to strengthen their commercial policy and make it easier to recruit?

Social responsibility
While it is an assumption difficult to verify, it is nevertheless probable that activities coming under the heading of 'social responsibilities' contribute to the firm's image and are highlighetd in the reports made to shareholders and disseminated to the public. For example, the Exxon report contains a statement of its directors' philosophy as regards social responsibility. In their view, society and the enterprise have shared interests. Admittedly for the enterprise the primary aim is economic, but it cannot overlook the fact that it operates in a social context. Thus educational activities are integrated in a broader policy for employment, consumption and environmental protection. Through its Education Foundation, Exxon has financed a large number of educational activities, in particular in the United States, but also elsewhere. Intercol, an Exxon subsidiary in Colombia, provides general education and basic technical education to children in the poor districts south of Bogotá. Similarly, financial contributions have been made in the Middle East, to the American University in Beirut and the American University of Cairo. The firm takes educational action on its prospection sites in Saudi Arabia and South-East Asia. Its directors uphold the idea that, in order to ensure its long-term survival and profitability, private enterprise must be increasingly sensitive to a wide range of public needs and desires, and be in a position to respond to them.[41] Exxon activities in the field of education and culture are also the subject of extensive publicity in the firm's publications, as witness the following extract from its French office's house magazine:

Exxon assistance to education and culture

For many years now, Exxon Corporation has been providing assistance to education and taking part in cultural activities of general interest. Its contribution increases yearly, and in 1976 the amounts it earmarked in the United States for this purpose exceeded $20 million, an increase of more than 20 per cent over the previous year.

Approximately half of this expenditure was allocated to education, including assistance provided through the Exxon Education Foundation, which allocated approximately $5 million to higher education, one of the aims being to encourage innovations. In particular, a new programme was introduced in 1976 to provide financial assistance for research into more efficient methods for financing higher education.

Exxon has also made donations to the famous Massachusetts Institute of

Technology, the Californian State Institute of Technology, Stanford University, the Texas State University and Chicago University, under a five-year programme for the financing of studies on energy policy and technology. Exxon has also continued its assistance to a teaching group, the Energy Task Force, whose aim is to help secondary and higher education institutions throughout the country to cut down on their own consumption of energy.

Other donations have been made to number of technical education institutions, either directly or through the governmental National Fund for Minority Engineering.

Exxon has contributed more than $4 million to financing television broadcasts dealing with the arts and scientific subjects, and has spent $400,000 on educational broadcasting, including bilingual serials for children.

As part of events organized to celebrate theb icentenary of the United States, Exxon contributed to the mounting of exhibitions in New York and Washington.

The Exxon group is also taking part in the travelling exhibition *The Treasures of Tutankhamen*, which is to be shown in six major towns in the United States between now and April 1979.

Elsewhere in the world, the group's subsidiaries also provide assistance to a great variety of activities on behalf of education and culture. In France, Esso S.A.F. has for many years now been conducting a very full programme including, for example, the holding of conferences in secondary and higher education institutions, organized tours of factories and industrial establishments for members of the teaching profession, participation in educational exhibitions, debates and experiments, the dissemination of pamphlets and audio-visual aids, etc.[42]

In another magazine of the same kind, F. P. Wilson upholds the idea that a well-run multinational corporation furthers the sole aim of helping to create a more dynamic international economy for the benefit of all. Education is also the best example of this aim with Union Carbide, which has built an elementary school at Rantsou, near the vanadium mines it works in South Africa. The education provided is intended almost entirely for employees or their children, and is not confined to technical subjects. Assistance is also given to the children of employees who wish to follow secondary studies. At its mine in Selukwe, in Zimbabwe, the Union Carbide subsidiary has introduced an almost complete education system, since it comprises primary and secondary schools and even a business school. Union Carbide Mexicana has financed a higher-education college at Apadaca, with emphasis on training for chemists and biologists.[43]

In its annual report for 1978, ITT groups together under the heading of 'social responsibility' its activities in the fields of public health, education and development, and its production of educational television broadcasts. Since 1973, ITT has financed and organized twenty-three series of keynote conferences on special subjects, held at the universities of Atlanta, New York, Seton Hall, Missouri and Washington, with reports disseminated in high schools. Since 1971 it has awarded 300 grants for study in the United States. Under a three-year programme organized by the Chicago Institute for Cultural Affairs it has launched vast development programmes for the villages of Ijede in Nigeria and Kohduheri in the Republic of Korea. During the first operational year (1979) emphasis was to be laid on the teaching of modern methods of cultivation, animal husbandry and hygiene.[44]

TABLE 31. The ten leading foundations in the United States in 1973 ($ millions)

Foundation	Capital	Annual budget	Activity
Ford Foundation	3 049	224	Motor vehicles
Robert Wood Johnson	1 302	20	Medical equipment
Lilly Endowment Inc.	1 139	31	Pharmaceuticals
Rockefeller Foundation	830	41	Banking
Kresge Foundation	658	26	Supermarkets
Andrew Mellon Foundation	636	27	Banking
Pew Memorial Trust	580	14	Petroleum
W. K. Kellogg Foundation	577	20	Food
Duke Endowment	367	19	Tobacco
Carnegie Corp. of N.Y.	338	16	Iron and Steel

Source: Business Week, 7 December 1974, quoted by A. Mattelart, Multinationales et systèmes de communication, p. 199, Paris, Anthropos, 1976.

All these 'adaptive' activities, now grouped together under the heading of 'social responsibility', have been particularly developed in countries such as the United States, where donations to charities or educational institutions can be deducted from companies' taxable profits.

In this respect TNCs have not made any innovations, but their size and the extension of their activities to Third World countries make them specially involved in development-aid projects. The overall importance of these activities is difficult to evaluate, but United States Senate reports estimate that contributions by American firms to charities are in the neighbourhood of 1 per cent of their pre-tax profits (0.66 per cent for the lowest contributions, 3 per cent for the highest). Altogether 1,500 firms in the United States have established foundations, 40 per cent of whose funds goes to education.[45] Between 1970 and 1974 the amount of these contributions in the United States rose from $1.4 billion to $2 billion.[46] A copious literature has grown up on the question of whether firms acted primarily in their own interests, or from purely altruistic motives in response to social expectations. From the perusal of this literature it is not possible to conclude one way or the other. Some directors consider that aid to education should be selective, since only too often firms send people to universities or institutions which denigrate the firms themselves, and are opposed to free enterprise.[47] Others, on the other hand, consider that the logic of self-interest is bound to fail, since in any case the provision of finance to private educational institutions is ultimately in the public interest. Firms should give aid to education as a whole, rather than try to control the use made of their funds.[48]

The case of Ciba-Geigy

The case presented below, taken from the firm's publications,[49] suggests that Ciba-Geigy proposes to go even beyond the concept of social responsibility, and to adopt a moral philosophy for its development activities.

1. *Ciba-Geigy in the Third World*

Ciba-Geigy's geographical presence in the Third World reflects the importance of its sales. Of its 44 affiliated and joint companies, two-thirds are in the countries in Group 1.* Its 93 technical assistance offices and agencies are also scattered throughout Groups 1, 2 and 3. Its turnover in Third World countries amounted in 1977 to 2.4 billion Swiss francs. The increase in turnover since 1972 (54 per cent) was more rapid than in the industrialized countries, and followed the growth rates for gross national product. Customers in the 'South' group suffered less from the recession than those in the 'North'. It is interesting to note that four-fifths of Ciba-Geigy's turnover in the Third World is in Group 1, the 'industrialized' countries, and that only a tenth, corresponding to 2 per cent of total turnover, is in Group 2 and a further tenth in Group 3 (thanks to India). Turnover by branch shows a similar picture.

2. *Ciba-Geigy's concept of its role in development*

With Roche and Sandoz, Ciba-Geigy has been participating since 1959 in the Basel Foundation for Aid to Developing Countries.

It was in 1974 that we formulated our 'business policy in Third World countries', thus giving specific form to the principle on which we operate, under which we are prepared to respect the special conditions in developing countries and agree to run higher risks there. This new policy made provision for our philosophy and our products and services to be adapted to the specific needs of Third World countries, and was aimed at bringing about closer commercial co-operation with these countries. It also laid down the criteria for a philanthropic type of aid, free from commercial considerations. This approach should have a positive effect on the development of the countries in which we carry out our activities (or attenuate the negative effects); its results should be worth while in relation to outlay, and should promote sincere co-operation. If an enterprise such as ours supports or maintains development aid projects of a philanthropic nature unrelated to its own work, it is not pursuing commercial objectives, but rather acting from the conviction that it is meeting its social responsibility and improving understanding of the needs of the Third World, so as to break down barriers of mistrust on all sides.

3. *Activities carried out*

Development aid projects:
Ifakara (Tanzania): School for medical assistance personnel ('bare-foot doctors') in co-operation with Hoffmann-Laroche, Sandoz S.A. and the Swiss Institute of Tropical Medicine.
Giyani-Gasankulu: Agricultural College, in co-operation with other Swiss companies and the Protestant churches of Basel.
Djakarta (Indonesia): School for medical laboratory assistants. Ciba-Geigy put up the capital expenditure and three years' operating costs, and then handed the school over to the state.

*Group 1: annual per capita income more than $375.
Group 2: annual per capita income less than $375 and more than $200.
Group 3: annual per capita income less than $200.

Ga-Rankuwa (Bophuthatswana): School of Arts and Crafts, in co-operation with Swiss companies.

Support given to specific projects operated by welfare societies, missions, doctors, etc., in Africa, Central America, South America and Asia.

The sending of United Nations experts to Mali, Indonesia, Ghana, the United Republic of Tanzania and the Economic Commission for Latin America (ECLA).

Are transnational education networks on the way?

With some enterprises, training activities are not confined to ad hoc actions, limited in time and usually made necessary by the recruitment needs of a subsidiary which is being established in an area where labour does not possess the necessary qualifications. Their training policy—some speak of education policy—is inseparable from their general policy, and each new local educational activity is integrated in a network designed and operated at worldwide level.[50] Thus, educational activity is a separate sector of the firm, with its own administration, teaching staff, programmes and research. In this case the size of the budget allocated to educational activities, which is decided centrally by the firm, depends only indirectly on a subsidiary's local needs; it transcends those needs, in the same way as it transcends the legislation in force in each country in regard to continuing education.

A transnational education network as defined above can only be created in cases where for example the firm itself is on a very large scale, employs large numbers of persons in many countries, occupies a dominant position in a given technology, is in the forefront of technological progress and lastly, and above all, has achieved substantial internationalization and also rationalization of production, necessitating uniform control and management procedures. However, these conditions are not enough to account for the greater investment in training by some firms than others. It appears rather that it is the actual type of product which, in both its external dimension, the development of the firm's market, and its internal dimension, the development of human resources, determines the need for an integrated training network.

Thus in the case of a United Kingdom based corporation[51] which produces tractors, combine harvesters, excavators, loading vehicles and diesel engines, vocational training is an integral part of its marketing practice. The fact is that it is necessary for customers to have the minimum technical knowledge to enable them to use and maintain the equipment purchased. A training centre was therefore established in the United Kingdom in 1947, and subsequently copied on a smaller scale in seven other countries (Australia, Brazil, France, India, Italy, South Africa, Spain). The United Kingdom centre is staffed by twenty full-time instructors; it receives 150 foreign students yearly, recommended by the company's distributors abroad or by a government. Courses are free of charge, and may last up to three months. The centres are supplemented by a mobile training team, used in major agricultural development projects in developing countries. The firm also supplies equipment, instructors, publications and short films to national establishments providing training in the use of agricultural machinery. In Colombia, the South American centre for training in agricultural mechanization is run jointly by the Servicio Nacional de Aprentizaje (management, premises, land), FAO (the financing of courses for Latin American students) and the firm (equipment and instructor). Similarly in Kenya, a training institute for peasant farmers was established on a tripartite basis by the Government of Kenya, the firm and the British Overseas Development Agency. This type of activity is to be found in varying degrees in all firms which have to disseminate a new or sophisticated technology to be applied under conditions which may vary depending on circumstances and regions.[52] For example ITT has established in Buenos Aires the only Latin American telecommunications institute that trains engineers, draughtsmen and repair technicians from all Latin American countries.

Those who obtain the diploma, and prove their ability, can continue their studies in ITT laboratories in Spain, in Madrid. Thereafter they have the choice between working for us or our customers or setting up in business on their own. . . . Our training programmes in Argentina and the rest of Latin America are not confined to telecommunications. They also include fields such as computer technology, hotel management, transport, food processing and the import–export trade. Our training activity is of no recent date. Over the years we have trained more than 55,000 people of both sexes throughout Latin America.[53]

Siemens has also grouped together its training activities for technicians in a centre in Argentina, where courses lasting approximately three months are held for all its subsidiaries in Latin America.[54] This is also the case for TNCs in the agri-business sector in developing countries, which have not only to convince farmers of the genuine worth of their products but also to persuade them to make sweeping changes in their cultivation methods. These firms accordingly try to act in the context of agricultural development operations sponsored by governments, international organizations or bilateral co-operation organizations.[55] Agricultural workers trained in these centres under the firm's programmes, and on its equipment, then recommend this equipment in their countries: 'when they go back home they act as instructors, or many become inspectors of agricultural mechanization projects or other development programmes'. Training has a two-way action, making it also possible for the firm to obtain information on the special conditions under which their product is used in particular markets; it is therefore important to constitute a fairly dense network of training centres.

The approach taken by IBM is much the same, though on another scale.[56] Training in computer technology, both in programming and in its applications, is an integral part of the firm's sales-and-service activities (Table 32). The constitution of a network of education centres is therefore directly related to the geographical distribution of IBM sales.

As IBM activities in Latin America are primarily sales-and-service activities, with only four of their subsidiaries engaged in production, the greater part of training is provided for customers. The Latin American area is covered by two regional centres, in Mexico and Brazil, and eleven local education centres. The number of man-days of training provided in 1972 was 92,000 for customers and 82,000 for employees. The courses provided

TABLE 32. Distribution of IBM activities

Activity	IBM in the United States	IBM World Trade Corporation
Sales agencies	280	336 (in 108 countries)
Factories	18	18 (in 13 countries)
Card-production centres	10	50 (in 41 countries)
Training centres	37	72 (in 38 countries)
Development laboratories	21	7 (in 7 countries)
Basic-research centres	3	1

Source: H. Bakis, *IBM, une multinational régionale*, Presses Universitaires de Grenoble, 1977.

concentrate on informatics (computer technology, programming and application); only 4,000 man-days are management courses.

The development of human resources within the firm is on a specially large scale in IBM.[57] In addition to compulsory staff training, two kinds of optional training are made available: the first confers a new qualification and promotion; the second is of a general nature, and employees are given very great latitude in the choice of subjects, which do not necessarily have any direct relationship with the nature of the work. This type of training is part of the firm's social policy designed to identify wage-earners with the firm and involve them as broadly as possible in its development. Working conditions and salaries, which are generally more favourable than in other firms, combined with social advantages (a broadening of tasks, the 'open door' policy, etc.), mean that, if employees adopt the 'IBM spirit', they make the firm their career. This enables IBM to prevent its graduate personnel leaving for rival firms, thus preserving the capital of skills it has built up, hence its technological advantage. IBM sets its educational activities in the context of social responsibility, which constitutes one of the four basic principles of its philosophy.[58] Research centres (each with a score of research workers) scattered throughout the continents work in co-operation with governments, research institutes and universities on subjects such as pollution, cancer, the detection of disease, the safeguarding of Venice, weather forecasting, etc. In Latin America for example, the Mexico centre is working on air pollution, agricultural models and the use of programmed languages in education. IBM sponsors conferences, university research centres and annual visits from teachers in South American universities to IBM establishments or North American universities. In Latin America it also disseminates a magazine in Spanish, *Think*, awards scholarships, receives trainees, etc. IBM strategy is clear for all to see, and totally unambiguous: by taking action in a great number of fields at present not directly related to its commercial policy, and by establishing relations with university or governmental bodies, it ensures the future extension of the fields of application of its technology, and improves its expertise in social-systems management.

IBM already has plans to develop a market in the educational field: a subsidiary, Science Research Associates Inc., has been set up for this purpose in Chicago (audio-visual aids and programmed instruction). Already in 1972, of the total of 260,000 employees working for the IBM group, it was estimated that there were 5,000 working on educational problems.[59]

The indirect impact of TNCs on education through the interplay between training and employment

A study of the indirect impact of TNCs on education involves considering the radical changes they may bring about in the education systems of the countries in which they take action, in particular through their action in the employment field. In the simplest sense of the term, this type of action takes the form of a quantitative change in the employment structure brought about by the recruitment carried out by the firm. Going beyond this first aspect, it is necessary to understand in what respect TNCs' recruitment methods, organizational structures, working practices and the value they attach to degrees and diplomas can influence the orientation of education courses.

The indirect impact of TNCs is transmitted through two channels: first, through the quantitative and qualitative changes that actually take place in the labour market and, secondly, through the ways in which the labour market is envisaged or represented by the various categories of agents (employers, managers, those responsible for education, students). For our purposes, we must leave aside the case in which the TNC generates a local employment flow without any demand for new qualifications, i.e. the case of a subsidiary with a highly contrasted employment structure, in which the very few supervisory posts would be occupied by expatriates, and the bulk of the new jobs created would be unskilled. It is obvious that in this case no great change should be expected in the education system. We shall on the contrary adopt the most favourable assumption, according to which a TNC establishing itself in a developing country expresses a demand for skilled labour (technicians, engineers, management personnel, etc.). We have seen above that the immediate and specialized nature of the demand for skilled personnel accounts for the firm having recourse in many cases to internal solutions, either by modifying its production procedures (a case which is, however, rare),[60] or by calling on support from the parent establishment in the form of supervisory personnel who train staff progressively under apprenticeship schemes or by working alongside them till they learn their job. Alternatively, the parent establishment may introduce training of its own, or arrange for some local supervisory personnel to be trained abroad. Sometimes the firm envisages a two-pronged solution, the second prong involving co-operation with the state education system. In such cases it helps to change the relevant course of study, bringing it more into line with the specialization it seeks by contributing technical assistance (curricula, materials, teachers). For example, the most immediate changes in the education system can be brought about by introducing training for adults, or out-of-school prevocational training on the lines described above.

Thus the impetus given to education by TNCs may go beyond their strict need for skilled personnel. They may strengthen existing institutions, or bring about the introduction of new courses, by co-operating through employers' organizations with the bodies responsible for training policy or management.[61] For example, Philips Brazil has concluded with the national training department a training agreement under which it receives financial and technical assistance, while for its part Philips Colombia provides the national training department in that country with advisory services and instructors.[62]

Co-operation may be informal, through the dissemination of new training standards or the participation of TNC professional staff in the advisory or decision-making bodies which institute the new courses. This presupposes that local employers and, as appropriate, the political authorities, have agreed that the patterns imported by the TNC as regards both the organization of work and the management of the work-force correspond to their firms' needs and also to development requirements. A specially important prerequisite is the spread of management philosophy. The activation of an out-of-school training sector closely geared to firms' needs accordingly appears to be inseparable from the emergence in Third World countries of a new managerial class trained in business schools. In order that there may be not only more rapid development of out-of-school types of training, or their introduction on the fringes of education systems, but that the whole impetus of these systems may be redirected, it is necessary for the impact of TNCs on the industrial system to be massive and lasting so that the employment structure may be radically transformed. This particularly concerns those countries that have received the most substantial flow of direct investment over the last ten years, most of which are regarded as being the new industrialized countries of the Third World.[63]

TNC involment in these countries is so extensive that it will predictably have direct or indirect consequences for the economic and social scene. By concentrating on these countries it is possible to deduce statistically a number of common features in the development of their education systems. At the same time, there may be a fairly wide range of educational changes in these countries. The differences are the result of the mix due to the nature of TNC activities, the socio-economic characteristics of the host country and, more particularly, its level of educational development at the time when foreign influences appear. Table 33 throws light on one set of differences, those resulting from the distribution of direct investment between the major industrial sectors.

As regard employment, the influence of TNCs is considerable in all these countries. In Singapore, they account for 30 per cent of jobs in industry as a whole (as much as two-thirds in textiles and electrical products). In Brazil and Mexico, the proportion of TNC employees in the manufacturing sector is in the neighbourhood of 10 per cent.[64]

The impact of TNCs on employment cannot be dissociated from the development of local firms in the modern production sector. It is nevertheless not possible to deduce directly the changes to be observed in these countries' education systems from changes in the growing demand for qualifications due to industrial development. In the first place, 'the relationship between

TABLE 33. Stock of direct investment in selected developing countries and territories, by major industrial sector, in selected years

Country or territory	Year	Total stock of direct foreign investment ($ millions)	Share of distribution (%)			
			Extractive sector	Manufacturing sector	Service sector	Other
Latin America						
Argentina	1973	2 275.2	5.6	65.0	24.5	4.5
Brazil	1971	2 911.0	0.9	81.8	14.9	1.4
	1976	9 005.0	2.5	76.5	18.6	2.0
Colombia	1971	692.0	27.3	50.0	19.0	3.7
	1975	965.0	36.0	44.2	18.3	1.5
Mexico	1971	2 297.4	5.9	75.2	16.4	2.5
	1975	4 735.8	4.1	77.5	18.1	0.2
Panama	1969	214.1	21.1	27.0	51.7	—
	1974	353.5	16.1	37.4	46.4	—
Asia						
Hong Kong	1971	759.5	—	100.0	—	—
	1976	1 952.4	—	100.0	—	—
India	1974	1 682.8	4.2	92.0	3.7	—
Indonesia	1970	1 581.4	74.9	19.2	5.5	—
	1976	7 077.0	37.5	57.0	10.3	—
Philippines	1973	146.0	5.7	39.2	52.5	2.6
	1976	513.0	12.6	48.7	34.0	4.7
Republic of Korea	1973	582.2	1.3	76.9	21.8	—
	1975	926.9	1.4	80.1	18.5	—
Singapore	1971	1 575.0	47.7	52.2	—	—
	1976	3 739.0	40.6	59.3	—	—
Thailand	1969	70.2	0.1	97.3	2.5	—
	1975	174.7	—	93.1	6.9	—
Africa						
Nigeria	1968	999.2	53.7	24.5	18.8	2.0
	1973	1 998.6	63.3	25.2	10.3	1.2

Source: United Nations, *Transnational Corporations in World Developments: A Reexamination*, 1978.

education and work is not simply a matter of the relation between the supply of and demand for workers with different qualifications, but expresses concordance/conflict or independence/domination relations between two institutions of the social system'.[65] According to J. Hallak and F. Caillods, assuming that production and technology come first in accounting for methods of division of labour, it is not possible to deduce any distribution of jobs by category of requirements (defined by technical data in respect of vocational qualifications and aptitude) from the level of production by sector of activity. In the light of the most recent research on the linkage between education and employment it appears that:

There is no typical distribution of jobs by occupation for any given level of development and production. Distribution depends on the technical charac-

teristics of the production sector, the interplay between the supply of and demand for labour at various levels of education, and the prevailing systems in regard to the organization of work.
There is not just one labour market but several, including that of the multinationals, each having its own operating characteristics in terms of levels of pay, career possibilities and stability of employment.
In a highly stratified world of work, employers expect job applicants to have not only vocational skills but also abilities and attitudes which will match the employee's social position in the firm; non-cognitive characteristics are very different, depending on occupational levels.*
School does more than merely inculcate vocational skills. It plays a role in the development of non-cognitive characteristics, which may or may not correspond to those sought by firms.

In the second place, possible mismatches between education and employment may be attenuated (for example, by the regulating role of the education system in operating social selection throughout schooling so as to adjust demand to the volume of industry's requirements), but they can also be increased by the time lag which appears between sweeping changes in the productive system and those in the education system.[66] This can be accounted for by the technical obstacles involved in the introduction of new training processes, particularly in the formal education system (teacher-training, curriculum design, the introduction of 'bridges', etc.), and by the inflexibility inherent in education processes which have become institutional. Above all, however, education systems develop according to a logic imposed on them by a demand for education which originates in a certain type of social stratification and particular systems of values and representation, and which does not always reflect the demands of the labour market.[67] For example, C. T. Bernheim considers that 'veritable enrolment explosions . . . and the proliferation of higher education establishments' in some countries of Latin America have not been generated by the demands of the production structure but by pressure for the expansion of secondary and higher education exerted by the recently formed middle classes, which seek 'to improve their relative position within the social hierarchy and to acquire greater political influence'.[68] B. Millot and F. Orivel consider that

education transmits and reveals the characteristics which help to gain access to the rungs of a ladder and to climb some of them, but those required to reach the top are neither taught nor encouraged in the types or levels of education where the demand from the middle classes is to be found; this epitomizes the ambiguous character of social demand, which is the result of an imbalance between the actual situation as experienced by the social group to which one belongs, and the actual or imagined situation of the reference group.[69]

Thus the indirect impact of TNCs on education systems must be apprehended qualitatively, with regard to both employment and demand. The fact is that the TNC transmits a set of new standards, not only as

---

* In particular, the role of education in filtering ability seems to apply much more in respect of high-level than low-level posts.

regards the organization of work but also as regards the social behaviour of a new managerial élite.[70] Just as TNCs represent the organizational model which local firms try to imitate in order to achieve the same efficiency, so their professional staff, usually trained abroad, represent the new élite with which students (or parents, who project their own views in the education they give their children) compare themselves, whether they accept this model or oppose it. Thus TNCs activate, and at the same time modify, both the demand for labour from local firms, which try by means of fresh recruitment to transform their management methods, and the demand for education from the middle classes, who see possible opportunities for social mobility. This tendency is moreover encouraged by the ideology of management. P. F. Drucker claims that in Europe in the 1950s management was, as it were, the counter-culture which was specially welcomed by young people and students as a battering-ram to break down the ramparts of privilege and the class structure, and with them the obstacles that lay in the way of opportunities.[71] Thus the ideology of management, from the individual aspect, merges with the concept of human capital, and gives the middle classes, who seek to identify themselves with the ruling classes, the vision of a mobile, competitive society where differences in income will stem from the differing amounts invested by individuals in their own education.

Section 2

TNCs and educational development

TNCs and the splintering of education systems

The education systems prevalent in most of the developing countries are inherited from the colonial era. It is generally recognized that in many cases the education provided does not contribute towards developing the full potential of the individual in the community.[72] Far from helping to even out the internal disparities which characterize different forms of underdevelopment, it appears that education only too often sets its seal on them, and may even accentuate them. The fact is that education systems are not all of a piece: structurally and functionally they reflect the forms of dualism which characterize the economies of these countries, such as, for example. the town/country dualism as regards the conditions governing the provision of education, the dualism between long and short courses, between well-equipped educational institutions and those with slender resources, and between 'modern' and traditional education.

As these economies become more fully engaged in the international division of labour they are subjected to a lateral shock which affects all these separate areas, in regard to both production and patterns of socialization. The way in which all these divisions are perpetuated, or become more pronounced, depends not only on the force of the sideways thrust and the speed with which an economy becomes integrated into the international division of labour but also, and above all, on the extent of the splintering

TABLE 34. Changes in the educational pyramid

Country	1960			1975			Growth 1960–75 Base 100 in 1960				III/I	III/II	II/I
	I[1]	II	III	I	II	III	I	II	III	T			
Argentina	79.4	65.7	4.8	66.6	23.1	10.2	126	220	437	153	3.46	1.99	1.74
Brazil	95.8	3.1	1.1	87.2	8.0	4.8	241	697	1 157	273	4.75	1.65	2.89
Mexico	89.2	9.3	1.4	78.8	17.8	3.4	237	511	636	268	2.68	1.24	2.15
Peru	85.8	12.1	2.1	71.1	24.1	4.8	211	509	572	281	2.71	1.12	2.41
Venezuela	86.6	11.5	1.8	69.7	23.6	6.7	166	421	740	211	4.45	1.76	2.53
Nigeria	94.5	5.4	0.1	88.8	10.8	1.4	177	374	937	188	5.29	2.5	2.11
Hong Kong	82.3	16.2	1.5	58.7	37.6	3.7	146	476	494	205	3.38	1.03	3.26
India	72.8	25.8	1.4	69.4	28.2	2.4	192	220	350	243	1.82	1.59	1.14
Indonesia	91.9	7.5	0.6	83.3	15.4	1.3	203	462	441	224.5	2.17	0.95	2.27
Iran	81.9	16.9	1.1	65.0	32.6	2.4	303	735	805	382	2.65	1.1	2.42
Malaysia	87.2	12.2	0.6	66.5	32.2	1.2	147	507	429	192	2.91	0.85	3.44
Philippines	81.6	12.5	5.9	71.7	21.2	7.2	182	352	254	207	1.39	0.72	1.93
Singapore	80.7	16.8	2.5	61.5	34.6	3.8	113	307	227	149	2.0	0.74	2.71
Trinidad and Tobago	87.8	11.8	0.3	72.4	26.2	1.3	119	318	786	145	6.6	2.47	2.67

1. I = primary; II = secondary; III = higher; T = technical.

Source: Unesco, *Trends and Projections of Enrolment by Level of Education and by Age*. September 1977. (CSR.E.21.)

and the degree of cohesion which existed in the society under consideration between a system of values, socialization patterns and a form of productive organization at the time when these countries entered on the internationalization process. A number of striking similarities emerge from a general observation of trends in the education systems of the countries we have been considering between 1960 and 1975. In Table 35, which shows changes in the educational pyramid, it will be noted that growth is greater for the higher levels of education than for primary education, even where primary education is still not universal.[73]

Activation of the higher levels of education; stagnation of schooling for all

It is a striking feature that most of the countries considered which have become industrialized and have opened up to external investment have not taken advantage of the growth of their product to obtain a more balanced educational pyramid so as ultimately to make possible the provision of schooling for all. On the contrary, they make increasing use of their resources to meet the growth of the higher levels of education (Table 35). Table 34 shows that during the 1960-75 period:

Educational pyramids, expressed in terms of enrolment, all changed in the sense of a strengthening of the higher levels of education.

This change reflects an increase in enrolment in higher education which is two to five times greater than that for primary education.

In most cases, the increase in enrolment in higher education is greater than that for secondary education.

Significant differences appear from one country to another: whereas this trend is extremely marked in Trinidad and Tobago, Nigeria, Brazil, Venezuela and Argentina, development is much more balanced in countries such as the Philippines, Singapore, Malaysia and Indonesia, where secondary education is expanding faster than higher education.

These trends characteristic of the élitist education systems which develop under the pressure of demand firstly from the higher classes of society, and then from the urban middle classes who emerge from the industrialization process, should be interpreted in different ways, depending on the country. For example, whereas in 1960 Argentina, Singapore, and Trinidad and Tobago had already reached a level of educational development that made it possible to provide schooling for almost all the 6-to-11-year age-group (see Table 36), at the same time Nigeria and Iran provided schooling for only 31.5 and 31.9 per cent respectively of children in that age-group. Thus, while for the former countries the substantial increase in higher education is bound up with a prolongation of schooling and a wider provision of education, with the latter this trend appears much more as the result of a combination of rapid industrialization and the furthering of class interests; in Argentina, for example, 'the effects of the extension of primary education and the spread of literacy were felt before the country became widely open to the international system and the stimulus of exchanges of a modernizing character'.[74]

TABLE 35. Public expenditure on education

Country	Percentage of GNP			Percentage of budget			Breakdown in 1976					
	1965	1970	1975	1965	1970	1975	Primary	Secondary	Higher	Special education	Adult education	Other types of education
Argentina	2.9	1.9	2.7	23.4	14.4	—	27.0	40.8	30.2	—	—	—
Brazil	2.4	2.8	3.7	11.9	10.8	—	45.5	16.9	23.6	—	—	—
Mexico	2.4	2.6	4.0	8.2	8.5	11.1	45.2	31.1	12.6	0.3	0.2	0.4
Peru	5.1	3.8	3.9	18.1	20.3	16.6	40.0	21.5	15.7	0.7	3.3	0.9
Venezuela	4.0	4.8	5.4	18.0	22.9	—	22.1	18.4	37.0	0.5	0.8	0.1
Nigeria	2.4	2.5	4.3	20.7	20.0	—	22.8	15.6	42.0	—	0.2	0.1
Hong Kong	2.5	2.9	3.3	14.8	22.8	20.7	48.7	26.3	20.6	0.9	0.4	2.1
India	2.5	2.8	2.8	9.2	10.7	11.6	—	75.1	17.2	—	1.0	1.7
Indonesia	2.0	2.8	3.3	—	—	12.5	47.8	33.6	7.9	—	—	—
Iran	3.2	2.9	—	—	8.6	—	33.4	28.3	18.6	—	—	—
Malaysia	4.7	4.8	5.8	18.5	18.6	17.0	43.3	33.3	12.4	0.2	0.1	—
Philippines	2.6	2.8	1.6	—	—	9.4	80.0	8.0	5.4	—	—	—
Singapore	4.3	3.1	2.9	—	11.7	8.6	38.1	34.3	17.6	—	—	—
Trinidad and Tobago	3.4	3.9	—	14.1	16.0	—	—	—	—	—	—	—

Source: Unesco, Statistical Yearbook, 1977.

TABLE 36. Enrolment ratios by age-group and by sex trends 1960–75

Country	Year	6–11 years			12–17 years			18–23 years			6–23 years		
		M/F	M	F	M/F	M	F	M/F	M	F	M/F	M	F
Argentina	1960	91.2	90.3	92.2	47.6	47.5	47.7	13.1	15.8	10.3	53.9	54.5	53.4
	1975	100.0	100.0	100.0	63.7	61.3	66.1	28.0	29.4	26.6	64.9	64.5	65.8
Brazil	1960	47.7	47.6	47.8	29.6	31.9	27.3	4.7	5.2	4.2	30.4	31.2	29.6
	1975	70.1	69.2	71.1	53.3	54.0	52.5	23.3	22.8	23.9	51.3	51.1	51.5
Mexico	1960	58.4	58.6	58.1	37.4	42.7	32.1	4.7	6.8	2.5	37.7	40.2	35.2
	1975	90.2	90.9	89.5	54.6	61.7	47.3	12.6	17.9	7.0	57.7	61.8	53.5
Peru	1960	56.7	62.5	50.8	43.2	52.2	34.0	12.9	17.4	8.4	40.6	47.1	33.9
	1975	79.8	81.2	78.4	73.4	80.0	66.6	33.1	40.9	25.2	65.1	69.9	60.1
Venezuela	1960	68.8	68.8	68.9	49.0	49.4	48.5	8.6	10.2	7.0	47.2	47.6	46.8
	1975	74.6	74.7	74.4	55.6	53.2	58.0	19.7	20.3	19.1	53.4	52.8	54.0
Nigeria	1960	31.5	39.2	23.9	13.2	18.0	8.4	0.9	1.5	0.3	17.2	22.0	12.4
	1975	38.3	45.0	31.7	18.9	24.3	13.6	2.5	3.6	1.4	64.9	66.5	63.2
Hong Kong	1960	68.7	72.3	64.8	53.9	57.0	50.3	14.1	16.9	10.7	52.8	55.8	49.5
	1975	89.3	89.3	89.2	81.1	82.7	79.4	21.2	24.7	17.4	64.9	66.5	63.2
India	1960	50.1	66.0	33.4	18.5	27.6	8.9	3.1	5.1	1.0	26.1	35.7	16.0
	1975	61.4	73.1	48.9	27.7	36.2	18.6	5.9	8.9	4.1	39.0	59.5	35.6
Indonesia	1960	50.4	58.7	42.9	24.1	33.9	16.3	2.1	3.5	1.0	27.1	34.0	21.3
	1975	62.0	66.3	57.6	36.9	42.0	31.6	6.7	9.3	4.1	39.0	43.3	34.6
Iran	1960	31.9	42.7	20.9	18.7	26.1	11.2	4.4	7.0	1.7	20.9	28.5	13.1
	1975	65.6	81.0	49.7	53.8	67.0	40.3	14.3	19.1	9.2	47.7	59.5	35.6
Malaysia	1960	86.0	95.3	76.2	32.1	41.8	22.1	1.3	1.8	0.8	47.1	54.3	39.7
	1975	92.7	94.4	90.9	50.2	55.0	45.1	3.0	3.8	2.1	53.5	56.0	50.8
Philippines	1960	71.7	72.7	70.8	39.4	40.6	38.2	13.3	13.7	14.8	45.4	46.3	44.5
	1975	78.1	78.4	77.8	60.1	59.8	60.2	22.7	21.8	23.6	57.7	57.5	57.8
Singapore	1960	84.9	90.4	79.1	62.0	72.0	51.5	12.2	16.2	8.1	57.8	64.2	51.0
	1975	99.9	100.0	99.8	56.8	57.6	56.0	9.5	13.2	5.6	54.8	56.3	53.2
Trinidad and Tobago	1960	89.5	89.5	89.5	51.8	54.7	48.9	3.3	4.2	2.5	55.1	56.6	53.7
	1975	95.9	96.0	95.7	67.1	69.8	64.4	10.3	13.2	7.5	62.7	64.8	60.6

Source: Unesco, *Trends and Projections of Enrolment by Level of Education and by Age Groups*. September 1977. (CSR.E.21.)

This style of development can be compared in varying degrees to what G. W. Rama calls a 'technocratic and/or training of manpower' style.[75] It is characterized by four features:

First, both the quantity and the quality of the educational services depend on the manpower requirements of the various sectors of the economy. Second, education is segmented as regards both subjects taught and standards of knowledge, and does not constitute a single system, since the labour market lays down specific conditions (as regards qualifications, pay, etc.) determined by social indexes deriving from the power structure. Third, education is not impartial, nor does it merely reflect society: it contributes actively to maintaining the differences between the social classes. Fourth, the social demand for education which—in a desire for culture, social mobility and training for participation creates a social market with demands independent of the economic system—is compressed by the government, which is responsible for providing appropriate educational facilities for each social group.[76]

Industrial growth, stimulated by transnational corporations, does not create sufficient employment, either by its contribution to the national product or by its technological characteristics, to integrate into the labour market the rural population and marginal groups of the urban population with a high rate of population growth. For G. W. Rama, 'the incoherence of the economic structure has its parallel in the educational system'. Certain social sectors whose services are not required in production are excluded from the system and condemned to remain illiterate.[77]

In most of these countries the effort made to provide primary schooling is inadequate to cover all the children in the 6-to 11-year age-group (Table 37). The aggregate figures in this table poorly reflect the exact situation in

Table 37. Level of illiteracy 15 years and above

Country	Year	Percentage of illiterates			
		Total	Male	Female	Rural
Argentina	1970	7.4	6.5	8.3	(60) 18.1
Brazil	1970	33.8	30.6	36.9	(70) 53.6
Mexico	1970	25.8	21.8	29.6	
Peru	1972	27.6	16.8	38.2	(72) 51.9
Venezuela	1971	23.5	20.3	26.6	
Nigeria	1962	84.6	75.0	94.0	
Hong Kong	1971	22.7	9.9	35.9	
India	1971	66.6	53.2	81.1	(71) 73.6
Indonesia	1971	43.4	30.5	55.4	(71) 47.8
Iran	1971[1]	63.1	52.3	74.5	(71) 79.6
Malaysia	1962	47.2	41.0	52.0	
Philippines	1970	17.4	15.7	19.1	(70) 21.3
Singapore	1970	31.1	17.0	45.7	
Trinidad and Tobago	1970	7.8	5.3	10.3	

1. 6 years and above.
Source: Unesco, *Statistics of Educational Attainment and Literacy*, No. 22, 1945-74.

primary schools: on the one hand, disparities in enrolment continue to be important between towns and rural areas, including the intermediate, outer suburban zone in its heavy concentration of marginal groups; on the other, the survival rate in primary schools is still low in certain regions (Table 38). Taking the completion of the fourth grade as the yardstick for the acquisition of literacy, it will be seen that nearly half the children do not attain this objective. For example, in the Philippines '200,000 7-year-old children each year do not go to school at all; and of those that do so many do not remain in school long enough to become functionally literate, in fact, 90 per cent of them leave school before reaching their highest educational potential level'.[78]

At the level of primary education, the exclusion process means that country children receive, at most, three or four grades of schooling, the minimum needed for a grounding in literacy. A similar fate awaits the children of the poorer quarters of the cities, for whom there are virtually no educational curricula which take their special circumstances into account. Dropping out and absenteeism, from socio-economic rather than academic causes, decimate the school population from the earliest grades onwards, so that many leave school before they have acquired functional literacy.[79]

TABLE 38. Approximate education survival rates for the 1965 and 1970 cohorts, both sexes

Region	Year	Grade 1	Grade 2	Grade 3	Grade 4	Grade 5
Less developed	1965	100	67	58	50	41
regions	1970	100	70	61	54	45
Africa	1965	100	78	71	61	52
	1970	100	83	78	72	64
Latin America	1965	100	58	48	44	33
	1970	100	64	54	47	41
South Asia	1965	100	67	58	49	40
	1970	100	69	60	52	41

Source: Unesco, *Trends and Projections of Enrolment by Level of Education and by Age Group*, September 1977, p. 37. (CSRE.21.)

Thus in countries characterized by economic and social disunity, the choice of a rapid rate of industrialization—a choice for which the TNCs are themselves partly responsible—encourages the forces contributing towards 'concentration' and 'marginalization'[80] while the avowed aim of education is social integration. Production growth is polarized in the sectors of activity most open to internationalization; these activities concentrate together into certain urban zones a more privileged population whose demands and needs stimulate educational development which increasingly excludes an illiterate population. Destructuring is accentuated, except in certain countries which, having reached a sufficient degree of societal cohesion before the impact of internationalization, are able to surmount these forms of educational underdevelopment.

Vocationalization of secondary education and strengthening of the dual educational network

Most states have promoted, with varying degrees of success, short vocational post-primary or secondary education with two aims in view: first, to meet the demand for skilled workers and technicians in productive sectors; second, to deflect part of the demand for education from general education courses which lead directly to higher education, towards a short course of education.

Any description of this type of education is extremely complex on account of the diversity of systems introduced. These differ as regards the level of integration in the formal education system, the type of educational method used (apprenticeship or full education), and the agents responsible.[81] As is clear from the relevant statistics (Table 39), there is great variety in regard to the way in which vocational education develops in the different countries we have to consider.

The case of Singapore
Singapore provides an example of a reform of the education system brought about with a view to creating an environment which would attract foreign investors, especially in the industrial sector. R. H. K. Wong describes the guiding spirit behind the adoption of a new policy:

In the re-orientation of the economic policy of the State, industrialization is vital. Industrialization is the key to survival. To increase industrial productivity, potential skill must be trained. So a start in developing the latent skills must be made in the schools. The new education policy would ensure that students have increased facilities for training as craftsmen, technicians, scientists and engineers.[82]

In secondary education the restructuring took the following forms:
All pupils in secondary schools followed the same course for the first two
  grades, consisting of both traditional disciplines and practical subjects.
Vocational secondary schools were provided for pupils who had been unable
  to obtain a primary-school certificate.
Commercial secondary schools offered a two-year business-oriented course
  following on two years of general education.
Training centres provided industrial apprenticeship in different trades or
  handicrafts.
Ten years later these technical education structures were made more flexible
  and more suited to the needs of industry:
A module system has been introduced into technical education whereby
  students with varying preparation and backgrounds can undertake
  industrial training at stages appropriate to their knowledge and skills.
An industrial training board has been established to interrelate the vocational

TABLE 39. Secondary education trends 1965–75, including percentages for technical and prevocational education

Country	1965 Total	1965 Technical	1965 %	1970 Total	1970 Technical	1970 %	1975 Total	1975 Technical	1975 %
Argentina	789 077	59 775	7.6	974 826	76 287	7.8	1 243 058	99 525	8.0
Brazil	2 154 430	380 459	17.7	4 086 073	682 548	16.7	1 681 728	782 827	46.5[1]
Mexico	1 002 610	236 159	23.6	1 584 342	—	—	2 938 972	321 456	10.9
Peru	328 104	56 437	17.2	546 183	93 182	17.1	813 489	186 430	22.9
Venezuela	267 240	93 120	34.8	465 861	168 565	36.2	669 138	—	—
Nigeria	250 917	22 610	9.0	356 565	30 201	8.5	568 303	20 423	3.5[2]
Hong Kong	166 620	11 437	6.9	230 894	14 104	6.1	368 655	21 509	5.8
India	4 126 299	293 444	7.1	6 391 441	200 219	3.1	—	—	—
Indonesia	1 453 834	393 645	27.1	2 459 875	544 830	22.1	3 361 308	722 193	21.5
Iran	576 727	15 160	2.6	1 056 787	30 579	2.9	2 183 137	150 509	6.9
Malaysia	355 189	9 143	2.6	538 865	17 025	3.2	759 676	24 184	3.2[1]
Philippines	1 183 307	141 961	12.0	1 714 875	—	—	2 254 543	662 949	29.4
Singapore	115 139	12 278	10.7	149 143	12 361	8.3	183 364	30 335	16.5
Trinidad and Tobago	46 116	2 601	5.6	52 639	2 829	5.4	54 584	2 794	5.1[3]

1. 1974.   2. 1973.   3. 1972.

training provided in all schools and the industrial training provided within industry; the board, whose members include representatives of the private industrial sector, promotes the training of an industrial work-force through the introduction of an extensive apprenticeship system.

The policy pursued as regards the vocationalization of education conflicts with the objective adopted by the Singapore Government of preserving language streams. Originally, English was to be the second language, and its use was encouraged only in the teaching of science subjects. At the same time the government promoted bilingualism in all curricula and the setting up of integrated schools. However, 'with the penetration of the economy by multinational corporations and as Singapore locks into the international network of trade and industry, the position of English, an official language inherited from the colonial era, has been consolidated and further entrenched'.[83] Or, as R.H.K. Wong puts it, 'parents came increasingly to perceive the growing interrelationship between on the one hand proficiency in the English language and the consequent mastery of technical skills, and on the other the well-paid jobs which will be provided by the rapid industrialization of Singapore.[84]

The increasingly restricted character of university education and the development of business-management schools

The expansion of higher education in the countries we have considered is not only quantitative, but is accompanied by structural changes in the distribution of enrolment in different courses, major modifications in regard to educational contents and the establishment of new institutions (Table 40). The question that arises is whether students opt for the subjects that are likely to be the most profitable in the industrial sector, such as for example training in engineering or management. It is difficult to give any exact answer, for a number of reasons. Figures for management and business training do not appear in statistics, since they are included under the social science heading; similarly, statistics do not reflect the important part now played by the short higher technological courses which have been instituted to meet the demand from firms. More basically, the relation between training and employment at the higher level is a complex one: on the one hand, most higher-education courses, even the least specialized can lead by means of supplementary training to a career in management; on the other, firms set as much store on social background and ability as on acquired skills for supervisory posts.

This being the case, one way of appraising the development of higher vocation-oriented courses is to study the development of non-university types of higher education in relation to that of university education (Table 41).

In Venezuela, Iran and Singapore, they appear to be developing much more dynamically than traditional forms of university education. In some countries this splintering of education is accompanied by a trend for higher education to move into the private sphere. Carlos Tunnermann Bernheim notes:

TABLE 40. Trends in the distribution of students by field of study, 1960-75

Country	Year	Total No. of students	Social sciences	%	Natural sciences	%	Engineering	%	Agriculture	%
Argentina	1961	180 796	30 565	16.9	6 653	3.7	26 205	14.5	3 334	1.8
	1975	601 395	119 996	20.0	25 334	4.2	83 627	14.0	31 605	5.9
Brazil	1960	95 691	14 380	15.0	5 339	5.6	18 667	19.5	481	0.5
	1975	1 089 808	119 996	11.0	89 335	8.2	89 319	8.2	18 885	1.7
Mexico	1961	94 073	20 276	21.6	5 339	5.7	18 667	19.8	2 859	3.0
	1975	520 194	200 826	38.6	17 525	3.4	154 146	29.6	20 784	4.0
Peru	1959	26 616	4 139	15.6	4 778	18.0	3 427	12.9	984	3.7
	1975	195 641	56 013	28.6	5 774	3.0	34 559	17.7	13 719	7.0
Venezuela	1960	26 477	5 574	21.0	446	1.8	4 648	17.5	1 121	4.2
	1975	199 889	42 520	21.3	7 438	3.7	38 107	19.1	6 227	3.1
Nigeria	1960	3 128	641	20.5	668	21.3	249	7.9	111	3.5
	1975	32 971	4 767	14.5	4 622	14.0	2 474	7.5	2 743	8.3
Hong Kong	1960	5 789	703	12.1	208	3.6	130	2.2	—	—
	1975	44 482	13 338	30.0	4 902	11.0	13 370	30.0	—	—
India	1960	1 028 660	86 486	8.4	296 849	28.9	43 619	4.2	26 845	2.6
	1975	2 903 551	348 871	12.0	922 764	31.8	83 528	2.9	48 971	1.6
Indonesia	1956	22 707	4 814	21.2	1 351	5.9	3 245	14.3	531	2.3
	1975	255 856	61 464	24.0	6 805	2.7	38 068	14.9	13 518	5.2
Iran	1960	24 885	819	3.3	2 264	9.1	2 224	8.9	1 150	4.6
	1975	154 215	27 093	17.6	27 317	17.7	34 411	22.3	6 837	4.4
Malaysia	1963	8 455	—	—	398	4.7	800	9.5	174	2.1
	1975	39 658	6 130	15.5	4 272	10.8	6 156	15.5	1 952	4.9
Philippines	1960	271 791	102 144	37.6	2 115	0.8	27 456	10.1	4 127	1.5
	1976	764 725	119 996	15.7	16 710	2.2	45 861	6.0	39 886	5.1
Singapore	1960	3 448	747	21.6	877	25.4	—	—	—	—
	1975	22 607	2 913	12.9	1 181	5.2	9 882	43.7	—	—
Trinidad and Tobago	1962	147	—	—	—	—	67	45.6	80	54.4
	1975	2 962	316	10.7	448	15.1	385	13.0	291	9.8

Source: Unesco, Statistical Yearbook, 1960, 1977.

TABLE 41. Relative development of university and other types of higher education

Country	Year	University education	Other types of higher education
Argentina	1965	246 680	6 621
	1970	274 634	7 012
	1975	596 736	8 471
	1976	601 395	9 989
Venezuela	1965	100 767	616
	1970	187 688	9 950
	1975	213 542	13 653
Iran	1970	74 708	26 292
	1975	151 905	85 533
	1976	154 215	85 522
Singapore	1965	13 807	3 208
	1970	13 771	4 875
	1975	18 195	9 166
	1976	22 607	9 425

Source: Unesco, Statistical Yearbooks, 1960, 1977.

To resist the thrust of the middle classes, the classes wielding political and economic power have encouraged the establishment of private educational facilities, which enjoy higher social standing and are designed to train the ruling élites.... This splintering of the educational system according to social stratification leads to increased compartmentalization in social terms, undermining the democratic objectives of egalitarian socialization.[85]

For example, in Latin America, where one-third of the institutions were set up between 1960 and 1970, the main driving force came from the private sector, the public sector's share of university enrolments falling from 89 to 78 per cent over the same period.

The universities of South-East Asia have rapidly adapted themselves to changes in the production system. Thus in Singapore the manufacturing sector now absorbs 25 per cent of the workforce, as compared to 15 per cent in the 1960s. To meet the demand from industry, which makes increasing use of technologies requiring high-level skills and services, universities have changed their intake: the more vocation-oriented subjects (engineering, accounting, law, business administration, architecture) have developed more rapidly than arts subjects or the social sciences.[86]

The Singapore Polytechnic has been enlarged, and the Ngee Ann Technical College, which previously catered only for students from the Chinese community, and offered courses in literature and business techniques, has also been converted into an institution of the polytechnic type. Plans for expanding Singapore University give priority to the departments of technology and business administration. Students who have received

TABLE 42. Number of graduates of tertiary institutions in Singapore

	1965	1969	1973
Universities			
Arts	330	440	613
Science	298	579	469
Law	58	47	87
Medicine	99	132	128
Dentistry	22	35	43
Pharmacy	35	27	20
Education	36	60	—
Commerce	121	321	501
Architecture, engineering	—	68	172
Singapore Polytechnic			
Engineering	162	263	1 105
Architecture	40	92	135
Accounting	52	90	—
Marine Engineering	26	45	70
Ngee Ann Technical College			
Engineering and management	—	134	210
TOTAL	1 279	2 333	3 553

Source: Philip Limb, 'The Employment of Graduates of Tertiary Institutions in Singapore', *Development Strategies and Manpower Needs. The Response of Southeast Asian Universities*, p. 82, Singapore, RIHED, 1976.

TABLE 43. Student admission to the four higher education institutions in Singapore, 1963-72

Year	Singapore University	Nanyang University	Singapore Polytechnic	Ngee Ann Technical College	TOTAL
1963	2 433	2 324	2 259	386	7 402
1964	2 572	2 273	2 299	688	7 832
1965	2 870	2 126	2 335	873	8 204
1966	3 012	1 851	2 642	852	8 357
1967	3 281	1 750	2 963	400	8 394
1968	3 714	1 991	3 374	353	9 432
1969	4 559	2 039	3 310	529	10 437
1970	4 680	2 310	4 094	598	11 682
1971	4 703	2 399	4 507	1 022	12 631
1972	5 226	2 596	5 764	1 185	14 771

Source: Philip Limb, 'The Employment of Graduates of Tertiary Institutions in Singapore', *Development Strategies and Manpower Needs. The response of Southeast Asian Universities*, p. 82, Singapore, RIHED, 1976.

technological training in English are on the whole better placed to find employment, whereas graduates from Nanyang University and Ngee Ann Technical College, which cater for those whose primary and secondary

TABLE 44. University graduates in Indonesia

Institutions	1969	1973	1978	1983
Public universities	4 000	5 200	7 050	9 540
Academies	200	200	400	400
Private universities	600	720	1 580	2 610
TOTAL	4 800	6 120	9 030	12 550

Source: Muhammadi Siswo Sudarmo, 'The Employment of University Graduates in Indonesia', Development Strategies and Manpower Needs. The Response of Southeast Asian Universities, Singapore, RIHED, 1976.

TABLE 45. Job opportunities for graduates in Indonesia

Employment groups	995	1969	1981
Engineering studies	6	10	30
Management	4	5	20
Administration	2	3	10
Trade	1	2	3
Agriculture, fishing, forestry	1	1	2
Industry	1	2	5
Services	2	2	5
TOTAL	17	25	75

Source: Muhammadi Siswo Sudarmo, 'The Employment of University Graduates in Indonesia', Development Strategies and Manpower Needs. The Response of Southeast Asian Universities, Singapore, RIHED, 1976.

schooling has been in Chinese, experience more difficulty in finding jobs.[87]

Employment prospects in the industrial sector govern the radical changes that have occurred in universities in other countries of South-East Asia. Thus in Indonesia, where enrolment has also increased most sharply in private universities (Table 44), the best job opportunities for students are again to be found in careers in management (Table 45).[88]

Similarly for Malaysian students, managerial posts in the private productive sector account for almost half the job opportunities.

Thus in countries where industrial development is stimulated from the outside, higher education at university, which had been expanding dangerously due to the demand from the new middle classes, now seems to be losing ground in favour of selective, vocation-oriented education determined by the technical division of labour in firms.[89]

TNCs and the extroversion of education systems

It is still common practice to depict education systems in the developing countries as dependent vis-à-vis the education systems of the former colonial powers.[90] This view proves to be entirely correct for most former colonized countries, particularly the less developed, which make use of a large number of foreign teachers, send their students to complete their studies in the former mother country, or call on the former colonial power to train their teachers and confer certain degrees or diplomas. However, this over-static analysis tends to disregard factors that make for change in international cultural relations and minimize the transformations affecting education systems, particularly in countries in the process of industrialization. The fact is that the perpetuation or widening of the technological gap between the more industrialized and the developing countries, combined with growing internationalization of their economies, gives fresh impetus to 'extroversion' of the inherited education systems.[91] We shall here confine ourselves strictly to studying an index of educational extroversion based on one of its most obvious forms: the sending of students abroad. As has often been stressed in this study, there can be no such thing as a nation whose gaze is directed solely inwards, so there is no intention whatsoever of criticizing the fact that students from developing countries go to complete their training in developed countries (the converse would moreover be highly desirable). This flow is obviously essential for communication between nations and for an open outlook among the leaders of developing countries. It is nevertheless a fact that the size of the phenomenon, and the forms it assumes in some countries may be an index of dependence. Furthermore, the question of the subsequent return of these students to their home country sometimes raises doubts as to the net gain derived by the developing countries from this outwards-directed training process.

In the countries we have considered, the number of students studying abroad, far from drying up, rose 2.89 times between 1969 and 1975, and doubled between 1973 and 1975 (see Table 46). This was all the more remarkable in that, as we have already seen, these countries have laid special emphasis on developing their higher education.

TABLE 46. Number of students studying abroad

Country	1969	1973	1975
Argentina	1 811	1 897	2 122
Brazil	3 064	3 948	5 583
Mexico	3 390	5 120	6 207
Peru	2 395	2 568	4 960
Venezuela	2 859	3 781	7 230
Nigeria	4 160	7 350	16 348
Hong Kong	11 120	16 980	21 059
India	15 720	15 160	14 805
Indonesia	3 183	3 183	6 820
Iran	12 330	19 680	33 021
Malaysia	8 840	13 620	16 162
Philippines	3 177	2 993	2 787
Singapore	1 958	1 328	2 421
Trinidad and Tobago	1 718	3 098	3 154

Source: Unesco, Statistical Yearbook, 1977; Unesco, Statistics of Students Abroad, 1969-73, 1976.

TABLE 47. Students studying abroad

Country	A No. of third-level students	B Students abroad	B/A (%)	C United States	C/B (%)	Significant countries
Argentina	601 395	2 122	0.35	560	26.4	France (909)
Brazil	1 089 808	5 583	0.5	2 160	38.7	France (1 122)
Mexico	520 195	6 207	1.1	4 620	74.4	—
Peru	195 641	4 960	2.5	1 700	34.3	Argentina (1 671)
Venezuela	199 889	7 230	3.6	4 680	64.7	—
Nigeria	32 971	16 348	49.5	11 440	70.0	—
Hong Kong	44 482	21 059	47.3	11 930	56.6	Fed. Rep. of Germany (6 644)
India	3 198 550	14 805	0.5	9 630	65.0	Canada (1 697) United Kingdom (1 437)
Indonesia	255 856	6 820	2.6	1 230	18.0	Fed. Rep. of Germany (3 324)
Iran	154 215	33 021	21.4	19 900	60.3	Fed. Rep. of Germany (3 845)
Malaysia	278 200	16 162	5.8	1 930	11.9	Australia (3 290) United Kingdom (6 394) Singapore (3 335)
Philippines	764 725	2 787	0.4	2 100	75.3	—
Singapore	22 607	2 421	10.7	400	16.5	United Kingdom (1 113)
Trinidad and Tobago	2 962	3 154	106.0	1 050	33.3	Canada (1 458)

Source: Unesco, *Statistical Yearbook*, 1977.

In each country the likelihood of student migration is partly determined by the level of development of its education system. The countries that have made the widest provision of education for the 18-to-23 age-group, such as Argentina, Brazil, Peru and the Philippines, have the lowest percentage of students abroad. Hong Kong, with 47.3 per cent of its students abroad, is an exception to this trend (see Table 47). By contrast, Iran and Nigeria, which underwent very rapid internationalization of their production machinery while their education systems were still barely developed, have a very substantial proportion of their students carrying out their studies abroad 21.4 and 49.5 per cent respectively). Iran, with 33,021 students abroad in 1975, exceeded all other countries in absolute figures. The students' choice of the former colonial power is still predominant in certain countries such as Malaysia or Singapore. This is however exceptional, and it is the United States that draws the majority of students, i.e. more than 60 per cent from Mexico, Venezuela, India, Nigeria, and the Philippines. The substantial percentage of students from Hong Kong (31.5) and Indonesia (48.7) who choose to study in the Federal Republic of Germany, notwithstanding language difficulties, indicates that it is the most industrialized countries, and the specialized types of training they can offer in certain technologies, which now exercise the greatest degree of attraction. Whereas Asian students abroad opt primarily for engineering (26 per cent), followed by the social sciences (22 per cent), of South American students abroad only 15 per cent choose engineering, and of African students only 9.5 per cent. The countries we have considered reflect the same differences, with however significant trends in Nigeria, India, Iran and Venezuela (see Table 48).

It is impossible to give a figure for students choosing management studies, since here again this subject is included in statistics along with the social sciences.

The industrial powers, which through their research potential maintain control over the production and renewal of scientific and technological knowledge, are able to provide in certain fields a quality of education which is still not to be found in the developing countries. However, the motivations that lead students to study abroad are not related solely to the gap between types of education. A no less important factor is the image that local élites have of study abroad, the attraction of a Western life-style and the benefit they hope to derive. Thus education should also be seen as a consumption of 'positional goods', in the sense used by F. Hirsh, that is to say goods the individual enjoyment of which depends on the degree of general availability.[92] For example, study abroad reflects the expectations of a certain social stratum whose consumption is oriented towards a Western value system, but in addition it is a practice that is all the more prized in that it is, for a minority, a visible means of distinguishing themselves from the mass of those now acceding to higher education in these countries. It is thus to some extent arguable that foreign degrees and diplomas acquire all the more value where there is democratization of higher education at the local level. For example, in developing countries where unemployment is

TABLE 48. Number of students abroad in social sciences and engineering, 1971

	A Social sciences	B Engineering	B/A (%)
Argentina	1 434	122	8.6
Brazil	3 048	394	12.9
Mexico	3 183	509	16.0
Peru	2 512	453	18.0
Venezuela	2 983	680	22.8
Nigeria	4 887	696	14.2
Hong Kong	10 750	2 895	26.9
India	13 882	5 867	42.3
Indonesia	3 693	1 083	29.3
Iran	14 115	5 260	37.3
Malaysia	9 790	2 788	28.5
Philippines	2 931	314	10.7
Singapore	1 543	417	27.0
Trinidad & Tobago	1 569	163	10.4

Source: Unesco, Statistics of Students Abroad, 1969-73, No. 21, 1976.

rife among university graduates, training acquired abroad makes it easier to accede to certain categories of employment, and particularly for local TNC subsidiaries, who thus find the trained qualifications on which they insist in their country of origin. To this should be added candidates' ability to use foreign languages, and a willingness to be internationally mobile. TNCs also encourage students to go abroad by awarding study fellowships. United States-based TNCs questioned at a Conference Board in 1968 considered that, in the countries where they operated, there was a shortage of skilled managers familiar with American working methods, due to the education systems of the countries in question and cultural or social differences. In particular, the basic concepts of American management, such as the delegation of authority, managerial initiative and profit as a measure of success in management, are not perceived spontaneously by large numbers of foreign directors but have to be assimilated through training or experience.[93]

But do students trained abroad in fact return to their home countries? It appears that in an initial phase, from 1960 to 1972, the non-return figures were so high that the 'brain drain' could be compared to a technology flow in the other direction.[94] The estimated value of the contribution represented by technicians who had emigrated from developing countries to the United States, Canada and the United Kingdom was $50.9 billion, whereas these countries' assistance to developing countries amounted to $46.3 billion. It is difficult to establish statistics on the non-return of students to their home countries. For the 1964–69 period UNITAR evaluated it at 30 per cent for Trinidad and Tobago, 20 per cent for the Philippines and 28 per cent for Colombia.[95] Quoting the work of the 1968 Lausanne Conference, T. Mende states that 90 per cent of Asian students who go to study in the United States never go back home.[96] L. Pearson estimates that 50 per cent of graduate engineers from Latin America work in the United States.[97] The reason commonly advanced by students who have decided to emigrate is the fact that their degrees receive no recognition in their home country, in other words that there are no jobs corresponding to their qualifications or salary requirements. Scientists stress the absence of research facilities as regards both equipment and the possibility of communication with others engaged in research.[98]

The causes of the brain drain are also cultural. Le Thành Khôi stresses that

training abroad, or else training on the spot but following a foreign pattern ... does not integrate the individual into his environment but, on the contrary, inculcates in him foreign and alienating values and hence turns his intellectual and material ambitions towards the outside world.[99]

According to T. Mende, a social divide can be created at the local level between scientific and technocratic élites trained abroad and the traditional ruling élites in their home countries.[100]

With developing countries which have recently become industrialized, are going through rapid transition and have opened up extensively to foreign investment, we are entering a second phase, in which the brain drain is tending to diminish; TNCs are replacing expatriate professional staff by local staff. In addition, job opportunities are appearing in local firms. R. Vernon detects in this movement the appearance of a new entrepreneurial class more obstinately determined to struggle for their countries' independence, but he nevertheless recognizes that the members of this class associate themselves with or compete against foreign firms depending on their own interests.[101] Indeed some authors stress the convergence of interests between these élites and the managers of multinational firms who have received the same education.[102]

In the educational field, degrees and diplomas acquired abroad are also prized in the more dynamic sectors of activity, and set a new standard, with local degrees and diplomas ranking beneath it. In this way a demand for education is created which leads students to expatriate themselves in order to acquire a particular type of training. This process only genuinely slows down once a comparable type of training has been established locally. In Latin America TNCs, with encouragement from the local entrepreneurial class, have for example promoted the establishment of management-training centres in the more industrialized developing countries.[103] This educational structure, based on external stimulus, is almost entirely cut off from the educational and cultural infrastructure of the country in which it is established. Courses are usually given in English, and programmes are copied from those of the foreign university that provides educational support.[104] T. Cullinan stresses that the organization of studies in management-training centres differs considerably from the traditional organization of higher education in Latin American universities. Though the integration of these centres in the traditional education system is valuable for prestige reasons and in order to obtain full recognition of diplomas, the author suggests that they should remain independent from the traditional university system on account of differences in methods and working conditions in universities (including student strikes).

In business schools, the case-studies used to impart a new slant to methods of instruction are produced and marketed on the basis of courses originating from the more developed countries. A leading business school will, typically, have been conceived from the outset in an international context. For example the Asian Institute of Management in Manila was set up in 1968 by local university institutions, government agencies and national and multinational firms (responsible for financing it) from nine countries.[105]

To sum up, five major conclusions can be drawn from these considerations:
First, it appears undeniable that TNCs now engage in a very substantial amount of activity in the educational sphere.
Secondly, TNCs participate in a form of education which is of a scientific and technical type, rather than a more general type, i.e. one postulating the oneness of knowledge.
Thirdly, educational action by TNCs passes less through the formal channels of the national education system than through the out-of-school and informal channels specially used for vocational training activities.
Fourthly, educational action by TNCs is matched within the developing

country by a trend towards the polarization of the education system. This is due to the more rapid, externally stimulated growth-rate of the modern system as compared with the development of the traditional education system.

Fifthly, educational action by TNCs has as its concomitant an extroversion of the national education system which manifests itself not only in curricula and institutions but also in attitudes, patterns of thought and ways of legitimizing the controlling functions in society.

Section 3

Promoting endogenous educational development

There is a preliminary risk in any attempt to suggest forms endogenous educational development might take for the Third World countries as a whole. The fact is that our thinking, even in its scientific and philosophical manifestations, 'has great difficulty in liberating itself from the prejudices that underlie the education we have received and the culture which encompasses us'. Thus we may well ask how we can be sure of escaping from the 'ethno-centric stereotypes which simplify history and social relations and forcibly enrol them in the service of a world-view that brings with it alienation'.[106] The cultural diversity of peoples, the distinctive economic and social situation of each nation, and its absolute right to be master of its own destiny, prompt the rejection of any universal model or solution for educational development, since a universal model would almost certainly be incapable of reproducing the diversity and would give rise to considerable difficulties in application. In this section, rather than present a universal educational model, we shall put forward a series of recommendations of a more practical nature designed to guide each state in its deliberate choices in respect of the development of its education system. This implies the rejection of homogeneity, hence the recognition of diversity and a resolve to develop, reproduce and disseminate original experiments in endogenous educational development. The difficulties involved in depicting so complex a phenomenon as the impact of TNCs on education systems make it necessary to insist, possibly to over-insist, on the similarities in the situations of different Third World countries, and also to give special recognition to the TNCs' ability to take action when compared with the cumbersome and ill-adapted character of these countries' education systems. In particular, we have made no reference to the experiments and innovations under way in a number of Third World countries, which tend in the direction of endogenous educational development. If these are taken into account, the result may be to make the processes seem less inevitable than may appear from the method of exposition we have adopted, and encourage this on-going movement of reform.

Conservation measures

The first series of proposals will be conservationist in character. They consist in inducing TNCs to respect the education policies of the countries in which they are established. The aim of these proposals is to bring the vocational training provided by TNCs closer to the principles contained in the Final Report of the Third International Conference on Adult Education, held in Tokyo in 1972:

Vocational training should go further . . . than simply preparing an individual for a productive role. The adult should be able to share in the control of all the processes in which he is involved. . . .

Trade union and occupational training for industry and agriculture [is] indispensable in any national system of adult education.

Adult education [should] help to induce a sense of national direction and purpose, weld the people together and assist them to participate more actively in public affairs.

An integral element of all adult education for nation-building is literacy.

Lifelong education and cultural development cannot be separated, and . . . are two facets of the same problem, i.e. the building up of free men in a changing society.[107]

In this context it would be desirable:

To request the publication of an annual review of TNC educational activities broken down by country.

To elaborate international legislation to govern the training contracts linked to the transfer of technology.

To provide states with legal means for supervising the funds made available for education in each subsidiary company.

To define a minimum percentage of total salary payments by foreign subsidiaries which should go to finance the education system in the host country in which they are established.

To determine a threshold beyond which the TNC should assume responsibility for training local teaching staff in technological disciplines.

To request a guaranteed minimum quota of general education in the language of the country, provided by teachers of the host country, in all the vocational training programmes of each firm, and in particular to request that plans be drawn up, as necessary, in each subsidiary as it is established, to provide literacy training for its personnel.

To recommend the use of the local language in the training and the textbooks provided by the TNC.

To allow trade unions freedom of expression and give them the means of supervising training programmes.

Measures to promote endogenous educational development

These proposals are inadequate unless accompanied by the creation of conditions making endogenous educational development possible. These conditions can be seen in relation to three ideas: (a) the idea of integrating education in the national development process; (b) the idea of preserving and developing the means whereby the state can direct and control the future of education; and (c) the idea of horizontal educational co-operation between countries in the same cultural region.

Integrating education in the national development process

The internationalization of the modern production sector reinforces economic dualism and encourages the splintering of the education system in favour of types of training which perpetuate forms of social inequality and furnish a supposed scientific and technological basis for legitimizing them. It is therefore necessary to promote education policies that will attenuate this destructuring, and above all bridge the widening economic and educational gap between affluent élites and the great mass of the population, consisting of peasants or an urban sub-proletariat, who do not benefit from the opportunities afforded by the education system. Educational reforms not only meet the requirements of greater social justice but are also aimed at reducing the burden on the economic development of the country represented by the cost of inadequate education, or no education at all, which marginalizes a substantial proportion of the population.

The specific forms to be given to educational reforms, and their extent, remain highly controversial. It is however possible to distinguish a number of principles emerging from the reforms introduced in certain Third World countries:

The need to promote education for the masses in rural areas. This cannot be done without a reform of educational contents and methods. In particular, such education should be participative, and form part of an integrated programme for rural development encompassing everything that can contribute to raising the standard of living of country-dwellers (improvements in housing, health, child nutrition, irrigation, the dissemination of agricultural techniques, etc.).

The use of schools for both primary education and adult education, involving the integration of formal and non-formal education. The community education centres in the United Republic of Tanzania are an excellent example of what can be done in this field.[108]

The development of technical education by making it an integral part of the curriculum, alongside general education, at all educational levels. This reform should make it possible to achieve three objectives: first, to avoid the creation of a dual educational network that selects on a basis of social background and increases inequality; next, to bring education nearer to actual production conditions and prevent its being possible for students to leave school without a genuine ability to perform productive work; and, lastly, to contribute towards providing a full education which will help to develop the individual's full potential. Examples are the measures designed to promote integrated science education in the primary schools of Kenya, Ghana, Sierra Leone and the United Republic of Tanzania.[109]

The reinstatement of local languages in all curricula, at whatever educational level, and in particular the decolonization of school textbooks.

The need to contribute to the country's educational independence by promoting research and teacher-training at the local or regional level.

The need to help all those concerned to participate in the definition of education policies and even in the dissemination of knowledge.

Preserving and developing the means whereby the state can direct and control the future of education

The power and mobility of TNCs make it possible for them to introduce rapidly the forms of education required by their strategies. The impetus they give locally to the modern production sector promotes the establishment of new educational institutions suited to their requirements and conforming to the educational model they bring with them. Since the initiative for establishing these institutions does not rest with the state, and is mainly directed to adults, they usually take their place within the framework of the non-formal education system.

In many Third World countries the growth of non-formal education appears to be greater than that of formal education. In the first place, non-formal education makes it possible to draw on new resources, in particular those of firms; secondly, it provides a means of reaching sections of the population previously without schooling; lastly, it enables instruction to be made more functional, more specifically oriented towards a goal. By contrast, the nation-state is saddled with a formal education system whose size, coupled with the great variety of functions for which it must be responsible, and the diversity of population groups it must reach, makes planning and administration extremely complex. This situation lends weight to the idea of a formal state system, hidebound by tradition and unsuited to its purpose, confronting a modern non-formal system, frequently in private hands, which corresponds to what is needed. To perpetuate this division would be to move towards the establishment of a dual education system that 'runs directly counter to the aim of achieving equality of educational opportunity. Such a policy is likely to legitimize existing social and class differences and to institutionalize inequalities.'[110] The decentralization and flexibility of non-formal out-of-school processes also mean that they are more sensitive to the forces of change and to external influences.

A closer look should therefore be taken, as regards out-of-school training projects, at what is the result of an analysis of countries' real situations, and what is the effect of the imitation of external models or of the application to under-developed countries of an analysis suited to the present-day situation of the industrialized countries.[111]

It is therefore necessary to seek ways of introducing an administrative reform which will bring together formal and non-formal types of education, and integrate them in plans for one and the same educational development. For the formal (school) system the aim should accordingly be:

To seek more decentralized, more participative methods of planning.

To decompartmentalize the various educational courses and open them up to the outside.
To bridge the gulf between teachers and students and reform the career structure of the teaching profession.
To encourage diversified use of educational premises.
For the non-formal (out-of-school) system it would be essential:
To encourage the logic of participation, so as to associate those concerned with defining the ultimate aims and content of types of training and give them more of a say as to the form they should take (for example in the firm, by bringing trade unions into the process of drawing up training programmes).
To determine minimum requirements to be observed in respect of general education; the fact is that only too often in out-of-school programmes the insistence that they should be functional (in particular, vocational) is met to the detriment of genuine instruction in the forms of expression, basic concepts and cultural knowledge which permit development of the full potential of the individual viewed as a whole in his work, leisure pursuits, and civic and family life.
To strengthen the means whereby the state exercises control over other agents providing education, be it in regard to the allocation of resources, the elaboration of programmes or the quality of the instruction provided.

Co-operation between countries in the same cultural region

Part of the TNCs' power is derived from the monopoly they hold in certain fields of knowledge and the control they are thus able to exert over the dissemination of this knowledge by means of training. In addition, TNCs tend to structure the flow of individuals and knowledge within their production sphere as a function of their own standards and in accordance with their organizational hierarchy, the ultimate stage of this process being the establishment of transnational education networks modelled on their individual strategy. Lastly, the publishing sector for school textbooks and educational materials is dominated as regards both production and distribution by a small number of major international firms. By contrast, the nation-state cannot cover the whole range of disciplines, especially when education seeks to reduce the gulf between itself and the world of work, subject as the latter is to major and rapid technological change. Thus the nation-state's education system does not always have the resources or organizational capability to make an effective response to new training needs. In particular, many Third World countries do not have the individual resources to develop a publishing sector for school textbooks, still less educational aids, since these would not be distributed on a scale sufficient to amortize production costs. Moreover these difficulties increase with the level and degree of specialization of education.

It is therefore essential to encourage regional co-operation among Third World countries belonging to the same cultural region. This proposal is probably not a novel one, and many efforts have been made in this direction in the educational and cultural fields. Yet too many co-operation agreements are still dominated by bilateral links with the more industrialized countries, which in most cases encourage the perpetuation of educational dependence. In addition, too many economic areas have been set up between Third World states on the sole basis of the free exchange of goods and capital, without establishing the foundations of a genuine community which would lay emphasis on development problems. In this way new spheres of mobility are created for TNCs, and in the fields with which we are concerned there is always the danger that these could even turn out to be prejudicial to endogenous national development. For this reason co-operation in educational fields among Third World countries in the same cultural region should form the linchpin of regional integration. As regards education it would therefore be desirable:

To facilitate the flow of individuals, both teachers and students, and knowledge between Third World countries.

To set up joint research centres whose aims are geared to development problems specific to the area, and in particular to make regional data banks available to those engaged in research.

To exchange information on educational experiences and achievements, and in particular to encourage joint planning of schoolbooks and materials.

To pool resources in developing a publishing and educational-materials industry.

To provide for co-operation between a number of countries in regard to higher education or very highly specialized forms of training, and at the regional level in regard to the training of teaching and research personnel.

To organize training centres at regional level to be responsible for both research and the further training of teachers.

NOTES

1. E. Durkheim, *Éducation et sociologie*, p. 102, Paris, Presses Universitaires de France, 1977. (Originally published in 1922.)
2. Chai Hon-chan, *Planning Education for a Plural Society*, Paris, IIEP, 1971.
3. M. Carnoy, *Education and Employment: A Critical Appraisal*, Paris, IIEP, 1977.
4. A. Meister, *Alphabétisation et développement*, p. 28, Paris, Anthropos, 1973.
5. F. Perroux, Qu'est-ce que le développement, *Études*, January 1961, pp. 17–18.
6. S. C. Dube, 'Theories and Goals of Education: A Third World Perspective', *Prospects, Quarterly Review of Education*, Vol. V, No. 3, 1976.
7. Durkheim, op. cit., p. 100.
8. J. Hallak, *A qui profite l'école?*, p. 163, Paris, Presses Universitaires de France, 1974.
9. M. Carnoy, *La educación como imperialismo cultural*, p. 21; Mexico City, Siglo XXI, 1977; J. Lesourne, 'Development of Economic Systems and the Dynamics of Knowledge', *Les systèmes du destin*, p. 407, Paris, Dalloz, 1976.
10. P. Bourdieu and J. C. Passeron, *La reproduction*, p. 185, Paris, Éditions de Minuit, 1970.
11. A. Benveniste, 'Côte-d'Ivoire, télévision extra-scolaire pour l'éducation des adultes ruraux: bilan critique'; J. C. Pauvert, 'The Progressive Renovation of Education in the Ivory Coast by Means of Television', *Education on the Move*, Paris, Unesco, 1975.

12. This programme, instituted by AID and Stanford University, is cited by A. Mattelart in *Multinationales et systèmes de communication*, Paris, Anthropos, 1976.
13. H. Cassirer, *Mass Media in an African Context. An Evaluation of Senegal's Pilot Project*, Paris, Unesco, 1974. (Reports and Papers on Mass Communication, 69.)
14. Unesco, *Learning to Be*, p. 122, Paris, Unesco/Fayard, 1972.
15. Unesco, *Statistical Yearbook*, 1977.
16. E. McAnany, *Radio's Role in Development; Five Strategies of Use*, Washington, D.C., The Clearinghouse on Development Communication. See reference by J. Gunter and J. Theroux in *Prospects, Quarterly Review of Education*, Vol. VII, No. 2, 1977, p. 289.
17. Bourdieu and Passeron, op. cit., p. 162. 'The sweeping changes in educational technology (audio-visual aids, programmed instruction) are triggering off a corresponding range of changes in the education system.'
18. J. Jouet, 'Critique de l'utilisation des média légers dans le Tiers-Monde', *Revue Tiers-Monde*, Vol. XX, No. 79, 1979, pp. 550–1.
19. Ibid.
20. Ibid., p. 561.
21. Mattelart, op. cit., pp. 170–80.
22. Quoted by Mattelart, op. cit., pp. 215–16. For the United Kingdom, see the *Guardian*, 22 December 1970. For Peru, typed document with the Peruvian Ministry of Education. A Mattelart and D. Waksman, 'Plaza Sesamo' and an Alibi for the Authors' Real Intention', *The Democratic Journalist*, Vol. 9, 1974.
23. ITT, 'Social Responsibility', *Annual Report*, 1978.
24. D. Gerdimis, *Transfer of Technology by Multinational Corporations*, Vol. 1, Paris, OECD, June 1977; C. A. Michalet, 'Firmes multinationales et transfert technologique', *Mondes en développement*. No. 12, 1975.
25. ILO, *Social and Labour Practices of Multinational Enterprises in the Metal Trades*, Geneva, ILO, 1976.
26. R. B. Helfgott, 'Multinational Corporations and Manpower Utilization in Developing Nations', *Journal of Developing Areas*, January 1978, pp. 235–46.
27. Ibid.
28. R. H. Mason, *The Transfer of Technology and the Factor Proportion Problem, The Philippines and Mexico*. New York, UNITAR (Research Reports, 10.)
29. ILO, op. cit.
30. D. T. Saint Rossy, A. K. Chakrabarti and A. H. Rubenstein, *International Transfer of Technology. An Evaluation of the Education and Training Component*, Evanston, Ill., Northwestern University Press, 1976.
31. For example, Philips has a pilot factory at Utrecht (Netherlands) to which nationals of European or developing countries come for training, where production conditions typical of certain areas of activities can be simulated. See ILO, op. cit.
32. A survey carried out with forty-eight firms in ten OECD member countries which have establishments in developing countries. According to the authors of this study, higher professional staff are usually trained at the TNC's headquarters, whereas lower-level staff receive training in the local firm. In the latter case, while training is often provided by staff members working on the spot, some TNCs use teams from headquarters. Approximately 70 per cent of the firms who took part in the survey organize training courses at headquarters for higher professional staff coming from developing countries, so as to take advantage of the special facilities frequently available at the corporate headquarters, and also to standardize to some extent the behaviour of managerial personnel throughout the group's subsidiaries. See 'Technical Assistance and Private Enterprise', *The OECD Observer*, December 1967.
33. Quoted in J. Masini, M. Ikonicoff, L. Jedlicki and M. Lanzarotti, *Les multinationales et le développement, trois enterprises en Côte-d'Ivoire*, Paris, Presses Universitaires de France/CEEIM, 1979.

34. S. C. Dilley, 'What is Social Responsibility', *A Magazine*, defines social responsibility as the implementation or non-implementation of activities by a private firm without any expectation of economic profit or loss, the aim being to increase the social welfare of a community or of one of its constituent groups. Such activities are generally recognized by the firm as contributing towards the welfare of society.
35. International Chamber of Commerce (ICC), *International Corporations and the Transfer of Technology (A). An International Petroleum Corporation operating in Venezuela*, 1972. The firm described was nationalized in 1975.
36. P. Furter, 'INCE and Technical and Vocational Training in Venezuela', *IBE* 1978. (Paris), No. 35.
37. P. Furter, op. cit., quotes R. C. Quintini, *Ideas por una segunda etapa*, Caracas, 1975.
38. R. A. Jackson (ed.), *The Multinational Corporation and Social Policy, With Special Reference to General Motors in South Africa*, New York, Praeger, 1974.
39. A United Nations report refers to their collaboration with the apartheid regime: *Activities of TNC's in Southern Africa and the Extent of their Collaboration with the Regime in the Area*, New York, United Nations, Economic and Social Council, Commission on Transnational Corporations.
40. H. Schreuder, 'The Social Responsibility of Business', in L. Van Dam and L. M. Stallart (eds.), *Trends in Business Ethics*, p. 79. Leiden/Boston, Martinus Nijhaff, 1978. He distinguishes between two different kinds of social responsibility: first, social responsibility in the narrow sense of the term: the private firm is expected to avoid certain activities, even though they may be profitable from the conventional point of view; secondly, social responsibility in the broad sense of the term: the private firm is expected to undertake certain activities on account of the resulting social benefit. Schreuder opts for the former definition; he considers that it is dangerous for a private firm to exceed the limits of its economic functions by taking action in the social, institutional or cultural field, since this may bring about a 'corporate society'. He also considers that when an organization pursues both social and economic aims there is a real danger that it will not be possible to make any clear choice. Lastly, to expect a firm to have social activities which mean an economic loss would imply approval of the fact that it has economic activities which are remunerated at a higher rate of profit than that strictly necessary.
41. Exxon, 'Social Responsibility', *Exxon Background*, 1973, 15 pp.
42. *Esso Informations*, 20 September 1977, (Internal Bulletin, No. 610.)
43. Union Carbide, *Union Carbide Profile—Special report: Social Progress*, December 1974, 32 pp.
44. ITT, op. cit.
45. 'The Role of Giant Corporations in the American and World Economies', Para 2B, Appendices, *Corporate Secrecy Overviews*, 9 November 1971, p. 3268. Washington, D.C., United States Senate Select Committee on Small Business.
46. R. H. Malott (Chairman of FMC Corporations), 'Self-interest should Guide', *Economic Impact*, No. 3, 1979.
47. Ibid.
48. L.W. Cabot (Chairman of the Board of Cabot Corporation), 'No Strings should be Attached', *Economic Impact*, No. 3, 1979.
49. Excerpts from the *Ciba-Geigy Journal*, No. 2, 1978.
50. When speaking of 'transnational education networks' we are concerned with their formal aspect, that is to say training centres, teaching staff and programmes. It is however obvious that any firm, when becoming transnational, institutes an informal network for the transmission of knowledge, consisting in a flow of information (technical documents, mail, telex) and a flow of personnel (meetings, training, courses, visits to other production units).
51. The case of the International Agricultural Machinery Corporation is quoted in *'International Corporations and the Transfer of Technology'*, 1972, a report by the Special Committee on International Corporations, approved by the Executive Committee of the International Chamber of Commerce.

52. A case in point is Air Liquide, whose training centres serve both to demonstrate possible applications of its products to potential customers and to train the staff of a subsidiary company. In the Ivory Coast, with SIVOA, an Air Liquide subsidiary, 'training is of a continuing nature and is provided in a local training centre. Educators from the parent establishment come to Ivory Coast to train African foremen, who in turn train workers. Training is not however limited to the subsidiary, since it is also provided for the users of the drilling equipment marketed in Ivory Coast.' See Masini et al., op. cit.
53. *Mecánica popular*, Miami, May 1971, quoted in Mattelart, op. cit., p. 168.
54. ILO, op. cit.
55. In *Food First: The Myth of Scarcity*, F. Moore Lappe and J. Collins give a number of examples of co-operation instituted between FAO and firms specializing in fertilizers, insecticides and agricultural machinery. S. George, in *Comment meurt l'autre moitié du monde*, pp. 184–223, Paris, Laffont, 1978, also gives examples.
56. The case of IBM is taken from J. P. Gunneman, *The Nation State and Transnational Corporations in Conflict with Special Reference to Latin America*, New York, Praeger, 1975, and R. A. Bennet (Vice-President, IBM World Trade Corporation).
57. There are three main criteria used for selecting and financing IBM projects in the field of social responsibility: (a) the project must be of vital interest to the country in which it is to be carried out (or else of world interest); (b) the firm must have sole competence in respect of the technical or scientific skills involved in the project; and (c) the project must not be directly related to the firm's commercial interests.
58. H. Bakis, *IBM, une multinationale régionale*, Grenoble, Presses Universitaires de Grenoble, 1977.
59. Ibid.
60. See the survey by Mason, op. cit. Also the ILO survey *The Impact of Multinational Enterprises on Employment and Training*, carried out on seventy-eight multinational enterprises with headquarters and subsidiaries in different countries which shows that fifty-seven of them had made no change in their production processes.
61. ILO refers to the resulting knock-on effect (*Pratiques de formation, Sociétés mères, filiales et développement de la formation*, Geneva, ILO, 1980.)
62. ILO, 1976, op. cit.
63. United Nations, *Transnational Corporations in World Development, A United Nations Review*, New York, United Nations, 1978.
64. ILO, *The Impact of Multinational Enterprises on Employment and Training*, Geneva, ILO, 1976.
65. J. Hallak and F. Caillods, *Education-Work-Employment in Panama*, Paris, IIEP, 1977. (Working paper.)
66. What M. Eliou calls 'asynchronism in the process of change', quoting J.-W. Lapierre, L'asynchronisme dans les processus de mutation', *Sociologie des mutations*, Paris, Anthropos, 1970 (see also M. Eliou, 'Educational Inequality, in Africa: An Analysis', *Prospects, Quarterly Review of Education*, Vol. VI, No. 4, 1976, p. 570).
67. P. Hugon, 'L'enseignement enjeu de la compétition sociale à Madagascar', *Options Méditerranéennes*, No. 21, Formation et développement, 1974.
68. C. Tunnermann Bernheim, 'The Problem of Democratizing Higher Education in Latin America', *Prospects, Quarterly Review of Education*, Vol. IX, No. 1, 1979.
69. B. Millot and F. Orivel, 'L'allocation des ressources dans l'enseignement supérieur français', p. 150, 1977. (Doctoral thesis, Dijon.)
70. The United Nations report *The Impact of Transnational Corporations on the Development Process and on International Relations* (E/5500/Rev. 1, ST/ESA/6), shows that TNCs introduce a 'business ethic'.
71. P. F. Drucker, 'The Managerial Era', *Economic Impact*, No. 27, 1979.
72. 'Development must therefore be aimed at the spiritual, moral and material

advancement of the whole human being, both as a member of society and from the point of view of individual fulfilment. It should result in, but also spring from, greater and more enlightened participation by the individual in the life of the community. Far from subjecting people to some form of external discipline, or alienating them by the attraction of foreign ways of life, it should help in emancipating them, enable them to seek their own way, and safeguard their dignity as free and responsible beings.' *Thinking Ahead*, p. 85, Paris, Unesco, 1977.
73. Tunnermann Bernheim, op. cit.: 'Latin American education reflects the paradox of high growth rates at the secondary and higher levels, together with the persistence of illiteracy and incomplete primary schooling.'
74. C. Filgeira, 'Educational Development and Social Stratification in Latin America', *Prospects, Quarterly Review of Education*, Vol. VIII, No. 3, 1978.
75. G. W. Rama, 'Education, Social Structure and Styles of Development', op. cit.
76. Ibid.
77. Ibid.
78. Pedro T. Orata, 'Barrio High Schools and Community Colleges in the Philippines', *Prospects, Quarterly Review of Education*, Vol. VII, No. 3, 1977.
79. See, Tunnermann Bernheim, op. cit.; also I. Deble, 'La déperdition d'effectifs dans le Tiers-Monde et ses ambiguïtés', *Revue Tiers-Monde*, Vol. XV, No. 59/60, July/December 1974; see also Unesco/IBE, *Wastage in Education: A World Problem.*
80. To quote G. W. Rama, 'The Project for Development and Education in Latin America and the Caribbean', *Prospects, Quarterly Review of Education*, Vol. VIII, No. 3, 1978.
81. *Developments in Technical and Vocational Education: A Comparative Study*, Paris, Unesco, 1978.
82. R. H. K. Wong, *Educational Innovation in Singapore*, Paris, Unesco, 1974. (Experiments and Innovations in Education, 9.) See pp. 7 et seq. for a description of the reforms.
83. K. P. Wong, *The Cultural Impact of Multinational Corporations in Singapore*, p. 41, Paris. (Unesco Working paper.)
84. R. H. K. Wong, op. cit., p. 16.
85. Tunnermann Bernheim, op. cit.
86. Pang Eng Fong, 'An Economic Perspective of Universities and Manpower Development', *Development Strategies and Manpower Needs. The Response of Southeast Asian Universities*, Singapore, RIHED, 1976.
87. P. Limb, The Employment of Graduates of Tertiary Institutions in Singapore', *Development Strategies and Manpower Needs. . . .*, op. cit.
88. Muhammadi Siswo Sudarmo, 'The Employment of University Graduates in Indonesia, *Development Strategies and Manpower Needs. . . .*, op. cit.
89. B. Laurier and R. Tortajada refer to building the education system 'from the top'. (*École, force de travail et salariat*, p. 150, Grenoble/Paris, Presses Universitaires de Grenoble/Maspero, 1978.)
90. Lê Thàn Khôi, 'Aid to Education—Co-operation or Domination?', *Prospects, Quarterly Review of Education*, Vol. VI, No. 4, 1976, p. 591: 'Education in the colonial era fulfilled a twofold function, first to boost European culture and downgrade local values in order to make subjection acceptable and, secondly, to train intermediate and lower grade personnel for administration and the economy. The ideological influence was so strong that even today, despite "independence", many of those in government and leading positions in the young states continue to put the culture of the former mother country above everything else, even speaking of "returning to the sources", "authenticity" or "cultural identity" to satisfy the needs of their internal policy. That this is simply words is proved by the fact that in the majority of countries, which are those where no revolutionary changes have taken place, educational systems have not changed greatly either in content or medhods.'
91. The figures, taken from a report by the French Agence pour la Coopération

Technique Industrielle et Economique entitled *Étude sur la formation professionnelle et l'exportation de biens d'équipement vers les pays en voie de développement* (April, 1975), reflect the amount of training activities generated by French exports of capital goods and industrial projects in 1976. These exports represented 70 billion French francs. If it is estimated that the cost of providing training represented on an average 10 per cent of the total cost, i.e. 7 billion francs, this corresponds to the activities of 25,000 to 30,000 educators over a year, which corresponds roughly to the number of technical and cultural aid personnel involved under bilateral co-operation agreements (38,000 aid personnel, including 25,000 teachers).

92. F. Hirsch, *Social Limits to Growth*, Cambridge, Mass., Harvard University Press, 1976.
93. M. G. Duew and J. Greene, 'Foreign Nationals in International Management —A Research Report from the Conference Board', *Managing International Business* (New York), No. 2, 1968.
94. J. Tinbergen (co-ordinator), *Reshaping the International Order, A Report to the Club of Rome*, New York, Dutton, 1978.
95. UNITAR, *The Brain-Drain from Five Developing Countries: Cameroon, Colombia, Lebanon, the Philippines, Trinidad and Tobago*, New York, p. 9, UNITAR, 1971.
96. T. Mende, *De l'aide à la recolonisation*, Paris, Seuil, 1972; *The Brain drain. Work of the Lausanne Conference*, European Reseach Centre.
97. L. Pearson, *Partners in Development. A Report on the Commission on International Development*, p. 96, New York, Praeger, 1969.
98. UNITAR, op. cit.
99. Lê Thành Khôi, op. cit.
100. Mende, op. cit. p. 154: 'Last but not least, in the social and political climate that prevails in most underdeveloped countries, it is very much the exception for doctors, engineers, agricultural economists and scientists to enjoy an income and social prestige comparable to those of politicians, the military and members of the ruling élite.' See also R. Vernon, 'Multinational Enterprises in Developing Countries', in D. E. Apter and L. W. Goodman (eds.), *Dependency and Interdependence. The Multinational and Social Change*, p. 50, New York, Praeger, 1976.
101. Vernon, op. cit.
102. Togba Nah Tipoteh, 'Multinational Corporations and African States. A Fusion of Interest', African Association of Political Science Bi-annual Conference, Lagos, Nigeria, April, 1976.
103. T. Cullinan, 'Latin American Management Education and Recruitment: An Environmental Perspective', *California Management Review*, Vol. XII, No. 3, 1970.
104. K. P. Sauvant, 'The Potential of Multinational Enterprises as a Vehicle for the Transmission of Business Culture', *Controlling Multinational Enterprises: Problems, Strategies and Counter Strategies*, Boulder, Colo., Westview Press, 1976. The training centres established on the model of American business schools form a 'business infrastructure' in the host country.
105. D. Germidis, *The Vocational Training Provided by Transnational Corporatarions and the Management Problems Involved*, Paris, Unesco 1976. (Doc. SHC 76/Conf. 635/11.)
106. I. Sachs, *La découverte du tiers-monde*, p. 80, Paris, Flammarion, 1971.
107. *Final Report of Third International Conference on Adult Education*, Tokyo, 25 July-7 August 1972.
108. Y. O. Kassan, 'Formal and Non-formal Education and Social Justice', *Prospects, Quarterly Review of Education*, Vol. VII, No. 2, 1977; G. R. V. Mhari, 'Attempts to Link School with Work: The Tanzanian Experience', op. cit., Vol. VII, No. 3, 1977; B. L. Hall, 'The United Republic of Tanzania; A National Priority to Education', op. cit., Vol. IV, No. 4, 1974.
109. H. M. Dyasi, 'Integrated Science Education in African Primary Schools', *Prospects, Quarterly Review of Education*, Vol. IV, No. 1, 1974.

110. C. Colclough, 'Basic Education—Samson or Delilah', *Convergence*, Vol. 6, No. 2, 1976; quoted by T. Simkins in *Prospects, Quarterly Review of Education*, Vol. VIII, No. 2, 1978.
111. P. Furter, *La formation extra-scolaire et le développement dépendant dans les modes de transmission*, Geneva/Paris, IED/Presses Universitaires de France, 1976.

Chapter 6

The role of TNCs in the production of knowledge and the division of labour in the developing countries: science and technology

From the theoretical standpoint, economic thinking today no longer dissociates the problems relating to the development and acquisition of technological potential from an analysis of TNC behaviour.[1] This attitude echoes the general agreement that exists regarding the active role played by TNCs 'in the emergence of a world economic system whose characteristic features distinguish it from the traditional international economy',[2] regarding, that is, the leading role that they play in the transfer of technologies from the developed world to the developing world. It is perhaps from this standpoint above all that TNCs are now considered to be chiefly responsible for the splintering of development into a modern sector and a traditional sector. The dualism is then founded on the difference in the relative productivity of these two sectors; a difference which itself depends on the technology used, on whether it is a tool technology or a machine technology.

Leaving aside for the present a few remote societies that are none the less of great interest for the light they throw on the hierarchy of social values assigned to the various activities, it seems practically recognized now that the Third World countries cannot achieve the development on which they have so fixed their hopes without aligning themselves to some extent on the Western techno-productivist model, even though they must not wholly accept it but adjust it to local socio-cultural structures. For it seems difficult to accept that development, of any type whatsoever, can be achieved without increasing production of the goods that are required if the social demand is to be met. In order merely to meet the basic needs of the 1,500 million starving human beings who will inhabit our planet in the first decade of the third millennium, prime consideration will have to be given to the resources of technology. Its importance is, if anything, enhanced by the fact that it makes it possible to increase productivity, and thus gives grounds for some optimism that the world economy may be able to expand production capacities to the point where it becomes possible to satisfy human needs more fully. However, productivity occupies a particular place in the productive process. Although the desirability of increased productivity is hardly open to question, it may happen that, if it is increased too suddenly, this may lead to traditional, participatory productive processes being replaced by large-scale, centralized, alienating productive processes whose efficiency may ultimately be questioned (see the debates on the green revolution). Moreover, the very place productivity occupies in the process of production will result in its having an altogether central socializing function. This is due to the fact that, at the micro-economic level, physical production, regardless of where it occurs in space and time, results from a combination of labour time and labour efficiency which itself results from a combination of labour intensity and labour productivity. Labour productivity then becomes the factor that divides working time from non-working time. Society is thus free to choose what type of productivity it will have, which again bears out the fact that a particular type of economic rationality is matched by a particular type of social rationality.

In contrast with Western societies in which the use of productivity has led to accumulation, anthropology provides us with examples of societies such as that of the Siane in New Guinea who used the time saved by the changeover from the stone axe to the steel axe to increase the number of their extra-economic activities—celebrations, wars and voyages.[3] In the developing countries the productivity gap between the traditional and the modern sectors corresponds to a differentiation of their respective ways of producing which results in technological dualism. In the traditional sector, labour productivity is the result of the combination of a tool that hardly develops with a know-how that presupposes a particular social process of training. In the modern sector, which is where TNCs operate, the labour process is at once a process of technically transforming matter and a process of labour organization.[4] Labour productivity, then, is the result of the technical process that combines machines with the organization of the workforce and labour skills.

As the use of machines changes, so science is applied to production and hence production is partly included in science, the organization of labour being used on the application of the social sciences of organization and management. As for labour skills, they presuppose that training has a social function.[5] The central question is whether the transfer of technology also embraces its latent content: scientific knowledge, techniques and methods. If so, the developing countries should eventually find themselves in control of a process of scientific and technological development. This way of looking at the question is tantamount to considering and differentiating between two levels of technological transfer: the first within the sphere of action of the firm, and the second outside the sphere of action of the firm, i.e. in the scientific and technological infrastructure of the host countries.

It is therefore necessary to turn away from the theoretical debate on TNCs and to pinpoint the concrete problems involved in the transfer of technology with reference both to its nature and to the ways in which it is acquired. Bearing in mind the relationship between machines and labour input, we shall then examine the impact of the science and technology used on the world of work.

Section 1

The nature of scientific and technological development

Science is a mode of apprehending reality that falls into the category of action. It is a particular system of representation that presents the aspect of 'a methodological space (sphere of representation) comprising theoretical constructions, figurations (diagrams), demonstrations, interpretations (transition from the formal to the intuitive or from one formal expression to another) and experimental illustrations'.[6] Whereas formerly technology was essentially a body of practical know-how with no true scientific basis, it has now become the concrete, material mediation between science and everyday life: in other words, technology in the modern sense. Technology therefore characterizes the interpenetration or, if one prefers, the cross-fertilization of science and a particular set of techniques.[7] This phenomenon is relatively recent. Until the eighteenth and nineteenth centuries there were few connections between techniques and sciences.[8] The major technical inventions of that period were generally 'the work of men seeking, by dint of trial and error, to find solutions to practical problems without the assistance of scientists, the latter being men whose aim was to understand and not to produce'.[9] In order for a technological element to find a place in the 'technical system',[10] that is to say, in the body of techniques employed in industry, it must be consistent with the socio-economic system. There exists therefore a link between the technical system and the socio-economic system which can be located by analysing the process of dissemination of technical knowledge,[11] and this link is one that is passed over in silence by economic theory.[12]

The sphere of innovation

The idea of a technique finding its place in the technical system brings us to Schumpeter and to the distinction that he makes, in the application of science to industry, between invention and innovation. 'While invention represents the creation of a new idea or a new technique, innovation consists in the application of that new idea or new technique to the actual processes of production.'[13] In this sense, the business undertaking is no longer, as in Walras's static world-view, a place where productive combinations are achieved, but one where new combinations are achieved, in other words, the sphere of innovation; and innovation assumes various aspects: the manufacture of a new machine, the introduction of a new method of production, the manufacture of a new product, the adoption of a new method for organizing production. Innovation is the culmination of a scientific and technological process, namely, research and development (R&D), conducted largely by firms. R&D has become for large firms a productive activity in its own right backed up by very substantial expenditure,[14] and one in the full throes of expansion.[15] R&D entails a twofold process of diffusion (absorption): horizontal and vertical.

Vertical diffusion

Vertical diffusion is that which starts with basic research and moves in three phases towards the industrialization of a product or a process.

Basic research
This is the scientific activity concerned with the general relations between phenomena. More specifically, basic research work is 'all that which is of assistance in analysing the properties, structures and mutual relations of the objects and living creatures that compose the universe for the purpose of organizing the facts emerging from that analysis into general laws by means of explanatory models and interpretative theories'.[16]

Applied research
This is 'activity that is conducted according to scientific methods with a view to a particular practical end, namely to make use of natural phenomena'.[17]

Development
Development 'covers an extremely large variety of activities ranging from the application of existing scientific and technological knowledge for the conception of design of a product or process to the engineering activities

TABLE 49. The top ten firms for R&D expenditure

Total budget ($ millions)		Percentage of sales		Expenditure per employee ($)	
1. General Motors	1 633	1. Waters Associates	16.1	1. Waters Associates	8 857
2. Ford Motors	1 464	2. Comten	13.9	2. Amdahl	8 410
3. IBM	1 255	3. Intel	10.4	3. International Flavors & Fragrances	6 836
4. American Telephone & Telegraph	841	4. Data General	10.1	4. Eli Lilly	5 830
5. General Electric	521	5. Systems Engineering Laboratoires	9.6	5. Upjohn	5 803
6. United Technologies	439	4. Fairchild Camera & Instrument	9.4	6. Merck	5 622
7. Eastman Kodak	389	7. AMP	9.2	7. Communications Satellite	5 584
8. Du Pont	377	8. Medtronic	9.1	8. Lubrizol	5 409
9. ITT	371	9. Hewlett-Packard	8.9	9. Church & Dwight	5 372
10. Chrysler	344	10. Instrumentation Laboratory	8.8	10. Comten	5 161

Source: Standard & Poor's Computast Services Inc., Business Week, 2 July 1979, p. 53.

needed to bring a product or process to the point where large-scale production can be undertaken'.[18]

Lastly, the final stage is that at which the product or process moves into the phase of industrialization.

Horizontal diffusion

Occurring at each stage in the vertical process, horizontal diffusion is 'diffusion with a view to the application of new knowledge, new processes and new products outside their original fields'.[19] In applied research one can refer by way of example to the 'achievement of Mexican port and waterway engineers in using *bolsacreto* for breakwater design, on the basis of the latest developments in polymer technology'.[20]

As this twofold process of diffusion is not confined to the individual nation-state but spills over into the international economy,[21] technological progress in a particular country results from any one of the following: (a) an endogenous innovation; (b) assimilation, when the host country adapts a process discovered elsewhere to its own needs; and (c) utilization, when the host country purchases the equipment and adapts it to its own purposes.

Endogenous innovation

In the developing countries endogenous innovation has played a fairly limited role up to now. This does not mean that there is no innovation in those countries but that it is not of the same magnitude as in the developed countries. In many countries there in fact exists a genuine capacity for innovation on the part of craftsmen who make 'watering-cans and buckets in Upper Volta and Niger, often starting from old pieces of corrugated iron that are patiently de-corrugated and welded. . . . And rifles in Togo and Upper Volta, their barrels being made from old metal steering wheels laboriously unrolled.'[22] These capacities remain limited, however, because in the developing countries the potential for innovation is small owing to the virtual non-existence of science. In the absence of science, explanations of natural phenomena are anthromorphic in nature, as individuals spontaneously and unconsciously project on to nature their own psychology and a frame of mind deriving from social tradition. To this characteristic corresponds action of a magico-religious type. Only by means of a 'psychoanalysis of knowledge'[23] is it possible to realize that scientific reality is not the reality of spontaneous observation but a constructed reality arrived at by transforming qualities into quantities and by substituting rational unification for empirical diversity.

In the productive sphere, local tools are generally of a fairly fixed and simple character, do not have a very specialized use and are geared to subsistence production.[24] This has a bearing on the inadequacy of the developing countries' scientific and technological research systems. While the number of research personnel per 10,000 inhabitants was less than two in 1970 in the developing countries, it was twenty-seven in the United States, ten in France and eight in Denmark.[25] But even though the gap in regard to science is considerable, between developed countries and developing countries it is also very large between developing countries, since countries such as India or those of Latin America have, for historical or cultural reasons, an appreciable advance in this field. The divergence is equally pronounced where financial resources are concerned: 'Most of the developing countries allocate less than 0.3 per cent of their gross domestic product to research, whereas in developed countries such as France, the Federal Republic of Germany and the United Kingdom the proportion is approximately 2 per cent.'[26] This situation, compounded by the fact that research is generally conducted in a small number of areas that have nothing to do with production, accounts for the very small impact of the research undertaken in developing countries on the evolution of their productive system. It will therefore be necessary to look more to the assimilation and utilization of imported technologies.

Assimilation and utilization

Cases of the assimilation and utilization of technologies imported from the developed countries are generally quoted with reference to Asian countries. The Republic of Korea[27] and Japan in particular are very often cited. Japan developed R&D activitiesfor the purpose of adapting imported technologies which have benefited the whole of Japanese technology.[28] This technological policy launched before the Second World War was assigned two objectives. The first, a short-term objective, consisted in assimilating foreign techniques and incorporating them in the productive processes used. The second, a long-term objective, consisted in strengthening national technological capability. To achieve this, the government took four types of measures:[29] (a) the application of advanced Western technologies; (b) steps to promote technological adaptation and creation of a national technology; (c) measures to encourage innovations and the dissemination of techniques in the traditional sector; and (d) the training of skilled labour.

This process of assimilation was made possible by an education system and research to which initial impetus had already been given.[30] However, the degree of adaptation largely depends on the sector and the product. It is therefore necessary to distinguish between traditional technology which is used by craftsmen working on a small scale in the developing countries (in the textile industry for instance), intermediate technology which is long-established in the industrialized countries (cement and steel production) and advanced technology highly geared to the world market, for which the degree of adaptation is very small, as is the case, for instance, in telephone exchanges where products have to conform to international specifications.[31]

For it to be possible to assimilate technology, certain conditions must first be met: (a) production must be on a sufficiently large scale; (b) the skill level of the labour force must be sufficiently high; and (c) there must be additional technical assistance.

Nevertheless, even if these minimum conditions are met, the country will be a long way from having sufficient technological knowledge if it does not have access to what is commonly known as 'engineering' skills which are characterized by a grasp of the various phases involved in project preparation such as general process know-how, knowledge of appropriate equipment, the ability to plan technical studies and to organize the project as a whole.

In the absence of these skills, recourse will be had to the importation of 'turnkey' or production-guaranteed factories and it will then be necessary to make an attempt to catch up technologically, something which is all too likely to prove very difficult in view of the initial differences and the frequency with which the knowledge required itself changes.

Section 2

The influence of TNCs on science and technology

The smallness of the developing countries' capacity for endogenous innovation and for assimilating technology leads them to purchase technology on the world market in one of the following forms:

Capital goods and sometimes semi-processed goods which are sold and bought on the market, particularly in the framework of investment policy.

Skilled, and in some cases very skilled, labour and semi-skilled labour, able to use the material correctly, to apply techniques properly and to pick up the algorithms of information processing and production.

Technical or commercial information that can easily be obtained on the market or that is covered by proprietary rights and is sold with restrictions.[32]

Ways and means of transferring technologies

Technology transfers correspond to transfers 'of techniques, methods and means, i.e. of techniques themselves—operational and managerial know-how—and their entire material environment—equipment, tools and materials—and their non-material environment—training, information and decision-making'[33]

Transfers of technology therefore involve operations relating to:

Quota, sales and licensing agreements covering all forms of industrial ownership including patents, certificates of invention, utility models, industrial designs, trade marks, service marks and brand names.

Agreements relating to the provision of know-how and technical knowledge in the form of feasibility studies, plans, diagrams, models, instructions, manuals, service contracts or specifications or entailing the provision of technical, advisory and supervisory personnel and staff training with the provision of training materials.

Agreements relating to the provision of detailed basic technical plans, and the setting up and operation of plant and facilities.

The purchase, rental or acquisition by any other means of machines, materials, semi-processed goods and/or raw materials in so far as they form part of transactions covering transfers of technology.

Industrial and technical co-operation agreements of all kinds including 'turnkey' agreements and their derivatives, international sub-contracting and the provision of managerial and marketing services.[34]

These different procedures for transfers of technology correspond to two ways of acquiring technology.[35] Either what is involved is a direct transaction on the basis of a contract with firms using the technology in their own production, or the technology is included in the products of suppliers of machines and consultancy or project-study services.

The first is the chief way of acquiring industrial technology. By way of example, a study concerning ninety firms belonging to the Andean group notes that forty-nine firms, i.e. 54 per cent, have recourse to it for one or more of their main products.[36] It generally occurs in the form of the granting of a licence and is called an 'integrated project transaction' as the technical process, project-study and construction are provided as a unit with technical assistance and are accompanied by different forms of control over management and agreements regarding the provision of materials, which are just so many restrictions whose purpose is to offset for the supplier the competition generated by the transaction.

The second way of acquiring technology covers two categories of transaction according to whether or not the purchaser of technology has the technical capacity to install the plant. If the purchaser does not need the services of a company to install the plant, he proceeds by way of direct agreements with the machine suppliers and project-study offices. This procedure is known as a 'simple direct transaction'.[37] In the opposite case, what is involved is an 'integrated process transaction' as the suppliers then market systems and not components. It should be distinguished from the 'integrated project transaction' as, unlike the latter, it does not usually entail the permanent monitoring of project implementation.

Simple direct transactions

The advantage of such transactions lies in the fact that the purchaser can control the procedure as the technology is not integrated in too large a package. Product differentiation leads to supply of an oligopolistic kind which may be hampered by:

Possession of a new and very specific technology by a supplier or of a new process by a project-study office which give them a dominant position on the market.

Import barriers resulting from aid tied to investment financing. In this case the purchasing country has to obtain its supplies from companies in the country granting the aid.

Agreements between suppliers which lead to the market being divided up geographically when it is very concentrated.

Integrated process transactions

This form of transaction which involves several degrees of integration—from the production line to the 'turnkey' factory—is more in line with conditions in the developing countries, where the know-how needed for simple direct transactions is rare. However, this type of transaction reduces proportionally the possibilities of using local project-study capability where it exists. This gives rise to a split between the purchasers' personal interest in minimizing the risks and the host state's interest in making savings on external economies thanks to the development of local technological know-how which would be obtained through the non-integration of processes. But this type of transaction is very often imposed by suppliers whose bargaining power results from a dominant position on the market. Several cases may arise:

A supplier who is in possession of an important innovation in respect of one the of components becomes very competitive and may decide to sell an entire system, i.e. a complete process, which eliminates the possibility of simple direct transactions.

The process is very special and its implementation calls for specific project-study and managerial know-how. In this case, the purchaser will opt for 'integration' which is less costly owing to the economies of scale achieved by the suppliers of the system.

The market for certain components is very concentrated and the suppliers consequently agree to deliver only complete processes.

The market is on the contrary very atomistic and the small firms that predominate do not have the means to market their components. On this account they prefer to conclude exclusive contracts with large constructors, who thereby benefit as in the previous case.

In addition to the problems already mentioned, this type of transaction leads to a decrease in competition on the components market. In some sectors the small number of suppliers who dominate the international market limit the range of integrated processes that would be available if competition existed. This means that some equipment could be more efficient than it is if different processes were combined in a manner more appropriate to the characteristics of the receiving countries.

Integrated project transactions

Also known as 'contractual transfers of technology', these transactions, more than the two other types, lead to negotiations between purchaser and seller that involve a certain amount of bargaining. The purchaser seeks, for instance, to obtain a licence on account of the commercial advantages linked to it, sometimes accompanied by industrial compensation agreements which compel the seller to buy part of the goods produced.[38] The seller for his part seeks to protect his innovations and to maximize the advantages that he may derive from them. He therefore inserts in the contract restrictive clauses in regard to his future competitor. As very few suppliers are able to obtain the commerical advantages sought by the purchaser, negotiations soon turn to the advantage of the seller. It is for this reason that this type of contract is a major source of concern to the developing countries, which set up administrative bodies with the function of overseeing this type of negotiation.

J. M. Chevalier provides us with a highly significant example of asymmetry in negotiations between a supplier and a recipient. He refers to the case of a tyre firm set up in a developing country, in joint ownership with the local bourgeoisie, which possesses 35 per cent of the subsidiary's capital. The investment costs calculated by the firm are overestimated—'in regard to project-study for instance, the proposed factory is a standard factory for which it is difficult to justify real project-study costs of 7.5 per cent'[39]—without the local authorities being able to check their accuracy, as in this field no market prices exist. Combined in addition with the 'impressive array of advantages that are put forward as a *sine qua non* for investment',[40] they allow the firm to possess '65 per cent of a factory which not only has cost it nothing but, what is more, brings it in between 1 and 2 million dollars yearly'.[41] As for the host country, such an investment 'siphons off local savings, increases the power of the comprador middle-class, gives rise to no new interindustrial exchanges, neither upstream at the pre-production stage, or downstream, at the post-production stage, and accentuates both technological and commerical dependence'.[42] In this context, Colombia, however, has introduced certain rules—subsequently adopted by the countries of the Andean Pact—with a view to increasing its bargaining power and reducing the cost of acquiring foreign technology. Thus for the years 1968 and 1969, the Committee on Royalties appraised 269 contracts for the transfer of technology, accepted 98 of them, rejected 19 and renegotiated 171, out of which 152 obtained a reduction in royalties, which made it possible to reduce the original cost by 37 per cent.[43] R. Montavon reaches the same conclusions with regard to Mexico when, speaking of the reaction of Mexican industrialists to the 1972 law on the control of technology transfers, he writes: 'They discovered with the passing of time that this law put a major trump card in their hands during negotiations with multinational enterprises and that their bargaining power had increased proportionally.'[44]

The effects of the firm's strategy

There is no longer any room for doubt as to the magnitude of the phenomenon of technology transfer under TNC auspices (see Fig. 14). According to a study carried out by the United States Tariff Commission, the TNCs achieve substantial revenue through transfers of technology, corresponding in 1971 to 90 per cent of all the royalties paid to the United States.[45]

This state of affairs is due to the fact that 'the majority of patents are in the hands not of individual inventors but of large multinational corporations'.[46] This in turn stems, as far as the pre-production stage is concerned, from the predominant share of TNCs in R&D in the industrial sector. To give an example, United States-based TNCs finance 80 per cent of total R&D in the industrial sector, 94 per cent of which is carried out in the United States, the rest being concentrated essentially in the major industrial-

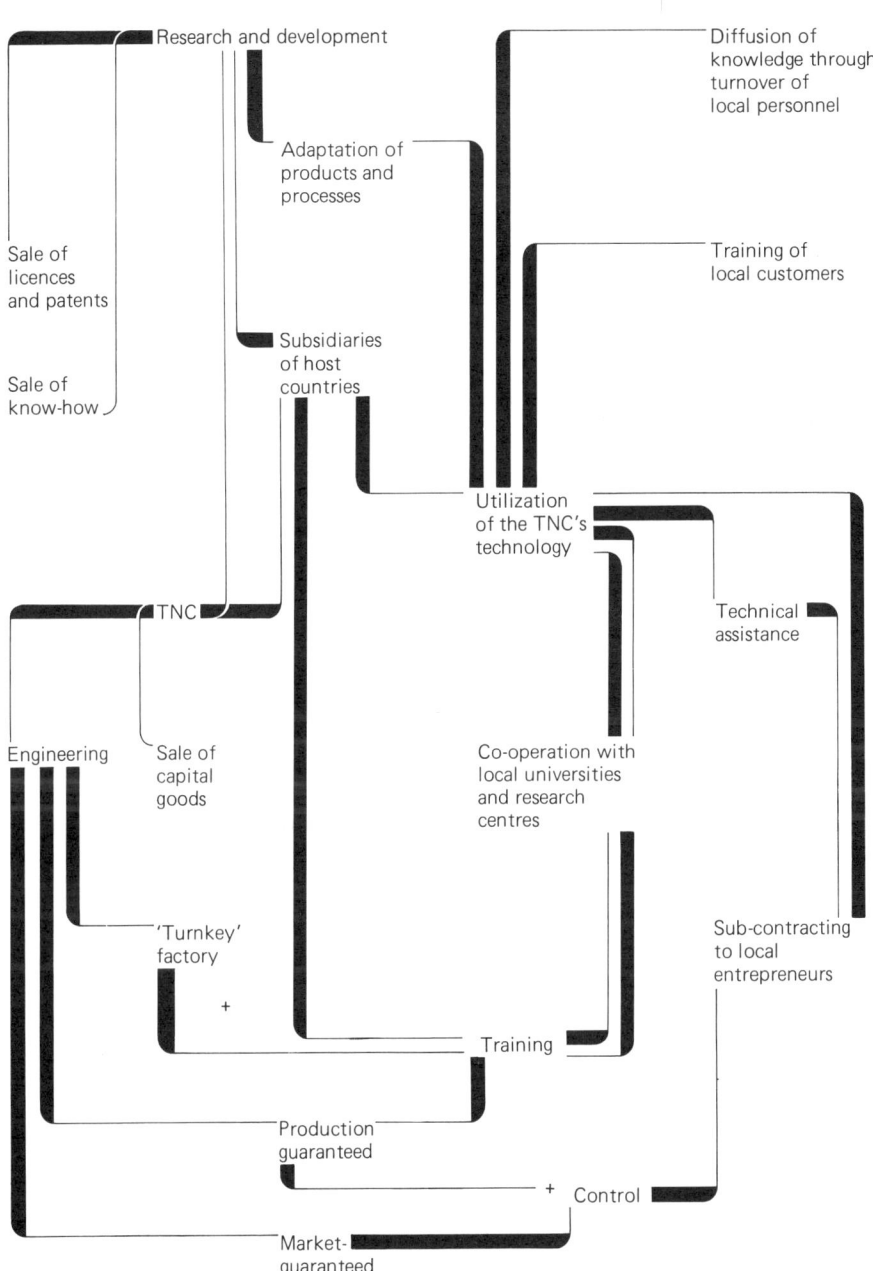

FIG. 14. Channels for Transfers of Technology from TNCs and their impact on local scientific and technological potential. (After: *Formation permanente*, No. 56, 1978).

ized countries.[47] Thus 'of the 35 million patents currently valid, only some 6 per cent of them were delivered in the developing countries'.[48] Of this number, 80 to 90 per cent are granted to TNCs and this percentage has been increasing over the last twenty-five years.[49]

It is clear that, worldwide, the production of technical knowledge is highly centralized. The general estimate is that 'between 95 and 98 per cent of total R&D spending takes place in the industrialized countries'.[50]

The industrialized world as a whole is estimated to possess ten times as much (i.e. 90 per cent) of the total stock of world scientists and engineers as the developing world, an imbalance which might take as long as a century to be reduced, at present respective rates of growth.[51]

This is borne out by the fact that virtually no R&D is carried out in subsidiaries. Sometimes there is indeed no alternative. Such, for example, is the case of a tea company in Kenya which, in order to use herbicides, engages in research on new crop techniques that cannot be carried out in the United Kingdom,[52] or of Nestlé which has no R&D located in Third World countries 'with the exception of research on tea in India (motivated by the existence of specific local raw materials)'.[53] This type of 'relocation', as it is called, is a fairly long-established practice, and generally takes place for enterprises

interested for one reason or another in agricultural produce. Thus the United Fruit Company has laboratories and experimental plantations in Costa Rica, Honduras and Guatemala where research centres on chemical means of combating the diseases that affect banana trees and ways of improving the species. In Peru, W. R. Grace and Company maintains a research laboratory and an experimental station where efforts are made to improve sugar cane. Anderson, Clayton and Co. has in Mexico a pilot farm where research is carried out on cotton but also on alfalfa, barley, sunflower, etc.[54]

These cases apart, the extent to which relocation takes place depends on the group's strategy as regards relations with its subsidiaries.

The relocation of industrial activity

may assume a variety of forms according to whether the subsidiaries concerned are branch subsidiaries oriented towards selling on the local (national or regional) market or workshop subsidiaries specializing in a particular sequence of the production cycle, whose products are re-exported to subsidiaries of the group located in the country of origin or in a third country.[55]

This typology resembles the standard distinction between market penetration, the exploitation of cheap labour and the exploitation of commodities. Both for natural reasons and for historical and/or socio-cultural reasons, the distribution of investments by category differs according to the region. Thus, for 1970, the distribution of investments in the developing countries was as follows: 42 per cent for the exploitation of commodities, 48 per cent for market penetration, and 10 per cent for the exploitation of cheap labour,[56] or by region as shown in Table 50.

TABLE 50. Distribution of investments by region

Region	Investment as a percentage according to type		
	Exploitation of commodities	Market penetration	Exploitation of cheap labour
Africa	60	34	6
Latin America	33	62	5
Middle East	91	9	—
Asia	30	36	34

Source: Y. Saboco, R. Trajtenberg and J. P. Sajhau, *The Impact of Transnational Enterprises on Employment in the Developing Countries*, p. 2, Geneva, ILO, 1976.

Lastly, in addition to the distinction between 'branch subsidiaries' and 'workshop subsidiaries', account should be taken of the direct sale of technology by TNCs, which has become an important means of transferring technology.

Units of the branch-subsidiary type

These subsidiaries are geared to local and regional markets. This is generally the case with European-based TNCs, for according to one estimate close on 97 per cent of the subsidiaries of companies based in continental Europe produce essentially for the local or regional market.[57] Mention may be made of the case of 'the Siemens factory in Mexico which produces and exports telex equipment, mainly to Latin America, and the Bosch factory in Malaysia which produces and exports cameras and projectors for Asian markets'.[58] This characteristic of European TNCs, which is bound up with their managerial structures, suited as these are to the purpose of circumventing tariff barriers, but not to global strategies,[59] distinguishes them from American TNCs, which are more oriented towards workshop subsidiaries. Nevertheless, it must also be said that European firms have started expanding in other directions, setting up for instance labour-intensive assembly subsidiaries producing for export. In units of the branch-subsidiary type, the parent company sometimes 'relocates' its research activities to the subsidiary for the purpose of adapting its products or processes to local conditions.

Product adaptation

It would be tempting to say that this corresponds to Vernon's 'product cycle',[60] in other words, that when it exists it concerns only 'mature products' or at best 'standardized products'.[61] To give an example: in the Philippines, a subsidiary that assembles vehicles has designed in its laboratories an automobile adapted to the regional market.[62] Similarly, food industries established in Mexico carry out research with a view to adapting food products to local consumer patterns.[63] However, it is not possible to generalize. Indeed, in a case-study on the S.A. Danone company in Mexico City, the author notes that the firm has a laboratory responsible for quality control but that this does not amount to research properly speaking.[64]

Furthermore, research on ways of adapting products to local conditions are supervised by the research centres of the parent company, which obtains proprietary rights over the inventions of the subsidiaries.[65]

Process adaptation

In some cases TNCs have adapted the size of their production units to the local or regional market.[66] Thus SIVOA, a subsidiary of Air Liquide in the Ivory Coast, is a production unit which is 'far less automated than those that currently operate in Europe, one reason being that the scale of production required by existing demand in the Ivory Coast is still too small to allow of greater automation'.[67] In the same way, a Japanese glass-making subsidiary established in India uses three times as many workers as the parent company unit for a plant half the size.[68] Research has also been conducted (in Africa for instance) with a view to using local raw materials that are generally not put to use.[69] It would appear that the subsidiaries of TNCs and national firms choose and adapt their technologies somewhat in the same way[70] because the degree of standardization of the product scarcely leaves any technological alternative.[71] The product thus appears to have a decisive effect on a firm's possibility of choosing a particular form of technology (a criterion characterized by its K/L ratio or any other ratio). The case of the soap industry in Kenya confirms this hypothesis: the manufacture of detergents and luxury soaps necessitates automated techniques whereas 'mere household soap can be effectively produced by means of labour-intensive methods. Thus the foreign subsidiary is more capital-intensive on account of the nature of the products that it chooses to manufacture.'[72]

For the directors of TNCs, the centralization of R&D at the level of the parent company is due to reasons of economy of scale but it also derives from the lack of skilled labour, resulting from the fact that education is not adapted to the needs of industry.[73] Here we speak of vertical transfer, as the subsidiary depends very heavily on the parent company for R&D activities. In the case of countries possessing scientific potential and a plentiful supply of cheap technically qualified labour, such as India, the relocation of R&D seldom goes beyond the stage of quality control and product adaptation.[74]

Units of the workshop subsidiary type

In contrast with the branch subsidiary, the organizational structure corresponds in this case to a horizontal transfer based on the interdependence of highly specialized subsidiaries, within a framework of international integration.

Generally this category includes the essentially labour-intensive assembly subsidiaries which have been established in developing countries largely for reasons of the wage differentials between developed and developing countries. To give a number of extreme examples average hourly wages in the cotton industry are 29.2 times higher in the Federal Republic of Germany than in Pakistan, 18.2 times higher in the electronic industry in the United States than in Taiwan, 11.6 times higher in the United States than in Singapore for semiconductors and plant assembly and 7.5 times higher in the United States than in Belize in the clothing industry; but in all the cases referred to the ratio is higher than 4.[75]

These wage differentials are all the more notable in that they are very little offset by productivity differentials. Thus, in Mexico's Border Industrialization Programme, labour productivity ranges between 80 and 140 per cent of that obtained in the United States, while in Morocco it ranges between 80 and 90 per cent of that obtained in Europe.[76] This is borne out by a study made by the United States Tariff Commission,[77] which, even though it notes that labour productivity in Mexico is only 60 per cent of that obtained in the United States in the clothing industry, nevertheless finds that in the electronic industry labour productivity abroad is equal to 92 per cent of that obtained in the United States and that for some products labour productivity is higher abroad than it is in the United States. Similarly, it is noted that, in regard to repetitive tasks in the electronic industry, labour productivity is between 10 and 25 per cent greater in Mexico than in the United States, and that the difference is even more considerable in the case of the Republic of Korea.[78] In this type of subsidiary the incidence of R&D depends on the complexity of the productive processes.

Complex products

Here we are concerned with firms that manufacture complex products using advanced technology and that split up their process of production at the world level. In the case of IBM, for instance, the relocation of research has very little chance of affecting the developing countries, as it calls for very highly skilled personnel. When relocation occurs, the firm's interest lies in recruiting high-grade personnel at low cost, resulting in a 'domestic brain drain'[79] that aggravates the international brain drain highlighted by the Club of Rome.[80]

Conventional products

We are concerned here with firms that use fairly unskilled labour. These firms, which typically produce articles of clothing and electrical household appliances, are increasingly establishing subsidiaries in the developing countries.[81] Here again, the effects on research are practically nil, as the subsidiary is almost always concerned with assembly operations.

The direct sale of technology

Those engaged in the direct sale of technology are satellites of the TNC (project-study and consultancy services and even embassies) that market its technical knowledge in connection with the sale of licences, know-how or 'show-how'[82] and provide the means of production ('turnkey' factories, production-guaranteed factories, etc.).

This type of action, which treats research as a productive activity, is very profitable and is tending to develop, either under the influence of the policies of the host countries (nationalization, joint ventures), or in the context of inter-state agreements, or because it makes the material presence of TNCs less visible while leaving them considerable negotiating power both at the pre-production stage (supply of raw materials, maintenance) and at the post-production stage (marketing of products when the domestic market is too small). At this point mention should be made of the importance currently assumed by international trading companies,[83] which establish international networks for the circulation of products—a precondition for the production of product packages—with a view to controlling the market. However, the most active of the TNC satellites in the field of science and technology are project-study departments and consultancies. Project-study comprises 'all the methods and organizational structures that make it possible to master the scientific, technical and economic information needed to plan and make optimum use of assets in the form of a coherent productive unit'.[84] In this sense project-study is a means of at once accumulating and disseminating industrial experience.

Project-study departments and consultancies that belong to or are closely connected to TNCs ensure the supremacy of the technological processes developed by the large firms and provide the means whereby the product is transformed into a 'product package' ('turnkey' or production-guaranteed factories, etc.). Thus, in France, project-study is 'highly concentrated among public and above all private, French and foreign, industrial and financial groups which have been set up or strengthened over the last twenty years or so',[85] as though 'the concentration of intellectual activity were developing apace with the centralization of capital'[86] or, rather, under the influence of the centralization of capital. As an example, of the twenty leading project-study offices, Paribas controls three (Heurtey S.A., SEMA, OTH), Empain Schneider controls two (Creusot-Loire, Speichim) and, of the first fifty, CGE controls four (CGA, GSI, Sogelerg). One of the results of this concentration is that the choice of technologies is fairly limited. For instance, in the steel industry, water-based metallurgy that necessitates ores of a grade higher than 60 per cent, new methods (steel works using oxygen) and high capacities (5 million tonnes) is imposed throughout the world.

The construction of major petrochemical complexes always depends on the same leading international project-study offices, Lummus, Kellogg, Power-Gas, SNAM, Projetti and Technip, which see that all new projects bear the imprint of the technologies of the large multinational firms and thus ensure their domination. . . . Any country wishing to produce aluminium today has to accept the conditions laid down by Alcan, Alcoa, Kaiser, Reynolds or Pechiney.[87]

Hence multinational firms are emerging as the major suppliers of both highly labour-intensive and highly capital-intensive technologies.[88]

Market prospects lead TNCs to sell their managerial know-how together with their technological know-how. We may refer to the case of Dow Chemical which has stated that the selling of licences is a thing of the past —at least in regard to the most modern technologies—and that consequently the company is not interested in selling only its process know-how. A company having the best technology might well not make a profit unless its technological know-how goes hand in hand with thorough knowledge of business management.[89] This centralization of technological creation accounts for the fact that, when the product is identical, there is hardly any difference between a national firm and a TNC.

The forging of links: relations between the subsidiary and the scientific, technological and industrial potential of the host country

There are four main ways in which a TNC's actions may impinge on the country in which its subsidiary is located in such a way as to increase the local scientific and technological potential and modify its absorption capacity. As in the previous case, the spillover for the country concerned differs according to whether the subsidiaries are branch subsidiaries or workshop subsidiaries, and whether the concern is with selling or with technical assistance.

The subsidiary's recruitment and vocational training policy

This point has been covered in Chapter 5. The vocational training provided by the TNC will have a multiplier effect if the recipients of such training transfer their knowledge to local firms. Some studies lay emphasis on the exodus of technicians towards rival firms,[90] as in the case of the five Kenyan senior personnel of the Bata Shoe Company who left in 1972 to found the Tiger Shoe Company, an enterprise financed by Kenyan capital.[91] But generally this type of mobility involves fairly unskilled personnel who wish to set up their own businesses. However, the trend is not very marked owing to the lack of financial resources. Senior technical sales personnel and engineers are regarded as having, in general, a very high level of stability.[92] A study concerning the Republic of Korea reveals that very few Koreans who have worked for a foreign firm subsequently work for a Korean firm.[93] As a general rule, the transfer of technology through the mobility of production personnel and managerial personnel between foreign and local firms seems to be negligible.

Relations between the subsidiary and public or private local research centres

The small degree to which R&D is relocated in subsidiaries, as seen earlier, leads to the virtual absence of a direct link with public or private local research centres in the form of either laboratories or universities. Financial relations exist but their main purpose is not production contracts, which alone are of interest to us here. The relations between the subsidiary and local research centres will clearly depend on the scientific and technological development of the host country, but also on the form in which the TNC establishes itself in the country.

Relations are generally most developed in the case of branch subsidiaries. In countries where the scientific and technological potential has been developed, such as India and Mexico, contracts with local research centres—as for the relocation of R&D within the firm—concern quality control or the adaptation of products to local tastes.[94]

It is very often asserted that it would be advantageous for foreign companies to transfer part of their R&D activities to India, a country where there is a plentiful supply of skilled research workers but where salaries are far lower than in the developed countries. This assertion, which does not take account of the role of R&D in competition, is valid only for a 'peripheral' technology and an 'import substitution' technology. The widespread use of sub-contracts for the production of technology will not be possible until the foreign company has full control over the use made of the technology, i.e. in the subsidiaries which it fully owns. However, owing to the danger that these companies may lose qualified local engineers to competitors, they generally hesitate to undertake research.[95]

The TNC will almost always avoid this kind of relationship in the case of a technological advance. Hence it does not always foster the developing countries' capacity for innovation, fearing an increase in their negotiating power and the promotion of a national scientific and technological system capable of developing an indigenous technology.[96]

Relationship between the subsidiary and local suppliers

The relationship between the subsidiary and local suppliers may, when sub-contracting is practised, constitute a means of upgrading the technological and industrial potential of the host country. For example, International Harvester, 'which assembles lorries in Rio de Janeiro, buys parts from about 200 Brazilian enterprises. This firm has a project-study department which distributes plans and technical information to its suppliers, corrects their mistakes, etc.'[97] By and large, the volume of sub-contracting is small. The subsidiaries ascribe this to the scant ability of national firms to comply with standards despite the technical assistance they provide. In some cases firms forced to sub-contract to local suppliers prefer to buy goods that have no relationship with the relevant sector of activity as the prescribed standards are not respected. Sub-contracting sometimes leads to intermediate technologies after local techniques have been improved through the TNC's know-how. The developing countries favour sub-contracting at present, but there is a great risk of over-specialization. In regard to project-study, which is generally of foreign origin, local project-study services, when they exist, are relegated pretty much to the sidelines. This is due to the fact that the transfer of technology usually takes place in the form of a 'technological package' and that for project-study recourse has to be had to the constructors of foreign capital goods. On this account, when local project-study services are used it is purely for the building and civil engineering components.

Sale of products

The sale of complex products by TNCs constitutes a means of disseminating technical knowledge to customers and distributors. It takes the form of two types of complementary action. The first type is directed to the customers, in the form of individualized after-sales service: for instance the secondment of technicians to assist the customer, and in the form of customer training such as that provided by computer manufacturers and manufacturers of farming equipment.[98] A 'consultancy' service may also be made available to customers. Thus, 'Celanese Mexicana S.A., a subsidiary of the Celanese Corporation, has a team of engineers whose function is to advise local industrialists on the processing of the plastics that it produces'.[99] The second is directed to distributors, in the form of assistance and further training courses, for the benefit, for instance, of automobile mechanics.[100]

Section 3

The influence of TNCs on labour

Viewed by some as resulting from the need for greater technical efficiency,[101] the division of labour was introduced, according to others, more for social than technical reasons.[102] Although this theoretical debate is of great interest if we wish to grasp the relationship between technology and the organization of society, on which the introduction of the technical division of labour is based, we shall leave it on one side, preferring to start off from the observation that the technical division of labour, deriving from the social division of labour and reflecting the level of a society's technical development, began to develop at the time of the Industrial Revolution.[103]

Similarly, for our purposes it does not seem appropriate to enter into: (a) the debate on the question of whether there is a strictly causal relationship between the advance of science and development of the productive forces,[104] which would bring us back to the problem of the congruence between the technological system and the socio-economic system; and (b) the debate —closely related to the previous one—centred on the scientific and technological revolution and the assertion that technological development is autonomous and that science has a universal status which allows it to impose its type of rationality.[105]

The fact of disregarding this theoretical debate does not detract from a study of the impact of TNCs on the division of labour, for the technologies transferred by the TNCs to the developing countries are, as we have noted, fairly similar to those used in the developed countries. This is borne out by D. Germidis: 'As a general rule the production techniques used in subsidiaries are entirely comparable to those which would be used in the country of origin, independently of the level of development of the country in which the subsidiary is established.'[106] In some cases, however, there exist technological differences, as is attested by a study focusing on 1,484 subsidiaries of American TNCs in eleven manufacturing industries.[107] That study indicates that in six industries the subsidiaries established in the industrialized countries are technologically different from those established in the developing countries, but that these differences do not necessarily result either from the extent to which they are capital intensive or from the way in which labour is used.

The link between the technology employed and the technical division of labour

Modes of production in the traditional sector

Although it is hardly possible to generalize, in view of the varying levels of development of the countries covered by this study, in most cases the specific production techniques employed by the developing countries involve the use of fairly simple tools and, at best, of 'universal machines'.

These modes of production, reflecting the state of technology in the traditional sector, correspond to individual craftwork or to micro-units of production of the workshop type in which the predominant pattern is one of unsupervised work by individuals who possess a know-how that gives them a total command over the finished product. Hence, in such societies, the division of labour involves principally the social division of labour into trades, with little in the way of technical division of labour.

Modes of production introduced by TNCs

As we have already pointed out, TNCs are now the main channel for the transfer of technology. This is the result of what we have already seen to be the marked extent to which technological creation is centralized, which leads to a national firm and a subsidiary of a TNC choosing much the same technology for an identical product. Even so, this does not mean that, in terms of overall statistics, the productive combinations of TNC subsidiaries and local firms are the same: for one thing, the branches in which TNC subsidiaries are active are not necessarily the same as those in which local firms are active; for another, within the same branch, the goods produced by a TNC subsidiary may be different from those produced by local firms. Lastly, in TNC subsidiaries and local firms the life-span of the technological capital may not be the same.

Types of technological equipment. By establishing subsidiaries and through the direct sale of technology, TNCs have now become the main vehicle for introducing modern forms of mechanization into the developing countries.

Mechanization should be understood as the bringing into operation of several tools (now automated so that there is no need for manual dexterity on the part of the worker who previously directly applied his strength to a tool) by means of mechanisms that transmit not a human force but a force based on the mechanical momentum produced by a motor.[108]

Nowadays mechanization is largely automated. The machine is incorporated within a system of machines which assigns to the worker a role of supervision and control, whereas in the case of conventional machine tools his activity related to start-up, loading, monitoring and similar operations. The degree to which automation occurs depends on the kind of processing involved.

In mechanical processing the productive act is discontinuous as it breaks down into the automatic mass production of parts on the one hand and, on the other, the mounting and assembling of those parts. The corresponding type of machine is: (a) for mass production, the transfer machine, i.e. an automatic system of machine tools organized in a sequence, which, after being first used in the automobile industry, subsequently came into widespread use; and (b) for the small-scale or medium-scale production of mechanical parts, the numerical control machine, the operation of which is governed and controlled by a program.

In physico-chemical processing, the productive act is continuous and it is possible to speak in this case of a wholly automated process. Such is the case in respect of intermediate industries such as the iron-and-steel and petrochemical industries.

Labour skills and principles of labour organization
When mechanization occurs the activity of production is broken down through the fragmentation of tasks and is reconstituted through the organization of labour. This division of labour corresponds to a dual movement. On the one hand, there is a drop in the necessary skill levels since, as the worker's responsibility is confined to a smaller aspect of what is produced, there is a corresponding reduction in the amount of know-how he needs, and hence he loses control over the manufacture of the product. On the other hand, there is an increase in the skill levels of a small number who are responsible for maintaining the technology.

This labour dichotomy gives rise to a dual labour market: a skilled and an unskilled labour market. The division of labour became increasingly predominant with the spread of Taylorism at the beginning of the twentieth century and then Fordism.

Taylorism. By transferring the qualitative characteristics of work to the machine, mechanization reduces work to a series of repetitive gestures characterized exclusively by its duration, i.e. the output norm'.[109] Taylorism is a principle governing the organization of work whose purpose is to 'step up the pace of the series of gestures corresponding to each work station and to reduce the number of gaps in the working day'.[110]

Fordism is at present the major form of labour organization in industry. It represents a stage beyond Taylorism in that it corresponds to the generalization of the production line, in other words, the automation of discontinuous productive processes. B. Coriat describes Fordism as follows:

So far as possible, all handling operations are performed by mechanized means (conveyors, mobile systems) and in any case are the responsibility of a service separate from that in charge of assembly operations proper. The works personnel are thus relieved of the need to move around the workshop and remain fixed at their stations . . . In addition (and this aspect is complementary to the previous one), the speed at which parts move from one point to another, i.e. the rate of work, is regulated mechanically, by a means external to the workers, and they are obliged to accept this fact.[111]

The methods of production of TNC subsidiaries are highly capital-intensive

Generally speaking, a consensus clearly emerges from comparative studies of local firms and TNC subsidiaries: TNC subsidiaries employ technical processes that are more capital-intensive than local firms. Thus S. H. Jo, in a comparative study of foreign firms and local firms in the Republic of Korea, notes, on the basis of data supplied by the Bank of Korea for 1973 and 1974, that the productive combination (K/L) of foreign firms is about twice that of local firms.[112] Similarly, C. V. Vaitsos gives for Mexico a figure of 2.5 to 1 for the industrial sector as a whole.[113] But these findings sometimes need to be qualified. For instance, H. Mason observes that American firms in the Philippines and Mexico use more capital per worker, but he points out that this difference is due more to investments in buildings and stock than to technological equipment. Vaitsos, for his part, analysing the productive combination (K/L) according to the size of enterprises, shows that in Peru, in 1973, the ratio between the two factors was higher in foreign firms, except for the largest, as is revealed by Table 51.

TABLE 51. Productive combination in Peru, 1973

Size of firms according to gross product (Y), (in millions of Peruvian soles)	Productive combination (K/L) (in thousands of Peruvian soles)	
	Firms in which Peruvian control is at least 80 %	Foreign firms and joint ventures
Y ≤ 5	68.6	142.4
5 < Y ≤ 25	98.5	152.5
25 < Y ≤ 100	174.8	216.4
100 < Y ≤ 500	218.0	291.0
500 < Y ≤ 1 000	297.5	435.8
1 000 < Y	757.2	304.3

Source: C. V. Vaitsos, *Employment Problems and Transnational Enterprises in Developing Countries: Distortion and Inequality*, p. 16, Table 2, Geneva, ILO, 1976.

The analysis by industry established by S. H. Jo reveals that certain branches are not affected by the general trend to which we referred earlier in respect of the Repulic of Korea.[114] For food industries, wood, clay and metallurgical products, and miscellaneous industries, the K/L ratio is lower in foreign firms than in local firms and is much the same in the petroleum, electrical and electronic industries.

Be that as it may, there is a tendency, as industrialization proceeds, to use increasingly capital-intensive processes both in local firms and in TNC subsidiaries in order to offset the lack of skilled labour in the developing countries.[115] Thus, in a case study on Iran, of twenty firms questioned, eighteen had adopted processes marked by greater capital intensity in order to make up for the shortage of skilled labour. However, this does not mean that there is no skilled labour in these countries but that the skills existing do not correspond to the product manufactured by modern industry. To this should be added the fact that the TNC, through the transfer of technology, helps to accentuate the social division of labour by contributing to the emergence of new occupations.[116] R. C. O'Brien even speaks of a problem of professionalism in the mass media in two African countries, Algeria and Senegal,[117] and P. Golding, examining the professionalism of journalists in Nigeria, defines it as the transfer of an ideology paving the way for the transfer of a technology.[118]

The spread of wage-earning

One of the notable consequences of technology is that, at the same time as it atomizes individual trades and renders the corresponding skills obsolete, it causes the worker to lose his free-lance status and become a wage-earner. J. Galtung refers to the highly significant case of a Norwegian fisheries-development scheme in the Indian state of Kerala. The scheme took the form of a technical-assistance programme whose purpose was to improve the productivity of the fishermen of Kerala by providing modern trawlers fitted out with electronic devices for locating fish. The result has been that the producers are no longer traditional fishermen moulded by the experience passed on from generation to generation. For the type of fishing introduced is industrial fishing and the fishermen are replaced by industrial workers.[119] This phenomenon, which is far from being peculiar to the developing countries, is the result of the concentration of technological capital. Through the effects of competition, large firms eliminate small firms, and of course to an even greater extent small workshops, by means of their technical efficiency and the dissemination of new products. Following the introduction of soya in Brazil, a report issued by the Centre Français du Commerce Extérieur noted: 'Over the last two years there has been a twofold trend: small factories are being closed and enormous processing units are being put into operation.'[120] But the evidence yielded by case-studies is contradictory.

On the one hand, some studies confirm this trend, as for instance that by P. B. Weinstein who asserts that the closure of a large number of local firms in Indonesia is to be ascribed to Japanese joint participation in the textile industry,[121] or the study by C. Brundenius who notes an identical phenomenon in the mining industry in Peru.[122]

On the other hand, some studies attest that the emergence of TNCs in the developing countries increases the number of entrepreneurs. K. Kumar notes that in countries like Brazil, Hong Kong, Malaysia, the Republic of Korea and Taiwan there is a positive correlation between the growth of foreign investment and the number of local enterprises.[123] Similarly, U. Kerdpidule reaches the conclusion that foreign capital has positive effects on the emergence of Thai entrepreneurs.[124]

This phenomenon would appear to be due to variables such as the degree of industrialization of the host country, government policy and the TNC's operating procedures. Positive effects can, for instance, be expected if the area is one in which the TNC relies on sub-contracting. Similarly, in countries marked by a small degree of industrialization, employees of TNC subsidiaries who have in the course of their employment acquired a skill may open their own business. Thus, according to D. Germidis, personnel such as electricians or other junior technicians are more apt to leave the firm from a desire to set up on their own and become independent, though he notes that lack of funds very considerably hampers this trend.[125] But once the country achieves a certain degree of industrialization, the trend may well be reversed. This is the kind of consideration underlying A. O. Hirschman's plea in favour of foreign disinvestment or 'divestment' in Latin America.[126]

The problem of urban unemployment

So-called modern production slowly throttles so-called traditional craft production in order better to destroy it. What is far more serious is that it also throttles the craftsmen for it is mathematically impossible for brand new factories to employ them all, even if they were to produce as much as the entire craft sector combined.[127]

The problem of unemployment is in this sense parallel to the spread of wage-earning. We are here at the heart of a veritable paradox with which the developing countries are faced in regard to the choice of the product that is manufactured.

On the one hand, they seek gains in productivity, which are possible through technology alone. On the other hand, as there is an obvious lack of the required skills, the technology cannot but be capital-intensive as we have seen, while in those countries what exists in abundance is labour.

Unemployment is thus the result of the elimination of previous forms of production by modern technologies which cannot absorb the labour surplus thus generated. The problem is a crucial one where the flight from the land is concerned. Even though one study, commissioned by the manufacturer of agricultural equipment, Massey-Ferguson,[128] on capital/labour substitution in agriculture, concludes that, apart from the use of combine-harvesters, mechanization is not always accompanied by a reduction in labour, farm mechanization allows of such gains in productivity that the outcome is obvious. In the Latin American countries traditional farm tools are very rudimentary:

The tractor-drawn plough is often unknown in the South Andes, the ploughman using the *chakitaccla*, a sort of spade of Inca origin. For harvesting the sickle is used, for threshing the thrail. The swing-plough is in use in Ecuador, but without the metal blade. Under these circumstances it is obvious that any gain in productivity is bound to lead to a displacement of labour. The mechanization of large estates will reduce employment for farm workers, peons, and lead to the eviction of tenant farmers. The introduction of more sophisticated farm equipment to serve medium-scale land-owning farmers will lead ultimately to an increase in the size of farms at the expense of the poorest sections of the population.... Studies conducted in Latin America[129] reveal that each tractor takes the place of five man-years. . . . If it is accepted that about one-third of the displaced workers find other employment in the agricultural sector, for each tractor brought into service between 3 and 4 men have to leave it.[130]

In addition, the runaway increase in the rural population[131] swells the number of those who are drawn to the town, either because they are in search of employment or because wages are higher there. As has been observed by F. B. Weinstein, referring to the countries of South-East Asia with the exception of Singapore, the concentration of foreign enterprises near the large cities has accentuated the disparity between rural and urban areas.[132] But very often the town is just a myth, for industrialization is capable of absorbing rural immigration, to which is to be added the large natural growth of the urban population. 'A vast marginalized urban sector is created.... But this marginality is not tied up with circumstances, is not a temporary phenomenon, but has structural features.'[133] While the employment offered by TNCs varies according to the region—the most fortunate regions being exporting areas, thanks to the establishment of assembly subsidiaries, which use the largest volume of labour[134]—it is interesting to note that, in the developing countries in 1970 only 2 million jobs were made available by TNCs,[135] while for the same year the estimated number of unemployed in those countries was 50 million.[136] While their relative share of the employment market remains stable, TNCs control a larger share of production. Thus, in Argentina in 1955, foreign firms controlled 18 per cent of production and 11 per cent of employment in the manufacturing sector; in 1972, while they still controlled 11 per cent of employment, their share of production had increased to 31 per cent.

The twofold division of the labour market

If the labour market can be seen as divided into a primary market, that of high wages and good working conditions, and a secondary market, that of low wages and poor working conditions, it can also, and to a greater extent in the developing countries than anywhere else, be seen as divided into a sector which looks towards TNC subsidiaries and one which looks towards local firms. The fact is that TNCs practise high-wage policies in Asia, Latin America and Africa alike:[137]

In the Third World the average earnings of wage-earners in the multinationals greatly exceed those of their counterparts in all national enterprises. The deviation is generally far greater than that to be observed in the industrialized countries and seems to be linked to the stage of economic development.[138]

A large number of country studies point to this being the general rule,[139] even if in some cases the wages paid by foreign subsidiaries are comparable to those paid in the same branch in the host country.[140] According to D. Lim, the wage level of TNCs is due to the high capital intensity of their productive processes which increases labour productivity, but also to the role they mean to play in keeping with their international status.[141] But it should not be forgotten that the size factor which allows of economies of scale also has a bearing on the happy position of TNCs in regard to wages. Moreover, when the wages paid by TNCs are compared with those paid by large local firms, differences in remuneration between the two types of enterprise are far less marked than they are when it is a question of overall averages.[142] On this account, 'wage-earners in multinationals are often considered to be a privileged minority'[143] particularly since advantages include social allowances and benefits and extend to working conditions.[144] This high-wage policy contributes to the emergence of a 'labour aristocracy'. Since those who are employed in the transnational sector occupy a privileged position, it is not surprising that TNCs attract the most experienced and most highly qualified workers in the developing countries while at the same time setting standards for other firms. But the influence that they thus exercise may have a destabilizing effect, for very often the pressure towards wage increases in local firms is unaccompanied by any increase in labour productivity, which results in the elimination of the firms in question.[145]

Section 4

Ways of achieving an endogenous technology

If by modernity we mean a rate of change that can be tolerated by the system; in other words if it is not to be harmful in socio-cultural terms, the developing countries must adopt a very firm attitude *vis-à-vis* science and technology as the spheres in which it finds material and non-material expression. It is all the more urgent and necessary for them to adopt such an attitude in that the structuring of the world technology market by TNCs affords those countries small opportunity to gain independent access to technology.

At this stage in the analysis it should be mentioned that once again it is not possible to make do with general proposals in regard to scientific and technological action. This truism leads us to distinguish clearly between two questions:

First, that of the rules it would be desirable to lay down internationally to counter-balance the abusive practices of certain TNCs and of the general principles governing science and technology policies, which can be discussed within the forum offered by international organizations.

Second, that of the specific decisions regarding science and technology, which depend on a consistent overall national policy and, on this account are necessarily an expression of the government's will.

Among the solutions proposed to improve the developing countries' position in the field of science and technology, mention is very often made of intermediate technology, which we shall now consider before taking a look at the general proposals.

Intermediate technology

Contrary to its original aims, the widespread introduction of the most advanced technologies in the developing countries, far from solving their problems, is, in many cases, a source of new forms of vulnerability. In view of this, there have been some who, following E. F. Schumacher, have advocated the use the intermediate technology with a view to limiting the fragmenting effects of progress. Several terms have been used to describe these different technologies: they have been referred to as soft, alternative or appropriate technologies; as ecotechnology or biotechnology.

The term 'intermediate technology' is explained by three factors which distinguish it from advanced technology:[146]

The cost of equipment per worker, i.e. the K/L ratio, while being higher than for traditional techniques, is far lower than in the case of advanced technologies. It is thus possible to spread out the capital by creating a large number of jobs.

The smaller size of the equipment encourages the introduction of technical advances in craft workshops and industries without giving rise to spatial concentration, which makes it possible to limit the flight from the land.

The simplicity of design enables indigenous workers to maintain the technical material, which makes it easier for them gradually to master the technological processes and thus acquire the ability to produce capital goods. In addition, this type of technology is in keeping with its specific environment (economic, social, cultural and ecological), a fact more clearly brought out by the term 'appropriate technology'.

When intermediate technologies are compared with advanced technologies they are very often regarded as symbols of impotence, the adjective 'intermediate' being replaced by 'backward'. This is a mistake, for intermediate technology does not turn its back on science:

[It] requires more scientific capability than is needed for mimetic transfer.... More generally, in order to give effect to project-study solutions calling for less capital, lower energy consumption, smaller size and simpler use, it is necessary not only to master the same basic scientific and technological principles but also to be able to innovate in the handling of local materials (coconut, bamboo, bagasse, jute, etc.), which are practically disregarded by conventional Western technology.[147]

On the one hand, then, intermediate technology calls for the cross-fertilization of modern scientific and technological analysis and traditional empirical know-how; on the other hand, it necessitates a precise analysis of needs with a view to redefining the technical nature of the services capable of meeting them. This point is a fundamental one, for, as we have seen, the choice of production techniques very often depends on the choice of manufactured products.

It should be made clear, however, that intermediate technology is not, in every case, the most suitable for the developing countries. As is pointed out in one of UNCTAD's reports, there does not exist, as is very often thought, a single type of technology (and technological development) for the developing and the developed countries or simply for the developing countries; it has been demonstrated that the three types of technology—modern, traditional and intermediate—are appropriate in certain cases and none of them inevitably takes precedence over the others.[148] This means that intermediate technology must be viewed from the standpoint of technological pluralism, and that it will not be appropriate unless it is integrated in its economic, social, institutional, cultural and ecological environment. Care must be taken not to be led astray again by the lure of widely marketed technologies into thinking that there can be 'for different needs, identical choices'. For all the aforementioned reasons, intermediate technology will not change the existing state of technological dependence unless it ceases, eventually, to be an imported product, for, as is noted by A. F. Ewing, TNCs are beginning to feel the need to propose different, i.e. appropriate, technologies.[149]

Proposals

In order to take steps towards improving their capacity for innovation, the developing countries should take two types of action: (a) the establishment of science and technology policies; (b) the formulation of rules to supplement these policies, relating to action by TNCs in the field of science and technology.

The establishment of science and technology policies

We cannot undertake here a detailed description of these policies, which must be in keeping with the choices made in regard to economic and social development, and with the specific features of each country. This does not mean, however, that general principles cannot be proposed. Science and technology policy should focus on four aspects: creating, evaluation, dissemination and storage. These four aspects are essential although, generally speaking, such policies are concerned only with the first or, at best, the first and the third. This partly accounts for their ineffectiveness and their failures.

Creativity

Scientific and technological independence cannot begin to be achieved where there is no creativity. The specific character of this factor in the developing countries stems from the co-existence of two ways of thinking which correspond to the production of two types of knowledge: scientific knowledge and practical traditional knowledge. Three types of creativity are therefore involved, creativity being understood as a state of mental responsiveness and receptivity culminating in the ability to form new combinations of elements: (a) creativity of a scientific type; (b) creativity of a traditional type; and (c) creativity of a composite type, resulting from cross-fertilization between the other two types of creativity. We shall not concern ourselves here with creativity of the traditional type as it does not come within the purview of science policy.

Creativity of the scientific type. Access to this type of creativity is gained through scientific and technological training prolonged by means of a research structure. The developing countries are highly dependent on the Western world in this connection and, although some countries have made considerable efforts in this direction, they will need to allocate vast resources in order to reduce the gap between them and the developed countries.

However, the incentive to do so varies according to the needs generated by the style of development. Two general cases can be distinguished: first, those countries that seek to develop an organic industrial fabric on the basis of advanced technologies must develop a complex scientific and technological system in order to increase their mastery of imported technology and subsequently achieve creativity in the matter of design, which will equip them with a capability for producing advanced technology; second, those countries that pin their hopes on the use of cheap local labour by sub-contracting (assembly) industries have a smaller need for creativity in that they are concerned with execution and not with design, a fact that is likely to keep them in a lasting state of dependence.

In order to gain access to scientific creativity, the developing countries, after deciding on the sectors to which to devote their efforts, have no other recourse than to develop a system of scientific and technological education and research institutions similar to those existing in the developed countries. In order to reduce costs—apart from the fact that it is essential to eliminate duplication of effort at the domestic level by setting up co-ordinating bodies that can decompartmentalize organizations and research fields by encouraging collaboration—the developing countries should pool their efforts to a far greater extent than they do at present by setting up joint reseach centres and universities. It will also be necessary to develop a project-study sector to plan the different phases involved in the preparation of industrial projects (general-process know-how, knowledge of the appropriate equipment, ability to plan technical studies, ability to organize the project as a whole).

So far as consistency or cohesion is concerned, science and technology policy should ensure, on the one hand, that pure and applied research are linked, and that development programmes are sufficiently sophisticated to allow the use of applied research. On the other hand, it should ensure functional cohesion, which calls for a certain distribution of research funds between operation expenditure and capital expenditure.

Creativity of the composite type. This is the result of the combination of information and scientific reasoning with traditional empirical know-how. This type of creativity leads to new (appropriate or intermediate) technologies in that it makes it possible to adapt advanced technologies to local natural, economic and cultural conditions or to improve ancestral techniques through the contribution of science. Thus, traditional techniques for water cooling and household refrigeration have been reinstated.

The development of this type of creativity presents a fair number of advantages, in particular because it makes it possible to enhance the role of scientific training and research at small cost without increasing foreign spending. It would therefore be desirable for the countries concerned to develop research institutions for this purpose and national project-study services dealing with specific technologies, which would enable them to reduce part of their foreign dependence. This type of research calls for multidisciplinary teams made up of scientists, sociologists and psychologists.

Evaluation

It is necessary for the developing countries to evaluate technology from the social point of view, on account of the many forms of socio-cultural and ecological vulnerability to which it gives rise. Special bodies should be set up for this purpose, comprising leading individuals in the country or region, though care would have to be taken to ensure that they shared the same general outlook; the task of such bodies would be to see that technological progress remained in line with science and technology policy or to take remedial action if it did not.

Dissemination

Dissemination should be assigned an important place in science and technology policy, partly because it is a prerequisite for the future exercise of creativity and partly because without it the results already yielded by creativity lead nowhere. Dissemination involves, on the one hand, the dissemination of knowledge and, on the other, the propagation of innovations.

The dissemination of knowledge. This is necessary both internally and externally. Internally, the aim is to make an inventory of the operational networks of scientific and technological operations with regard both to results and to trends, and to facilitate exchanges between universities and research centres. Externally, scientific publications of an international standard are an important means of disseminating knowledge. The countries concerned could therefore use part of their budgets to enable their scientific and technical personnel to have access thereto. In the same way, it would be valuable for such personnel to participate in forums on science and technology which promote relations between research workers and also between research centres. It is therefore desirable that national policy-making should pay serious attention to scientific documentation but also to scientific information in the broad sense, including the organization of personal exchanges between research workers.

The propagation of innovations. The approach here differs according to whether it is the modern sector or the traditional sector that is involved. In the modern sector, it is necessary to remove the institutional barriers that prolong the 'lead time' before an invention is brought into use. Furthermore, the developing countries must have 'state of the art' information in regard to the advanced technology available at the international level, and for this purpose must join in technological information systems. In the traditional sector, new technology is not used unless an effort is made when it is introduced to explain it, to develop the population's awareness of it and to secure the participation of the people at large so as to make them receptive to a selected form of modernity. It is therefore necessary to improve communications by setting up suitable dissemination machinery; this may take the form of extension services (mobile exhibitions), the mass media (press campaigns or audio-visual packages to attract the public's attention) or further training for adults. While general education plays an important role in the dissemination of technology (according to a study carried out in the agricultural sector), it will be necessary to rely on other methods for countries that have not attained a sufficiently high level of education owing to the amount of time required for training. In this case efforts should focus on the training of instructors, familiarizing them with methods for communicating messages that are suitable for the social environment in which they are called upon to act. It might also be desirable to organize intermediate technology fairs among developing countries.

Storage
The institutions responsible for administering research administration are not usually much concerned about storage. This omission came to be recognized when the concept of appropriate technology developed. Former Western techniques of production, better suited to the local conditions of certain developing countries (resources), could not be put into practice as all trace of them had been lost. To avoid such a misadventure and enhance the potentialities of intermediate technology, it would be necessary for the developing countries to develop systems for preserving their technological heritage. It would also be desirable for appropriate measures to be taken at the international level and for an agency to keep a classified record of production techniques as they evolve.

The framing of rules governing the activities of TNCs in the field of science and technology

As we have noted, the practices of TNCs, although controversial, do not as a general rule contribute to the scientific and technological development of the host countries. Rules could therefore be drawn up to foster the equal distribution of science and technology, and in this connection it would be desirable to encourage relocation of the TNCs' R&D activities by providing that firms whose R&D expenditure in the country over a given period falls short of a prescribed amount should contribute to a fund a given percentage of their turnover (the percentage varying according to the branch of activity).

In addition, in order to guard against certain abuses resulting from the TNCs' dominant position, the developing countries should set up centres to monitor transfers of technology. These centres, which would have ample documentation at their disposal, could also adapt business practices governing transfers of technology to the needs of the country concerned.

NOTES

1. G. Corm, 'Les firmes multinationales et l'accès du Tiers-Monde à la technique moderne', *Le monde diplomatique* (Paris), November 1978.
2. C. A. Michalet, 'Les firmes multinationales et la nouvelle division internationale du travail', Geneva, ILO, 1975. (WE.P. 2-28/WP5.)
3. See in this connection M. Godelier, *Rationalité et irrationalité en économie*, Vol. II, p. 158, Paris, Maspero, 1974, which reproduces M. Salisbury, *From Stone to Steel*, Melbourne, Melbourne University Press, 1962.
4. C. Palloix, *Travail et production*, p. 64, Paris, Maspero, 1978.
5. R. Fossaert, *La société*; Vol. II: *Les structures économiques*, p. 231, Paris, Seuil, 1977.
6. P. Raymond, *L'histoire et les sciences*, p. 33, Paris, Maspéro, 1978.
7. M. Daumas, *Histoire générale des techniques*, Vol. II, pp. xvi, xvii, Paris, Presses Universitaires de France, 1965.
8. R. Mousnier, *Progrès scientifique et technique au XVIIIe*, Paris, Plon, 1968.
9. D. Furia and P. C. Serre, *Techniques et sociétés*, p. 201, Paris, Armand Colin, 1970. (Collection U.)
10. The term is taken from B. Gille, 'Prolègomènes à une histoire des techniques', in 'Histoire des techniques', *Encyclopédie de la Pléiade*, p. 24, Paris, Gallimard, 1978.
11. Cf. D. Dufourt, 'Transfert de technologie et dynamique de systèmes techniques', *Prévisions, Choix, Planification* (University of Lyon-II), No. 6, October 1978, p. 3.
12. We may refer here to R. Findlay, 'Relative Backwardness of Direct Foreign Investment and the Transfer of Technology: A Simple Dynamic Model, *Quarterly Journal of Economics*, Vol. XCII, No. 1, 1978, p. 1: 'Economic theorists, however, have on the whole not devoted much attention to the formulation of explicit analytical models of technological diffusion.'
13. B. R. Williams, 'Conditions de l'innovation industrielle', *Économie appliquée*, Vol. XIV, April–September 1961, p. 307. (Article based on C. F. Carter and Williams, *Industry and Technical Progress*, Oxford, Oxford University Press, 1957, and *Science in Industry*, Oxford, Oxford University Press, 1959.
14. This productive activity is measured by its costs owing to the difficulty of estimating R.&D output. A. Weber defines 'the R&D service production of an enterprise, a facility or a body as its intramural R&D activity estimated at its cost' in an INSEE note of 4 May 1970, quoted by Dufourt, op. cit., p. 33.
15. According to an estimate in *Business Week* based on 683 firms, R&D expenditure increased by 16.4 per cent between 1977 and 1978 (*Business Week*, 2 July 1979, p. 52).
16. OECD, Scientific Affairs Directorate, *Model method proposed for research and development surveys*, Paris, 1963; reproduced by Dufourt, op. cit., p. 34.
17. F. Russo and R. Erbes, 'Le concept de recherche, développement', in F. Perroux (ed.), *Recherche et activité économique*, p. 20, Paris, A. Colin, 1969.
18. Ibid., p. 21.
19. Dufourt, op. cit., p. 35.
20. Ibid., p. 38.
21. As is noted by B. Gille, the phenomenon is not a recent one: 'The immigration of foreign techniques and technicians was one of Colbert's major concerns between 1665 and 1670.' 'Centre International de Synthèse, L'encyclopédie, dictionnaire technique', *L'encyclopédie et le progrès des sciences et des techniques*, p. 88, Paris, Presses Universitaires de France, 1952.
22. F. de Ravignan, 'Autour d'une petite lampe', *La fin des outils*, pp. 321–2, Geneva/Paris, Presses Universitaires de France, 1978. (Cahiers de l'IUED, No. 5.)
23. To borrow Bachelard's expression.
24. To give an example, in Black Africa local farming implements are the hoe, the adze, the axe and the machete. Cf. J. Binet, *Psychologie économique africaine*, p. 45, Paris, Payot, 1970.

25. S. Thébaud, 'Les systèmes de recherche scientifique et technique des pays en voie de développement', *Revue Tiers-Monde*, Vol. XVII, No. 65, 1976, p. 129.
26. Ibid., p. 130.
27. W. R. Loon and W. R. Yung. *Data Development for a Study of the Scope for Capital Labour Subsitution in the Mechanical Engineering Industry*, Seoul, February 1972.
28. K. Oshima, 'Technological Innovation in Japan', *International Aspects of Technological Innovation*, pp. 57–61, Paris, Unesco, 1971. (Science Policy Studies and Documents, 26.)
29. UNCTAD, *Case Studies in the Transfer of Technology: Policies for Transfer and Development of Technology in Pre-war Japan (1868–1937)*, New York, United Nations, 1978. (TD/B/C.6/26.)
30. Care should be taken not to make too much of the Japanese experience in the sphere of technology, for the international development context was altogether different at that time from that now experienced by the developing countries. For this there are several reasons. On the one hand, the technological advance of the developed countries was not so great at the time, and technology, which was essentially mechanical, could be assimilated by productive practices. On the other hand, at the end of the nineteenth century the system of industrial ownership was not so well established as it is today and the process of assimilation was therefore far more flexible. Lastly, Japan was not affected in the sphere of consumption as the developing countries are at present. On this account the savings available through accumulation have had a leading influence on the rate of technological development through the maintenance of traditional consumer habits (cf. UNCTAD, op. cit.).
31. N. Jequier, *Transfer of Technology in the Telecommunication Industry*, OECD, November 1975. (Mimeo.)
32. UNCTAD, *Guidelines for the Study of the Transfer of Technology to Developing Countries*, New York, United Nations, 1973. (TD/B/AC.11/9.)
33. D. Carrière, 'Une erreur à dénoncer: le transfert pour l'acquisition des techniques', *Options méditerranéennes*, No. 27, pp. 29–30.
34. Dufourt, op. cit., pp. 11–12.
35. UNCTAD, *Handbook on the Acquisition of Technology by Developing Countries*, New York, United Nations, 1978.
36. L. Krieger Mytelka, 'Licensing and Technology Dependence in the Andean Group', *World Development*, Vol. 6, p. 449, Oxford, Pergamon Press, 1978.
37. According to the term used in UNCTAD, *Handbook on the Aacquisition of Technology...*, op. cit.
38. B. Chaillou, 'La sous-traitance, élément intégré de la politique de l'entreprise', University of Lyon-II, 1978. (Doctorat d'État thesis.)
39. J. M. Chevalier, 'La stratégie d'implantation d'une firme multinationale. Étude de cas', *Firmes transnationales et développement*, pp. 792–3, 1975. (Mondes en développement, No. 12.)
40. Ibid., p. 795.
41. Ibid., p. 797.
42. Ibid., p. 798.
43. J. Carlsen, 'Les différents modes de transfert de technologie', *Symposium on Multinational Corporations in Africa, Dakar, 25 September–5 October 1974*, United Nations/IDEP. (CS/2562-12.)
44. R. Montavon, 'Implantation de deux entreprises multinationales au Mexique', p. 158, Paris, Presses Universitaires de France/CEEIM, 1979.
45. A. Ribicoff, *Implications of Multinational Firms for World Trade and Investment and for United States Trade and Labor*, Committee of Finances of United States Senate, Washington, D.C., Ninety-third Congress, first session, February 1973.
46. Study carried out by the Cartagena Agreement Board for UNCTAD, pp. 24–5, quoted by P. Judet, 'Transfert des technologies et processus d'internationalisation', *Options méditerranéennes*, No. 27, p. 49.

47. See, *Report of the United States Senate, 1973*, pp. 61, 81–3, and K. Pavitt, 'The Multinational Enterprise and the Transfer of Technology', in J. A. Dunning (ed.), *The Multinational Enterprise*, London, Allen & Unwin, 1971.
48. *Les transferts de techniques*, p. 24, Brussels, World Confederation of Labour, February, 1976.
49. Carlsen, op. cit., p. 9; B. Kapp, 'Après bien d'autres, les pays du Tiers-Monde remettent aujourd'hui à l'ordre du jour le procès des brevets', *Economia*, June 1977.
50. Carlsen, op. cit., p. 9.
51. Unesco, *Thinking Ahead*, p. 167, Paris, Unesco, 1977.
52. R. Kaplinsky and S. Chishti, 'Technical Change and the Multinational Corporations: Some British Multinationals in Kenya and India', in D. Germidis (ed.), *Transfer of Technology by Multinational Corporations*, Vol. I, pp. 77–150, Paris, OECD, 1977.
53. J. Masini et al., *Les multinationales et le développement. Trois entreprises en Côte-d'Ivoire*, p. 97, Paris, Presses Universitaires de France/CEEIM, 1979.
54. R. Demonts, 'La recherche dans la firme plurinationale et la propagation des techniques', in Perroux, op. cit., p. 410.
55. C. A. Michalet, 'Le mythe de la firme transnationale', *Firmes transnationales et développement*, 1975, p. 726. (Mondes en développement, No. 12.)
56. Y. Sabolo and R. Trajtenberg, *The Impact of Transnational Enterprises on Employment in Developing Countries*, Geneva, ILO, 1976. (WEP 2-28/WP6, No. 2.)
57. L. G. Franko, *The European Multinationals, A Renewed Challenge to American and British Big Business*, London, Harper & Row, 1976.
58. P. K. M. Tharakan, *La division internationale du travail et les entreprises multinationales*, p. 124, Paris, Presses Universitaires de France/CEEIM, 1979.
59. Franko, op. cit., p. 127.
60. R. Vernon, 'International Investment and International Trade in the Product Cycle', *Quarterly Journal of Economics*, May 1966.
61. This image would appear, however, to be more relevant to the 1960s. E. Mansfield (University of Pennsylvania) shows on the basis of a study of sixty-five innovations transferred abroad that in 75 per cent of cases the products have a life-span of less than five years. This means that the export phase in the product's life-cycle has been at best shortened and at worst eliminated. 'The Profitable Lure of Exporting Innovation', *Business Week*, 25 June 1979, p. 90 B-1.
62. B. Willegas, 'Multinational Corporations and Transfer of Technology: The Philippine Case', in Germidis, op. cit., pp. 151–60.
63. A. Nadal, 'Multinational Corporations and Transfer of Technology: The Case of Mexico', in ibid, pp. 219–50.
64. Montavon, op. cit., p. 87.
65. Kaplinski and Chishti, op. cit.
66. S. A. Morley and G. W. Gordon, 'The Choice of Technology: Multinational Firms in Brazil', *Economic Development and Cultural Change*, Vol. 25. No. 2, 1977, pp. 239–64.
67. Masini et al., op. cit., p. 168.
68. T. Ozawa, *Transfer of Technology from Japan to Developing Countries*, UNITAR, 1971. (Research Reports, No. 7.)
69. W. Chudson, in H. R. Hahld et al. *Nationalism and Multinational Enterprise*, pp. 131–61, Dobbs Ferry, N.Y., Oceana Publications, 1975.
70. L. T. Wells, 'Don't Over-automate Your Foreign Plan', *Harvard Business Review*, Vol. 52, No. 1, 1974.
71. L. T. Wells, 'Economic Man and Engineering Man: Choice of Technology in Low Wage Country', *Public Policy*, Vol. 21, No. 3, 1973, pp. 319–42.
72. S. Langdon, 'Firmes transnationales, transfert de goût et sous-développement: une étude de cas au Kenya', *Options méditerranéennes*, No. 27.
73. Germidis, op. cit., pp. 28–9.
74. Carlsen, op. cit., p. 31; Kaplinsky and Schishti, op. cit.

75. These data are derived from a table compiled by Tharakan, op. cit., p. 131, on the basis of two studies: for the cotton industry see, B. Boltron, *The MNCS in the Textile and Leather Industries*, p. 84, Brussels, International Textile, Garment and Leather Workers' Federation, 1976 (mimeo), and for the other industries, see Sabolo et al. op. cit., p. 23.
76. M. Sharpston, *International Sub-Contracting*, pp. 8–9, May 1974. (IBRD and IDA Bank Staff Working Paper, No. 181.)
77. United States Tariff Commission, *Economic Factor Affecting the Use of the Items 807,000 and 806,300 of the Tariff Schedules of the United States*, September 1970.
78. D. W. Baerresen, *The Border Industrialization Program of Mexico*, p. 33, Lexington, Mass., Heath Lexington Books, 1971.
79. In the words of C. A. Michalet *(fuite de cervaux à domicile)*, in *Le transfert international des techniques et la firme multinationale*, A report submitted to the Symposium of the Association Française des Sciences Économiques, Lille, October 1974.
80. J. Tinbergen (co-ordinator), *Reshaping the International Order, A Report to the Club of Rome*, New York, Dutton, 1976.
81. G. Breinstein, 'International Division of Labour and Structural Unemployment', *Inter-Economics* (Hamburg), April 1976, p. 117.
82. 'Know-how' is defined by a French decree of 26 May 1970 as 'all the scientific and technical material accompanying the acquisition or transfer of industrial property rights—technical studies, essays and research, scientific and technical information'. As for 'show-how', B. Gille (op. cit.), states that it consists in 'showing how to use equipment over a period varying between ten months and three years according to the plant'.
83. 'International trading companies, after helping suppliers to gain a footing in foreign markets, may propose services that fall within the category of project studies and that result in a genuine transfer of technology': Dufourt, op. cit., p. 8.
84. Cf. J. Perrin, 'Un pas vers la maîtrise du transfert de connaissances: la création de sociétés d'ingénierie dans les pays en voie d'industrialisation', *Options méditerranéennes*, No. 27, p. 58.
85. J. P. Gilly, 'Recherche, ingénierie et stratégies industrielles', *Économie et humanisme*, January/February, 1979; reproduced in *Problèmes économiques*, No. 1622, 9 May 1979, p. 10.
86. M. Freyssenet, *La division capitaliste du travail*, p. 64, Paris, Savelli, 1977.
87. P. Judet, 'Transfert des technologies et processus d'internationalisation', *Options méditerranéennes*, No. 27, pp. 50–2.
88. G. K. Helleiner, 'Manufactured Exports from Less-developed Countries and Multinational Firms', *The Economic Journal*, March 1973.
89. *Eastern Europe Report*, 21 September 1973, p. 273.
90. T. Ozawa, op. cit.; International Chamber of Commerce, *International Corporations and the Transfer of Technology, Report of the Special Committee on International Corporations*, ICC, 1972.
91. N. Swainson, *The Bata Shoe Company. Types of Production and Transfer of Skills*, Paris Unesco, 1978, (Report TNC.6).
92. Germidis, op. cit., p. 92.
93. C. Jee, *Direct Foreign Investments in Korea*, Seoul, 1975, quoted by S. H. Jo, *The Impact of Multinational Firms on Employment and Incomes. The Case Study of South Korea*, p. 44, Geneva, ILO, 1976. (WEP 2-28/WP 12.)
94. Kaplinsky and Chishti, op. cit.
95. Carlsen, op. cit., p. 31.
96. Nadal, op. cit., p. 271.
97. Demonts, op. cit., p. 413.
98. International Chamber of Commerce, op. cit.
99. Demonts, op. cit., p. 414.
100. D. Germidis, *Multinational Firms and Vocational Training in Developing Countries*, Paris, Unesco, 1976. (Doc. SHC-76/CONF. 635/11.)

101. The first person to put forward this thesis was Adam Smith in the famous example of the manufacture of pins (*Inquiry into the Nature and Causes of the Wealth of Nations*, Book 1, Chapter 1).
102. This thesis is upheld by S. Marglin ('Origines et fonction de la parcellarisation des tâches', in A. Gorz (ed.), *Critique de la division du travail*, Paris, 1973) for whom the fragmentation of labour was originally the first stage in the loss of control by the worker over production.
103. We take our cue here from a remark by Karl Marx in *The German Ideology*: 'The most explicit way of recognizing the degree of development attained by the productive forces of a nation is the degree of development attained by the division of labour.'
104. Cf. a letter of 25 January 1894 from Engels to Borgius: 'If, as you say, technology depends largely on the state of science, the latter depends even more on the state of the needs of technology.'
105. Cf. in this connection B. Coriat (*Sciences, techniques et capital*, Paris, Seuil, 1976) who criticizes the theses of R. Richta (*La civilisation au carrefour*, Paris, Anthropos, 1969).
106. Germidis, op. cit., p. 33.
107. W. H. Courtney and D. M. Leipziger, *Multinational Corporations in LDCS: The Choice of Technology*, Washington, D.C., 1974. (Aid Discussion Paper, No. 29.)
108. C. Palloix, *Théorie du système productif*, Vol. I, p. 217, IREP/CORDES, 1977.
109. M. Aglietta, *Régulation et crises du capitalisme*, p. 93, Paris, Calmann-Lévy, 1976.
110. Ibid., p. 94.
111. B. Coriat, 'Un développement créateur du taylorisme: le fordisme', typewritten note, January 1975, quoted by Palloix, op. cit., p. 229.
112. Jo, op. cit., p. 30.
113. C. V. Vaitsos, *Employment Problems and Transnational Enterprises in Developing Distortion and Inequality*, p. 17, Geneva, ILO, 1976. (WEP 2-28/WP 11.)
114. Jo, op. cit., p. 30.
115. International Chamber of Commerce, *Realties—Multinational Enterprises Respond to Basic Issues*, ICC, 1974.
116. K. Kumar, *A Working Paper on the Social and Cultural Impacts of Transnational Enterprises*, pp. 48–9, Honolulu, East-West Center, East-West Culture Learning Institute, August 1978.
117. R. C. O'Brien, 'Communication de masse: mécanismes sociaux d'incorporation et de dépendance', *Revue Tiers-Monde*, Vol. XX, No. 79, July-September 1979.
118. P. Golding, 'Media Professionalism in the Third World: The Transfer of an Ideology', in J. Curran et al., *Mass Communication and Society*, London, The Open University, 1977.
119. J. Galtung, 'Technology and Dependence', *CERES*, September-October 1974.
120. P. Vautrin and J. P. Guilhamon, *Le développement de la production de soja au Brésil*, Centre Français du Commerce Extérieur, 1973. (Collection 'Enquêtes à l'étranger'.)
121. F. B. Weinstein, 'Multinational Corporations and the Third World: The Case of Japan and South-East Asia', *International Organization*, Vol. 30, No. 3, 1973.
122. C. Brundenius, 'The Anatomy of Imperialism: The Case of Multinational Mining Corporation in Peru', *Journal of Peace Research*, Vol. 9, No. 3, 1972.
123. Kumar, op. cit., p. 79.
124. U. Kerdpidule, *Thailand's Experience with Multinational Corporations*, p. 26, Bangkok, Kasetsart University, Department of Economics, 1974, quoted by Kumar, op. cit., p. 79.
125. Germidis, op. cit.
126. A. O. Hirschman, 'How to Divest in Latin America and Why', in A Kapoor and P. Grub (eds.), *The Multinational Enterprise in Transition: Selected Readings and Essays*, Princeton, N.J., Darwin Press, 1972.

127. De Ravignan, op. cit., p. 323.
128. Massey-Fergusson, *The Pace and Form of Farm Mechanization in Developing Countries*, Toronto, Massey-Fergusson.
129. K. C. Abercromble, *Agricultural Mechanization and Employment in Latin America*, Geneva, ILO, 1974.
130. C. Auroi, 'Mécanisation agricole: le modèle européen et l'Amérique Latine', *La fin des outils*, pp. 40–1, Geneva/Paris, Presses Universitaires de France, 1978. (Cahiers de l'IDED, No. 5.)
131. P. Bairoch, *The Economic Development of the Third World since 1900*, Chapter 9, London, Methuen, 1975.
132. Weinstein, op. cit., p. 400.
133. Auroi, op. cit., p. 43.
134. In South-East Asia, for instance, the share of TNCs in factory employment varies from 31 per cent in Malaysia (cf. M. Hui,'Multinational Corporations and Development in Malaysia', *Southeast Asian Journal of Social Science*, Vol. 4, No. 1, 1976, p. 59) to 44.3 per cent in Singapore (cf. W. S. Fan, 'The Multinational Enterprise in Singapore', in E. Lim Poh Tim (ed.), *Multinational Corporations and their Implications for Southeast Asia*, p. 23, Singapore, Institute of Southeast Asian Studies, 1973). (Current Issues Seminar, No. 1.)
135. Sabolo et al., op. cit., p. 4, reproducing L. G. Franko, *Comparative Multinational Enterprise Project*, Geneva, Centre for Education in Industrial Management, 1974.
136. Y. Sabolo, 'Employment and Unemployment 1960–1990', *International Labour Review*, December 1975.
137. G. L. Reuber, *Private Foreign Investment in Development*, Oxford, Clarendon Press, 1973.
138. ILO, *Wages and Working Conditions in Multinational Enterprises*, p. 59, ILO, Geneva, 1976.
139. For India: B. M. Richman and M. Copen, *International Management and Economic Development*, New York, McGraw-Hill, 1972; for Thailand: R. Hirono, *Industrial Relations in Foreign Corporations. Case of Thailand, Foreign Investment and Labor in Asian Countries*, Tokyo, The Japan Institute of Labour, 1976; for the Republic of Korea: Jo, op. cit.; for Malaysia: E. Lim Poh Tin (ed.), 'Multinational Corporations and Their Implications for South-East Asia', *Papers and Proceedings of a Seminar Organized by the Institute of South-East Asian Studies in Singapore, 1973*; for the Philippines: E. T. Ramos, *Filipino Trade Unions and Multinationals, Foreign Investment and Labor in Asian Countries*, Tokyo, The Japan Institute of Labour, 1976; and for the Latin American countries: G. Standing and T. Koija, 'Labor Market Effects of Multinational Enterprises in Latin America', *Nebraska Journal of Economics and Business*, Vol. 12, No. 4, 1973.
140. Montavon, op. cit.
141. D. Lim, 'Do Foreign Companies Pay Higher Wages than their Local Counterparts in Malaysian Manufacturing?', *Journal of Development Economics*, Vol. 4, No. 1, 1973, p. 64.
142. ILO, op. cit., p. 59.
143. G. Caire, *Multinationales et relations professionnelles*, p. 14, Working Group on Multinationals and Development, EADI and IEDES, 1977. (Working Paper, No. 12.)
144. Caire, op. cit., p. 14, and Masini et al., op. cit., p. 176: 'In the three cases (CAPRAL, SIEM and SIVOA) the social benefits enjoyed by wage-earners in firms are on the whole somewhat higher than they are on the average for wage-earners in Ivory Coast.'
145. R. Jolly, 'The Problem of Job Creation, Industry and Employment and the Developing World', *Report of the Seminar Jointly Sponsored by IBM (United Kingdom) and ODI (Oxford, 20–22 November 1974)*, p. 20, London, Overseas Development Institute, 1974.
146. D. Thery, 'Du transfert mimétique à l'auto-détermination technologique:

quelques points de repère', *Actuel Développement* (Paris), No. 14, July/August 1976.
147. Ibid.
148. UNCTAD, *Transfer of Technology: Its Implications for Development and Environment*, Geneva, UNCTAD, 1977.
149. A. F. Ewing, 'Appropriate or Inappropriate Technology: Some Recent Contributions to the Debate', *Journal of World Trade Law*, Vol. 12, No. 3, May–June 1978.

GENERAL CONCLUSION

In conclusion we should like to stress the need for a follow-up to this study in two directions. First, it is clear that we are far from possessing a comprehensive picture of the socio-cultural impact of TNCs. This is due to the lack of objective information regarding all the activities of relevance. Lack of information is the source of all prejudice. The literature that we have consulted on this matter and the case-studies that have been conducted as a basis for this work plainly come up against the TNCs' fear that their action will be distorted and misinterpreted. As a result, the research worker's approach is unduly influenced by whatever his views were before ever embarking on analysis. Further research is therefore necessary along two lines. The first involves the collection of a uniform general body of information concerning the activities of TNCs in Unesco's fields of competence. The second entails a thorough-going study of individual cases where subsidiaries have been established with a view to ascertaining the relationship between the various economic and socio-cultural effects to which they have given rise. As a direct result of not having this knowledge, states are virtually powerless to assess, select and, where necessary, counteract some of the TNCs' forms of action in this field. The recommendations that we have put forward may perhaps provide an initial framework for action. They will still need to be assessed on a case-by-case basis, no doubt with the co-operation of the United Nations, and geared to the circumstances and concrete situations directly concerned. For it seems to us that the scale of the TNC phenomenon in the cultural sphere necessitates an awareness and a form of control that go far beyond the national context.

There is nothing paradoxical about this. Taking the world system as the necessary basis for promoting national autonomy means basing the evolution of that system upon real differentiation rather than homogenization. It means accepting the deliberate, conscious participation of each national entity in the construction of the system. It means, finally, recognizing that the enduring quality of the system will depend on the degree of autonomy and communication existing between the nations that constitute it.

GENERAL BIBLIOGRAPHY

ABERCROMBIE, K. C. *Agricultural Mechanisation and Employment in Latin America.* Geneva, ILO, 1974.
ALTBACH, P. Publishing in Developing Countries. *International Social Science Journal* (Unesco), Vol. 26, No. 3, 1974.
——. Literary Colonialism: Books in the Third World. *Harvard Educational Review*, Vol. 45, No 2, May 1975.
ALTBACH, P.; McVEY, S. (eds.). *Perspectives on Publishing.* Lexington, Mass., Lexington Books, 1976.
AMIN, S. *Le développement inégal.* Paris, Les Éditions de Minuit, 1973. 365 pp.
APTER, D. E.; GOODMAN, L. W. *Dependency and Interdependence. The Multinational and Social Change.* New York, Praeger, 1976.
BADER, M. Breast Feeding: The Role of Multinational Corporations in Latin America. *International Journal of Health Services.* Vol. 6, No. 4, 1976.
BAERRESEN, D. W. *The Border Industrialization Program of Mexico.* Lexington, Mass., Heath Lexington Books, 1971.
BAKIS, H. *I.B.M., une multinationale régionale.* Grenoble, Presses Universitaires de Grenoble, 1977.
BARNET, R. J.; MÜLLER, R. E. *Global Reach: The Power of the Multinational Corporations.* New York, Simon & Schuster, 1974.
BECHTOS, R. International Advertisers Change Consumer Ways. *Advertising Age*, Vol. 46, No. 20, 1975.
BELL, G. *The Cultural Contradictions of Capitalism.* New York, Basic Books Inc., 1976.
BELTRAN, L. R. Communication and Cultural Domination: USA–Latin American Case. *Media Asia, An Asian Mass Communication Quarterly*, Vol. 5, No. 4, 1978.
BELTRAN, L. R.; DE CARDONA, E. F. Mass Media and Cultural Domination. *Prospects, Quarterly Review of Education* (Unesco), Vol. X, No. 1, 1980.
——. Latin America and the U.S.: Flaws in the Free Flow of Information. Paper presented at the Conference on Fair Communication Policy for the International Exchange of Information, Honolulu, Hawaii, March–April 1976. East-West Communication Institute, East-West Center.
BERQUE, J. Towards a Better Transfer of Knowledge and Values. *Prospects, Quarterly Review of Education*, Vol. VI, No. 3, 1976.
BREINSTEIN, G. *International Division of Labour and Structural Unemployment.* Hamburg, Inter-Economics, April 1976.
BRIGAUD-ROBERT, M. *Méthodologie de la mesure de l'impact de la publicité des S.T.N. du tourisme sur les valeurs socio-culturelles des pays en développement.* Paris,

Unesco, Division for the Study of Development, 1978. (French only.) (TNC-5.)
BRUNDENIUS, C. The Anatomy of Imperialism: The Case of the Multinational Mining Corporation in Peru. *Journal of Peace Research*, Vol. 9, No. 3, 1972.
BRZEZINSKI, J. *La révolution technétronique*. Paris, Calman-Lévy, 1971.
BUCKLEY, P. J.; CARSON, M.W. *The Future of the Multinational Enterprises*. London, Macmillan, 1976.
CAIRE, G. *Multinationales et relations professionnelles*. Working Group on Multinationals and Development, EADI and IEDES, 1977. (Working Paper, No. 12.)
CARLSEN J. Les différents modes de transfert de technologie. *Colloque sur les sociétés multinationales en Afrique, Dakar, 25 septembre–5 octobre 1974*. United Nations/IDEP. (CS/2562-12.)
CARNOY, M. *La educación como imperialismo cultural*. Mexico City, Siglo XXI, 1977.
CARTAPANIS, A.; EXPERTON, W.; FUGUET, J. L. *Méthodologie de recherche sur l'influence des sociétés transnationales sur les systèmes éducatifs des pays en développement*. Paris, Unesco, Division for the Study of Development, 1977. (French only.) (TNC-4.)
———. *Transnational Corporations and Educational Systems in Developing Countries: An Annotated Critical Bibliography*. Paris, Unesco, Division for the Study of Development, 1977. (TNC-2.)
CASSIRER, H. *Mass Media in an African Context—An Evaluation of Senegal's Pilot Project*. Paris, Unesco, 1974. (Reports and Papers on Mass Communication, 69.)
CENTRE ON TRANSNATIONAL CORPORATIONS. *National Legislation and Regulations relating to Transnational Corporations*. New York, United Nations, 1978. (ST/CTC/6.)
CHANNON, D. F.; JALLAND, M. *Multinational Strategic Planning*. London, Macmillan, 1979. 344 pp.
CHEVALIER, J. M. La stratégie d'implantation d'une firme multinationale, Étude de cas. *Firmes transnationales et développement*. 1975. (Mondes en développement, No. 12.)
CLASTRES, P. De l'éthnocide. *L'Homme*, July–December 1974.
COMMISSION ON TRANSNATIONAL CORPORATIONS. *Report on the Second Session (1–12 March 1976)*, United Nations Economic and Social Council. (E/5782-E/C.10/16.)
CONTRERAS, E.; LARSON, J.; MAYO, J.; SPAIN, P. *Cross-cultural Broadcasting*. Paris, Unesco, 1976. (Reports and Papers on Mass Communication, 77.)
CORIAT, B. *Sciences, techniques et capital*. Paris, Seuil, 1976.
COUNTERINFORMATION SERVICE (London), SOMO (Amsterdam) (in co-operation with the Transnational Institute). *Unilever's World*. London, 1977.
COURTNEY, W. H.; LEIPZIGER, D. M. *Multinational Corporations in LDCs: The Choice of Technology*. Washington, D.C., AID, 1974. (Discussion Paper, No. 29.)
DRUCKER, P. F., The Managerial Era. *Economic Impact*, No. 27, 1979.
DUEW, M. G.; GREENE, J. Foreign Nationals in International Management, A. Research Report from the Conference Board, New York. *Managing International Business*, No. 2, 1968.
DUFOURT, R. Transfert de technologie et dynamiques des systèmes techniques. *Prévision-Choix-Planification* (University of Lyon-II), No. 6, October 1978.
DYMSA, W. D. *Multinational Business Strategy*. New York, McGraw-Hill, 1972.
ENG FONG, P. An Economic Perspective of Universities and Manpower Development. *Development Strategies and Manpower Needs: The Response of South-East Asian Universities*. Singapore, RIHED, 1976.
FAN, W. S. The Multinational Enterprise in Singapore. In: E. Lim Poh Tim (ed.), *Multinational Corporations and their Implications for Southeast Asia*. Singapore, Institute of Southeast Asian Studies, 1973. (Current Issues Seminar, No. 1.)
FIELDHOUSE, D. K. *Unilever Overseas, The Anatomy of a Multinational*. London, Croom Helm, 1978.

FINDLAY, R. Relative Backwardness, Direct Foreign Investment and the Transfer of Technology: A Simple Dynamic Model. *The Quarterly Journal of Economics*, Vol. XVII, No. 1, 1978.
FLICHY, P. *Contribution à une étude des industries de l'audio-visuel*. Paris, Ministère de la Culture et de l'Environnement, Institut National de l'Audio-Visuel, 1978.
FRANK, A.G.; AMIN, S. *L'accumulation dépendante*. Paris, Éditions Antropos, 1978.
FRANKO, L. G. *Comparative Multinational Enterprise Project*. Geneva, Centre d'Études Industrielles, 1974.
GABEL, J. L'idéologie. *Encyclopedia Universalis*. Paris, 1968.
GALTUNG, J. Technology and Dependence. *CERES*, September/October 1974.
GARCIA, N. R. *Technologia, comunicación y publicidad: formas ocultas de dominación*. Caracas, Escuela de Sociología y Antropología, Facultad de Economía, 1975.
GEORGE, S. *Comment meurt l'autre moitié du monde*. Paris, R. Laffont, 1978.
GEORGES, R. *Hétérogénéité culturelle et communication*. Paris, Anthropos, 1978.
GERMIDIS, D. *Multinational Firms and Vocational Training in Developing Countries*. Paris, Unesco, 1976. (SHC-76/CONF. 635/11.)
——. *Le Maghreb, la France et l'enjeu technologique*. Paris, Cujas, 1976.
GIRLING, R. Mechanisms of Imperialism: Technology and the Dependent State. *Latin American Perspectives*, Vol. 3, No. 4, 1976.
GODFREY, M.; LANGDON, S. Partners in Underdevelopment? The Transnationalization Thesis in a Kenyan Context. In: J. Villamil (ed.), *Transnational Capitalism and National Development*. Brighton, The Harvester Press, 1979.
GRONOW, P. *The Record Industry, Multinational Corporations and National Music Traditions*. Vienna, International Institute of Music, Dance and Theatre in the Audio-visual Media, 1975.
GROUPE DE TRAVAIL, TIERS-MONDE. *Nestlé contre les bébé*. Paris, Maspero/Presses Universitaires de France, 1978.
GUBACK, T.; VARIS, T. *Transnational Film and Television*. Paris, Unesco, 1977. (Mimeo.)
GUNNEMAN, J. P. *The Nation State and Transnational Corporations in Conflict, with Special Reference to Latin America*. New York, Praeger, 1975.
HAHLD, H. R.; SMITH, J. G.; WRIGHT, R. W. *Nationalism and Multinational Enterprise*, Dobbs Ferry, N.Y., Oceana Publications, 1975.
HEAD, S. W. *Broadcasting in Africa*. Philadelphia, Temple University Press, 1974.
HELFGOTT, R. B. Multinational Corporations and Manpower Utilization in Developing Nations. *Journal of Developing Areas*, January 1978.
HELLEINER, G. K. Manufactured Exports from Less Developed Countries and Multinational Firms. *The Economic Journal*, March 1973.
HIRONO, R. Industrial Relations in Foreign Corporations. Case of Thailand *Foreign Investment and Labour in Asian Countries*. Tokyo, The Japan Institute of Labour, 1976.
HIRSCHMAN, A. O. How to Divest in Latin America and Why. In: A. Kapoor and P. Grub, (eds.), *The Multinational Enterprise in Transition: Selected Readings and Essays*. Princeton, N.J., Darwin Press, 1972.
HOOD, N.; YOUNG, S. *The Economics of Multinational Enterprise*. London, Longman, 1979.
HUI, M. Multinational Corporations and Development in Malaysia. *Southeast Asian Journal of Social Science*, Vol. 4, No. 1, 1976.
ILO. *Wages and Working Conditions in Multinational Enterprises*. Geneva, ILO, 1976.
INTERNATIONAL CHAMBER OF COMMERCE. *Realities—Multinational Enterprises Respond to Basic Issues*. ICC, 1974.
——. *Report of the Special Committee on International Corporations*. ICC, 1972.
IUED. *La fin des outils*. Geneva/Paris, IUED/Presses Universitaires de France, 1978. (Cahiers de l'IUED, No. 5.)
JACKSON, R. A. *The Multinational Corporation and Social Policy, With Special Reference to General Motors in South Africa*. New York, Praeger, 1974.
JANUS, N.; RONCAGLIOLO, R. Advertising, Mass Media and Dependency. *Development Dialogue*, No. 1, 1979.

Jo, S. H. *The Impact of Multinational Firms on Employment and Incomes. The Case Study of South Korea.* Geneva, ILO, 1976. (WEP 2-28/WP 12.)

JOLLY, R. The Problem of Job Creation, Industry, Employment and the Developing World. *Report of the Seminar Jointly Sponsored by IBM (United Kingdom) and ODI (Oxford, 20–22 November 1974).* London, Overseas Development Institute, 1974.

JOUET, J. Critique de l'utilisation des medias légers dans le Tiers-Monde. *Revue Tiers-Monde,* Vol. XX, No. 79, 1979.

JUDET, P. Transfert des technologies et processus d'internationalisation, *Options Méditerranéennes,* No. 27.

KAPLUN, M. La Comunicación de Masas en América Latina. *Educación Hoy,* (Bogotá, Asociación de Publicaciones Educativas), No. 5, 1973.

KATZ, E.; WEDELL, B. *Broadcasting in the Third World.* Cambridge, Mass., Harvard University Press, 1977.

KINDLEBERGER, C. P. *Economic Development,* New York, McGraw-Hill, 1965.

KLETTER, R.; HIRSCHHORN, L.; HUDSON, H. Access and the Social Environment in the United States of America. In: F. J. Berrigan (ed.), *Access: Some Western Models of Community Media.* Paris, Unesco, 1977.

KOUYATÉ, B. *The Components of Poverty and Socio-cultural Values among the Bambara Populations of the Ségou Region (Mali).* Paris, Unesco, Division for the Study of Development, 1977. (POV.1.)

KRIEGER MYTELKA, L. Licensing and Technology Dependence in the Andean Group. *World Development,* Vol. 6. Oxford, Pergamon Press, 1978.

KUMAR, K. *A Working Paper on the Social and Cultural Impacts of Transnational Enterprises,* East-West Culture Learning Institute, East-West Center, Honolulu, August 1978.

LADRIÈRE, J. *The Challenge Presented to Cultures by Science and Technology.* Paris, Aubier-Montaigne/Unesco, 1977.

LANGDON, S. We've Got What She Wants . . . And It's All Yours. *The New Internationalist,* 1972.

——. Firmes transnationales, transfert de goût et sous-développement: une étude de cas au Kenya. *Options méditerranéennes,* No. 27, 1975.

LAPPE, F. M.; COLLINS, J. *Food First: The Myth of Scarcity.* London, Souvenir Press, 1980.

LEDOGAR, R. *Hungry for Profits: U.S. Food and Drug Multinationals in Latin America.* New York, IDEC North America, 1975.

LEE, J. *Towards Realistic Communication Policies: Recent Trends and Ideas Compiled and Analysed.* Paris, Unesco, 1976. (Reports and Papers in Mass Communication, 76.)

LESOURNE, J. *Les systèmes du destin.* Paris, Dalloz, 1976.

LIM, D. Do Foreign Companies Pay Higher Wages than their Local Counterparts in Malaysian Manufacturing?. *Journal of Development Economics,* Vol. 4, No. 1, 1977.

LIMB, P. The Employment of Graduates of Tertiary Institutions in Singapore. *Development Strategies and Manpower Needs, The Response of Southeast Asian Universities.* Singapore, RIHED, 1976.

LIM POH TIM, E. *Multinational Corporations and their Implications for Southeast Asia: Papers and Proceedings of a Seminar Organized by the Institute of Southeast Asian Studies in Singapore, 10 December 1972.* Singapore, Institute of Southeast Asian Studies, 1973.

LORENZI, J. H.; LE BOUCHER, E. *Mémoires volées, satellites, micro-ordinateurs, robots, télématique, séries TV. US., réseaux vidéo, banques de données . . . Et demain la France.* Paris, Éditions Ramsay, 1979.

MACLENNAN, B. N. *The Impact of Transnational Corporations on Developing Countries: A Selected Review of the Literature and Annotated Bibliography in the Areas of Education, Science and Culture, and a Report on the Science and Technology Research and Training Policies of Transnational and Multinational Corporations.* Paris, Unesco, Division for the Study of Development, 1977. (TNC-1.)

MASINI, J.; IKONICOFF, M.; JEDLICKI, C.; LANZAROTTI, M. *Les multinationales et le développement. Trois entreprises en Côte-d'Ivoire*. Paris, Presses Universitaires de France/CEEIM, 1979.
MASON, H. *The Transfer of Technology and the Factor Proportion Problem: The Philippines and Mexico*. New York, UNITAR. (Research Reports, No. 10.)
MATTELART, A. *Multinationales et systèmes de communication*. Paris, Anthropos, 1976.
MATTELART, M.; MATTELART, A. *De l'usage des média en temps de crise*. Paris, A. Moreau, 1979.
MAZRVI, A. The African University as a Multinational Corporation: Problems of Penetration and Dependency. *Harvard Educational Review*, Vol. 45, No. 2, May 1975.
——. The Impact of Transnational Corporations on Educational and Cultural Processes: An African Perspective. *Prospects, Quarterly Review of Education*, Vol. VI, No. 4, 1976.
MICHALET, C. A. *Le capitalisme mondial*. Paris, Presses Universitaires de France, 1976.
——. Le mythe de la firme transnationale. *Firmes Transnationales et Développement*. Paris, 1975. (Mondes en développement, No. 12.)
——. *Les firmes multinationales et la nouvelle division internationale du travail*. Geneva, ILO, 1975 (French only). (WEP 2-28/WP5.)
MIGNOT-LEFEBVRE, Y. Vers une communication à double sens ? Mythes et réalités. *Revue Tiers-Monde*, Vol. XX, No. 79, July/September 1979.
MODELSKI, G. International Content and Performance Among the World's Largest Corporations. In: G. Modelski (ed.), *Transnational Corporation and World Order*. London, Freeman, 1979.
MONTAVON, R.; WIONCZEK, M.; PIQUEREZ, F. *L'implantation de deux entreprises multinationales au Mexique*. Paris, Presses Universitaires de France/CEEIM.
MORLEY, S. A.; GORDON, G. W. The Choice of Technology: Multinational Firms in Brazil. *Economic Development and Cultural Change*, Vol. 25, No. 2, 1977, pp. 239-64.
MYRDAL, G. *The Challenge of World Poverty*. London, Allen Lane/The Penguin Press, 1970.
NORDENSTRENG, K.; VARIS, T. *Television Traffic—A One-way Street? A Survey and Analysis of the International Flow of Television Programme Material*. Paris, Unesco, 1974. (Reports and Papers on Mass Communication, 70.)
NURSKSE, R. *Problems of Capital Formation in Underdeveloped Countries*. Oxford, Basil Blackwell, 1966.
O'BRIEN, R. C. Domination and Dependence in Mass-Communications: Implications for the use of Broadcasting in Developing Countries. *Institute of Development Studies Bulletin*, Vol. 6, No. 4, March 1975.
——. Mass-Communications: Social Mechanisms of Incorporation and Dependance. In: J. Villamil (ed.), *Transnational Capitalism and National Development*, pp. 129-43. Brighton, The Harvester Press, 1979.
——. Communication de masse: Mécanismes sociaux d'incorporation et de dépendance. *Revue Tiers-Monde*, Vol. XX, No. 79, July-September 1979.
——. Mass Media, Education and the Transmission of Values. *Prospects, Quarterly Review of Education*, Vol. X, No. 1, 1980.
OECD. *Facing the Future*. Paris, OECD, 1979.
ORDÓÑEZ, M. *El rol de la comunicación en la sociedad*. Quito, CIESPAL, 1975.
OZAWA, T. *Transfer of Technology from Japan to Developing Countries*, UNITAR, 1971. (Research Report, No. 7.)
PAGES, M.; BONETTI, M.; DE GAULEJAC, U.; DESCENDRE, D. *L'emprise de l'organisation*. Paris, Presses Universitaires de France, 1979.
PALLOIX, C. *Théorie du système productif*, Vol. I. IREP/CORDES, 1977.
——. *Travail et production*. Paris, Maspero, 1978.
PAVITT, K. The Multinational Enterprise and the Transfer of Technology. In: J. A. Dunning (ed.), *The Multinational Enterprise*. London, Allen & Unwin, 1971.

PERLMUTTER, H. V. The Perplexing Routes to Legitimacy: Codes of Conduct for Multinational Corporations Regarding Technology Transfer and Development. *Codes of Conduct for the Transfer of Technology: A Critique.* New York, Council of the Americas, 1976.
PERRIN, J. Un pas vers la maîtrise du transfert de connaissances: la création de sociétés d'ingénierie dans les pays en voie d'industrialisation. *Options Méditerranéennes,* No. 27.
PERROUX, F. *Recherche et activité économique.* Paris, A. Colin, 1969.
PREISWERK, R. Relations interculturelles et développement. *Le savoir et le faire. Cahiers de l'IUED.* Geneva/Paris, IUED/Presses Universitaires de France, 1975.
RAMA, G. W. Education, Social Structures and Styles of Development. *Prospects, Quarterly Review of Education,* Vol. VIII, No. 3, 1978.
RAMOS, E. T. *Filipino Trade Unions and Multinationals, Foreign Investment and Labor in Asian Countries.* Tokyo, The Japan Institute of Labour, 1976.
REUBER, G. L. *Private Foreign Investment in Development.* Oxford, Clarendon Press, 1973.
REYES MATTA, F. The Information Bedazzlement of Latin America: A Study of World News in the Region. *Development Dialogue,* No. 2, 1976.
RIBICOFF, A. *Implications of Multinational Firms for World Trade and Investments and for United States Trade and Labor.* Committee of Finances of United States Senate, Washington, D.C., Ninety-third Congress, first session, February 1973.
RICHMANN, B. M.; COPEN, M. *International Management and Economic Development.* New York, McGraw-Hill, 1972.
ROBINSON, R. D. *International Business Management.* Cambridge, Mass., MIT Press, 1973.
RONCAGLIOLO, R.; JANUS, N. Z. Transnational Advertising, the Media and Education in Developing Countries. *Prospects, Quarterly Review of Education,* Vol. X, No. 1, 1980.
SABOLO, Y. Employment and Unemployment 1960-1980. *International Labour Review,* December 1975.
SABOLO, Y.; TRAJTENBERG, R.; SAJHAU, J. P. *The Impact of Transnational Enterprises on Employment in the Developing Countries.* Geneva, ILO, 1976. (WEP 2-28/WP6.)
SAINT ROSSY, D. T.; CHAKRABARTI, A. K.; RUBENSTEIN, A. H. *International Transfer of Technology, An Evaluation of the Education and Training Component.* Evanston, Ill., Northwestern University Press, 1976.
SAMPSON, A. *The Seven Sisters.* New York, Viking Press, 1975.
SANTOS, M. *L'espace partagé.* Paris, Éditions Génin, 1975.
SAUVANT, K. P. Multinational Enterprises and the Transmission of Culture: The International Supply of Advertising Services and Business Education. *Journal of Peace Research,* Vol. XIII, No. 1, 1976. International Peace Research Center, Oslo.
——. The Potential of Multinational Enterprises as Vehicles for the Transmission of Business Culture. In K. P. Sauvant and G. Lavipour (eds.), *Controlling Multinational Enterprises; Problems, Strategies, Counterstrategies.* Boulder, Colo., Westview Press, 1976.
——. His Master's Voice, *CERES,* Vol. 9, September/October 1976.
SAUVANT, K. P.; MENNIS, B. *Socio-cultural Investments within the International Political Economy of North-South Relations: The Role of Transnational Enterprises.* Colloque de l'Association Française pour l'Étude du Tiers-Monde sur 'L'information et le Tiers-Monde', 30 May-1 June 1979, Dijon (France).
SCHAUPP, D. L. *A Cross Cultural Study of a Multinational Company.* New York, Praeger, 1978.
SCHILLER, H. *Mass Communications and American Empire.* New York, Beacon, 1971.
——. *Communication and Cultural Domination.* White Plains, N.Y., International Art and Sciences Press, 1976.

SCHREUDER, H. The Social Responsibility of Business. In: L. Van Dam and L. M. Stallaert (eds.), *Trends in Business Ethics*, 1978.
SCHUMACHER, E. F. *Small is Beautiful*. London, Blond and Briggs, 1973. 255 pp.
SCHWANN, H. *Entreprises multinationales, les codes de conduite*. Geneva, Institut Universitaire d'Études Européennes, 1977.
SHARPSTON, M. *International Sub-contracting*. Washington, D.C., IBRD and IDA, May 1974. (Bank Staff Working Paper, No. 181.)
SINE, B. *Impérialisme et théories sociologiques du développement*. Paris, Anthropos / IDEP, 1975.
SISWO SUDARMO, M. The Employment of University Graduates in Indonesia. *Development Strategies and Manpower Needs: The Response of Southeast Asian Universities*, Singapore, RIHED, 1976.
SKOLIMOWSKI, H. Cultural Values, Science and Technology. *Cultures* (Unesco), Vol. VI, No. 1, 1979.
SMITH, D. *The Economics of Book Publishing in Developing Countries*. Paris, Unesco, 1977. (Reports and Papers on Mass Communication, 79.)
SMITH, K. The Impact of Transnational Book Publishing on Knowledge in Less Developed Countries. *Prospects, Quarterly Review of Education*, Vol. VII, No. 2, 1977.
——. *The Impact of Transnational Book Publishing on Intellectual Knowledge in Less Developed Countries*. Paris, Unesco, Division for the Study of Development, 1978. (TNC-3.)
SOMAVIA, J. The Transnational Power Structure and International Information. *Development Dialogue*, No. 2, 1976.
STANDING, G.; KOIJA, T. Labor Market Effects of Multinational Enterprises in Latin America. *Nebraska Journal of Economics and Business*, Vol. 12, No. 4, 1973.
SUNKEL, O. Transnational Capitalism and National Disintegration in Latin America. *Social and Economic Studies*, Vol. 22, March 1973.
SUNKEL, O.; FUENZALIDA, E. *Transnationalization, National Disintegration and Reintegration in Contemporary Capitalism*. Brighton, Institute of Development Studies, 1974. (Internal Working Paper, No. 18.)
——. *The Effects of Transnational Corporations on Culture*. Paris, Unesco, 1976. (Doc. SHC-76/CONF. 635/6.)
——. Transnationalization and its National Consequences. In: J. Villamil (ed.), *Transnational Capitalism and National Development*. Brighton, Harvester Press, 1979.
SWAINSON, N. *The Bata Shoe Company: Types of Production and Transfer of Skills*. Paris, Unesco, Division for the Study of Development, 1978. (TNC-6.)
THARAKAN, P. K. M. *La division internationale du travail et les entreprises multinationales*. Paris, CEEIM/Presses Universitaires de France, 1979.
THEBAUD, S. Les systèmes de recherche scientifique et technique des pays en voie de développement. *Revue Tiers-Monde*, Vol. XVII, No. 65, 1976.
TINBERGEN, J. *Reshaping the International Order, A Report to the Club of Rome*, New York, Dutton, 1976.
TORNEDEU, R. *Foreign Disinvestment by US Multinational Corporations*. New York, Praeger, 1975.
TURNER, L. *Multinational Companies and the Third World*. New York, Hill & Wang, 1973.
UNCTAD. *Guidelines for the Study of the Transfer of Technology to Developing Countries*. New York, United Nations, 1973. (TD/B/AC.11/9.)
——. *Handbook on the Acquisition of Technology by Developing Countries*. New York, United Nations, 1978.
UNESCO. *Intergovernmental Conference on Institutional, Administrative and Financial Aspects of Cultural Policies, Venice, 24 August–2 September 1970, Final Report*. Paris, Unesco, 1970.
——. *International Aspects of Technological Innovation*. Paris, Unesco, 1972. (Science Policy Studies and Documents, 26.)
——. *Intergovernmental Conference on Cultural Policies in Asia, Yogyakarta, 10–19 December 1973. Final Report*. Paris, Unesco, 1974.

UNESCO. *Moving Towards Change: Some Thoughts on the New International Economic Order.* Paris, Unesco, 1976.
——. *Intergovernmental Conference on Cultural Policies in Africa, Accra, 27 October–6 November 1975. Final Report.* Paris, Unesco, 1976.
——. *Thinking Ahead.* Paris, Unesco, 1977.
——. *Intergovernmental Conference on Cultural Policies in Latin America and the Caribbean, Bogotá, 10–20 January 1978. Final Report.* Paris, Unesco, 1978.
UNESCO/UNITED NATIONS. Preservation and Further Development of Cultural Values. Note by the Secretary-General. New York, United Nations, 1976. (General Assembly Resolution 31/39 of 30 November 1976.) (Doc. A/33/157.)
UNITED NATIONS. *Multinational Corporations in World Development.* New York, United Nations Department of Economic and Social Affairs, 1973. (Sales No. E.73.II.)
——. *Transnational Corporations in World Development, A Reexamination.* New York, United Nations, 20 March 1978. (E/C.10/38.)
——. *Corporations in Advertising.* New York, United Nations, 1979. (Technical Paper, ST/CTC/8.)
VAITSOS, C.V. *Employment Problems and Transnational Enterprises in Developing Countries: Distortion and Inequality.* Geneva, ILO, 1976. (WEP 2-28/WP11.)
VARIS, T. *The Impact of Transnational Corporations on Communication.* Paris, Unesco, 1976. (Doc. SHC-76/CONF.635/7.)
VERNON, R. International Investment and International Trade in the Product Cycle. *Quarterly Journal of Economics,* May 1966.
——. *Storm over the Multinationals, The Real Issues.* Cambridge, Mass., Harvard University Press, 1977.
VILLAMIL, J. *Transnational Capitalism and National Development.* Brighton, The Harvester Press, 1979.
WALTER, H. Marketing in Developing Countries. *Columbia Journal of World Business,* Winter 1974.
WEINSTEIN, F. B. Multinational Corporation and the Third World: The Case of Japan and Southeast Asia. *International Organization,* Vol. 30, No. 3, 1973.
WELLS, L.T. Economic Man and Engineering Man: Choice of Technology in Low-wage Country. *Public Policy,* Vol. 21, No. 3, 1973. pp. 319–42.
——. Don't Over-automate Your Foreign Plan. *Harvard Business Review,* Vol. 52, No. 1, 1974.
——. The Internationalization of Firms From Developing Countries. In: T. Agmon and C. P. Kindleberger (eds.), *Multinationalization from Small Countries.* Cambridge, Mass., MIT Press, 1977.
WONG, K. P. *The Cultural Impact of Multinational Corporations in Singapore.* Paris, Unesco Division for the Study of Development, 1979.
WONG, R. H. K. *Educational Innovations in Singapore.* Paris, Unesco, 1974. (Experiments and Innovations in Education, 9.)
WORLD CONFEDERATION OF LABOUR. *Les entreprises multinationales du secteur tabac.* Brussels, WCL/CMT, 1977.
ZIEGLER, J. *Main basse sur l'Afrique,* Paris, Seuil, 1978.
——. *Le pouvoir africain.* New rev. ed. Paris, Seuil, 1979.
ZIOLKOWSKI, J. Cultural Dimension of Development. *Cultures* (Unesco), Vol. VI, No. 1, 1979.

SS-81 / D-123 / A